"*Acting the Michael Chekhov Way* is a simply masterful step-by-step introduction to the many wonderful tools of the Michael Chekhov technique. A game changer in the classroom, this detailed textbook not only offers a clear scaffolding from abstract physical exploration through to direct application into scene work but also offers actors a beautiful philosophy on self-guidance, self-assessment, and autonomy. This healthy and positive approach to actor training (a hallmark of Chekhov's work long ignored) is a welcome antidote to the many problematic approaches to actor training that exist today. Equally perfect for personal study or in the classroom, this marvelous text provides endless opportunities for exploration, growth, and the expansion of artistic discoveries for years to come."

**Anjalee Deshpande Hutchinson**, *Department of Theatre and Dance Bucknell*

"In *Acting the Michael Chekhov Way*, Dalton lays out an easy to follow progression through the entire Chekhov canon that culminates with the SART, a stunningly efficient process we used in *Small Town Boys*. Rehearsing the climactic moments does more than unite all the elements of a show. Lisa's approach gives an actor the rhythmic soul of the performance. Ms. Dalton is a brilliant teacher and director!"

**Sean Casey Leclaire**, *The SCL Coaching Group*

# Acting the Michael Chekhov Way

Rooted in Chekhov's Guiding Principles and Laws of Composition, *Acting the Michael Chekhov Way: A Playbook for Healthy, Sequential Training* offers a step-by-step pathway for actors, directors, and teachers with an emphasis on the health and wellbeing of the performer.

Developed over 30 years within the National Michael Chekhov Association's renowned certification training, this clear, accessible training sequence for Michael Chekhov's techniques is designed to support artists at every level. The chapters build logically and functionally, layering in benefits for artistic and personal growth. Central to the approach is the Chart of Inspired Action, created by Chekhov for his student and estate executrix, Mala Powers, who co-founded this pedagogy with Dalton and Professor Wil Kilroy. In these pages, Dalton introduces *SynthAnalysis*™, a groundbreaking synthesis of Stanislavsky's analysis and Chekhov's methods, bridging theory and practice tested through decades of global application. She also shares anecdotal insights from her 45-year acting/stunt career and draws on Chekhov's esoteric inspirations—elements often absent in most books and teachings on Chekhov. The book presents mystical concepts like the goblet in playful, functional ways, empowering artists to use them as imaginative metaphors and explore their deeper potential.

A helpful tool for both solo and classroom use, *Acting the Michael Chekhov Way* will speak directly to the actor and their teachers, guiding them on a transformative journey into the heart of inspired action and creative freedom.

The book includes access to detailed discussions, additional activities, downloadable templates, and suggested syllabi and tips for instructors, available at www.resourcecentre.routledge.com/books/9781032844480.

**Lisa Loving Dalton** has made profound contributions to the performing arts through her extensive work with the Michael Chekhov technique. As president and co-founder of the National Michael Chekhov Association (1993), and Certifying Master Teacher, she has been instrumental in advancing Chekhov's methods globally. Her ground-breaking documentary *From Russia to Hollywood* and the creation of the Chekhov.net video archive underscore her dedication to preserving and promoting Chekhov's legacy. Applying Chekhov over her rich and diverse 45-year career as a film and stage director, actor, and stuntwoman deeply informs this innovative pedagogy.

**The Michael Chekhov Playbook Series**
Series Editors: Lisa Loving Dalton and Wil Kilroy

*The Michael Chekhov Way Playbook Series* is the result of over thirty-five years of collaboration between Wil Kilroy and Lisa Loving Dalton, developing a fun, healthy, and comprehensive way of training and applying Michael Chekhov's (acting) techniques to stage, film and the artist's life.

The series focuses on various aspects of performance art training, such as core concepts for actors, improvisation, script analysis, directing, devising, dramaturgy, design and applications for specific use in style, marketing and media. Each playbook offers step-by-step guidance and tips for "free styling" the integration of the concepts.

**Improvisation the Michael Chekhov Way**
*Active Exploration of Acting Techniques*
Wil Kilroy

**Acting the Michael Chekhov Way**
*A Playbook for Healthy, Sequential Training*
Lisa Loving Dalton

For more information about this series, please visit:

# Acting the Michael Chekhov Way

A Playbook for Healthy, Sequential Training

Lisa Loving Dalton

NEW YORK AND LONDON

Designed cover image: NMCA Photos & Art

First published 2026
by Routledge
605 Third Avenue, New York, NY 10158

and by Routledge
4 Park Square, Milton Park, Abingdon, Oxon, OX14 4RN

*Routledge is an imprint of the Taylor & Francis Group, an informa business*

© 2026 Lisa Loving Dalton

The right of Lisa Loving Dalton to be identified as author of this work has been asserted in accordance with sections 77 and 78 of the Copyright, Designs and Patents Act 1988.

All rights reserved. No part of this book may be reprinted or reproduced or utilised in any form or by any electronic, mechanical, or other means, now known or hereafter invented, including photocopying and recording, or in any information storage or retrieval system, without permission in writing from the publishers.

*Trademark notice*: Product or corporate names may be trademarks or registered trademarks, and are used only for identification and explanation without intent to infringe.

*Library of Congress Cataloging-in-Publication Data*
Names: Dalton, Lisa author
Title: Acting the Michael Chekhov way / Lisa Loving Dalton.
Description: New York : Routledge, 2025. | Series: The Michael Chekhov playbook series | Includes bibliographical references and index.
Identifiers: LCCN 2025018770 (print) | LCCN 2025018771 (ebook) | ISBN 9781032844497 hardback | ISBN 9781032844480 paperback | ISBN 9781003512745 ebook
Subjects: LCSH: Acting
Classification: LCC PN2061 .D255 2026 (print) | LCC PN2061 (ebook) | DDC 792.08--dc23/eng/20250602
LC record available at https://lccn.loc.gov/2025018770
LC ebook record available at https://lccn.loc.gov/2025018771

ISBN: 978-1-032-84449-7 (hbk)
ISBN: 978-1-032-84448-0 (pbk)
ISBN: 978-1-003-51274-5 (ebk)

DOI: 10.4324/9781003512745

Typeset in Goudy
by KnowledgeWorks Global Ltd.

Access the Support Material: www.resourcecentre.routledge.com/books/9781032844480

# Contents

Acknowledgments ix
Chekhov Technique Abbreviations x

## PART I
## PREPARATION: WELCOME AND ONLINE RESOURCES 1
Introduction 5
1 Preparing your imagination, your body, and the ensemble 35

## PART II
## PSYCHO-PHYSICAL BODYBUILDING FOR ACTORS 57
2 Expanding/Contracting 59
3 Qualities/Kinds of Movement 69
4 Archetypal Gestures 73

## PART III
## EMOTIONAL LIFE FOR ACTORS 85
5 Three Sister Sensations of Equilibrium 87
6 Qualities and Sensations 95
7 Atmospheres: Overall and Personal 99
8 The Four Brothers of Art 113

## PART IV
## ESTHETICS 139
9 Ensemble 141
10 Truth 148
11 Style 154

## PART V
## TRANSFORMATION: CHARACTERIZATION AND GESTURE — 165

12  Transformational characterization: Ideal Self, Centers, Imaginary Body, Trinity of Psychology—Thinking, Feeling, Willing — 167

13  Radiating and Receiving Radiance — 201

14  Tempo and Rhythm — 211

15  Focal Points of Concentration — 220

16  Objectives "What for?" — 228

17  Psychological Gesture — 234

18  Improvisation/Jewelry — 245

## PART VI
## PUTTING IT ALL TOGETHER — 249

19  SynthAnalysis™ for the part-Composition — 251

20  Love, laughter, and the MC way hereafter — 274

Appendix 1   POA Journal-Flyback Playsheet — 288

Appendix 2   Wil Kilroy's rehearsal outline — 289

Bibliography — 290

Index — 292

# Acknowledgments

This book is dedicated to my loving friends, colleagues, and mentors in the work of Michael Chekhov, whose guidance and support have been invaluable to me over the years. In particular, I wish to honor the late Mala Powers and my very alive, dear friend Wil Kilroy, my co-founders of the National Michael Chekhov Association (NMCA). Their vision and dedication have been a constant source of inspiration. To Charlie Bowles, our current NMCA Executive, thank you for being my steadfast knight in shining armor, transforming my prolific ideas into reality through the images in this book, publishing assistance, and the live trainings NMCA presents. Our collaboration has been a gift beyond measure.

I am deeply grateful to the dozen "first generation" students of Michael Chekhov who mentored me, including Deirdre Hurst du Prey, Beatrice Straight, Eleanor Faison, George Shdanoff, and Jack Colvin. Their insights helped flesh out the wisdom gained from my earliest explorations into this work alongside Wilfred A. Hunt in 1980. Trisha Gray, my dear clown partner, thank you for smacking me upside the head when I dismissed your suggestion that Michael Chekhov was my answer—who knew there was someone besides Anton! Introducing me to your other clown partner, Ted Pugh, changed all of our lives. God bless you, Ted, for our years together in New York and all your contributions since.

To my colleagues in the International Michael Chekhov Association—Joerg Andrees, Jobst Langhans, Vladimir Baicher, and Sarah Kane—thank you for laying the groundwork for global conferences that have influenced this pedagogy and seeded its growth worldwide since 1992. Your enduring support for the work and for me personally has been a cornerstone of my journey.

To my students over the past 45 years, especially the Los Angeles and San Diego Dalton Gangs and our sponsors, Odessa Ferris and Lesha Sand, thank you for testing these theories and bringing them to life. I thank the international Michael Chekhov Studios' Coop who inspires me weekly online.

I extend my gratitude to Nicholas Wilde, whose previous training with me informed his patient editorial support during times of doubt and disarray. Thank you, Anjalee Deshpande Hutchinson, for inviting me to contribute to your previous books and for your editorial encouragement on this project. Thank you Justina Kasponyte for sharing your Lithuania research. Gratitude to HeathMath.org for your research that supports so much of this work.

My gratitude is truly extensive, and I invite you to explore the online resources for deeper acknowledgements. This book is a testament to the power of collaboration, mentorship, and shared passion, and I am forever thankful to everyone who has been part of this journey.

Mr. C, I love that you brought love into the work and my dream is to speak that into the future.

*With hope,*
*Lisa Loving Dalton*

# Chekhov Technique Abbreviations

| ABBREVIATION | DEFINITION |
|---|---|
| 3Is | Inspiration, Imagination, Intellect as a means to discovering choices |
| 3S | 3 Sister Sensations of Equilibrium: Falling/Yielding, Balancing/Teetering, Floating/ Weightless |
| 5GPs | 5 Guiding Principles |
| A-SART | Actor's SynthAnalysis™ Run-Through |
| AAA | Activity/Action, Archetype of Character, Atmosphere for Auditions |
| AC | Archetypal Character |
| AG | Archetypal Gesture: Push, Pull, Reach, etc. |
| ASC | Access, Select, Convey |
| ATMO | Atmosphere |
| BEEF | Beauty, Ease, Entirety, Form |
| BBEEP | Breath, Body, Extreme, Effort that is P.A.S.S.ed |
| CG | Compositionary Gestures |
| C.I.R.C.L.E | Concentration, Imagination, Radiation, Centeredness, Love/Lightness, Ease |
| DA-SART | Director's Active SynthAnalysis™ Run-Through |
| FP | 5 Focal Points for Concentration |
| GA | General Atmosphere |
| HG | Harmonious Grouping |
| IAC | Ideal Artistic Center |
| IB | Imaginary Body |
| I-Sphere | Unlimited Sphere of Imagination/Higher I/Higher Ego |
| L.E.A.D | Lines, Emotions, Activity/Action, Desires |
| LQ | Leading Questions |
| MC | Moveable Centers |
| MFFR | Molding, Flowing, Flying, Radiating |
| NMCA | National Michael Chekhov Association |
| OA | Overall, Objective, General Atmosphere |
| O.R. | Online Resource |

| ABBREVIATION | DEFINITION |
|---|---|
| PA | Personal, Subjective, Individual Atmosphere |
| PASS | Prepare, Act, Sustain, Stop |
| PPE | Psycho-Physical Exercises: X/C, MFFR, AG |
| PG | Psychological Gesture |
| POA | Practice, Observe, Apply |
| QP | Quantum Peek Chart |
| Q&S | Qualities and Sensations |
| QOM | Quality of Movement (MFFR) |
| RAD/REC | Radiating/Receiving |
| RG | Japanese Rock Garden |
| SA | SynthAnalysis™ Stanislavsky System of Analysis with Chekhov Composition |
| SART | SynthAnalysis™ Run Through |
| SBV | Stick Ball Veil |
| STAC/LEG 6 | Staccato/Legato Six Directions Exercise |
| TFW | Thinking, Feeling, Willing |
| TIP | Transform, Inform, Perform |
| ToP | Trinity of Psychology |
| TPT | Triplicity, Polarity, Transformation |
| T/R | Tempo/Rhythm |
| UFO | Unidentified Focus On (Atypical Eye patterns) |
| WiP | Work-in-Progress |
| X/C | Expanding/Contracting |

# Part I
# Preparation: welcome and online resources

## Welcome

Welcome, dear player-reader, to this dynamic world of *Acting the Michael Chekhov Way*. Will you agree with the idea that the performing artist is a gymnast of thoughts, feelings, and desires? If so, you know it isn't an art one can master by sitting on the sidelines. See Figure P.1, the Chart of Inspired Action that will serve as the floor plan of our actor's gymnasium. In this first part, we hope to prepare you to play well. One can think of it as a warmup that energizes your body, mind, heart, and soul, preparing you to fill your artistic dreams with empowered action.

I had the pleasure of interviewing hundreds of Hollywood casting directors at the American Film Institute over an 18-year period. Every single one of them said that "lack of preparation" was the single, most evident flaw of actors. Our preparation is like the inhale so necessary to sing, speak, and laugh. All athletes cycle through the process of preparation, action, sustaining, and finally stopping for some rest. This will be our method. We hope that you now know this sequence sets you up for success—strong preparation makes the action effortless. If you are new to Michael Chekhov, it ventures into a world unlike any other acting technique and yet will feel so familiar to every human as we recognize how we once did all of this as little children. If you are deepening your Chekhov experience, welcome, and thank you for expanding your love of the work. May this book reward you with ever more images on your journey to know thyself.

This introductory part gives you the ideas, guidelines of play, and an overview of what's to come. It reveals some unique pathways to understanding why Chekhov's techniques are so healthy and effective. Have fun because if it isn't fun, it isn't Chekhov!

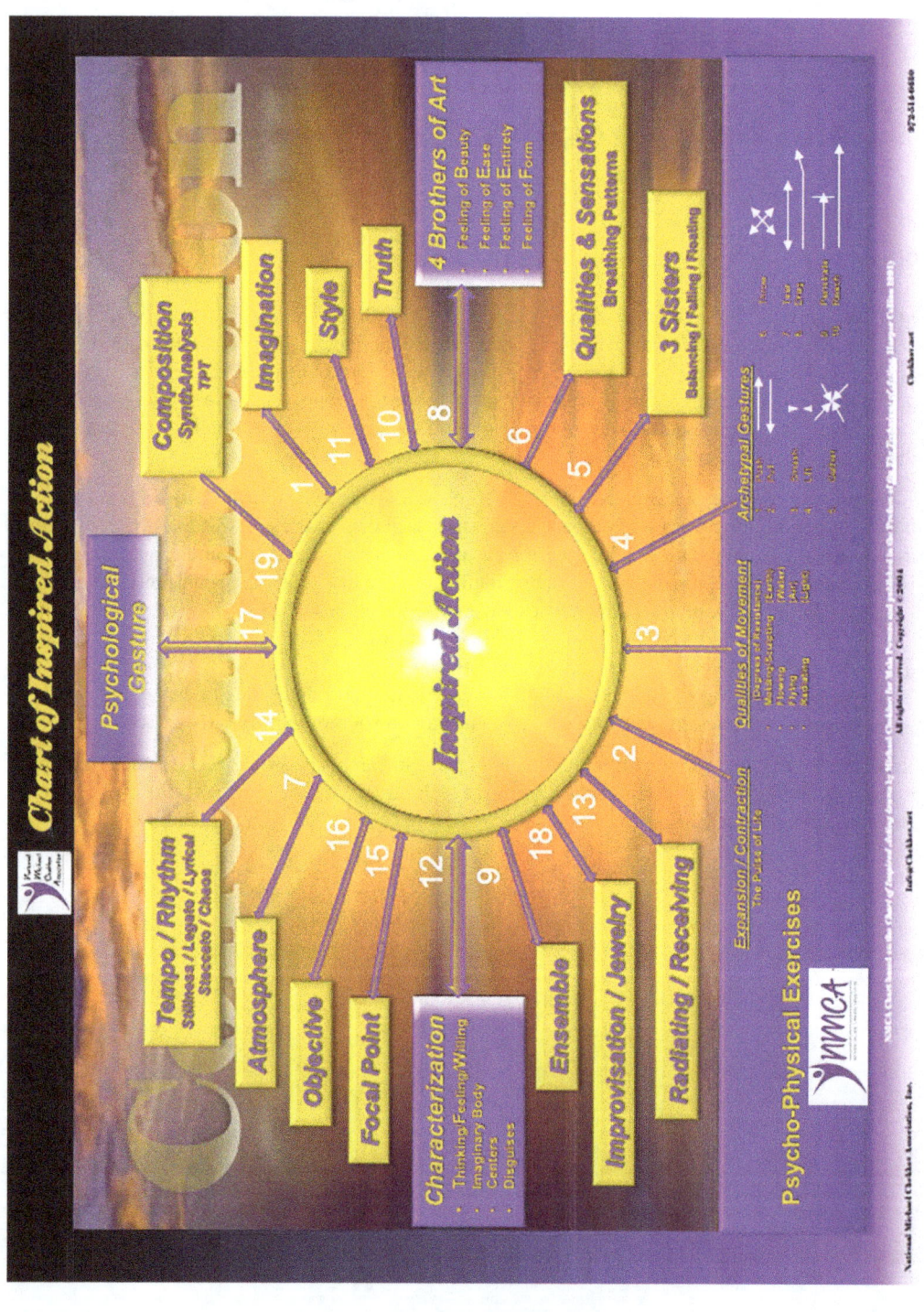

*Figure P.1* National Michael Chekhov Association Chart of Inspired Action with numbered sequence to match chapter numbers. (Copyright Lisa Dalton & Charlie Bowles.)

## Online Resources

Some **deeper detailed discussions** and **advanced activities** have been placed in the **Routledge Resource Centre as online resources** along with practical **worksheets**. Watch for this cue:

- See **OR + Chapter.Doc#.**

**These OR Documents can be accessed at** the link to the password-protected Routledge Resource Centre www.resourcecentre.routledge.com/books/9781032844480.

In fact, if you are deeply curious about how this got started or a teacher,

- See **OR 0.1-.04** for Deeper Acknowledgments, NMCA Pedagogy Origins, Link Resources and Extended Author Bio.
- See **OR 0.8** for To the Teacher—AMCW Use in Class.
- See **OR 22.0-2** for Teacher Tips.

# Introduction

**IMAGINE**

**You are on fire!**

**On a roll! In a role!**

**Everything you are doing is perfect.**

**How do you make this happen again?**

It's never come out of you this way before. It feels like you aren't even in your body. Part of you is hovering above. Another part is in the audience, poking someone in the ribs, saying, "Look, look. That's me!" And that part hovering above you is very calm and pleased.

Meanwhile, your body is raging, sobbing, seducing, or uplifting the other characters in the scene. Inside, you are doing a big *whoop-dee-doo*, surprised at how effortlessly everything is coming out of you, unlike any other time. You are in *the zone*, in flow, at peak performance, and have "IT" happening. It's fun and free, and yet, you are doing nothing. It is entirely effortless, beautiful, perfect, and delightful. And you want it to last forever.

Afterward, you don't have a clue what just happened. You know something extraordinary happened. You know that everyone there knows it, too. You don't need them to tell you that it happened. You have no *need* for anything. You, of course, enjoy the flood of attention and recognition from peers and audiences, but you don't need any of it. So full was your experience that you will know it as long as you live. You may never know the details, but that's not the point. When someone says to you, "You remember that moment where you did that thing with your hand? That was amazing," you will nod and say, "Uh-huh," and you will smile and say, "Thanks, I am so glad you liked that moment."

Isn't this what actors live for? Those moments when things flow through us to our audiences and colleagues that send everyone into an elevated state? I know you know what I am talking about because this is why you are here, reading this book. Because you want to learn how to get there again. Often. Regularly. Safely ... without driving yourself insane. And that's what this book is here to help you do. Chekhov calls those moments "happy."

Those happy moments seem to have a more significant *you* in them. What I mean by that is, in our daily lives, we go along thinking about our bodies, our feelings, and what's on our minds. We need to eat, sleep, feed ourselves, pay the bills, interact socially, and keep our heads on straight. But, we rarely experience those other parts that appear so viscerally during those happy times. As actors, we know we can train our bodies, cultivate our feelings, and develop our minds. However, it rarely occurs to anyone in any leading acting technique to train those intangible aspects of the self that one experiences in those peak moments. Thus, the door is open for Chekhov's most unique gifts, which we will be exploring.

Chekhov examines the concept that these happy moments happen when four aspects of the human being align simultaneously in perfect harmony. These encompass our physical body, our mind, our emotional soul and our sense of self or "spirit." Whether or not one believes in Chekhov's ideas is not critical at all to the success of employing his approach. It can be learned with or without agreeing with his understanding of these elements. The invitation to you as an artist is to play with the possibilities. Why would you not, if just pretending they exist and playing fully with them leads to your happiness?

As a student of Konstantin Stanislavsky, Chekhov knew about asking "What if?" Here, I suggest you employ this same idea by setting aside the need to believe any of what is offered here and asking, "What if it were true? What could happen then?"

We aspire to a field of play rather than work. Long before the comedy improv age, children gathered to play, asking, "What if?" "What if we did this?" or "What if I did that?" So, what if you employ the attitude of a child and really pretend that what we are playing with has an invisible superpower? Engaging in this approach with this attitude may allow you to discover the gifts hidden inside you. Moreover, it may free up your mind to allow you to embody the images you are tasked with conveying to the audience. This is critical to all that the artist does. If you can't reveal the power of what is within you, if it is getting stuck inside, it is probably very painful for you. Here, you will find the salve to heal that pain and the tools to be free of that pain in the first place.

Also here, you can find a step-by-step approach that has a very logical flow to it.

When I started exploring the Chekhov work, I was blessed to train with many of his direct students. However wonderful they were as artists, there were hardly any professional teachers among them. I learned many powerful exercises, but in no particular order. Nor did we apply them to speech and the practical work I was doing for a living: auditioning and performing on stage and in film. I yearned for a more structured, coherent pathway, a step-by-step sequence that would go from discovery to application, prioritizing its practicality, logic, and healing empowerment. Each step here solves our challenges as actors at play on stage or in film. I offer you my 40+ years of acting, directing, and teaching experience so that you can find the happine$$ I have enjoyed through it.

Ultimately, by following this sequence around the Chart of Inspired Action, you will learn how to apply it to the many different needs an actor has to meet. That is if you truly want to learn. Do you?

To help you learn, we included a set of useful tools: We created abbreviations/acronyms that will make it easy to take notes and use with other artists who share your language. There is an abbreviation list in the front of the book.

We have also included self-reflection prompts for your notes, journal, or discussion, each of which is shown with a *Flyback* icon for easy identification. Finally, you will discover key phrases to facilitate your study, which we have labeled with an atom as our *Axiom* icon. These takeaways are essential concepts or mantras. Whatever the name we give them, their truth will give you strength. Repeat them frequently to help you feel confident and creative. This first one reminds us of how ancient and significant the art we love is to the evolution of humanity.

>  **Axiom 0.1: We storytellers are needed to guide the souls of humanity.**

Many actors fear loving acting. We may be filled with self-doubt regarding our talent, future security, or the value of our professional dreams. We may be bullied and shamed by family, peers, and the public for loving a "vain and useless" art. What if this is the truth? What you can learn here will nurture your talent so that as an actor, you can teach humanity more than any single teacher, defend more causes than any lawyer, heal more wounds than any doctor, and inspire more goodness than any preacher.

This is a sacred profession that began in caves as a necessity of humanity, and it isn't going away just because artificial intelligence is out there.

- See **OR 0.5** for Antidote to AI.

When you know the significance of your role in society, you feel the courage needed for a great purpose in life and can access the will to be the best at what you love.

Michael Chekhov exhibited this will on the stage. He was actually a superstar who enjoyed curtain calls that lasted HOURS, and then, at the height of his career in 1917, he lost his mental health. He could not work until he found the truth of our purpose, which is that we are in a sacred profession with a profound social responsibility. He found balance through his teaching and spiritual research and returned to create a healing training process. And now, over a century later, the world is finally ready to expand toward healing.

The task of finding a better way to train actors has been documented over the millennia via archeological research, such as that conducted by notable behavioral archaeologist Yann-Pierre Montelle, who, through his studies of the use of caves by humans in Prehistory, especially related to rock art, states in his book, *Paleoperformance*:

> Theatricality, as practice, finds its first tangible evidence in the deep caves of the Upper Paleolithic, c. 30,000 years ago. It is my belief that a direct line of interrelated "landmarks" can be established between the cave and the *theatron* (or *cavea*).[1]

Only the past century brought about what has become known as the iconic style of realism that launched our film industry. This style became famous for its extreme limitations and potential psychological dangers induced by the techniques. Today, some actors brag about how much pain they choose to go through to be "authentic." Some succeed. Some die for their efforts. Some teachers rebelled and created their own techniques to foster a safer way to rise to the acting challenge. They, unfortunately, haven't fared much better in resolving the vast challenges facing the performer. Trends are generated to fix this or that acting problem. For example, one technique is only about accessing an actor's emotional life. Another is about safely training an expressive body. There's a technique for awareness of spatial surroundings. There's another about following impulses from a partner. Generally, this wave of gap-filling techniques cultivates thinking, feeling, or willing within the artist, but none puts it all together. As you will learn here, the actor trains in all three aspects of essentially being human for daily living as well as for artistic excellence. This is evidence that the world is now ready for one comprehensive training that builds upon the strengths of Stanislavsky and fills in all the gaps: connecting the body, mind, and spirit of the artist with the writer, director, and designer in one unified language for stage or film.

Chekhov's work provides us a path to fulfilling human potential, making your entire life a work of art where the path is living an artistic life. Because you are an artist how many hours a day? Yes, 24/7. You never actually stop being an artist, even while you sleep. We know this because we sometimes wake up with great ideas, right? And, while you are washing the dishes, images appear to you of this or that moment of art—one yet to come or one that came and went. You are always a whole human being: a spiritual being with a life force in a physical body, and you are always an artist—all at the same time. If you train yourself for peak performance in all you do, chances increase significantly that you will achieve that same peak experience on the stage. Doing this training is a gift for you, your family and friends, and your audiences. When they participate with you in those happy moments on the stage or on camera, we are all uplifted, healed, educated, and enlightened.

## Preparing the foundation for *Acting the Michael Chekhov Way*

### ✒ Journal/Discuss/Flyback

Chekhov's work will allow you to expand the skills you currently know and will add so many possible ways to reach that peak moment that you will be able to solve any problem that arises. This is why jotting down your current challenges is such a great thing to do now. The entire process of being able to use Chekhov's ideas for your artistic life requires you to want to know yourself. Keeping a journal, especially handwritten, is a handy way to get to know yourself. In this book, questions will appear. These are ideal opportunities to reflect—to ask and respond in your journal and in discussion with others. We call this reflection a *Flyback*. We'll go into more detail on *Flybacks* a bit later.

### ✒ Journal now for later review

Self evaluation

- *What do I like about my acting now?*
- *What do I want to add, strengthen, or eliminate?*
- *Where could I use help?*
- *What was my favorite acting moment?*
- *What are my greatest strengths as an artist? As a person?*
- *How do I hope this approach will serve me?*
- *What do I like about my ability to get creative, story-appropriate images?*
- *What was the coolest idea I ever had?*
- *What do I like about how I use my imagination? My body? My creativity? My voice? My breath?*
- *Could I use help with any of these?*
- *What do I wish I could do?*
- *What am I most afraid of as an actor?*
- *What do I worry about regarding my skills? My opportunities? My body? My voice? My future?*
- *How do I feel about exploring this technique?*
- *What do I wish for my audiences?*

You may also want to know something about the life of those whose techniques you are exploring. They are now your artistic ancestors, whose legacy you are adopting. There are many great resources for Chekhov's biography, so this book doesn't cover that in detail.[2] What I will say is that Chekhov's life was deeply challenged by his health—mental and physical—and by a society amid revolutions, epidemics, and world wars. He evolved this technique to help himself heal and cope. Chekhov offers us an actor's language by an actor. His technique itself provides strategies to identify your own artistic genetics and those of artists who have gone before you. When you discover who you are in terms of thought, feeling, and will, for example, you will also see how perhaps Laban or Viewpoints[3] train the thinking life. Or Suzuki or Grotowski train the will. With Chekhov, the aim is to train all three of your *soul forces* that make up your psychology to work in harmony and to provide the stimulation you need. And we train them in the body, mind, soul, and spirit all at once.

### Our health

Worry about the self? Will you be able to do this? Will you be safe physically? Mentally?

Yes. The amazing thing about this work is that if you, as an artist, are willing to play, it is adaptable to any physical and mental condition and often leads to greater health. We have successfully trained children in kindergarten, senior citizens in wheelchairs, adults on crutches with MS, and a broad range of otherly abled learners.

What you do want to have is a desire to play freely and an understanding that each of us has a body that we might call an energy body. This energy body is something you might recognize in, for example, shocking moments when you say something like, "My heart flew into my throat when the car almost hit us." This statement about your heart refers to the energy in your physical heart that has moved well beyond where it normally is. The physical heart did not literally *fly*, but you felt the energy flying, and that's a mighty shift, right?

> ⚛ Axiom 0.2: I have a body, an energy body. I can move. I transform energy with my imagination.

The energy body is sometimes called an etheric body, kinesphere, or a light body. Today, we have Kyrlian cameras that can literally photograph this energy, changing its form based on your thoughts and images.

In our work with, among other things, the energy body, we will cultivate the power of our thoughts, our concentration, and our imagination with the aim of being aware of this energy and what we are doing with it at all times.

Have you noticed that we might be more able to recall a dream's details than our peak performance? Studies show that there are changes in the brain in peak performance "flow," such as "a hemispheric shift away from the frontal left evidenced by a resulting reduction of left frontal activity and an increase in frontal alpha."[4] This shift can support an increase in activity in the visual-spatial right brain area. We go into high levels of concentrated efficiency (no short-term memory needed). Building skills through increasing challenges is the best way to cultivate "flow." Multi-tasking diminishes the ability to flow.

Why is this relevant? It helps us to understand that developing extraordinary powers of concentration is highly desirable, and our ability to achieve our objectives will be proportionate to our mastery of concentration. There are many clearly outlined concentration exercises that actors can do. However, we don't usually take the time to experience these in a classroom or through books for many reasons. Here, you are invited to trust that the word "concentration" underlies all we do. Take a moment to find it on the Chart (see Figure P.1).

## Concentration destroyers

All the exercises are concentration exercises regardless of whether presented as such. Several elements often fracture our concentration when we are trying to achieve a level of mastery that requires a unified focus.

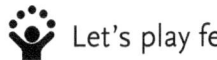 Let's play feeling focus

Imagine concentration as a stream of energy emanating from our body toward a single point. Every cell of our being unites with that outward flow focused on a single point. Anything that distracts us, we want to remove. Picture this energy flowing from the center of the chest, about three or four inches below the collar bone, over the thymus gland. Let's use our hands to make this more visible. See Figure 0.1 for reference. Allow one hand to reach upward to the sky as if grasping that light bulb of a great idea above you. Simultaneously, reach down with the other hand to the Earth to anchor your will force. Draw the forces above and below together until your palms are at the center of your chest, and then extend them forward, pointing them to a spot you focus on in front of you. Imagine that great idea flowing into your arms toward

Center    Reach & Gather from Earth & Sky    Unite Energy toward Focal Point

*Figure 0.1* The artist has gathered forces above and below and now sustains focus as they radiate to a single point.

the point. Sense the ground beneath you, and a stream of will force traveling up from the legs into the chest and through the arms to your point. Sense the force of your creativity flowing from your chest, uniting the thoughts and the will to that single point. You are welcome to pretend you feel it even if you don't. Try this gesture three times and think or say,

> *All peak performances come through a unified field of focus.*
>
> *I gather and focus everything to one point, to unify.*

Notice how the movement starts in the opposite or polar place from where it ends.

Now, play with the gesture above as if your focus fractures and your upper hand doubles back, pointing to your head. Then, with your willpower, refocus your energy on your previous focal point, moving your hands back together united in one direction. We can use this gesture to recover from moments when we feel weak or lost.

When self-doubt arises, it's as if this flow splits apart, sending a portion doubling back into your brain and activating a distracting inner commentary, often very concerned about needing approval, getting it right, or not feeling stupid. If this occurs, I have several suggestions.

## Needing approval

So many actors are driven by the search for approval that this issue is a rampant disease in our industry, leading to severe addictions, among other kinds of aberrant behavior. It leads to vulnerability and susceptibility to rip-offs from a variety of merchants, representatives, and employers. Building the awareness to self-assess will help you stay focused on your task, keeping all your energy concentrated in the best direction.

> ⚛ Axiom 0.3: Where attention goes, energy grows!

Remember this little mantra and keep it close to you. Whatever you pay attention to becomes more powerful. You are choosing with every thought to focus on what you love or fear. Your power is in your concentration and awareness. As you practice choosing love-based thoughts, your power will get stronger and stronger. Your impact on the audience and on your partners will grow in strength too. Eventually, that power will radiate through you like it did for some of Chekhov's most famous students like Marilyn Monroe, James Dean, Anthony Quinn, and Clint Eastwood.

## ✒ Journal/Discuss/Flyback

Power

*Who are some of the actors whose work I most admire? Why do I admire them? Do I feel their power? What kind of power is it? Does it draw me into them, or does it knock me back in my seat? Does it lift me or send me deep within? Do I want the power to uplift audiences? This kind of power does require practice to build it up to its fullest potential. Am I willing to invest the awareness necessary to cultivate that?*

Notice, we are not asking as much for "time" per se as for your attention. Will you choose to notice the world around you as you gas up your car? Will you eat your breakfast or brush your teeth with awareness that will build this power in you? Because that is truly what it will take to release the genius that is inside of you, when you need to have it available—on command, on cue, take after take, or night after night, and matinees too. Consistent practice of focused attention.

This book can lead to fully freeing your artistic, creative individuality only if you follow the path of embracing the practices fully in the gymnasium of life. The technique is the floor plan of a gym, and we are the trainers. You are the member who must show up to train. We cannot do it for you. You are also the one who will walk away "buff" if you choose to show up, consistently. In your early stages of training, it is important to just show up—no worries about where you are on the path of life and career. Perhaps you are fresh in university, confident and planning to take on the drama department, and think you already know all about acting—that was me at 17. Or perhaps you are a retiring acting professor ready to refresh your acting chops and step onto your local community theatre's stage after years directing. Or you may be an accountant who just needs a break from the numbers, or a curious, free spirit coming to play.

Whatever the case may be, as you begin, rejoice in the fact that you cannot get this "right" and there are almost no ways to fail in this approach. Normally, I say that failure isn't an option, but there are, in truth, a few ways that will make studying this useless—one of them being NOT showing up! Another is not being willing to play. If you show up and are willing to play and are ok with not being right or wrong, then we are going to get along just fine.

Most folks are a bit nervous or skeptical when coming to a new approach, so that's perfectly normal. Know that you are not alone. I do invite you to consider pretending that you really like the playful nature of the information and, that your nervousness is in fact secretly excitement.

I also advocate that we, as Crosby, Stills, Nash, and Young sang, "Love the one you're with."

Journal/Discuss/Flyback

Clean slate

*Am I willing to release my current understanding of acting and pretend I know nothing, and that everything I am learning now is perfect? Am I willing to release any attachments to other teachers and techniques, even other Chekhov teachers and this author? Is it ok to "play the fool"?*

Why would we ask this? Because who you are today is different from who you were when you learned what you already know. Does that make sense? And today's teacher is a creative individual who will share with you their own way of understanding these concepts. Allow your "naïve" appreciation of what is being offered today to keep you in the moment with the exploration. Only if you can free yourself of prejudice or bias about what is being offered and how it's being offered will you truly discover the nuances and gifts available in Chekhov and revealed through today's lens.

> ⚛ Axiom 0.4: Most people who think they are being led in the wrong direction miss all the beautiful scenery along the path.

After you complete your walk on a director's or teacher's path, you can sort out more definitively what resonates with you as a creative artist. Then, what you already know and what you have newly discovered can coalesce in a creative collaboration rather than a battle of displacement. When we release all we think we know about what an exercise is, discoveries will grace us each and every time, regardless of how many performances or years we have explored this technique. Rest assured that you will be able to be integrate and value everything you already know.

While using this book with an active class or before you try things out yourself, your reading will prepare you for what you are about to learn. Rereading after learning it in a class or after playing with it on your own or with a group of other interested artists, you will hopefully deepen your experience and understanding of the material.

## Contact—Be in it to win it

The art of acting is like all other arts and athletics in that it is a contact sport that must be played. Making contact or connecting with your body and your voice creates your art. Connecting with fellow cast members, actors, creatives, teammates, spectators, and fans builds your skills. Learning a contact sport from a book always has its challenges. Can you master basketball without ever shooting the ball? How will you know where you to throw the ball and develop a feel for how to get it just the right distance and location? An athlete has to feel it in the body. Equally, as a musician, a pianist for example, you can learn to play the notes, but what will define your brilliance is much more than just striking the keys in the right order with the right speed and duration. The nuances you embody through practice are what your genius reveals.

## Train your inner genius

In a study of genius, where all different kinds of amazing geniuses in all fields were included, there were two notable consistencies in how they were trained. The first element of the study was to identify what was most important to the student who was just beginning. The key was to cultivate enthusiasm. En + Theos (from the Latin, "in" + "god"), or as Earl Nightingale suggests, "And the happiest, most interesting people are those who have found the secret of maintaining their enthusiasm, that God within."[5] If you are beginning your journey in Chekhov, the most important thing to do is play and have fun with it. When a child has fun playing soccer in kindergarten, getting them to have perfect technique is completely unnecessary. If they don't have fun, they will not love it enough to keep playing. They will quit if their parents let them.

> ## Rock guitar
>
> My friend, Rick, really wanted to play rock 'n roll guitar in elementary school, but his parents made him take piano. He hated piano and kept asking for the guitar. He quit piano. At 12, Rick got his guitar, but his parents made him study classical guitar. He quit. By the time he got to high school, Rick got interested again in music and finally got a rock guitar on his own. He loved it and then wished he had been able to learn more about music, piano, and classical guitar. By then, however, his hormones were more important than the undeveloped musician inside, and being on the football team was sexier to the gals. Rick never learned to play any instrument very well; nor did he find a productive job while hanging out backstage with musicians but ended up couch surfing most of his life, and at 65 listens to other musicians all day and night. If Rick's parents had given him a rock guitar in grade school and cultivated his love for any kind of music, he most likely would have reached the stage where he really wanted to know more, seeking a level of mastery, and fully committing to the effort. We might even be listening to Rick's music today.

**Don't let your inner parent or perfectionist take your love from you.** Dare to do something badly or wrongly many times over, and it will be just perfect, I assure you. Remember that you gotta be in it to win it. If you are free of worrying about whether you are good at acting and allow yourself to love it and play regardless of your skill level, then you will be enthusiastic in your feelings, curious in your thinking and have the will force to build the discipline for mastery. In college, I was never cast in a main stage play. When I learned this technique after college, I paid my rent in New York and Los Angeles for over 30 years as a performing artist. I continue to be willing to be a naïve actor so that I can leave behind my fears and grow in love for the art.

That's where the second common element of training that these geniuses had comes in. After they had demonstrated perseverance based on their love for what they did and their desire to get better, they were given good foundational skills. If they loved that and still wanted to get better, then, they were mentored by a master teacher to give them masterful techniques. Master teachers break down the art or game into micro bits. They dissect the skills required into minute particles that are unrecognizable as the whole. Everything goes into slow motion. The piano maestro requires the developing, passionate pianist to play G with their little finger repeatedly, to discover just how the degree of the curve of the little finger and a precise amount of pressure affect the tone. Then, they change the degree of the curve and the amount of weight on the key to see how that is different. Can you make 100 different tones from G alone? This nuanced precision lifts the skill set into consistent brilliance. An emotional impact rises beyond the mechanics of striking the right note at the right time. *Acting the Michael Chekhov Way* takes all the elements of genius in acting, of peak performance, and dissects them into doable exercises for the beginner to play with, for the intermediate artist to polish skills, and for the advanced actor to master. If the love is there, your results will generate extraordinary experiences for you and your audience alike.

Are you willing to get up on your feet? Will you venture with me in a game of Follow the Leader?

Would you enjoy playing a game you may never have experienced without knowing what the game is? With the only guideline being to imitate what the leader is doing as best you can? It should last about three to five minutes. If you are playing alone, perhaps you might record the following at a fast pace, maybe around three minutes for the whole sequence, taking about a second in between each action. And then, whip through the sequence freely, believing you know what you are doing and that it is perfect.

##  Let's play Follow the Leader

Ok, Ready? Spread your body out as big as it can get. Tuck up into a tiny, hard ball. Pretend you have to go through heavy mud to stand up. Now, a wave catches you, washing you off, and then you float up and start to fly like an eagle. Suddenly, you turn into lightning. Now you are fire, laser, sunlight. Push something huge. Now pull it. Lift it. Smash it. Throw it. Gather it. Penetrate it. Tear it apart. Drag it. Reach for it. Start to flop around like you want to fall down but you don't. Now, walk on a tightrope trying not to fall. Now, pretend you are in outer space with no gravity. Now, look at your hands. Move them slowly, cautiously. Let your whole body move that way. Look at your hands again and make sharp fists, grunting and stomping; start sobbing; now, giggle and make light, silly movements. Look around. You are walking in a cemetery late at night. Now it's a shopping mall; now it's a rock concert; now, a funeral. You are a commanding king, a shy orphan, a condescending bitch. You move easily through space. Now, make forms that start somewhere, have a middle and an end. Now you are in awe and beauty. You move like you are on top of the world. You follow the tip of your nose, bouncing as you go. Now, your groin juts out in front and drags you around. Now you are a lion. A tin man. A scarecrow. A professor. An excited cheerleader, a two-year-old in a tantrum. You are a stick, a veil, a ball. Now, you send beams of light out. And now, you draw beams of light in. Now you throw those beams of light somewhere way far away. Now you thrust forward, right, left, down, up, back, and to the horizon. Look at your clothes on your body while adjusting them. Look straight into a partner's eyes. Look at something in the room where you are. Imagine where you had your last meal. Glance briefly up to the universe and toss your hands up. Now you imagine tearing a part of your body away. Now you gather a dying child. Now you cheer up the world with joy.

##  Journal/Discuss/Flyback

*What was that? What was your experience? What happened? What did we do? Was it fun? How did that feel?*

---

 **Axiom 0.5: If it isn't fun ... it isn't Chekhov ...** 🙂

---

Our work is play, and Chekhov often said, "Don't Toil!" We love to play hard with full commitment, and when it is fun we can do it for hours. Jack Nicholson, known to use Chekhov, is said to have done 12 to 14 hours of repeating his famous "You can't handle the truth" speech from the film *A Few Good Men* at full performance every take, while off camera. When the director Rob Reiner reminded Jack that he didn't need to go full force every time, Jack responded "You don't understand, Rob. I LOOOVE to act." He was able to turn it on and off, to be goofy between shots and then deadly serious. You too can build this kind of skill set while having some serious fun.

What we have just done is to whip completely around the entire Chart of Inspired Action (Figure P.1). Everything you will be doing from here on out, you will already have done on some level, at least once. Chances are, as you play with these tools discovering ever more about them, you will recognize many things as familiar to you. Perhaps you did this under another name. Or maybe it was the way you intuitively used to do things before someone said to do it in another way. You certainly did all these things in some way, unconsciously, when you were in peak performance states. Now, we are here to be conscious of the energies that happen in those moments and to be able to access those energy patterns on command.

In 1955, Chekhov recorded a series of audio lectures[6], outlining his Five Guiding Principles for mastering his technique. This training sequence is built upon these principles. As you read them now, they may not make much sense; however, as you continue to discover *Acting the Michael Chekhov Way*, we will refer to these, and they will become more and more intuitive for you. GP1: We practice full-bodied movements called psycho-physical exercises (PPE). They awaken and connect our body and imagination. GP2: We use images and ideas that we can't literally touch, yet they produce a powerful effect in the storytelling process. GP3: We play with a sense of the creative spirit and higher self as real powers that unite the many different parts of our performance. GP4: We discover that any single part of the *Michael Chekhov way* appears to awaken all the other parts at once, like a hologram. The whole is in every part. GP5: We explore each of these parts to figure out how they help us feel free and happy on the stage. When we know how much a skill helps us, it makes us want to play with them even more. For example, when we build our basic concentration skills and see how important they are for doing the more intricate techniques like psychological gesture (PG), that's when we will happily sit down again and do the long, still, intense focusing exercises that we were bored with in the beginning.

- See **OR 0.6** for deeper 5 GP handout/training integration

> **Axiom 0.6: Five Guiding Principles for *Acting the Michael Chekhov Way***
> - Practice psycho-physical exercise to affect artistic states (GP1).
> - Use intangible means of expression to produce tangible results (GP2).
> - Employ creative spirit and higher intellect to unify various aspects of your performance (GP3).
> - Use each point on the Chart of Inspired Action to awaken all other points on the circle (GP4).
> - Go over each point on the Chart of Inspired Action and ask each, *"To what degree and by what means do you free my talent?"* (GP5).

## Foundational concepts

Before embarking on learning each tool and its application, having some basic terms and policies to share will help keep things moving efficiently, creating an environment conducive to hearty play and growth.

## The universal being

There is an ideal self that each of us can be, become, once were—the best possible expression of us. This self is unencumbered by the everyday self, perceives no limitations of expression, and holds the highest ideals for us and others. When we are operating from this self, we are in a peak performance state. Our energy seems to be centered in our chest, about three inches below the collarbone, inside. It has a quality like the sun, radiating and receiving. We call this our **Ideal Artistic Center (IAC)**. It is from this point that we imagine our impulses emanate when we play with our techniques and perform our roles.

When we use the term IDEAL; what is ideal is specifically unique to you. Your body, mind, and spirit have their own blueprint of perfection. We each have vulnerabilities that we have developed over our lifetimes which can block our natural, ideal self. These are present when we are hanging out casually. When we wish to get into some serious play, you are invited to allow your highest, uninhibited self to come to the party.

Whenever possible, bring this part of you to the practice session with the confidence that it wants to come play in a field of safety. Imagine that when you enter the play space, you are crossing a threshold into a safe playground where all the rest of reality is left outside.

## Three levels of attention

In the time dedicated for play, we can maximize our energy use to make everything more efficient. In essence, we are in one of three levels of attention:

1. Hang time = loosely attentive
2. State of readiness/standby = active with our awareness of our IAC
3. In action = fully concentrated while exercising or performing

In *hang time*, we are in a more dispersed level of focus, with low levels of concentration. We are released, possibly resting, recollecting, and conserving our resources. In *standby*, we are focusing fully, actively preparing to cross a threshold into an artistic act. We are centered in our universal self. In *action*, we are transformed into the art, fully focused on our playing. We can consciously shift between levels, but we sometimes unconsciously shift levels, depending on our concentration. You can use this in two ways. First, monitor your own attention level and shift it into the level that supports your current work. Second, notice that any character is also subject to these levels. You can put your character into the level appropriate to the scene so you, the artist, are *in action* of being a character in *hang time*.

## ✒ Journal/Discuss/Flyback

*Take some time to observe how these three levels of attention are at play in everyday life. Can I use my attention more efficiently?*

## Silence as a tool

Keeping in mind the following will also help. Staying silent during transitions between segments of class, between being given directions for an exercise and beginning the exercise, will help you grow faster. These three levels of attention are very clear on a film set or in a rehearsal when we are between takes/scenes, on stand-by or in places, and when action is called, and when we play the scene. Learning to conserve energy, when possible, allows us to focus it powerfully when in action.

## ✒ Journal/Discuss/Flyback

*What happens to your energy and focus when you chitchat for a moment during transitions? How could being silent change things?*

Here's an example of the power of conserving focus in transitions. The leader invites the ensemble to form two rows facing each other, which we will call an alley and select a partner who will go first (see Let's play silent alley, below). Normally several minutes of chaos follows before everyone figures it out and gets the form and partners clear, etc. Could this be done more efficiently, without words? Yes, and our concentration remains more focused. When we verbalize the selection process, many extraneous words are used, the general hubbub of the larger group inspires extra chatter, and the atmosphere dissipates instantly. There is a loss of form, rhythm, and entirety. The leader then needs to corral the group back into focus. Regardless of how careful the leader is, such "corralling" might be experienced as reprimanding, and might curtail freedom, beauty, and ease. It also challenges the focus and flow of the leader, possibly allowing loss of ease and a gain of guilt, disappointment in having to "command" the group or a Rodney Dangerfield sense of "getting no respect."

## Let's play silent alley

Try (or imagine) you and an ensemble of actors fluidly and quietly form an alley in absolute silence by

- Moving into an alley with two lines facing each other
- Finding a partner
- Selecting who will lead

## Journal/Discuss/Flyback

*What do I notice? Was it possible? How did it feel? Was forming the alley a little piece of art? Could I imagine a future where we are so aware of each other that we are able to arrive from any point in the room at precisely the same moment and settle into any form suggested in a state of readiness for the impending action? Continuously creating little pieces of art?*

Transitions in silence circumvent the possible consequences of noisy dispersion mentioned earlier. Silence builds the tool of concentration. Concentration skills build and strengthen synaptic connections in the brain. Remember our gesture for strong focus? (See Figure 0.1.) All peak performance has complete concentration on a single focal point. If one breaks the stream of concentration on the game being played, it can create a chain reaction among the whole ensemble. Having the self-discipline to not talk, especially during transitions, can be quite a relief in fact. It creates a powerful atmosphere of respect among the team.

This is also an important professional skill. When we are doing our exercises, imagine that we are on stage (or on camera). When we have a transition to make in class and we would like to keep the focus strong; we can pretend that we are backstage (or off-camera) while the play is still going on (or the camera is still rolling), so that we must move and communicate quietly and efficiently using non-verbal communication. This idea might be a fun way to get our whole ensemble to maintain silence, build powers of concentration, imagination, and radiation while supporting the whole, easy, and efficient flowing form of a beautiful play session. For those of us who have health conditions that challenge our concentration and focus, making a game out of it that we know will pay off in the real world can be inspiring.

You may notice efficiency is a recurring value in our system. In fact, the entire technique is designed to help us efficiently manage our energy with health and safety. Peak performances use only as much energy as necessary, no more, no less. It is very ecological in this way and saves us a great deal of stress. We learn to turn on our attention through preparation, focus it with the exact amount of effort needed for the action, then sustain it and then stop it, releasing, back into *hang time*.

>  Axiom 0.7: All peak performance has maximum efficient use of energy.

## Kinds of imagination

### Orphan

One time, my Chekhov teacher guided my class through seeing an image of an orphan, watching them walk to a trash can, do something, and return. I sat there, trying my best to see this orphan. I got nothing. I felt terrible. I would never be able to do this technique because I couldn't see anything in my imagination. I was really dropping the ball on this and hated myself for being untalented. I kept

> trying but kept seeing nothing. When it was my turn, I decided to totally fake it. I stood up, became the orphan I pretended to have seen, walked to the trashcan, did whatever it was in the trash and then went to turn around. Suddenly, I was—only very briefly—confused as to whether to turn left or right to get back to where I began. I turned left just for the heck of it, trying not to miss a beat, and returned. The teacher said, "Good, it was very clear that you saw everything but which way the orphan turns to come back."

Wow, that was a shock. What I learned was that I had a kinesthetic imagination rather than a visual one; and, that I could imagine in an equally powerful way—not wrong, just different. The inspiration for my "pretending to see" had been real. I had gotten hung up and limited by what I thought I was supposed to do because of the words "See the image." Today, I have done this activity so many times that I can now see, hear, smell, and feel the images one way or another. I don't even think about limiting how images arise for me. However your imagination works now is perfect and can be developed further if you want to do so.

##  Journal/Discuss/Flyback

### My imagination

*How does your imagination operate? Are you visual? Aural? Symbolic? Kinesthetic? Other? Are you happy with the way your imagination works? Or are you mad that it doesn't operate a different way? What can you do to accept what you are doing and add more?*

## The primary laws of composition

> ### ⚛ Axiom 0.8 The Three Primary Laws of Composition (TPT)
> - Triplicity—Law of Threes
> - Polarity/Contrast—Yin/Yang/Opposites
> - Transformation—Law of Change

Michael Chekhov integrated TPT into all his work. Many things are seen in threes, or triples, called *triplicity*. Many laws describe triples in nature. In composition of artistic works, one knows of beginning, middle, and end or introduction, body, and conclusion. In verticality, we have top, middle, and bottom. We also experience polarity and contrast, up/down, in/out, good/bad, yes/no, etc. The law of polar opposites is required to make a work interesting. Finally, transformation must occur to make a story compelling. Something significant must change across the arc of the story—a character, something between characters, or with the world must transform as a result. These primary laws are seen in all dramatic works, in scene work, and throughout Chekhov's methods and techniques. They are even in athletic competitions. Things start with an even match; the game is played. There is a halfway point and then an ending with a winner. Thus, any event that ends in a tie is somehow less than ideal.

Always search for these three laws we abbreviate as TPT. With the Michael Chekhov way, we can access unlimited creative images. We will ultimately need to select the best ones for our performance. TPT will become our compass for making great choices. When in doubt, choose three for your rhythm and polarity/contrast for your dynamics. This creates transformation in the story. Don't worry, we will explore this in detail as we go.

## Journal/Discuss/Flyback

*Where do I see TPT in the world around me? What things come in threes? What are some polarities in my own personality? What do I see changing/transforming regularly, gradually, or suddenly?*

## PASS the energy

Chekhov used a key concept in all his movement exercises, from body movement to moving energy, from ball-toss to physical gestures. And, in fact, one will see this concept throughout our work when an action is taken at any level. Before you begin a move, **prepare** by reaching mentally or physically in the opposite direction of the movement. Inhale at this step to draw in enough breath to express the action.

Insufficient preparation weakens the expression. We must work harder during the action to make up for lack of preparation. That's when things don't come out the way we hope.

> ⚛ Axiom 0.9: Strong preparation makes easy.

Follow the inhaled preparation with your **action** while exhaling. Extend this movement fully toward the receiver of the action (e.g. when tossing a ball across the circle to a partner extend your hand fully toward, reaching the receiver). This action ensures that the energy you send reaches the receiver. This is radiating. Once the action is radiated to the receiver, then you **sustain** the reach as the energy carries to the receiver, usually three beats. Sustaining is the same as an athlete's follow-through. The ball can't reach its destination and lands short of the target without the correct follow-through. When acting, failure to sustain the energy causes the end of lines to fall or disappear affecting the flow of conversation of characters. The actors lose energy at the end of the scene, or the energy never reaches the audience.

Finally, **stop** by fully releasing the energy and any physical force (e.g. drop the arms to the side).

> ⚛ Axiom 0.10: PASS the Energy.
> - Prepare—inhale images
> - Action—exhale expression
> - Sustain—radiate three beats
> - Stop—full release

By using this Prepare-Act-Sustain-Stop (PASS) method, you can ensure that the energy and the action (e.g. lines in a scene) are delivered strongly to the receiver and audience.

## Journal/Discuss/Flyback

*Where do you see this PASSing of energy in the world around you? When one of the parts is missing, what happens?*

## Spatial awareness

Today, many people live their lives with very little awareness of anything that is not right in front of them. In this world of alternative staging, site specific, theatre-in-the-round, etc., you want the ability to impact the audience regardless of what view they have of you. Since you are always an artist and your whole body is your artistic instrument, let's be 360-degree actors. To help build spatial dynamics, we use six directions: your back space, right- and left-side space, above and below, along with front space. If we imagine our unseen inspiration flows from our above and our back space, developing that becomes crucial to our creativity.

 Journal/Discuss/Flyback

*What is your spatial awareness level? Where does it focus? How many degrees of awareness are you using in daily life? When you are training? When you are performing?*

 Sandwich Cookie Flyback

Giving value to your efforts is imperative to freeing your inner creativity and allowing full expression of it. Chekhov rarely raised his voice to a colleague or identified something as "wrong." Self-abuse was one exception, and our policy is to be very firm on this subject. Self-criticism and abusive criticism from anyone toward yourself or another are not tolerated in our reality. It is antithetical to fostering a field of freedom that must be grounded in safety first. Kindness has deep meaning for us.

So much time, energy, and heartbreak have been thrust into the player's training that the entire profession has been considered dismal. We were told to toughen up and get a thick skin. We lived in a state of paranoia about being judged horribly. We justified our paranoia by hiring teachers who systematically tore us apart. We were told it was for our own good. We created vicious inner critics to try to fix us before others attack us. These days we are even applauded for saying "My bad." Let's let go of making ourselves bad. Let's say "No more shame!" As soon as we accept that things come out differently than we hope, we can transform it into a lesson, and every lesson transforms into love. That's TPT in inner action. We grow healthier and happier for it.

## Let's play criticize or evaluate

Stand up for a moment. Center yourself and close your eyes. Now, listen to someone or say the word "**criticize**" with the energy of intense judgment. Hit the K and T sounds harshly. Allow your whole body to react as if the sounds were actual physical weapons.

Simply listening to the auditory impact of the harsh K and T in "criticize" makes us cringe. What does the term "to criticize" mean? It seems to connote a negative judgement.

Center yourself and close your eyes again. Now, say the word "**evaluate**" with the energy of simplicity. Allow your whole body to react as if the sounds were actually giving value to you.

What happens to the auditory flow of evaluate? What does evaluate mean? To give value to.

## Journal/Discuss/Flyback

*What is the difference in your body's response to* criticize *versus* evaluate? *Which do you want to experience more?*

Self-talk and word choices are deeply impacting on our psyche, and here is one of the most significant learnings that Chekhov offers us. Sticks and stones may break my bones … and those bones often heal more quickly than the wounds of words. In the beginning was the word. It has the power to give life.

When we find a way to give value accurately to what we have given to our audience, and creatively ask "What more can I offer?" then we get very interested in a "second take." We are also completely independent of needing outside input. If we get hit with criticism, we can develop dread and want to avoid the second take. We invest heavily in getting approved of by others and getting it right according to what we think they think is right. This is dangerous thinking, for how can we know what anyone else is really thinking? How many actors take a scene study class and self-direct the scene specifically to avoid getting criticized for things they have seen that teacher attack in other scenes?

How is learning *how not to get attacked by this teacher* going to help you with your next director? Most directors hope you will show them something surprising and perfect beyond what they could have imagined; and they will be with you only briefly over the span of your art. The great risk you take in being creative is rewarded when surprises happen. When you cultivate greater and greater understanding of what works and what doesn't, you will be able to self-direct. This entire way of learning leads you to this, the theatre of the future. Then, any additional help you get from a director is a wonderful guiding blessing and springboard to even more fun.

With the Flyback process, the teacher/director's job is to guide you through your self-evaluation and reflect back the accuracy of it. We artists who immediately trash ourselves, apologize or blame, need to pause and find what we can appreciate overall about how we played the scene. I like to think in terms of sandwich cookies. They have three parts. So, using this as an image, ask yourself to identify the bottom cookie: "What did I like overall?" Once you discard the "It sucked," sandwich and replace it with the "Well, I liked this overall," then, ask, "How would I double stuff it, making it even tastier the next time?" You are ready to review objectively and create a plan for your next rehearsal or take. Top the cookie by asking, "What was my favorite moment?" Watch the state of self-appreciation open up a healing flow of creativity that inspires your future activity. It also builds the very necessary skill for discovering sparkling, spontaneous moments we call jewels, and for instantly making wonderful choices, as you will learn.

This Cookie Flyback in three self-appreciating parts can take time to do. It is very well worth doing. However, in productions, in semesters and intensive programs the practicality of coaching each person may fall to the wayside. You as an actor can continue to Flyback personally and in journals, etc. regardless of whether or not there is time in class or rehearsal. The teacher/director can give notes, keeping in mind this basic formula of observing an overall positive, giving growth-producing suggestions, and ending with a special moment that you liked. You also might ask your director or coach the three questions.

Jack Colvin[7] used the word "Spyback," and Mala Powers used "Flyback." There are points in Chekhov's writing where either is used. Experiment for yourself to see if one word inspires you more. And, as for the cookie, perhaps a cherry-topped hot fudge sundae is more your taste!

The Cookie Flyback is a guide to healthy self-evaluation that "appreciates what you've done and excites you for what is to come." We are using the image of something most people enjoy (see Figure 0.2).

Build from the ground up with the base cookie, add extra filling and then the top cookie. Ask three questions in the order described or change the order as you wish.

---

 **Axiom 0.11: Cookie Flyback**

1. The bottom cookie: **What did I like overall?**
2. Double-stuff the middle: **What can I add next time to make it more delicious?**
3. The top cookie: **What was my favorite moment?**

*Figure 0.2* Double-stuffed sandwich cookie for the Flyback, a three-part healthy self-reflection. Art by Author.

This teacher, that director, even your parents—all those folks you hope will approve of you and your acting, won't be with you forever. Ultimately, you are the only one who is going to be with you your whole life. And you are the only one who truly needs to appreciate what you do. Experience alone does not create growth. Repetition grows power—good or bad. Experience and repetition with self-reflection create healthy empowerment. Being able to self-assess frees you from needing their "approval." When you are in the zone, in peak performance, you are free from needing anyone else's affirmation that you went there. Of course, it is nice to know they went there with you, even though you already knew in your heart.

> **Missed audition**
>
> One day in Los Angeles, I was so "high" from a wonderful class I taught at the American Film Institute that on the way home I decided to drop by my agent's office to say Hi. I walked in and she said to me, "Oh, they liked you, but they went a different way." I stood in shock, not understanding whom she was talking about. My mind began to race, chattering: "Who liked me? When? Oh … CRAP! I completely forgot to go to a producer meeting at Warner Brothers for a TV series!" I asked her, "What do you mean, they liked me?" She repeated that they said I did a good job, but they chose someone else. I asked if it was another actor from this same agency? Yes. And then I said, "Ok, but did they actually say they liked Lisa Dalton's audition?" Yes, they said you specifically. "Well, I am embarrassed to say, I forgot to go." She stared at me, trying to clarify what I just said. "It's true, I never went." She looked at me, and after a pause, said, "Well, let's not tell them that!"

A producer meeting at a studio is usually limited to five actors per role, each actor having been selected from 20 to 40 previous auditioners and possibly 1000 to 3000 submissions. It is a prized opportunity to meet the directors and producers and to strengthen relationships with the casting directors. And I got good feedback from Warner Brothers without even phoning it in. The moral of the story is that good feedback from others may not be true! It serves us well to receive it all gracefully while building faith and trust in accurate self-reflection.

Introduction    23

> ⚛ Axiom 0.12: Healthy Growth/Power = Repetition + Reflection

## Afraid of overacting?

One of the most common fears an actor has is being accused of overacting. It just sucks when that happens. Because this technique invites you to be huge and powerful, you might be a bit scared of looking like you are overacting. Don't worry about that to start with. Imagine this fairy godmother has cast a spell on the whole group, making big, powerful acting into perfect magic! And the secret is that big, powerful acting is different from overacting.

**Overacting** happens when the player has not engaged the entire body, usually abandoning the lower body by over-charging the upper body. The lower body is then relegated to the task of keeping the actor's face off the floor and from falling forward. More than just a cliché, there is a physical sense that you did fall on your face in that scene.

We could say the lower body is not engaged in anything the character is doing; rather it is solely struggling to balance the actor. We might imagine that 95% of the character's energy inhabits the upper 50% of the actor's body. Maybe 5% of the character remains in the lower body. The antidote here is to distribute the veiled energy through the entire body by literally "bringing it down" and saving face! (see Figure 0.3.)

When most actors hear "Bring it down," they usually bring it "in" and decrease the energy while staying "over the top." Imagine instead, that the energy of the tool is rising from the Earth into your legs and groin simultaneously with the energy shooting from your IAC into the Earth. This empowers the lower

*Figure 0.3* Acting over the top? Stop, and literally bring your energy down into the whole body.

body and allows the actor to radiate intensity while barely moving and they might even be speaking in a whisper.

## Veiling—adjust your style and size of acting

Chekhov gave Mala Powers a very strong image of how to make these big physical exercises into usable acting forms for different styles. He called it veiling.

**Veiling** is when you make the tool less visible in the body while keeping the energy at high intensity.

Imagine that you have a very bright light on the stage. If it is too bright for the scene, there are several ways to make it less bright. You could lower the switch on the dimmer board. This will decrease the light by decreasing the amount of power or electricity going into the light. Do you want to decrease your power? Or you could put something over the light, like a gel or a gobo, limiting the amount of light without decreasing the energy. This is what Chekhov prefers. He suggests that a veil will soften the energy without decreasing the power. Make the veils thicker or thinner as needed.

 Let's play veiling

To practice veiling, expand with both your energy body and your physical body in a fully unveiled manner. Then decide to veil it lightly; perhaps only 10% is veiled. The physical body now reveals only 90% of the movement while the energy body is imagined doing 100%. Increase the degree of veiling by percentages in increments based on your time available. First veil only 25%, 50%, 75%, 90%, and 99%; all the while, the energy body remains at 100%. Allow the 1% that is revealed in a 99% veil to "leak" through the IAC.

Chekhov suggests that our hands need special training because, after the eyes, they are the main thing people look at. I suggest that the next thing we look at are the feet. Consider what gets a closeup first? The eyes. Second, the hands. Third, the feet. So, wouldn't it be important to give extra attention to training those three areas? Keep this in mind when veiling and unveiling in the large abstract full-bodied explorations. Let the eyes, hands, and feet be the place where things stay a little less veiled. Things leak out through these three key places. Each person in life has a special way of using their eyes, hands, and feet. We call it **eye life, hand life, and foot life.**

## Journal/Discuss/Flyback

*What is your eye life? Hand life? Foot life? How does it differ from your character?*

Dial the veiling up or down to meet the style. For a soap opera you may be very veiled. For A *Midsummer Night's Dream* you may be very unveiled. You will use this modification process throughout your career. It will enable you to use more power in a closeup on camera than you use in a French farce. This veiling gave Clint Eastwood his whole career. As a shy musician, it took him some time to get it authentically powerful in his eye life. He worked with the Chekhov tools and when he honed radiation to an art, he became a world-renown superstar. So, knowing you can do this, I am sure has *made your day*. "Do you feel lucky?"

## Tips for technique mastery

If you truly seek a path to happiness via mastering your art, take the following suggestions to heart.

> ⚛ Axiom 0.13: Know your goal, objective, aim or purpose, your "What for?"

Chekhov often asked the question "What for? What for are you doing this?" We are accustomed to asking *why* our character is doing something. Here, we are using slightly weird words—somehow, they make a difference. Perhaps it inspires a clear goal, aim or outcome? *What for* are you doing this training? *What for* is this exercise? Once you know what skills you are building, what purposes you want to achieve in your training, then you adjust the exercises to address your *what for*.

"I want the audience to totally get me!"

Maybe it sounds selfish, egotistical or whatever, but on some level, to want that is absolutely a sacred act. Let's go for it! More will be shared later on how true this is. Suffice it to say, the "me" you ask them to "get" lives in you as an **image**.

## The acting job description

The artist's job is another triplicity: to convey **images** from your highest creative individuality to the audience; therefore, let's learn to access, select, convey (ASC):

> ⚛ Axiom 0.14: We train to Access, Select, Convey images.

1. **A**ccess, conjure, create, receive, and allow images to appear and inspire. Here is where our creative concentration and imagination truly shine.
2. **S**elect from amongst the many images that appear; choose an ideal image for the story being told. This is where our application of TPT helps us make great choices that are a perfect fit for the whole story. Our creative individuality takes the spotlight here.
3. **C**onvey, reveal, radiate the chosen image truthfully in communion with the script, director, mise-en-scene, audience, and your higher self. This fixes that horrible problem of getting great ideas and them not coming out right. No more ouch!

## The learning curve

Some acting approaches begin with training to focus and respond to your partner so that you are fully in a state of re-acting to your partner. In *Acting the Michael Chekhov Way*, we expand the definition of partner to include different parts of our self, the space, the author, and the other actors in that order. We begin by developing artistic sensitivity to our imagination and bodies first. When we are succeeding in allowing our imagination to lead us, then we learn to respond to the space, the text, and our partners. The more sources that can inspire us, the better. You can learn a great deal working solo during the exercises while also cultivating sensitivity to an ensemble.

**Michael Chekhov's Chart: A Map to Happiness (Figure P.1)**

Chekhov's approach evolved over a lifetime on three continents through extraordinary socio-political-technological change. His writings, recorded lectures, and the notes taken of his live teaching are very extensive. Like the famous story of the group of blind men touching an elephant and arguing over what it is, if you sample random Chekhov workshops and books, you may never know what the larger whole truly is. This is where the Chart of Inspired Acting saves the day, as it unites single elements of his method into a solid and fluid technique. Shortly before Chekhov died, he drew a chart by hand for Mala Powers[8]. A version of this original Chart of Inspired Acting was published in the book, *On the Technique of Acting* in 1991 as a reminder of all the resources Michael Chekhov offers. It serves as a treasure map for anyone wanting *to be "happy on the stage"* (Chekhov 2004).

## Overview of the book: Understanding the chart as a pathway into the zone—a clear sequence

The chart is sun-like in its depiction. If we want our sun to shine or, in contemporary terms, if we want to get into "the zone," all we need to do is to focus on a single point on this chart. Your focus creates a chain reaction by igniting the light in that box, which sends sparks into the center. This ignites all other points instantly and effortlessly. Chekhov offers us a holographic technique where the whole is in each part. Each box on the periphery describes a tool, a concept, or a universal law representing one or more elements of inspired "happy" states. The National Michael Chekhov Association (NMCA) motto of bringing the spirit of Michael Chekhov into the 21st century has led to transforming the original black-and-white chart into a multicolored one. Numbers on the Chart of Inspired Acting identify the training sequence presented.

In his actor training, Chekhov looked at what energy patterns are present in peak performances, identified these patterns, and created exercises to activate them at will. Thus, we create the favorable conditions to coax inspired images by replicating the energy patterns of inspiration. To develop the rich psychophysical sensitivity required, the actor awakens the energy by exaggerated use of the body with strong concentration on the image and gradually lessens the physical movement to achieve the style of the performance. These fundamental principles are the fastest way to build your skills.

## ✒ Journal/Discuss/Flyback

*How do you feel about moving in big, exaggerated movements? Making weird and abstract movements and sounds that you may have never done before? Are you willing to go for it? Wait ... didn't we just do that?*

In truth, if you did the Follow the Leader exercise (Let's Play Follow the Leader), you did just do all the above. We whipped around the whole sequence. From here on out, everything we will play with, you have already done successfully.

Below is a brief orientation to the tools on the chart. Following that will be an in-depth exploration of each concept and its application. This sequential flow is designed to make everything you are learning into a practical, efficient, inspiring energy management system for peak performance.

You can see a set of numbers on the chart. In the text are the corresponding numbers in parenthesis. These represent the basic order of learning the tools. Some of the elements, however, we will use throughout the whole process and will be merged in as needed. Specific recurring ones include the following:

- Warmups, including the Ball Toss and yoga, both practiced by Chekhov himself (#2)
- Images of the Quantum Peek Pie chart and the Goblet of Inspiration (#1)
- Ensemble (#9), Truth (#10), Improvisation (#18)
- Compositional laws of Triplicity, Polarity, Transformation (TPT) (# 19)
- Prepare, Act, Sustain, Stop (PASS) the energy (#2)
- Full voice, energy, and body integration (#9, #10)
- Openhearted contact (#9)
- Flyback–reflective self-evaluation (#8)

The teaching uses Chekhov's Law of Triplicity. First, an introduction and exploration of each element is rhythmically followed by second, improvisation to deepen the skill with the tool, and then third, a scene/monologue study to explore and develop application skills. Wil Kilroy, Co-founder of National Michael Chekhov Association, has a companion book, *Improvisation the Michael Chekhov Way*, which offers many additional improvisations and games to go with this sequence.[9] Appropriate complementary chapters will be suggested with each detailed exploration of the tools and will be forthwith noted as

- See *Kilroy Improv* Chapter #.

You will also see acronyms or abbreviations in parenthesis next to terms introduced. In the front is a list of what these abbreviations mean. For a system to be useful, having easy-to-remember ways to notate becomes quite handy. These abbreviations are intended to become a kind of shorthand for artists to collaborate, making notetaking, direction-giving, and concept-sharing very efficient.

One of Chekhov's bold ideas is that the images of the story, the characters, situations, etc., already exist independently in the collective unconscious, an unlimited sphere of imagination that we will call our **I-sphere**. If we accept this or pretend to accept this, then making contact with the images, and then conveying these images to audiences becomes the actor's greatest task (Axiom 0.14).

## Journal/Discuss/Flyback

*Do you know how it is when an image arises but doesn't come out right? Has this happened to you? How does it make you feel?*

It happens when there is a disconnect between your imagination and your body's ability to express it. After establishing a field of safety with the Ball Toss, solving this image–body gap is where we begin the journey.

## Part I—Preparation: welcome and online resources

(#1)[10] *Preparing Your Imagination, Your Body, and the Ensemble* relies upon the vast unlimited possibilities of the imagination, offering the means to expand it, increase its creativity, and nurture the uniqueness of each artist's gifts. You need never toil or fret that your imagination is dry or small. You can stimulate your imagination simply and rapidly, by asking it questions. The entire Chart of Inspired Action reminds us of all the questions we might ask. TPT will help us choose from the many answers which may flow into us. The PPEs will help us reveal the answers we choose: ASC (Axiom 0.14).

**The Goblet** exercise is an experiential process of understanding our aims. We follow this with an exploration of the **Quantum Peek Pie Chart** where we build an image of ourselves in relation to who we are, our sense of identity, and what our aim is in creating characters with their own identities. With that, we discover the value of expanding "our piece of the pie." This leads us to

## Part II—Psycho-physical Bodybuilding for Actors

The Psycho-Physical Exercises (PPEs) are

- (#2) *Expanding/Contracting*—<u>What</u> the most basic pattern of all motion is.
- (#3) *Qualities/Kinds of Movement*—<u>How</u> the motion meets resistance using Earth, water, air fire/light as a metaphor.
- (#4) *Archetypal Gestures*—<u>Why</u> the motion is done: to push, to pull, to smash, etc.

Doing the PPEs restores the artist's ability to move or speak in any way that a character might. Like a vocalist mastering the scales allows them to sing any note confidently, the artist here restores to themselves the ability to freely convey any image without inhibitions. The PPEs train the imagination, energy body, and physical body to play interactively with each other. PPEs prevent the pain of having a great idea and it not coming out the way you knew it could.

> ### Smash
>
> Matthew was a very gentle, soft-spoken actor frustrated with his failure to book auditions. He was a six-foot-five, very dark-skinned body builder, constantly auditioning for physically dominating and aggressive characters like bodyguards, cops, and bullies. But he had avoided expressing aggression in his life for so long that he was afraid he might lose control of it when acting. His own energy body was small and gentle. After practicing the smash gesture, Matthew learned how to turn his aggression on safely and instantly while acting and to turn it off when done. Within one year he was fully supporting his family as an actor.

With mastery of the Psycho-Physical Exercises, Matthew's problem of being unable to convey the image of aggression was solved. Learning to use these three foundational tools will restore to you all possible ways for your characters to move. These tools release the psychophysical blocks of your everyday personality. Like dancers who practice the barre exercises throughout their careers, actors who practice the PPEs regularly are ready to perform any role.

## ✒ Journal/Discuss/Flyback

*What would you need to believe right now to want to hone your skills to a level of mastery?*

## Part 3—Emotional life for Actors

The next step in becoming an energy management master is cultivating the emotional life. "Not feeling the moment" is one of the greatest lifelong fears that actors have. Three main tools to awaken artistic feelings are the Three Sister Sensations, Qualities and Sensations, and Atmospheres. These all work on an objective level, freeing the artist from using personal pain as a stimulant for a process that is an in-the-moment creation.

(#5) *Three Sister Sensations of Equilibrium* (3S) tool examines gravity as the law of physics that most affects us, and it is non-directional. The tool can be applied three ways: to great emotional effect, as an element of characterization, or to segue between gestures.

- *Falling* is yielding to gravitational pull from any direction.
- *Balancing* is teetering, struggling for balance.
- *Floating* is weightlessness in any direction, distinct from the *elemental quality of movement of flowing/floating/water*.

(#6) *Qualities and Sensations* (Q&S) free us from the fear of not feeling the emotion and remove the need for psychologically disturbing recall and substitution approaches. Moving body, breath, and voice with a quality awakens a sensation which cultivates a feeling and radiates it out.

These Feeling Life Tools, 3S and Q&S, activate the emotional energy artistically within the artist—from center to periphery.

(#7) *Atmospheres: Overall and Personal* (ATMO) are the feeling energy in a space that results from the combination of the elements of that place plus the events happening in the space. Actors create atmosphere through imagination and then respond to these atmospheres accordingly. Atmospheres linger in the soul of the audience and are the single most missing element in storytelling today. Atmospheres will become increasingly necessary to draw audiences to see performances. The Overall ATMO (OA) affects all in its scope.

*Personal Atmosphere* (PA) is the name for another type of atmosphere, the human aura. It can be connected to the enduring essence, personality or archetype of the character.

These Feeling Life Tools, OA and PA, activate the emotional energy of the space, awakening the artists' response from the periphery to the center.

With the PPEs and the Feeling Life Tools, the artist can now perform any character, objective, and emotional requirement called for on the job. But what about a tool for a healthy life?

(#8). *The Four Brothers of Art*: Beauty, Ease, Entirety, and Form (BEEF) are four concepts present in all peak performances and help the artist thrive in meeting the challenges of life. Fully embracing these keeps you stable and healthy through all crises, strengthening your relationship to self and others. Creating safe spaces that inspire brave engagement is cultivated with multiple exercises like the Ball Toss, Making Friends, Cookie Flyback, and the objective Feeling Life Tools.

## Part IV—Esthetics

(#9) *Ensemble* connects with the *Feeling of Entirety and Form* and incorporates the *five communions* the artist cultivates. Every performance is an ensemble act in communion with the audience, writer, co-actors, director, and the *higher self/creative individuality*. All communions engender inspiration, a feeling of truth and wholeness, beauty, and form. All Michael Chekhov way training builds a feeling of ensemble—our place in the cosmos. Exercises such as the Ball Toss, Golden Hoop, Harmonious Groupings, and Improvisations all build ensemble.

(#10) *Truth* is relative to the style, since what is true in one style, such as soap opera, is not in another, such as farce. Truth rises and falls on commitment to the whole: style, ensemble, body, voice, as we see in our Over the Top (Figure 0.3). Meisner, in *Sanford Meisner on Acting* (p. 10), says it was "Michael Chekhov who made me realize truth, as in Naturalism, was far from the whole truth."[11] With this understanding, all styles can exist truthfully with full commitment.

(#11) *Style* is an element of feeling of form, such as classical theatre, film, and avant-garde works, on stage or on camera. All styles are greatly supported by Chekhov. A future publication in this series will specifically address style for various applications. During this initial training, styles are introduced as needed for the material being addressed. *Veiling* is the process of masking or revealing the degree of expression which the spectator sees. Using the power of the imagination, you, the actor, can shift to any style, on camera or on stage, by increasing or decreasing your veiling, without ever losing creative power. Growing comfortable with different styles becomes easy the Chekhov way. Style defines truth in production.

## Part V—Transformation

(#12) *Transformational Characterization* satisfies the yearning to transform that all artists carry within themselves. This area is where the Michael Chekhov way wins Oscars! How the characters pursue their goals, expresses their emotions, and responds to success or failure is unique for each character.

- *Ideal Artistic Center* (IAC) awakens the universal in your creative individuality. It clears your canvas so you can create exactly what you want the audience to experience. Playing with your "on top of the world" walk brings an easily available healthier way to walk on a daily basis.

- *Moveable Centers* (MCs) have a quality, location, and degree of mobility to inspire characters and are quickly accessible.
- *Imaginary Bodies* (IBs) help you fully become the character in movement, posture, and speech. Drawing the characters was a favorite activity of Chekhov. Playing with costume pieces, portraits, and found objects tickle unlimited possibilities.
- *Thinking, Feeling, Willing* (TFW) is the *Trinity of the Psychology* (ToP) that defines the soul forces of each character. This concept appears in all metaphysical/spiritual/mythological traditions globally. It is a game changer for understanding ourselves and each other, defining body language, speech patterns, and design elements.

(#13) *Radiating and Receiving Radiance* (Rad/Rec) is the key to star quality, riveting the audience. Marilyn Monroe and Clint Eastwood trained themselves to turn this on and off. Your charisma can be strengthened here. These can also be used to free undue stress, revitalize from exhaustion, and activate focus.

(#14) *Tempo and Rhythm* (T/R). We train to be comfortable moving and speaking with the rhythms of staccato, legato, stillness, lyricalness and chaos. Tempo is speed. Many people avoid certain patterns and therefore limit their repertoire of expression. Being able to speed up or slowdown in any rhythm opens us to take direction easily and improve dynamics in performance.

(#15) *Focal Points* (FP) *of concentration* expand Stanislavsky's Circles of Attention with five distinct focal points where a character can look in a scene. Stanislavsky introduced the first three circles; Chekhov's interpretation adds two more circles:

- FP 1. Looking at one's own body/clothes
- FP 2. Looking at your partner
- FP 3. Looking at the immediate present environment
- FP 4. Looking into memory or imagination at some specific object not present
- FP 5. Looking into the great beyond, the unknown, the gods, the void, the big duh!

Focal points are also applied to our humanity to support healthy and wise choices of where to put your energy, for example: Should it be on your character (FP1), your new acting tools (FP2), finding an agent (FP3), your health (FP4), or your spiritual life (FP5)? Sometimes, we need to phone home. Other times we need to be at rehearsal on time and not grab that coffee on the way. How do we decide what is the best focal point?

(#16) *Objective* is ultimately the decision maker for where to focus our energy. We find it through gesture. We rephrase the word "objective" several ways for a variety of insights. What is the problem? *What for* is the character doing this? What is the seed of the character's need? What is their dream fulfilled? Their nightmare dreaded? Chekhov's distinct contribution to objective has to do with how one discovers it, which is imaginatively rather than intellectually.

(#17) *Psychological Gesture* transforms the artist instantly into the character in one large movement, with one inhale and exhale. It is a culmination and unification of all preceding tools and happens through GP3. In the Michael Chekhov way, there are three ways to discover the gesture:

The 3Is

- Inspiration—it appears instantly and effortlessly.
- Imagination—it is revealed via meditative communion with the character.
- Intellect—it develops as a compositional sequence of gestures embodying the character's objective. This gives a surefire step-by-step process for finding activating PGs.

(#18) *Improvisation/Jewelry* (improv) has multiple meanings, building various skills, and is used continuously in the training.

- The artist is most alive when inwardly in a state of "as if" it is the first time, moment-to-moment discovery, while maintaining the integrity of the text, direction, and the feeling of the whole mise en scene. When using a tool such as X/C #1, imagine one is expanding now, rather than remembering yesterday's expansion and replicating the results.
- Explore the tools with games and improv to deepen skill sets.
- Explore the subtext and scene dynamics as a rehearsal technique using different tools.
- Unique discoveries appear during the improv which sparkle in our minds and stand out with our spectators. These *jewels*, when discovered, are psychologically true for the character and can become shining moments in your performance. When we identify our favorite moment in step 3 of the Cookie Flyback, we are cultivating the skill to recognize the jewels discovered from the tools.

## Part VI—Putting it all together

(#19) *SynthAnalysis™ for the Part-Composition* embraces the Stanislavsky System of analysis and synthesizes the multidimensional approach of *Acting in the Michael Chekhov Way* to lift the page onto the stage. Where many books discuss the Chekhov tools, this book brings us into direct and systematic integration with Stanislavsky analysis. It is an advancement of the practical application for actors. Future publications in the Michael Chekhov way series expand upon this process for actors, directors, designers, writers, and dramaturges.

(#20) *Love, Laughter, and the MC Way Hereafter* is the invisible element at the heart of *Acting the Michael Chekhov Way* and unites all of the elements of the chart with the spirit of the artist.

## Feeling of Entirety: Work-in-Progress (WiP)

Bringing in an audience completes the necessary ingredient to act. This is why I hope your training culminates in a WiP the Michael Chekhov way.

See **OR 9.1 for a** deeper work-in-progress plan.

## Introduction conclusion

In the same way that you are an artist 24/7, you are also an artist until you die. So, ultimately, your commitment to excellence requires learning some concepts to remember all one's life and practicing skills to stay in shape for performance.

In this book, you can learn a whole new vocabulary that will become an awesome shortcut for you in your own work and highly useful when you are collaborating with other Chekhovites. Your creativity will expand, and you will see life in a new language, one made just for you, the actor, with guidelines to free your creative individuality, cultivate your love and joy of the profession, and the joy of sharing that love. We will even show you some science revealing the healing power of positivity. *Acting the Michael Chekhov Way*, with its beauty, positivity, practicality, and creativity has helped thousands of artists around the world. This is because Chekhov needed to heal himself, as did I. And perhaps you do, too?

> ### Louis B. Mayer
>
> While I was interviewing one of my teachers, George Shdanoff, for my documentary *From Russia To Hollywood: the 100-Year Odyssey of Michael Chekhov and George Shdanoff*, Shdanoff told me this story. He was so very pragmatic and earnest that Chekhov called him, Doctor. He and Chekhov taught many contract players for the Hollywood studios, including for Metro-Goldwyn-Mayer (MGM). One day, as they were walking on the studio lot, Shdanoff sadly complained, "What are we doing—making better actors for Louis B. Mayer?" and Chekhov responded, "No, Doctor, we are helping people become healthier and happier human beings."

Healthy artists find ways to live life to the fullest, whether they make a profession of it or not. Their talent seems to blossom when they are happy, and they make others happy in the process. They play hard and heartily, and their love lets them do that. To be that kind of artist, you may want to completely redefine yourself psycho-physically, like a body builder. Learning the Michael Chekhov way is similar to joining a new gym. There are many tools that build certain artistic muscles, and once learned, those muscles need to be practiced in the same way that any dancer, athlete, or musician does. **The Chart of Inspired Action** is like the floor plan of an actor's gym. This book is your trainer giving you a tour of the Chekhov gym. We show you the different tools, help you try them out with a few reps, and help you learn what muscles these help you build. However, ONLY YOU CAN BUILD YOUR MUSCLES. These muscles are not usually highly developed after only one round on the circuit of machines with your trainer.

>  **Axiom 0.15: Repetition is the growing power.**

And, like most folks, you may experience a little muscular tenderness. Pace yourself and share concerns. To help you engage in repetition try using the following approach—and, by the way—rather than homework, let's homeplay!

> ### Homeplay: Use POA©
>
> For those wishing to master the Chekhov technique by **practicing, observing and applying (POA), our goal is to train our imagination and our body to inspire each other so that we can access, select, and convey images powerfully to our audiences.** Some new ideas may be very challenging to our current way of thinking and experiencing the world. We won't want to do the ones we don't understand or feel good about (GP5). The following guidelines are developed with the intent to
>
> - Convince our everyday mind that these concepts have value to us as artists.
> - Train our bodies and voices to reflect images. The POA process will enable you to observe and express/respond to the inner world as fast as to the outer world.
> - Build a toolbox of resources for getting great images that you can then convey.
> - Help you gain the deepest, most rapid understanding of these tools in **thought, feeling,** and **will,** so that you can use them instinctively and unconsciously.
> - Awaken your life of continuous artistry because you are an artist 24/7.

**Once each week, take a moment to plan the playdates with yourself.** Look at the Chart for Inspired Action and select topics for the next five or six days. Write them in your calendar.

For example:   Monday: Expanding/Contracting        Tuesday: Molding
                Wednesday: Flowing/Floating          Thursday: Flying
                Friday: Radiating                    Saturday: Ideal artistic center
                Sunday: Celebrate your dedication!

1. **Practice** the physical movements and exercises with the images and energy body for at least five minutes each day, preferably morning. This builds your **feeling** for the tool.
2. **Observe**—look consciously—for one minute, three times during the day (once in morning, once midday, once in evening) for the tool expressing itself in life. For example, notice how Mom eats breakfast in terms of contracting or expanding. Observe co-workers or servers at lunch; notice the traffic at rush hour, the person walking across the street, the plants on the side of the road, something on TV. Try to discover where it is happening in the world naturally, without conscious choice. This builds your **thinking** force.
3. **Apply**, by consciously doing the tool while executing a practical task for one minute, three times during the day. This is different from observing. Now you are using your **will** force to do the tool intentionally in a place where it might not naturally be used. Brush your teeth contracting and end expanding; mold your breakfast or fly up to change the channel at night. **Please practice responsibly**. Avoid pranks on others. Being unkind is not art. Employ the feeling of beauty and ease in the form of this whole practice.

## ✒ Journal/Discuss/Flyback

*When you journal, the impression these playdates have on you strengthens. Whenever you share your observation and experience with someone in writing or speaking, you also deepen the experience.*

You are welcome to email me any observations you like at info@chekhov.net or post on the National Michael Chekhov Association Facebook page.

- See **Appendix 1** for sample POA form.
- See **OR 0.7** to download POA forms.

One year from the day you commit to this, you will have attained a level of mastery that will last a lifetime. You will have developed the concentration and self-discipline to prepare on your own for your auditions and jobs. Your strong preparation will make your action easy (Axiom 0.9). Your POAs will be a springboard to being a **powerful organic artist**!

> ⚛ Axiom 0.16: Homeplay: In 11 minutes a day, be a POA!

This section began with us yearning for a way to awaken that feeling of being on fire, on a roll, in a role, again and again. You now know you can consciously replicate the energy patterns of peak performance and by doing so, you can look like and sound like you are in it. This increases the likelihood of it "happening," and audiences feel like it is even when you are consciously acting the Michael Chekhov way.

## Summary

In your "Introduction," you have come to understand that

- The power is within you to train your artist in a healthy and logical sequence that will prepare you to perform in any capacity.
- You have the confidence of knowing there are consistent steps to take which will lead to practical skills for art and life itself as an art form.
- There will be active exploration, improvisation, applications, journal prompts, and fun improvisations to do.
- You have the opportunity to learn how to work solo, as so much of our career calls upon us to do such as for self-taped auditions and on-camera jobs.
- With your solo playtime and POA homeplay, you will be learning how to self-evaluate, so you won't need outside affirmation.
- You have gotten a complete overview of the entire Chart of Inspired Action.
- A few personal stories aim to help you understand you are not alone and maybe the stories will save you from some ugly challenges in the future.
- There are axioms to help you remember key takeaways.
- There are acronyms and abbreviations such as PASS, ASC, and TPT to help you remember essential concepts and take quick notes. (PS: There's an acronym/abbreviation list in the front of the book. Perfect!)

## Notes

1. Schechner, Richard, *Performance Theory*, Routledge, 2004.
   Montelle, Yann-Pierre, *Paleoperformance: The Emergence of Theatricality as Social Practice*, Seagull Books, 2009.
2. References to Lithuania, 1932-34; Dartington, 1936-38; Ridgefield, 1939-42; Hollywood, 1942–55.
3. https://actorstoolkit.co.uk/the-ultimate-guide-to-acting-movement-practitioners/
4. https://pmc.ncbi.nlm.nih.gov/articles/PMC7551835/#sec4-behavsci-10-00137
5. Nightingale, Earl, *The Strangest Secret*, Sound Wisdom, 2020.
6. Chekhov, Michael, *On Theatre and The Art of Acting*, Applause Books, Copyright © MCMXCII, MMIV, Book Publishers Enterprises, Inc.
7. Jack Colvin, Actor, director, designer, artist was a student of Michael Chekhov in the 1950s and mentor to Lisa Dalton for six years. He is most famous for playing Jack McGee in the original *The Incredible Hulk* series.
8. Mala Powers, author, actor, director, was the executrix of the Chekhov Estate and co-founder of the National Michael Chekhov Association with Dalton and Wil Kilroy.
9. Kilroy, Wil, *Improvisation the Michael Chekhov Way: Active Exploration of* Acting Techniques, New York, NY, Routledge 2024.
10. # Denotes the number located on the Chart of Inspired Action, Figure P.1.
11. Meisner, Sanford and Longwell, Dennis, *Sanford Meisner On Acting*, Random House, 1987.

# 1
# Preparing your imagination, your body, and the ensemble

Have you ever gone into a place that totally creeps you out?

Do you feel overwhelmed by it or maybe chilled?

Or perhaps we are at home, alone, in very familiar surroundings that don't inspire our creativity?

What if we are in an online class at home and not feeling it?

Or maybe we are easily distracted by a bit of mess we wish wasn't there?

Sometimes places just make us uncomfortable, you know what I mean? Maybe you are feeling that now. Or maybe you felt it at an audition? Imagine how your energy body can feel when it enters a space that makes you nervous, like the waiting room. Maybe you think others are out to sabotage you, to beat you, or best you? Or ignore, humiliate, or judge you? How would your performance be?

Let's fix this the Michael Chekhov Way right now by making friends with our space. And yes, this may look or sound downright wacky, but I am hoping you will play along with me.

 Let's play making friends

Pause momentarily to look at everything around you and sense how the room feels. Decide to say hello to the space, speaking out loud. "Hello, space. How are you today?" Have fun walking around and introducing yourself to different elements. "Hello, window. Thank you for being my friend and letting air flow in here. Hello, uneven wood that I might trip on. Thank you for being my friend. Hello, light. Thanks for shining on this place so that I can see. Hello, Zoom cam. Thanks for connecting me with others who are learning. Hello, gum on the chair. Thanks for taking such an interesting shape for me to explore."

Make a note of any particular area that may cause you a challenge. "Oh, and thanks, pile of mess, for keeping it real." If you've been in this space 1000 times, try to notice and befriend something new. Now, come to a pause and breathe in the space. No matter how silly that may have been, see how different the space feels.

Most people feel more comfortable and accepting in the space after making friends with it. Sometimes, the air feels lighter and more welcoming, and we feel calmer inside. If the space is familiar, this activity can refresh our appreciation of it. Think of space as a friendly puppy eagerly awaiting your arrival. Their tail wags briskly, and they pant, saying, "Hi, hi, hi!" even if it's only five minutes since you were gone. Imagine that the space is so welcoming to you that it feels like a big, warm hug and a firm pat on the back. Maybe it gives you a high five for showing up. If it is your best friend—your BFF—how might your performance be? Generally, we will do our best when we feel our best. With less tension in our bodies, our creative light can shine. So, this little "making friends with" exercise Chekhov offers can apply to all kinds of situations.

## In daily life

Can you imagine yourself walking into a biker bar? Maybe that place would scare you? Or maybe you are a biker, and it's filled with your friends? What if that were the case? Suppose you had to get up on that stage in the biker bar and give a talk about improving the safety of the riding formation. Being a biker myself, I would be in familiar territory; however, we will each react differently to different places. For instance, this space might feel intimidating if you were not a biker. But, if this were a hall of friends who always placed safety first, who live to ride and always want you to ride well and want to ride well themselves, so they all don't kill each other; and, if you knew they had your best interests at heart, your immediate safety would not be an issue.

Well, that sense of safety and support that a space can give is available anywhere. Instead of allowing spaces to intimidate or depress you, take a few moments to make the space your friend. Just like any great friend, the space will support you fully when you do. It will have your back and keep you safe everywhere you go. The way to do it is straightforward and yet not to be overlooked. Simply think, as you take in the details of the space, that you are saying in your mind, "Hello, space, thank you for being my friend." Having said it out loud here in your training, all you need to do is think the words, and they will have the same power.

> ### Homeplay
>
> Try this on your own in places that you go today. Take a few minutes to imagine future opportunities where this could help. For example, if all audition waiting rooms were filled with friendliness, how might that help you? How might it help all the performers and people so desperately seeking a great cast?

## ✒ Journal/Discuss/Flyback

*What places do you go to where you don't feel comfortable? Make a note in your journal, and the next time you are in one of those places, try making friends with it.*

Remember, you are an artist. How many hours a day do you work? Yes, 24 of them. So, use every moment of your day to see, smell, taste, hear, and feel the world through the filter of your artistic self. This is what Chekhov means by Continuous Artistry.

In Michael Chekov's technique, we focus a great deal on tension-decreasing tools. These all fall under the category of a *Feeling of Ease*. Making friends with various styles, different kinds of directors, different shapes of performance areas, other teachers, and different wardrobes or sets will come in quite handy throughout your whole life.

## The Ball Toss

Playing with a ball is a practice that we know goes at least as far back as 1924 for Michael Chekhov. He used it in rehearsals for his Hamlet production at the Moscow Art Theatre. It is frequently used as an icebreaker in Chekhov to help everyone make friends with each other. Tennis balls, especially junior tennis balls, are highly visible. Colorful foam balls are gentle. Bean bags can be firmer and roll less. It's fun having a variety of objects for different activities.

When playing solo, you can toss the ball up, bounce it off the ground or a wall, or toss balls onto a couch or net and modify these exercises, imagining the surface you use is your partner. The best deal, however, is to find a Chekhov buddy or ensemble to play ball with you. We can also imagine this ball toss as a conversation.

## 👐 Let's play ball

Let's gather into a circle, allowing a comfortable space between yourself and any walls or object behind you and giving the folks around you enough room to catch. For safety purposes, use an underhand toss that arches across to your partner as a default approach in a group environment.

To begin with, check in with yourself to see how you feel just seeing the ball and knowing you are going to play catch.

*Are you excited to see how good you are? To show everyone else that you can do this well? Or maybe you are intimidated because you've dropped the ball so many times in your life?*

## It's perfect

Guess what? We are not playing *catch*! We are playing *miss the ball badly*.

Yes, the first task is to make a mess of this attempted catch and follow it with the words and thoughts, "That's perfect!" Let yourself speak it out loud.

Toss the ball and mess up the catch. (If you accidentally do catch it, just drop it, pretending to have missed it.) Say, "Perfect!"

Now, pause for a moment and check in with your body.

*Did you just lie? Did you actually think that totally sucked! Did your body language wince, cringe, or fall when you missed? Was it a relief that missing it was perfect?*

Why are we doing this?

Because one of the most painful moments an actor gives to an audience is a moment of self-consciousness. When actors think they messed up, the audience does too. It's awkward! Awkward is unpleasant; it is uneasy. We want to develop this self-awareness to know when our physical and energy bodies are showing the audience that we messed up. We want them to believe every moment is perfect and precisely as we intended. So, this first step—playing with the "perfect ball drop"—becomes a fundamental lesson you will want to master for life.

Make friends with dropping the ball. Be curious. Every actor will drop lines. It happens. How we handle it is what makes one artist perfectly brilliant and another an unskilled actor. Every person has weird moments in conversations. It happens. Making friends with our awkwardness opens our ability to connect with others. Be curious.

Allow your first throws to be a mess, and with each subsequent throw, think or speak aloud to the ensemble, "PERFECT." Check in. Is your body showing any mannerisms that conflict with the idea that missing the ball is perfect? It may take a good amount of time to catch all the betraying signals you are throwing to the audience if you judge things as imperfect.

## ✏ Journal/Discuss/Flyback

*Do you do something with your mouth, make a little sound, make a small gesture of helplessness, laugh, or groan? Does your chest fall? Like a poker player, know your "tells." Be a detective and make notes in your journal about any "I messed up" little apologies for being imperfect.*

Let's expand our guidelines for playing ball:

- If you are nearest to it, it's yours to play. Whether or not the ball is intended for you, if you are closest to it by accident on the floor or bouncing off someone else's hands, pick it up. No need to hand it to the intended recipient. Play it, own it. And if you were the original sender, you can just pretend that person was the one you were sending it to anyway. If our scene partner misses a line and we pick up their line to keep the scene going, we need to deliver it as our own.
- You now have the option to miss or catch the ball, and either choice will be…perfect!
- Continue acting like whatever happens is perfect.
- Ask yourself, "What might I do next time to get this ball where I want it to go?"
- Add in your name as you throw. Imagine that the ball is your name, and it carries the sound of your name into the other person's hand. Let your name sound out until they have the ball in their hand. This might require you to extend the sound of your name differently than you usually say it, especially if they need to chase the ball. That's perfect. As you give and take the ball, learn each other's names.
- Add a second ball of a different color or texture and say the name of the person to whom you are throwing the second ball. Begin their name as the ball leaves your hand and let the sound travel in the arch across the circle into the hands of your partner.
- What do we need to do first, before we throw? Especially if we start throwing before we say the name? Make eye contact. Yes, this starts the process and gives us a clear beginning. It helps us clearly decide to whom we are throwing. Our line begins well before the sound ever comes out. And it lingers until we know what we have said has landed in our partner. Our partner catches or misses what we send. It's perfect.

## ✒ Journal/Discuss/Flyback

*Why are we even throwing a ball in an acting class? What does the ball signify? How does it apply to what we do as actors?*

The ball is energy. Can we agree that we are all made of energy? The ball symbolizes the energy we have and exchange with others. As artists, we are pursuing mastery of energy management. This is a primary skill-building game.

- Next, we might ask, How much of our body is an *actor's body*? All of it!
- Then how much of it would an actor want to use to exchange energy? All of it.

Take a moment to reflect on how much of your body you have been engaging in this ball toss.

## ✒ Journal/Discuss/Flyback

*What parts are not in use as fully as they could be? Were you using your feet? Your hips? Your non-dominant hand?*

Next time your body gets to toss the ball, try engaging all of it. Check the legs, hips, and non-throwing hand to see how they are helping focus the energy.

All peak performance arises when the body, mind, soul, and spirit are aligned toward a unified field of focus.

Pause the game, setting the balls aside, and repeat the Focus Gesture (Figure 0.1) from earlier. Reach one arm way up to the sky and the opposite one down into the earth. Pretend they are very wide and broad enough to gather all the energy above, around, and below you and bring them together as if you can take all the energy of creation into your core and send it toward a single point, your partner. Notice how the ball toss is its own expression of this gesture.

Try this: practice throwing "air balls" for a few moments, exploring these questions:

*How can I toss the ball using this idea of getting every part of my body and imagination to all work together to get the ball exactly where I want to send it?*

*How must I prepare to do that?*

*How must I end? How much effort do I need to use?*

All peak performances use energy efficiently. They use as little as possible and as much as necessary to complete the task.

*Am I using too much energy or not enough? Maybe I am using too much in the beginning and not enough in the end. Or vice versa?*

If the ball is not going far enough, maybe it is losing energy at the end. Check your fingers in the follow-through. Are they extending toward your partner or maybe curving up? Is your preparation reaching all the way into the back space, or is it too weak at the beginning?

Notice that there are three parts to the throw. It ends with the follow-through, where your throwing hand is extended and radiating in front of you, sustaining the energy all the way to your partner. The beginning is the Preparation, the opposite of the end. Here, the throwing hand moves into the backspace to the equal and opposite degree of Sustaining. The forward-moving throw, the middle part, is the Action. Say to yourself as you throw your air balls,

> *I prepare. I act. I sustain. I stop.*

Try this as many times as you need to get comfortable with it. Try it with both hands.

Allow your weight to shift and arms to counterbalance each other. Try a step with the throw. Try a throw without a step. Play with variations using the Prepare-Act-Sustain-Stop sequence. Notice what the first letters of that sequence spell? PASS. Yes, we PASS our energy. Remember this acronym as we will use it throughout our playing time to remember for all that we do, we are becoming masters of energy management. Peak performances require us to PASS the image, the energy, the contact, the character, and the gesture.

---

### ⚛ Axiom 1.1: We PASS with our energy.

**P**repare **A**ct **S**ustain **S**top

---

Once again, begin exchanging real balls using PASS and add a few more balls into the circle if there is a large group. If you have a large group, you might add more balls earlier in the process, while names are being learned, so that more people get more activity and so names are repeated more frequently. Alternatively, if you have an ample supply of balls, you can pair up in two lines facing each other, each pair having a ball. In this way, our focus is just on building the PASS skills.

Let's call this formation of two lines facing each other: a **hallway** or **alley**. We will use this form often; sometimes, it will be a narrow hallway or alley so close you can touch. Other times, a wide one. For now, allow it to be as wide as the space permits.

## A note about the kind of balls to use

Soft balls that are the size of tennis balls or a little larger are ideal. Bright colors help them to be visible in various lighting conditions. Foam and yarn balls are light and soft, so they don't hurt when they make contact. Adult tennis balls, juggling beanbags, and lacrosse balls can be painful. Try junior tennis balls. They are a little larger, softer, and very brightly colored. It is fun to have different colors, shapes, textures, and weights of balls that travel through the space with different dynamics.

For many of the ball toss variations, you don't need balls with bounce. Non-bouncing balls may be easier to retrieve when they go perfectly awry. However, there are many variations of the ball toss, which you might do with a bouncing ball and additional tools. We will explore where bouncing balls are useful.

Keep safety always first and make friends with the new toys.

It is ideal to have at least half as many balls as players to create pairs of two. However, groups of three to four can also work for some hallway formation variations.

## The ball greeting

This exercise is another step in the making-friends-with and ensemble-building process that is useful early in the course or rehearsal period.

Have every fourth person in the circle step to the center, forming an inner circle. Give each one of them a ball. With 12 artists, three would enter the center. Have the inner circle and outer periphery circle face each other. The center players toss their ball to someone opposite them, saying their own name as the ball travels. Here is a perfect moment to add pronouns as an option. The outer circle receives the ball and tosses it back, echoing precisely the words received from the artist in the center. The center person steps to their right, continuing around the circle, greeting and introducing themselves to each person. When the inner circle arrives back at their start point, they exchange places with the first person they greeted. The new inner circle continues in the same fashion until all participants have been in the center and on the periphery.

Note that those who reach the inner circle simultaneously may miss each other in this sequence. One can accept that or invite anyone who missed someone to step in and find them and complete the process until all have greeted and been greeted by everyone.

## Increasing efficiency

In a wide hallway formation, play by first throwing an imaginary ball, an *air ball*, to your partner. If you bring your arm back behind you, parallel to the floor at shoulder height and allow it to drop and swing forward just using the gravitational, centripetal, and centrifugal forces, where does it stop?

Most likely at the equal and opposite place—shoulder height, parallel to the floor in front of you.

Try now, only preparing half-way back and release. What is the difference? Can you feel the weight of having to lift the ball forward if you don't use any back preparation? The ball will almost throw itself if you prepare fully by taking the arm back behind you to shoulder height.

Try throwing a real ball with this full, solid preparation. Try it again, but only do it with half the prep.

*What is the difference?*
*What kind of actor do you want to be?*
*With a half-prep, what is the difference in how much effort it takes to get the ball across the room?*

If time permits and you have a very safe space to play in, try facing a wall without a partner and allowing yourself to toss that ball with the great force of energy that arises by doing a complete preparation.

Chances are that when you throw these actual balls with only the dynamics that the universal laws of force and gravity create, putting all your effort into the preparation, the ball could go anywhere—if you fling the ball fearlessly—it could even go behind you, or straight up, or be like a bowling ball. Nonetheless, it will be perfect. You will learn to love being a little out of control. At least, I might say, I encourage you to fall in love with not being in control.

Why do I support "yielding control" to the universal forces? Well, I bet you have been in peak performance at least once, right? You might not have been there long or many times, but at least once. In that "zone" moment, you were in a flow and barely knew what was happening. Most of us don't remember what we did specifically. But we sure do remember the feeling—the high—afterward. And maybe we felt like part of us was outside ourselves, in the audience or hovering above our body, watching it do its thing.

## Journal/Discuss/Flyback

*When was that first moment when you knew something extraordinary had happened?*

It might have been very long ago when it first happened. And maybe it wasn't in a formal "acting" setting. Perhaps it was playing a game of *pretend* with other kids. Maybe it was telling a story at a party, athletic event, or musical recital.

I would stake my life on the fact that you wouldn't be reading this if you hadn't had at least one moment when you felt the magic. It happened; somehow, it wasn't you as you know yourself in everyday life. It was happening through you effortlessly, easily. And, very importantly, it was in control, and you were not. Perhaps that scared you? Maybe you fell out of the moment because you got freaked out, excited, or confused.

Essentially, these moments of peak flow happen when your body, mind, and spirit all align toward the single field of focus and the everyday part of you, which Chekhov calls the "lower ego" or "everyday personality," disappears and your highest best self or, as Chekhov says, "your higher ego" is allowed to flow through you to your audience. That is why they all know it when it happens too. And your knowing is so rich and deep that you never need to ask anyone afterward how it was. You never need outside confirmation that you did well. You, as your everyday self, were not in control. It was in the "now."

When we look to use the laws of gravity to help us do the ball toss, rather than trying to push the ball to the other person, we align with those forces, and we let them take control. We are practicing to consciously imitate the energy pattern of peak performance.

Does this sound like a bright idea? Once we become familiar with the knowledge that giving control to the universal guiding principle makes things so much easier, more fun, and fulfilling for us and the peeps around us, we will feel safe allowing ourselves to be in that state more frequently for more extended periods of time. If you want that, you will benefit from understanding and practicing those principles. You will want to go to your peak performer's gymnasium frequently.

So, back to the toss.

Let's look at the ending process. This is the *sustaining*, also known as the *follow-through*. Do some tosses and notice where your hand and arm go when you are done. Do any of your tosses go left or right rather than center? If so, what has happened in your follow-through? Maybe you will notice that your hand curved off in that direction.

Try extending your hand at shoulder level toward your partner until they get the ball. This may mean until they get the ball from under the stack of chairs in the corner. No problem, allow your hand and the energy body in and around your hand to keep extending light to the person until they get that ball and make eye contact with you to complete the moment.

Then, open yourself to receive the ball again.

You have noticed that one of these universal principles is that *strong preparation makes the action effortless.*

---

> ⚛ **Axiom 1.2: Strong preparation makes the action effortless.**

Repeat this several times as you now throw the ball with beautiful Preparation, Action, Sustain, and Stop.

Receiving the ball is another act that we must also prepare.

If the event begins with eye contact first, observe how you inwardly respond when someone holding the ball looks at you.

## ✒ Journal/Discuss/Flyback

*How does your body language reveal or conceal your inner response? Do you shy away, contracting into anxiety? Do you reach forward early to catch it, and if so, does your body move forward to the sender before they have released the ball?*

If you find yourself having the ball bounce off your fingertips, this might happen because your body has begun to anticipate where the ball will be and moves forward to meet it in an effort to get there in time to catch it. Moving forward before the ball is released creates a misalignment in the process. You have been moving your energy body too soon; your physical body follows it and gets there too soon. The sender has been aiming to send it where you were, and now you are closer than you were earlier and closing your hands around the energy ball before the real ball has arrived. Your forward motion makes it difficult to adjust if the throw is higher or faster than anticipated.

The anticipation is essential to notice. How would this be reflected if this were a scene of dialogue being exchanged? Have you ever anticipated a line? And then stepped on your partner's line? Or perhaps you are so ready to deliver the line in response to the way it was said the last time, but now it is sent to you in a completely new way, and you aren't in the moment.

Everything you are doing in the ball toss is a metaphor for how you are acting. It is revealing your energy management tendencies. Yes, it is fun and delightful; however, stay alert for the discoveries you can make about yourself.

Are you continuously underthrowing? Perhaps being too cautious or "precious." This preciousness happens when we slow down the entire event and make each moment connect very deeply. It is a wonderful phase to explore. The challenge is, *Can I still toss the ball rather than place or push that ball and retain the sense of connection that this reverent exchange so sweetly produces? Can I maintain the reverence and grow the dynamics? Can I retain the strong preparation, the use of the gravitational principles and dynamics, and the depth of the connection?*

This is a worthwhile goal to be sought and requires an understanding of catching or receiving that is equally apparent as the sending.

## Receiving soundlessly

Listen to the sound that the ball makes when you catch it. Notice what others are doing when they first catch the ball. Do the hands go to meet the ball, or do they welcome it into them? What is the difference between the sounds made in these two variations?

The sound of a catch reflects the quality of the efficiency of the energy transfer. This means if a ball is efficiently caught, it makes less sound than a catch done inefficiently. The sound will be louder when the receiver's hands go forward to meet the ball. The sound will be moderate when the hand stays neutral, moving perhaps higher or lower, right or left, but not forward. When the catch is made by allowing the ball to land in the hand as the hand draws the ball in the same direction as it was thrown, drawing back behind the receiver (or down toward the ground for the person tossing the ball up and catching it themselves,) cradling it as it were, the ball will be silent.

This silent receiving of the ball, which draws the energy through its center into its backspace, is the most efficient energy transfer.

Try tossing a ball up and catching noisily by moving up to catch it. Notice that, after you have caught it, you need to lower your hand to throw again. This requires several moves to execute.

Try catching it silently by cradling it. Notice that by cradling, your catch brings your hand down into the perfect place to start your next throw. No unnecessary steps.

Play for a few moments, pretending to receive an "air" ball in this manner. Allow it to come toward the middle of your chest, where with both hands, you draw it into you and then smoothly, without stopping, transfer it into your throwing hand, continuing to keep it moving behind you into your backspace. Suddenly, you find that this strong, fluid receiving move has taken you right into your precise preparation mode. And your *strong receiving becomes strong preparation for you*.

> ⚛ Axiom 1.3: Strong receiving becomes your strong preparation.

What is this *catching the ball* akin to in a scene?

This is listening to the energy sent to you by your partner, listening with more than your ears, with your whole body. You are allowing the way that this line is coming to you today, and only today, to prepare you to respond anew.

Practice this receiving now with a partner in a hallway formation as earlier, or if solo, bounce off a wall. See if you can send and receive without ever stopping the ball in its course.

*How is this like the story you are playing?*

The energy should always remain in motion without ever coming to a stop.

See if you can change up the speed and dynamic of this exchange with a partner.

Ideal receivers

- Have eye contact.
- Have openness in the center.
- Are centered like a tennis player ready to move in six directions: up, down, back, forward, right, or left.
- Respond and adjust as needed based on your visual, audio, and kinesthetic impulses guided by the flow of the energy coming to you now.
- Draw the ball into the space behind you as you make eye contact with the sender, then select and make eye contact with the next sender, keeping the ball moving in fluid action.

Many Chekhov artists begin every class or rehearsal with a ball toss as a warm-up and ensemble-building activity that helps cross the threshold from the outer world into some serious play. Here are some variations to develop over time.

Advancing your skills

- Send the ball to the next person, sustaining your hand until they receive and make eye contact with you.
- If they neglect to make eye contact with you after receiving, remain radiating to them with your hand extended.

Yes, this will be awkward and weird. However, it is essential that we build the courage to be heard, and they need to help develop the awareness to listen and acknowledge that we have been heard. This eye contact completes the whole exchange between us and does not need to become an entire dialogue of body language with head nods, etc. It is an efficient, direct connection through the eyes that can be made instantly with no other obligations. It will have to be that efficient if we are to build tempo and dynamic. Our willingness to stand with our palm open, full arm extended toward a partner who is ignoring us will help them become conscious that they must complete their contact with you. It will help everyone build awareness and self-acceptance. (It's hard to feel perfect when we realize we left someone hanging out there! This gives us a chance to accept that it was perfect and that we don't need to repeat that! Can we make the missed contact and move on without apology?)

As the tasks of the game increase in challenges, these fundamentals may be more challenging to accomplish while simultaneously more critical to meet the increasing skills being called for.

- See **OR 1.0** for Advanced Tossing with Moving Circles, Freudian and Observational Toss, Baptizing balls, Throw 'n Go, Repeat Patterns and Objects/Sticks.

## Warm-up wake-up

On days when time is short, a lengthy warm-up to activate your body-mind-spirit may not happen. Playing ball for about five minutes can still be effective to wake up the energy and get everyone focused. Try moving in a circle to the right while continuing to toss the ball. Notice you now need to anticipate where the receiver will be and throw it there. Reverse directions and alter speeds as skill builds. Count completed ball tosses and restart if the ball touches the ground.

Warming up is an excellent idea for any physical artist when there is more time. We are athletes of thoughts, feelings, and desires. And all actors must be that. After all, we are forms moving through the space and creating sounds that carry the story. These body parts and the energies that operate in us are subject to getting stiff, tight, slow, or choppy. In effect, they can get cold. If you are coming in cold, chances are you won't start at the top of your game. If you seek to be in a show, onstage, or on-camera, once you are in front of an audience, there is no tolerance for "warming up" to your peak level of engagement. This is part of a strong preparation.

What needs to be warmed and awake for the performer? Yes, the literal body is ideally warm when it is moving easily through the space. And the voice is fluid, flexible, and audible. We can hear and understand you. For the Chekhov actor, the call also includes a warmed-up imagination and energy body working together with the physical body.

This energy body travels beyond your skin. Scientifically, it is measurable and photographable. It is in layers and includes your aura. This is a bubble around your being, like an egg, that goes everywhere with you. It helps your energy get sent out into space, and it enables you to get energy coming from space to you. Sometimes, this kinesphere gets tight and cold, contracting in on itself with a sense of depression, anxiety, or impatience. With that around you, the likelihood of a peak performance will diminish.

Similarly, sometimes that kinesphere can be overheated, expanded, over-inflated by ungrounded moods, warm, inviting days where the outside just beckons to play, or big distracting things like drugs or alcohol. Ultimately, this kinesphere will serve you best when it is warmed up to a balanced state of readiness to play.

As an actor, you might want to adopt responsibility for arriving early enough to warm yourself up because, in the world beyond a class, school, or rehearsal where warm-ups might be included, you are on your own most of the time. No one will oversee you and ensure that you are adequately prepared. And what have I learned about preparation?

> **Strong preparation makes the action effortless.**

Our task as actors is to convey images, as stated previously. We want to get great images to convey. So, warming up by activating the imagination is exciting, and when you imagine the animals that inspire many yoga movements, for example, you are warming up the imagination.

- See **OR 1.1** Kilroy's Warm-Up for a full day of heightened activity, an extended body-mind-voice awakening. Try thinking in terms of Chekhov language as you loosen and enliven.

I love doing the Five Tibetan Rites. These are five simple yoga movements that are done 21 times each. I can do the whole sequence in five to six minutes or slow it down to 10 or 20 minutes. Yoga was a regular warm-up at the Moscow Art Theatre under Stanislavsky and Chekhov. These are included in the **OR 1.1** above.

*As you do your warm-up activities, what Chekhov terms might you use to describe what you are doing?*

When done with images corresponding to the movements, the exercise is lifted into the art realm and prepares you to continue this body-mind pathway. The use of imagination with movement is the central skill set that distinguishes all peak performances. It is the magical part of any great acting moment where you are so entirely synergized with the character that the audience experiences your character in this story and their personal inner story, awakened by the character. This part of the energy management training is essential to having charisma and radiating star quality.

## Ideal Artistic Center

In *Acting the Michael Chekhov Way*, we work with the concept that there is a higher ego—the very best part of our humanity. Where does this higher ego live? Is there a place in the body where it tends to reside?

While this higher ego is so powerful that it can be thought of as all-encompassing, there does seem to be a particular part of the body that is a connecting point or center for this "I/Me" sensation in each person.

Try this exercise. If solo, stand in front of a mirror. If with a group, space yourselves anywhere in the room. Let your hands hang loosely at your sides. Close your eyes and pretend someone says to you something that you will answer with the words, "Who me?" When you do, allow your body language to respond, and use your hand to point to yourself and say, "Who Me?" out loud. Hold there for a moment, then open your eyes and look at yourself as if what you just said and what was said to you were true.

Ready? Here are some statements to play with:

*I heard you won a million dollars!*

*You are an amazing person.*

*You are getting an Oscar!*

Where did you point? Most people will point to somewhere in the center of the chest.

Maybe you pointed there without reaching all the way to touching your chest. Chances are, if you kept your elbows in place and finished moving your hands in the direction they were going, you might have ended up right there in the center of your chest. Maybe your point was a little higher or lower, no worries.

There is a point in the chest, Mr. Chekhov suggests, that is about three inches below the collarbone in the center, three inches deep. This is the spot where, if anywhere in the physical body, the Ideal Artistic Center (IAC) can be found. Imagine that this is the portal into your highest self and that all your ideas that come from moving your body, or from a script-inspired image, flow through this portal. It is at the intersection of the vertical line streaming from above, through your fontanelle, between your ankles into the Earth's core, and the horizontal line of your arms extended to the sides, right middle fingertip to left middle fingertip.

This point seems to be unique from the physical heart. In Chapter 7 of *Science of the Heart*, the HeartMath Institute[1] inspires us to trust the soul's wisdom contained in our "energetic heart" (see Figure 1.1).

> Our experience suggests that the physical heart also has communication channels connecting it with the energetic heart. Nonlocal intuition, therefore, is transformational, and from our perspective, it contains the wisdom that streams from the soul's higher information field down into the psychophysiological system via the energetic heart and can inform our moment-to-moment experiences and interactions. At HeartMath Institute, this is what we call heart intelligence.

## Electromagnetic Field of the Heart

Our thoughts and emotions affect the heart's magnetic field, which energetically affects those in our environment whether or not we are conscious of it.

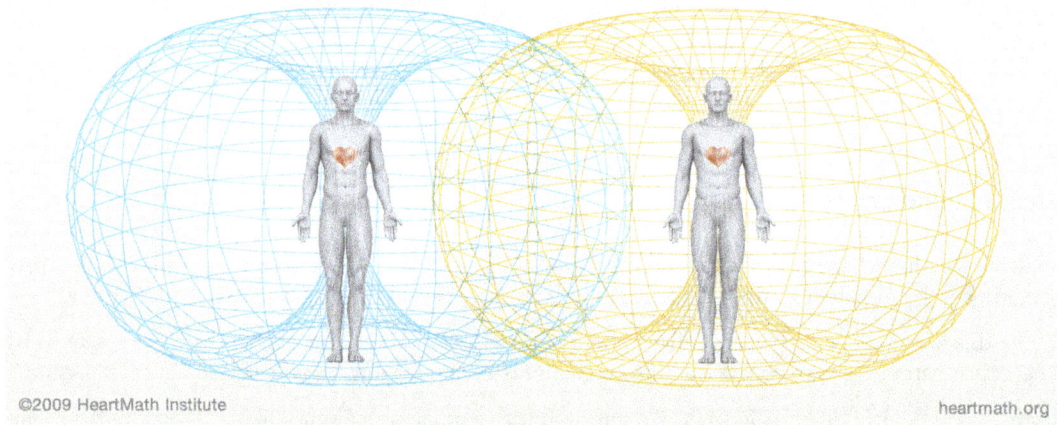

*Figure 1.1* The heart is the most powerful source of electromagnetic energy in the human body, producing the largest rhythmic electromagnetic field of any of the body's organs. It produces 60 times more amplitude than the brain. An electrocardiogram (ECG) measures any body surface. The magnetic field of the heart is 100 times greater than that of the brain. Magnetometers detect that energy from three feet. (Image courtesy of the HeartMath® Institute—www.heartmath.org.)

One hundred years ago, Chekhov called it our IAC. Some like to tap gently to help it activate if you like. It may be pretty tender. If you want, you can also think of it as a search button. If you have a question, ask it through the IAC and pretend the IAC answers you. Just like entering a question into the search engine on your computer, your IAC will generate various answers depending on how specific the question is. Maybe you will check out several of the answers. Try them on, like shopping for a new outfit with free shipping and free returns! It's a good deal.

Your IAC resides like an awesome, bright, shining sun inside of your energy body, filling it with power, moving your blood, breath, and heart. And, when you are in the zone, in that flow or, as Mr. C. would say, "happy" on the stage, that inner sunlight shines brilliantly for all to see.

Now, is the sun shining at midnight? Is the sun shining when it is a dark, cloudy, stormy day? Yes, it is shining. You might not be able to see it at any given moment. You might have to rotate the Earth or tear off the roof to see that sun. But does the sun need to do anything differently to be seen? No, it is already there in full power, just as the whole of you is all here, even if you are only using one slice to play your game of life.

The power of that sun-like quality within you, that star quality, is a little like Tinker Bell in *Peter Pan*. It can be helpful to think that what keeps us from seeing Tink, like our sun, can be cleared away by cheering and clapping for it. By saying, "Yes, we love you and want you to be here," that part of you can grow big and strong. Where attention goes, energy grows.

What happens when our ideas don't come out right? We fail to express our images to the audience. Play this next game with an ensemble to understand what happens when we can't really convey our images.

##  The trapped image game

Designate teams of five to seven persons.

Have each team select a representative to send to the leader.

The leader explains to these representatives that they are the directors of this game for their group.

Give each director an image of a large object. If you wish, you could have a picture for them or verbally describe it secretly to each director. Giant buildings like Notre Dame, the Taj Mahal, statues like Lady Liberty, the Eiffel Tower, or a giant oak. Keep the image secret so that only directors know what they have. The directors return to their groups and position the groups so no one group can see the other groups.

Now, each director goes to their actors and asks each one to create by themselves their own physical expression of this object, keeping it a secret from other groups. The director can show a picture, or it can be described. The actors are "auditioning" for the director by shaping their own body into a representation of that image.

Give them about 60–90 seconds. Each actor presents their own image to the director simultaneously and holds it, sustaining and filling them with the unique energy that the image represents.

The director now selects the best actor from the group, in their opinion, to be the image. Let everyone release for a moment and then have the chosen actor from each group recreate the image. The rest of the cast, including the director, now surrounds the actor holding the image. The cast links palm-to-palm and toe-to-toe like a membrane trapping the image inside the circle, blocking it from being wholly seen.

Now, the director invites the "image-actor" to escape the membrane and show itself. However, any adjustments they make to get out of the mass blocking it must be adopted permanently. If they squat to get under the arms, they must stay in the squat. If they bend to get through, they stay bent when they escape. The ensemble wrapped around the image can be of limited degrees of help, closing its spaces or making more room while keeping palms and toes touching the person on either side of them. The actor with the image must adapt to escape and retain changes in their form and any emotions and other energies that came up while escaping. Once they escape, they are suspended in their new position.

When all images have escaped and can now be fully seen, have everyone look at the images of the other casts in their current form. What do they see? What images come to their minds when they see this form? For example, Cast A will look at the mangled image of Cast B and describe what they "get" from Actor B, while Cast B looks at the mangled image of Cast A and describes what they "get."

Then, after comments have been made about each of the actors in their mutated image, have them release and restore the image to its original form. Now, Cast A and B see the original form of each other's artist. What is this image that can now be seen in its full, pure original shape?

Then, reveal each director's object to the group.

Compare the difference between what the director was seeking, what the original image was, and what the mangled, escaped image was.

Our creative higher self is our inner director, asking for images. Our creative higher self is the actor who provides an expression of that director's image. Our lower everyday personality and body comprise the ensemble wrapped around all that, the membrane blocking and mangling our images with doubt, habit, and all the other things.

*Do you want to live with that extraordinary talent and creativity trapped inside you, unable to be seen, heard, or shared with the world? What if there were a way to free yourself of those trappings? Would you want to? Why does it happen in the first place?*

## Quantum pie

Here is a mind map offered as a way of understanding where/when these blocks develop and how we can use the process of freeing ourselves as a springboard to our peak performance. (See Figure 1.2.) You might think of it as finding a way to access your own unlimited I-cloud with full, free image access capabilities faster than any computer ever will have.

Let us imagine that the top circle (A) represents the entirety of all that is, our supreme unbounded self, what Mr. Chekhov calls the higher self, higher I, or EYE.

From there, we want to come to the Earth for a while. But to do that, we have to make some choices about which parts of our many possible energies we could and will use most often. We need to do this because our human bodies simply can't vibrate fast enough to hold all of that power consciously and stay visible. Imagine that coming into the Earth means having to slow way down. Kind of like racing along a highway at 125 miles an hour; things are a blur. Wave your hand as fast as you can, and it too will be a blur. Slow it down, and you can see it just fine. Let's pretend that slowing down uses up a lot of your hard drive, so you will have to leave a lot of your information—a lot of your energy in your I-cloud (A).

How much of your potential will you be able to consciously access and how much remains unconscious? This combination of consciousnesses evolves into our personality, what we will call our "lower ego" or everyday self. If we think of consciousness as an iceberg, most say we only see/know the top five percent. Let's pretend we are cooking a pizza pie and we can choose only 5 of 100 add-ons. May be we can expand that to 8.

Imagine the lower circle (B) is our arrival on Earth, where we select for our piece of the pie 5%–8% of our personality potential.

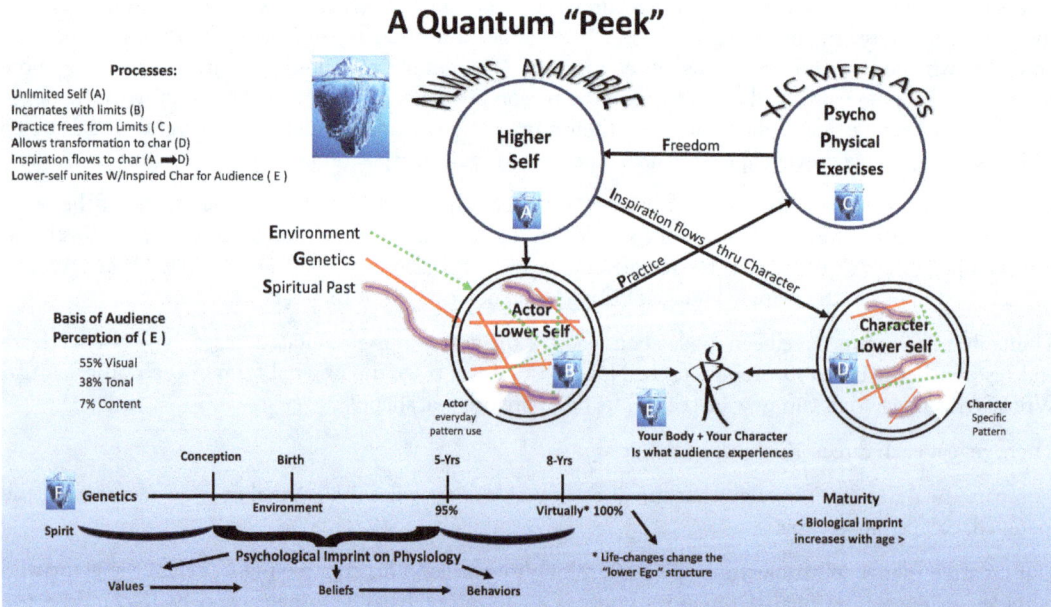

*Figure 1.2* The Quantum Peek chart shows the relationship between the higher ego (A) and lower ego (B). Three elements influence the form of our "personality." (A) can flow directly into the artist's expression of the character (E) because the artist has prepared their body (B) by doing psycho-physical exercises (C) to express all possible impulses the Character (D) may need in any given moment. Section F below the circles is a timeline of influences that limit the expressivity of the Lower Ego (B). (Courtesy of NMCA, Dalton with Charles Bowles.)

How do we choose which 5%–8% of all the possible personalities a human can have?

There are three basic influences on this selection process.

1. Genetics: Your genes will determine the starting point for the body you grow, and that will influence some of the choices that form your personality (B).
2. Environment: Where/with whom you grow up will influence what works and what doesn't work for your personality to survive and thrive.
3. Spirit: There is some invisible thing that we are talking about here when we say spirit. We are not talking about religion and things like that. We are not interested in you believing anything differently than your own beliefs. We are suggesting, however, that twins—genetically identical—who grow up in the same environment, magically turn out to be two different human beings. Right? Whatever it is that makes them two distinct beings is what we mean by spirit, influencing them invisibly and inspiring different ingredients in their piece of the pie.

When do these influences start taking effect?

In section (F) of the chart, we see how young we are when our essential personality forms, affecting our body. Perhaps at conception the genes and environment start making an impact. When the spirit forms is your choice, as you understand it. Maybe before, maybe during, or maybe after, but we can agree that at some point, those twins are different, and most parents can see the subtle differences within hours, if not in the womb.

Current psychological studies suggest that the decisions regarding which personality traits work and which don't tends to be 95% complete by age four or five, and the other 5% by the age of eight. Your choices lead you to generate certain beliefs about the world. Those beliefs create values or priorities. Your behavior develops to meet those beliefs and values.

What this means is that essentially who you are in kindergarten is who you remain, with a final polish by third grade or so. Only with a "life-changing" event are lower-ego personality changes generally seen. One could imagine that a personality transformation in our metaphor means that you change the ingredients of your "piece of the pie."

With each ingredient you select for your piece of the pie, the flavor of you changes. And the body itself changes. The energy patterns that you repeat over and over make a biological imprint on your physical life. If you pick aggression, your body grows more forward and expands. If you pick shyness, your body grows downward and inward. The longer you keep this ingredient on your menu, the more deeply it will affect your body, your way of moving and speaking. The biological imprint on your hardware increases with age.

Have you ever gotten a great idea that didn't come out right? Yes, that old, trapped-image situation. Now consider:

*Have you ever learned about a habit you have that is unhealthy and decided to get rid of it? Only to find out that you can be free of it for a short time and then you backslide right back into it, no matter how much you swear you won't?*

It happens all the time because the old habit is biologically built into how you walk, sit, think, and breathe. That's your hardware. It will need an upgrade to express new behaviors.

When you imagine a character, and you go to do it and that image clicks perfectly, it's because your piece of pie has matched the image's requirements for conveying it to your audience (E). We all know how frustrating it is when it doesn't come out the way we meant. I call it *the big Dis-Click*. Ouch!

The psycho-physical exercises (PPEs) (circle C) are the Chekhov way to clear the dis-clicks, old habits, and upgrade our expressive body.

The main PPEs cover all the basic energy patterns using metaphors from nature. By doing these repeatedly, we introduce to our body and mind—our energy body—the many possible ways of moving that we didn't include in our ingredient list. Some of these we use so often in our piece of the pie that it doesn't feel inspiring. Or maybe you use it so rarely that it's weird. You might like them or not. I enjoy hiking mountains, but it's hard. These things might be outside your piece of the pie. Through repetition of the PPEs, you have fun expanding your ingredient list. It's like an artist going from a pencil to primary colored paints. Eventually, you'll access unlimited combinations of colors. PPEs awaken all the potential ways of moving that are in the unused part of your everyday self (B), the same as it is in the higher self (A). Then, when you have a character you want to create (D), you will make up their own piece of the pie out of your whole higher pie (A).

This character's piece of the pie will always overlap yours but will never ever be the same because no two beings are the same. Even playing yourself on the stage in a solo show will draw from a slightly different part than your everyday personality. All your characters will share your physical body, and that's where the necessary overlap comes (E). The audience sees the artist's body merged with the character's image.

When you have practiced your tools like a great musician or athlete, with precision and an aim to improve your skills so that they become unconsciously present without you even trying, you have created a direct connection that will download straight from your higher self (A) into you as the character (E).

This quantum peek represents our journey to who we are today as psycho-physical beings. With this map to guide us, we can draw a correlation between our highest artistic being and our everyday self. We can also sense the relationship between our influences, behavior patterns, and their impact on us as artists. Through Chekhov's most basic exercises, we can restore a fluidity to ourselves that enables the desired transformation into the character. This is the magical benefit of uniting the imagination and the body's movement in a conscious way.

Are you willing to use *Acting the Michael Chekhov Way* to free your talent? If so, this next experience can lay the foundation for your empowering transformation.

##  The goblet

###  Let's play dissolving the gunk—erecting the goblet

Find your creative space in the room where you would love to lie down. Use mats if that helps you to be comfortable. Allow yourself enough room to move a bit without colliding with a colleague. If solo, record the guidance slowly while imagining leading someone through it. Then replay as you play.

Close your eyes if that works for you.

1. Now imagine you are wrapped in gunk, bound to the ground in mud and doubt.

    Inside of you are brilliant ideas that want to rise up and express themselves. They are shining inside your chest. You have everything already within you, but it is stuck. You need help.

    Imagine, high above is your star, a cosmic special helper just for you. Listen carefully as your star guides you to discover somewhere near you the perfect tool. Move your hand in search of it.

    Wow! You found it. Now take it and begin to scrape off the muck that's holding you down. Imagine freeing yourself from whatever is wrapped around you.

    Be thorough. Get it off every part of your body.

    You know what you have inside is worth working to free and share it. Maybe now your arms and legs are free enough to start getting up.

Inside of you is an amazing talent, and if you can clear this stuff off, you will be so happy, and everyone who sees you will be happy.

2. Keep rising, clearing, and freeing yourself with this tool until you are standing up freely on your own two feet.

Now imagine the power of all that you have freed yourself from is forming into a solid platform beneath you, supporting you. Feel the strength you have gained while freeing yourself.

As you stand upright, you can now access more images coming from your star. You are now free to perform something specific. You ask for more help.

3. Imagine your creative angels, beings, and images are gathering to send you the perfect inspiration for this moment in your acting.
4. You extend your arms out into the space and lift them to the sky, forming a cup, a goblet to catch the inspirations flowing from above. They flow into your own unlimited IAC, into your arms, into your imagination, pouring through your head, chest, heart, and full torso deep into your powerful base.

Streams of light and power shower down upon you. You catch them in your chalice and send them deep into the earth.

5. Then you radiate this to an audience. A volcanic power begins to return to you. First, it is two miles down, now one mile, now half a mile. It's getting closer, now 500 feet, now coming through the building's foundation, now through the floor, now into your foundation, your chakras, your feet, your calves, your knees, your thighs, your groin where you feel connected to the earth, your belly where you feel connected to your tribe, your spine, your diaphragm where you feel connected to your feelings, your heart where you connect to love, your throat where your power of speech resounds, your mind where your higher self sees the creative world, your crown where the light meets these amazing creative spirit energies coming down. The energy shoots into your arms and up to the magical place from which it came.

There, your star and the creative cosmic world grows stronger because of what you send back to them. Expressing these creative images is like sending food, like manna, to the heavenly spirits.

Sustain this moment, imagining the energy flowing back and forth through you up to them.

And now: Release.

*(Note: It may be useful to imagine this energy flowing in all directions and without directions at all yet still allowing you to scoop up all you need into your Goblet.)*

## ✒ Journal/Discuss/Flyback

*How did you experience that sequence? What happened for you? How did it feel when you were trapped? When you found the tool? Did you want to use it? How did it feel when you finally got up? When you opened your arms? When you discovered that imaginary forces would help fill you with images? And that when you let them help you, they get stronger? Is that a cool idea? You don't have to do this by yourself.*

## Let's discuss the goblet

You may notice that our erecting the goblet exercise has five parts. These numbers coincide with five pictures from the early 1930s.[2] In Figure 1.3. Panel 1, we see our star and the red base representing our basic self. In Panel 2, a stem is growing as we build our skills with the tools, while above creative beings are gathering toward our star. In Figure 1.4, Panel 3, we form the cup of the goblet when we ask for specific images for this moment, and our star gathers to send them to us. In Panel 4, our star brightens as the images flow into us. In Figure 1.5, Panel 5, our whole goblet is glowing, radiating to those star beings and helping these "special helpers" grow too.

*Figure 1.3* Panel 1: Our blue star above the red base represents our basic self. Panel 2: The stem grows as we build our skills with the tools; creative beings gather around our star. (From Lithuanian Theatre, Music and Cinema Museum Archive, courtesy of Justina Kasponyte.)

The goblet is a metaphor that Michael Chekhov used at least as early as the beginning of the 1930s in Lithuania. The in-depth secrets about the goblet images have been effectively hidden for nearly a century. By 1936, Chekhov stopped revealing that there are "special helpers" and your "unique star" became your "creative soul." The goblet as an image fell into obscurity. Whether you believe in it or not, I am here to say: having a personal star helper to do some of the work is empowering, so you might play "as if" you do and see if it makes you "happy."

The Goblet reminds us of the steps we take toward inspiration. While we cannot command ourselves to be inspired, we can create a ready receptacle to receive inspiration by building our natural talents through mastering the tools Chekhov has given us. Practicing the tool today will build your stem; using the tools for a specific character or situation strengthens and broadens the arms of the goblet. All you do now becomes part of your base for tomorrow. Your base and foundation will strengthen as you grow and use the tools.

 Axiom 1.4: Today's inspiration is tomorrow's foundation.

## Tools

Each of Chekhov's concepts, each physical movement, each tangible doable task, each intangible idea, each guideline for how to work, each principle is a tool. We want to allow the tool to rule, while we respond to its inspiration.

 Axiom 1.5: Allow the tool to rule.

# Preparing Your Imagination, Your Body, and the Ensemble

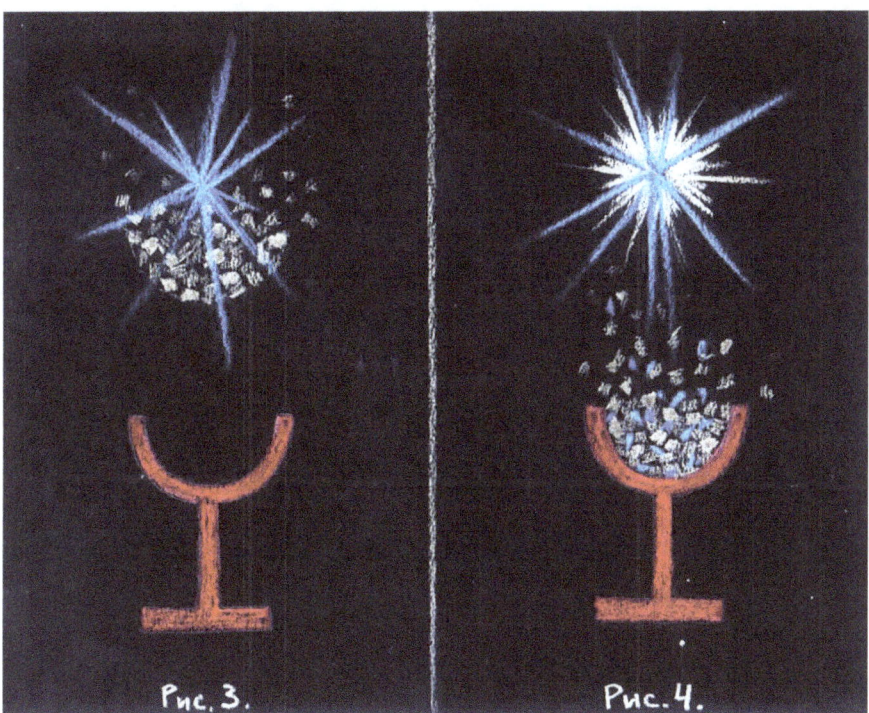

*Figure 1.4* Panel 3: The cup of the goblet forms; our star gathers images to send down. Panel 4. Our star brightens; images flow into goblet. (From Lithuanian Theatre, Music and Cinema Museum Archive, courtesy of Justina Kasponyte.)

*Figure 1.5* Panel 5: Our whole goblet glows, radiating to the star. The "special helpers" grow from the glow. (From Lithuanian Theatre, Music and Cinema Museum Archive, courtesy of Justina Kasponyte.)

Remember that when we look at the Chart of Inspired Action (Figure P.1), the rays of that sun-like center each have a toolbox at their outer point.

*But how many tools are in the center?*

None. The center is the inspired state where no tools are needed. The image helps us understand that tools are there to help us get inspired!

***If it ain't broke, no need to fix it.***

These tools are problem solvers if we aren't inspired. If you don't know how the tools work, they have no way to help you.

## ✒ Journal/Discuss/Flyback

*When you are in peak flow states in performance, are you able to allow them to last? Are you ok with not being in control? Does it make you uneasy?*

If you fall out of a "happy" state, simply choose a new tool to focus your energy on, and allow it to play you. *Imagine the Concentration and Focus Gesture (Figure 0.1) points to a tool.*

## Summary

In this chapter we have "warmed up" as preparation for launching into the tools on the Chart of Inspired Action:

- Imagination is #1 on the Chart. Developing it is our aim throughout this journey.
- We learned that "making friends" with spaces, ideas, our own bodies, and more brings us across the threshold into a field of safety, leading us to the freedom to grow.
- Through the ball toss, we moved closer to mastery of how to send and receive energy. We have many take-aways that will apply to nearly everything we do in the future, such as
    - Perfect Ball Drop
    - PASS: Preparation, Action, Sustain, Stop
    - Strong Prep makes Easy Action,
    - Strong Receiving Becomes the Preparation
- With the "Who Me?" experience, we discovered that most of us instinctively point to our chest, in the same place Chekhov identified as the location of your sun-like Ideal Artistic Center.
- Our Quantum Peek journey leads us to understand how our everyday lower self has adopted the personality we have and that it impacts how our bodies grow. We know the PPEs can free us from any limitations if we practice. Where focus goes, energy grows.
- We understand that the great ideas are our talent and the challenges to expressing talent are overcome through psycho-physical exercises.
- We played the Trapped Image Game, where we experienced how our great ideas can get mangled trying to make it from our brain to the audience.
- We gained insight into Chekhov's ideas that all the images exist in an I-sphere outside the Earth's ozone layer
- Through the Goblet Process, we became powerful receptacles for receiving those images and are affirmed that we serve the highest good in doing so. This part of Chekhov has been hidden for almost a century. We can experience this goblet with every use of our imagination.
- We don't need to really believe it. We can pretend and see if it works for us.

Next up—Start the chart on our feet with the PPEs!

Wait ... what? What is a PPE? Let's dive in...

## Notes

1. https://www.heartmath.org/articles-of-the-heart/global-interconnectedness/each-individual-impacts-the-field-environment/ and Science of the Heart, 2016 HeartMath Institute, Ch. 6,7.
2. Kasponyte, Justina (2011) *Stanislavski's directors: Michael Chekhov and the revolution in Lithuanian theatre of the 1930s.* MPhil(R) thesis, University of Glasgow. Original images found at the archives of Lithuanian Theatre, Music and Cinema Museum, Vilnius.

# Part II

# Psycho-physical Bodybuilding for Actors

> Help! Why didn't my great idea come out right?
>
> Why do all my characters seem the same?
>
> How is my objective supposed to change my acting?

In our next unit, we focus on understanding and beginning to master our mind–body connection. As we experienced in the trapped image game, there's nothing worse in acting than getting a great idea of how to do something, and it just doesn't come right! This happens when the body doesn't communicate the images from the imagination. As we understand from the Quantum Peek, we begin our training with this part of the Chekhov technique that seeks to resolve this disconnection of images and body.

## Part II Aims

1. Introduce the primary means of training the imagination and the body to respond to each other. The artist requires special training of the whole self to meet the demands of transformation.
2. Develop a knowledge of how to exercise and improvise with the tools of

    – Expanding/Contracting (X/C)
    – Qualities of Movement (QoM) (MFFR)
    – Archetypal Gestures (AG)

3. Use monologues, open scenes, or scripted scenes to practice the tools.
4. Develop the habit of daily practicing, observing, and applying (POA):

    a) Practice a tool to enhance psycho-physical skills.
    b) Observe a tool in the environment to train the thinking forces of the artist to perceive the self and environment in terms of the tools.
    c) Apply tools as a means of cultivating the skill to use the tools in performance.

Psycho-physical work aims to restore to the body the original flexibility and expressiveness with which we are born, as laid out in the Quantum Peek Figure 1.2. We eliminate specific energy patterns from our repertoire through life and focus on others more intensely. This interferes with our ability to fully inhabit a character because the character's energy management system differs from our own. If you want to be always ready to perform with a moment's notice, do these Psycho-Physical Exercises (PPEs) as a lifelong artistic practice, in the same way a musician practices their scales or a dancer their barre.

The tools in this section are based on patterns of natural impulses and elements found in all of creation. Through homeplay of practice, observe, and apply you develop your awareness of when to use your new skills in performance. Use the POA sheet to support your process. All the rest of the tools we will learn will use these three chapters as a foundation.

# 2
# Expanding/Contracting

## Expanding/Contracting (#2)

 Let's play opening and closing

Stand with arms and legs spread. Just move them into this position and then check in on yourself. Ask silently, *How does it feel? What comes to your mind? Does it remind you of anything? Do you like it? Does anything change when you have your chin lifted up? Are your eyes open? Closed? Head down? What do you want?*

Release and then tuck up into a ball on the ground. Pull yourself in as stiff, tight, and small as possible. Sit on a chair if you have knee challenges. Silently check in: *How does it feel? What comes to your mind? Does it remind you of anything? Do you like it? Does anything change when you have your fists over your eyes? Your eyes? Eyes open? Closed? What do you want?* Release and restore yourself to chat or write about what you experienced.

## Journal/Discuss/Flyback

*Did the two positions change how you experienced things? Did it change the invisible things in you, like your feelings, thoughts, and desires? Did you like one more than the other? Did you feel power or vulnerability in one or the other or both in each?*

## Discussion

Your response may be entirely different than that of the person next to you.

In any case, we have surely experienced a change because of a "mechanically" executed movement. Understand this fundamental premise as the basis for all of our psycho-physical training.

> **Axiom 2.1: Any physical movement will stimulate a psychological response.**

One of the most watched TED Talks by Amy Cuddy addresses using this concept for power poses. At last count, her talk had 42 million views. That is a lot of interest in this formerly dismissed concept that Chekhov began developing over 100 years ago. From this point forward, we always want to add images to our movements. "Psycho" is the imagination, and "-physical" is the body. With a conscious concentration on an image, we will multiply the psycho-physical effect of movement.

DOI: 10.4324/9781003512745-5

Expanding/Contracting (X/C) is the grand archetype of all motion, the black and white of the artistic palette of movement.

>  **Axiom 2.2: Expanding/Contracting is the pulse of all creation.**

### The implied question on the Chart of Inspired Action

Each tool on the Chart of Inspired Action could be a prompt for a question you might have. For example, if all energy is in motion, then *what* is the most basic pattern of motion representing? Expanding/Contracting. So, we begin learning X/C as "what" the energy is doing.

All tools on the chart will involve Expanding and Contracting, which is why it is the #2 point on our path around the chart, following Imagination in Chapter 1 (see Figure P.1, #1 on the Chart in Part I).

### ✒ Journal/Discuss/Flyback

*What things in the universe expand and contract?*

From the big bang theory to the cell dividing itself, we have examples of Expanding/Contracting everywhere.

*Take some time to contemplate this and share ideas. Call out or jot down a list of things with X/C, such as the heart, weather, reproduction activities, oceans, clouds, etc.*

> **Homeplay**
>
> Contemplate and seek out these energy patterns in yourself and the world around you. Notice that giggling tends toward contracting, and fear can activate expansion, especially in the senses. Where else do you see X/C expressing itself with a quality different from your own first impressions of it?

There are many synonyms and manifestations that can be useful in broadening one's understanding of the concept.

- Opening/closing, growing/shrinking, blossoming/wilting, bigger/smaller, oak/seed
- Encroaching/withdrawing, amplifying/diminishing, widening/narrowing, increasing/decreasing
- Aggrandizing/belittling, diffusing/distilling, waxing/waning, ebbing/flowing

In our initial responses, you might have noticed that how you reacted, positive or negative, is associated with your everyday personality. It reflects how Expanding and Contracting have each been used in your "piece of the pie." That is why it may be different from other people's responses. Your responses may be different from your character's, as well. The motion of X/C itself is an entirely neutral action that we then color with good and bad as appropriate in the context.

What we did initially was a mechanical move. The guidelines said rather bluntly, do this, do that without any image connected to it. It was essentially purely physical. And yet, it did awaken different experiences inside us. Hopefully, that will be the last time we do a purely mechanical move. We are looking to unite the imagination, the mind and the body with every movement from here on so that we multiply the power of our body language to consciously radiate energy across time and space.

Expanding/Contracting 61

Repeating the Expanding/Contracting process with different images such as light and dark, playing with clouds and snuggling into a cloud blanket, growing from a seed to a tree or flower—any of these can help us know the potential this tool provides. Varying the tempo of the transitions, from Expanding to Contracting, as well as the rhythms of the transitions, is critical to developing complete freedom of expression. It is essential to discover your personal relationship to any tool you learn. Your aim will eventually be to use the tool with no specific plus or minus reaction to it based on your personality. This way, you will be able to allow the imagination to select and color the tools according to the character and the story. You will freely allow the character to contract when you might expand in the same situation.

All movements of a character and the essence of the character itself can be described by their degree of Expanding or Contracting. A basic 10 scale, using 0 as the deepest Contracting and 10 as the grandest Expanding, creates a simple system to identify the extent of the opening or closing. I love to use Dicken's character Scrooge from *A Christmas Carol* as an example of a role that might use Contracting or Expanding, demonstrating the application of a 10-scale for the character's evolution. Most people know the basic story quite well, so it is easily communicated. Each actor playing Scrooge could craft their own unique Expanding and Contracting score (see Figure 2.1).

A **score of tools** is, like a musical score, a chart or notation of the sequence of notes (tools) the actor will play. These can be made on a graph, the side of a script, or on the blank back of a previous page. One can use the shorthand abbreviations, numbers, and symbols as noted on the chart (see Figure 2.2).

- See **OR 2.0** For X/C Graph Template.

*Draw your own graph based on what you remember off-hand for Scrooge's story or any other character.*

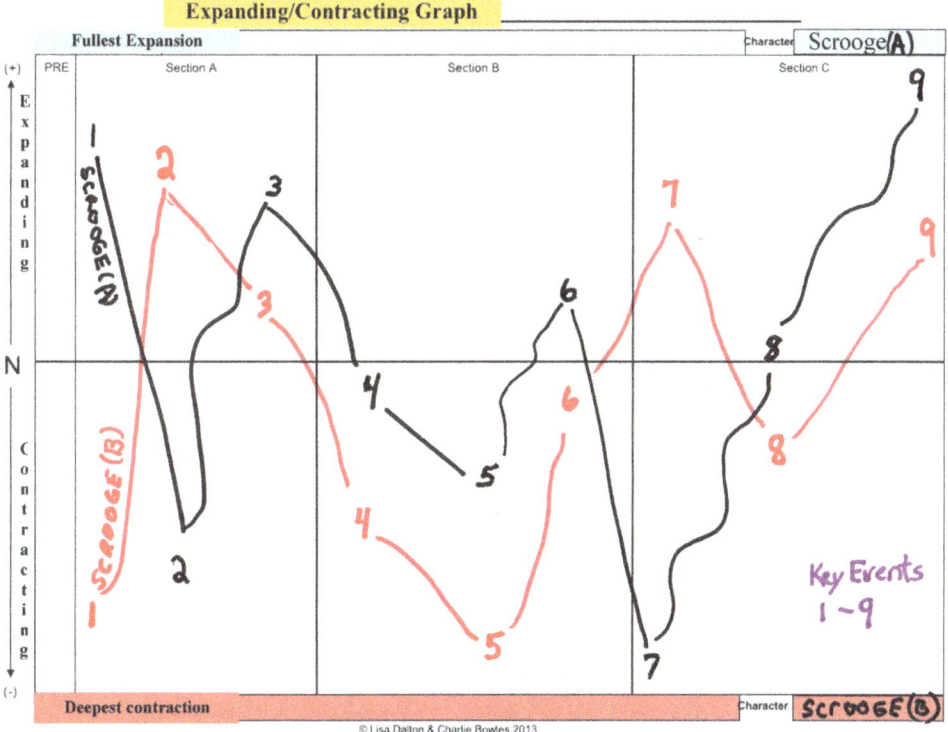

*Figure 2.1* X/C Graph for Scrooge. There are two different choices here to show there is no wrong way to do it. It is your imagination and creative individuality.

Courtesy of author.

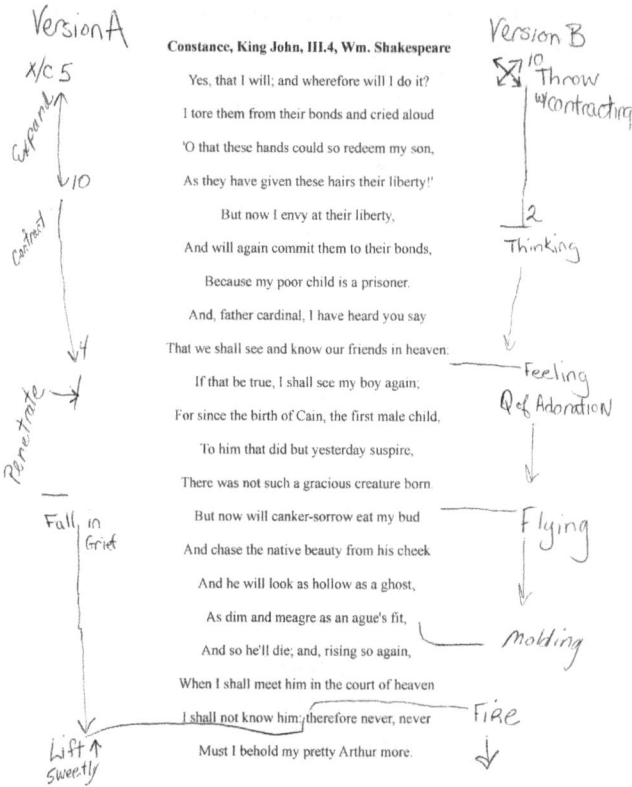

*Figure 2.2* Shakespearean monologue, Constance, from King John, with contrasting scores on either side, also using tools taught in upcoming chapters.

Score by author.

## Ways to play with this tool

 ### Let's play Expanding light

Standing in your universal stance, allowing awareness of your Ideal Artistic Center (IAC) with its sun-like radiance flowing through you, imagine you have a tiny seed in your chest. Very gradually, allow that little seed to expand its light in all directions, filling every cell in your body, moving in all directions. It flows through the body, Expanding the energy in every bone, muscle, organ, and fluid. It pours through your whole being as if you expand to fill this whole room. Now it travels beyond the walls, through the floor into the Earth, up through the ceiling into the sky. It expands more, with more and more space between the molecules of you, encompassing the city, the state, the country, the planet. It goes beyond the ozone layer out to the solar system. Now it is so big the whole Milky Way is inside of you. Now the universe. And beyond.

Begin moving with full-bodied abstract explorations. Add random sounds like the alphabet or numbers. Imagine the sound wave itself Expanding from and through you to the farthest reaches.

Gradually, imagine you can keep your energy body fully expanded and simply walk through the space the way your physical body wants to when its energy body is hugely Expanding. Perhaps you greet someone in passing or say a line or two of text, allowing the voice to reveal the Expanding.

Begin to contract the energy now. Draw it in from the farthest reaches of the universe, knitting each molecule back to another, closing out the light, tightening, darkening, shrinking the energy until you are in a tiny, hard, dark ball on the ground taking as little space as possible. Your energy body is now a hard dark dot. Keep Contracting that even smaller as you stand up through a series of contractions. Walk around the room. Say some of the random sounds in a way they can be heard. Pretend the sound wave itself contracts away from you into the space. Perhaps you greet someone or say that same line or two of text.

Gradually begin Expanding the energy body, allowing the light to grow, until you are back to your universal stance. Shake it all out.

## Journal/Discuss/Flyback

*Did you allow your body to move as fully as possible? How was your concentration on the image? Were you able to keep concentrated on how expanded you were? Did you expand into back and side space too? What was your experience? How did you feel? Were you contracting as fully as possible? What happened? Did your voice express the image?*

Practice veiling and unveiling in increments. Since this may be your first practice of veiling, gradual steps can help. Revisit the veiling in the introduction (page 24).

Practice transitioning from an Expanding 10, Contracting down the scale to 0, in a staccato (choppy) rhythm, then legato (smooth) rhythm. Practice Contracting to Expanding the same way. Call out random numbers and a speed to it so you are, for example, doing staccato Expanding slowly, and then quickly Contracting. Remember to Flyback often. Sometimes in our eagerness to do it again, we miss reflecting on what we have done and miss the potential growth opportunity. We encourage the Flyback because practice makes permanent, and we don't want to go on repeating an undeveloped approach.

Explore physicalizing the different images for X/C listed above and add your own. Make note of any interesting discoveries you have as you play. Try to enter the game free of preconceptions as to how the images may affect you.

Add sound to your expression to allow the voice to reflect the images. Start with random words, numbers, or letters. Try a nursery rhyme or phrase of text. Allow the image to influence the sound, the phrasing, emphasis, pitch, tone, intention. Allow the complete vocal and physical impact to express itself. Add in a partner and play with contrasting tools that transform in the middle. Play with partner in a nonverbal dialogue of Expanding versus Contracting, using various degrees of veiling and styles. Add in generic dialogue, monologues, scenes or verbal improvisation. Repeat the same activity using a different tool in different places in the scenario. Note how the tool changes the way the scenario unfolds.

**Use these basic ideas for all sessions playing with the tools:**

- Do it as fully physically as possible with strong concentration on the tool. Flyback.
- Add random sound, eventually text, improvisation, monologues and scenes. Flyback.
- Each time you play with a tool, assume you know nothing about it.
- Gradually veil the tool as you apply it to text and blocking.
- Try using the same and contrasting tools with your partners.
- Our goal is to allow the tool to guide how the text and activities express through us.

> Axiom 2.3: Let the tool rule.

## Surprising

One thing to be aware of is the tendency to think we know what an image will produce, and so we produce that. An example here is "I think my voice will get loud when I expand." And therefore, when I play with Expanding, I make my voice loud and I force the physical expression to follow the loudness of my voice. The limitation in doing what we *think* the image will produce is that we will rarely ever surprise ourselves. Our choices will always be within the framework of our everyday thinking skills. Though using the tools this way will increase our range of expression, we will be unlikely to experience the freedom and creativity that playing with a tool can spark. When you expand, you are actually imagining the energy Expanding right now. The next time you are Expanding; this will still be true—you can only be Expanding in the present moment. Anything else could be, in effect, a process of recalling past expansions and repeating the behavior you exhibited in the past. Using the words Expand*ing* and Contract*ing* keeps the concept in motion. Expan*sion* and Contrac*tion* may limit us to an immobile state of inaction.

>  Axiom 2.4: Our peak performances surprise us.

In your Flybacks, regularly ask,

*"Did anything surprise me? Did something happen unlike any other time?"* Did it come out exactly the way I thought it would? If so, was I controlling the tool or did I let the tool rule?

##  X/C Improvisations and Variations

### The plant

Standing in your universal stance, allowing awareness of your IAC with its sun-like radiance flowing through you, imagine that you have a small seed within your chest. It is floating in the air but yearns to bury itself deep in the Earth. Let the seed travel gently down toward the Earth allowing your whole body to follow it. Bring it down to the Earth and burrow into the Earth as if your entire body now is the seed.

Imagine your entire energy field and body are now nestled in the perfect place to take root. Some fresh water pours in and the impulse from the center of the seed begins to grow, spreading first some roots and then a stem. Notice the roots seek deeper earth and the stem seeks the light. Follow the plant as it grows in all its directions. Allow your body to follow the image. Gradually bring the body into full expression of this plant in its fullest expression. It is healthy, receiving the light, the rain and the earth and transforming the light into its body. Imagine the fragrance and allow your plant's energy body to travel into the atmosphere, wafting through space. Imagine the delight, the colors, the beauty, the shade that the form gifts to the cosmos. Imagine the shelter, the food, the amazing presence of this plant shares with all that lives.

Now imagine the pleasure and satisfaction, the playground it has been for beings of all kinds. Imagine is it satisfied and now it wants to rest. It floats or falls or crumbles or dehydrates, giving its disintegration to those who will enjoy it. Now new creatures grow from its decay. Until at last, in the roots and stem and leaves, it rests and gradually dissolves into the cosmos, yielding one tiny seed.

### The clouds for crowds

You are all particles in the air. You are hovering above and completely open, expanded, you are air unformed and shapeless. A yearning comes to connect to other molecules, to gather closer to other molecules. This you all do. The elements combine and you form a denser mass, a cloud. What kind of cloud are you? Allow the atmosphere to be discovered amongst you. Sense the pulse of all that the ensemble is creating.

Will this cloud stay in one large mass, or will it break up into ephemeral forms? Will a storm be brewing in this mass and generate lightning, thunder and hail? Allow the group to play out the possibilities. Using no leader.

## Cloudlet—solo

You are an individual cloudlet, dense and resting on a mountain hillside. You are a child tucked up in a ball, lonely and hoping someone will come to play. Gradually you become aware that someone has wrapped themselves around you hugging you. It is an invisible cloudlet. This cloudlet wants to play. Will you rise and let it, opening yourself to play with it? You can run by holding its hand; you can send it up until it floats back to you again. Send it all over the mountainside in hills and valleys, and when you want, you can wear it as a superhero cape or a snuggly blanket in a cove. Play with this cloudlet until you are ready to take a nap, then, snuggle into on the ground.

 ## Cookie Flyback

*How was your experience playing with Expanding and Contracting with images from nature?*

## The letter étude

This improvisation can be done solo, by everyone in the room themselves, or in pairs.

Use one piece of blank paper folded in three. An envelop is optional. Create a score for yourself in advance and declare it out loud, e.g. "I am going to begin fully expanded and gradually contract." Prepare yourself by physically Expanding and then allowing the large expression to veil so about 5%–10% is visible, especially in the chest and breath, keeping the energy Expanding fully. Enter the stage and approach the letter. Take and open it. Gradually, move your eyes as if reading from the top while beginning to contract your energy. Continue moving your eyes across the page to the bottom as you contract. When you are fully Contracting, place the letter down and exit in your contraction.

If working with a partner, Person A brings the letter to Person B and then watches as B reads the letter, returns the letter and they both exit. Person A may choose the same or a contrasting score as Person B. Both artists are either Expanding or Contracting at all times.

 ## Games and Improvisation

Chekhov's classes in his last Hollywood years focused on lectures, learning the tools, improvising with the tools and applying the tools to scenes and monologues.

When we play games and improvise with the tools, we are building our understanding of the possibilities of the tools, and we are building our strength and skill set for using them.

Use the basic guidelines for clean and safe improvisation such as

- Yes, and … Accept what is coming as truth and add to it.
- Always use fictitious names for yourself and others.
- What happens in an improv, stays in Vegas. Take nothing personally.
- Use real names only in an emergency to stop the game.

Pairs of actors can improvise in the shared space. Group improvisations like the ones above can be used. Solo explorations help actors develop the habit of playing with the tools alone. The sky is the limit as to the scenarios for these improvisations. When in doubt, simplify by limiting the given circumstances to a relationship. The rest will take care of itself. Here are three examples:

- A boss and disgruntled employee
- A server and hungry patron
- A costumer and set designer

Further information about improvisation and its meaning and role on the Chart of Inspired Action will be in Chapter 18.

- See *Kilroy Improv* Chapter 1 to expand your fun!

 Let's apply tools to monologues and scenes

Follow your improvisations by applying the tool to a scene or monologue. For your first time applying tools we suggest you start developing your skills by memorizing the last eight lines of your scene (four lines each partner), or the last four lines of your monologue. No matter how well you have it memorized, keep a printed or handwritten copy of your text nearby or even taped on a wall. Best to avoid relying on digital technology for this. As you continue around the chart to new tools, add a few more lines before the last section, until finally you are doing the whole script from start to finish.

- See **OR 2.1** Reverse Memorization.

**Use the following ideas for the application process with all your Chekhov tools:**

- Continue to develop your skill with X/C by veiling it while doing an "étude" (a sequence of behavior with a clear beginning, middle, and end.) Walk to a water bottle, pick it up, open it, take a sip, close it, set it down, and return to the start point. Try this same sequence Expanding and Contracting at different times and speeds.
- Add text. Keep flying back after each round of your game.
- Try a monologue unveiled and gradually veiled with one gesture all the way through. For example, decide on a pattern or score for how you will apply the tool. Say out loud to someone what that is. "I will begin my monologue fully unveiled at a 5, using a scale of 0 to 10, 5 being neutral. Start contracting into a 0 by the middle, expanding up to a 10 at the end."
- Now, play your score and Flyback with questions such as this:

 Cookie Flyback

*What did I like about what I did overall? What would I do differently? Did I contract all the way down, expand all the way up? Did my voice reflect the images of X/C as I did them? What was my favorite moment-my special surprise?*

- Try the same score veiled. Decide how veiled—will 50% be showing, or can only 30% be seen? Maybe 90% at the beginning is veiled (maybe only my chest and a little bit of my arms show I am Expanding) and it becomes unveiled gradually so only 10% is veiled. Flyback. If you feel like the energy of the tool disappeared when you veiled, try unveiling more.
- Try different scores—reverse your first score or switch for different beats, veiled and unveiled. Flyback.

- Try Expanding where you are sure it would not fit, and Contracting where you are sure it is best Expanding.
- Try a scene. For scene practice, each player chooses their own score. It can be the same or contrasting. Do the same pattern of beginning with unveiled large movements and gradually veiling with blocking, trying polar gestures.
- Initially, it is not your task to respond to your partner's gesture. If you were playing in a chamber ensemble, you first would focus on how to play the music on your instrument. After you mastered the music on your own instrument, then you would focus on listening and responding with your partners.
- Clarify with your scene partners your plan, including whether you will be responding or focusing first on allowing the tool to free you of a preconceived idea about the scene.
- If the energy of the scene gets lost when veiling, unveil by degrees until it returns and try again to keep the invisible power as you veil once more. Remember these are all muscles that will strengthen with *repetition*.
- Release any obligation for blocking, characterization, eye contact and having the scene make sense. Holding onto the meaning of the scene and the character at this stage would be like a first-time pianist worrying about playing the symphony. We are just looking to yield ourselves to the inspiration of the tool and let it rule. That is all.

## Voice and Body Unity

In addition, for freeing our body, our goal is to free our conscious self from forcing or controlling the sound of the text. We would like to allow the tools to guide our dialogue. When veiling, try keeping the voice inspired by the unveiled imagination. Then try the voice veiled to the same degree as the body. Keep the will of the invisible gesture strong. If the tempo, pitch, and rhythm remain the same when you use the same dialogue with a different gesture, then you know that you are controlling the text. Perhaps it always sounds like the way you memorized it. Each change in gesture, tempo, rhythm, and quality should affect the voice in its own manner.

Imagine as you speak that you can see the sound wave flowing across the space as it might appear on a graph. If your sound was being recorded, would the waveform reveal the tool you are imaging, e.g. the Expanding and Contracting, the quick or gradual transitions? With every run through, the sound wave would be unique depending on your tools.

Be careful to truly follow the image, allowing it to influence the speech. Intelligent actors can figure out what a tool might likely produce and then adjust the gesture to match their mind's prediction. When this happens, the actor experiences the text as coming out exactly as they wanted. This is good if you want to be in absolute control. It is not, however, the truth of inspired action, which comes out in a surprising way, unlike any other time. In states of inspiration, the text merely flows in some previously unknown way, surprising both the players and the audience. The player has yielded control to the image. It is the vulnerable and scary and delicious part of the highly prized state of inspired action.

### True confessions

The first five years I studied this technique, I made a lot of money performing in New York using it for stage acting, commercials, soap operas, stunts, clowning, and impersonations. I would use the tools that made sense to me, and my acting was very intelligent. I was also still taking acting classes in other non-Chekhov studios, where I got less and less criticism because I was delivering intelligent, skillful work. One day at an Equity Principal Audition, typically a two-minute event, after I did my dramatic monologue, the director asked me for a comedic, then a classical monologue, then something with some circus skills, and more. He gave me directions, which I took. I felt great. I nailed everything he asked for. It all came out exactly as I planned. I even had to, more or less, improvise a monologue from eight years earlier. I thought for sure I was getting this part! After about 25 minutes, he said, "Can I be honest with you?" "Please do" I eagerly responded. "You took every direction I gave perfectly, but I can't hire you because you never surprised yourself once!" "Thank you." I humbly uttered. These words were an amazing gift to me. They helped me understand what I am now hoping you will understand. I hope to save you five years of doing Chekhov in an intelligent, economically successful, but limiting way. I was controlling the tool with my intellect, and he was right, I was never surprised. I discovered that *allowing the tool to rule* freed up my control-freak self. I started having more fun and more success as an artist and economically.

# 3
# Qualities/Kinds of Movement

 Let's play Qualities/Kinds of Movement (#3)

Lying on the ground, imagine you are enveloped in rock-solid earth and feel completely natural in this firm state. You are made of this rock-like substance, yet you wish to create a form by moving, so you try; however, you meet such resistance that you can barely move. You try with every muscle and body part to shape the earth-like space around you, using your body as a sculpting tool. Ah! The rock gradually becomes more malleable, and you can move more fully, carving, Molding, and sculpting the space with your body. Your ears can shape this space, creating a form in it. The backs of your legs give the space form. Your shoulders mold the space. Can you sense the forms you are creating?

Gradually add in a Molding sound. Let the sound wave be earth-like, Molding its way through the space, shaping all it meets. Allow it to sound bizarre and inhuman. It may feel like rigid, slow motion, using a lot of willful effort. That's fine. Maybe the earth becomes more clay-like and less resistant to your efforts. Eventually, as if a little more water is being added to the space, it becomes more like molasses. It still resists your movements, and you mold them with your body and voice.

More water is added in, and eventually, it begins to carry you. You can go with the flow, allowing your movements to flow and your voice to flow, too. You can go against the current or float on top of it. Your body is Flowing like water. Now, a lily Floating on the surface or a wave rushing to the shore, you become a waterfall.

Suddenly, you are in the air, evaporating from the water into the air above the water, Flying. The air catches you under your armpits and lifts into flight like a pelican first, then soaring higher like an eagle, then zooming like a jet. You fling an arm or leg into space, letting it fly freely, with barely any resistance to your movement. You pause for a moment and let just your eyes fly across from one corner to another.

You take off like a rocket bursting through the ozone layer Radiating lightning, then fire, then laser beams. Your walk, your look, small movements, and gigantic abstract moves light up the room as you radiate through as lightning, or as fire and then sunlight. Now, you are sunlight, walking through sunlight, meeting no resistance, offering no resistance. You come to rest, sustaining this Radiating light. You release.

✒ Journal/Discuss/Flyback

*What did you experience in this sequence? Did you like one more than the others? Was one more challenging than another? Did your voice reflect the quality? Did you use your whole body?*

## Discussion: The implied question on the Chart of Inspired Action

The task of Expanding/Contracting answers "what" is the motion of the energy? The Qualities of Movement (QoMs) answers "how" the energy is moving, how much resistance does it meet? QoMs also can be called **kinds of movement**. They are Molding, Flowing, Flying, and Radiating (MFFR). These are named after the elements of earth, water, air and fire/light and used as a metaphor to express the full potential "how" of the Expanding/Contracting. The quality of the movement is related to the **degree of resistance** the movement meets. So, you will see that on the National Michael Chekhov Association (NMCA) chart as a subtitle.

The heaviest resistance generates an earthy Molding movement. The degree of resistance decreases as the molecules of the elements expand from earth to water to air to light. There are as many interpretations of the QoMs as there are expressions of these four elements. For our purposes, imagining a gradient scale will yield a broader range of playable qualities than limiting the expression of Molding to one tempo of heavy resistance or Flowing to one slow and legato movement. Molding can range, for example, from solid rock diamond to dirt, clay, and sand. Flowing can be an ocean wave, a lily on a pond, or a flood. Flying can be a heavy, slow pelican, a jet plane, or anything. Radiating can be light manifesting as lightning, fire, laser, or sunlight. In all cases, the QoM is universally neutral and, like Expanding/Contracting (X/C) may initially evoke a plus or minus reaction from our personality. We want to sensitize our bodies to be able to express objectively these Qualities of Movement. If X/C is the black and white of an artist's palette, these are the medium of the artist—the clay, oil, watercolor, or laser art.

Since *all* movements can be described as being more like earth, water, air, or light, it is possible to imagine you are moving through the space, which is resisting you to the degree that earth, water, air, or light does. You may also imagine your body itself as that medium that your body is moving as rock, clay, water or air, etc. A movement can refer to a physiological motion, as well as to a psychological movement. Our thoughts, feelings and desires are Expanding/Contracting, but how? Are they Molding, Flowing, Flying, or Radiating?

Any image that comes to you whether observed through your senses or arising in your imagination can be identified by how much resistance it meets in movement. If we can do all possible variations of these four kinds of movement, we can express any image we wish.

Each character will have a default QoM.

 Journal/Discuss/Flyback

*What are your personal QoM patterns? Can you compare and contrast them with your characters? Who are people you know that mold, float, fly or radiate as their basic QoM? When in your life do you find yourself Molding, Flowing/Floating, Flying, and Radiating? Where are these evident in the world around you?*

### Let's play deeper exploration

Divide the space into quadrants, defining as precisely as possible where one starts and the other ends. Baptize each quadrant with a QoM. Enter one quadrant exploring more deeply how this element moves around you, through you and as you. Perhaps first you are your everyday self, Molding through earth-like substance, making artistic forms. Then maybe you are the earthy clay moving through everyday air. Then you are the clay moving through the clay. Are these experiences different? What is awakened? Add random sounds, words or a monologue if you wish, allowing the voice to experience the tool.

Eventually move through each quadrant, stepping distinctly over the line and instantly transitioning into the new QoM. Examine more and more deeply the vast variety of ways this QoM can inspire your movement. Having played with all four, try moving quickly from one to the other with instant changes. Add your speech practice when ready.

Now, step out and gaze at the four quadrants. Imagine the sharp lines blur. Now the water mixes on one side with earth and on the other with air. And the fire mixes with air on one side and earth on the other. The section furthest from any other element is where the element is in its purest form. As you approach the center, the elements are mixing more and more. Explore moving through the space now, adding sound.

This exploration can advance into scene work where partners move through the space. A full monologue can be developed unveiled and eventually veiled.

Play additional games and improvs using Molding, Floating, Flying, and Radiating. Decide whether you want to do improvs using only one QoM at a time and then rehearse with it or Improvise with all the QoMs and then rehearse.

 ## Full-bodied contact improvisation

Find yourself a partner, and establish your safety parameters about making contact. (We can be creative and use a gentle object if touch is off limits. During pandemic times, we used foam pool noodles as extended arms.)

When ready, in silence, decide who will be the sculptor and the model. Imagine that you are both made of clay. Pretend the sculptor is a molded, baked clay instrument. The model is a hunk of formless malleable clay that will take the form the sculptor creates. Together, both actors, using the entire body and perhaps non-verbal sound, allow the sculptor to mold the model into a beautiful form. Mold two to three minutes, then the sculptors can step back and review their work.

Switch roles in silence. After the second set of sculptors review their models, release and chat for two minutes with each other about your experience. If energy and time permit, play again and using different QoMs.

### Samples of four-way improv

Create groups of four. Absorb and distribute extra players as needed. Assign a different quality of movement to each player in the group of four. Begin the improvisation with a prompt for the circumstances only. When the leader calls "Switch," the players, while staying in the same stream of the story, move to the next QoM in the sequence of Molding, Flowing, Flying, Radiating, back to Molding. Here are some sample circumstances:

- A big storm is coming, and preparations need to be made.
- A surprise birthday party needs to be planned.
- A political rally is coming up.

 ## Journal/Discuss/Flyback

*What did you discover about Molding? Floating? Flying? Radiating? Were you able to hold your QoM while the others held theirs or did you start to synchronize with some one? Was your whole body engaged in the QoM?*

- **See *Kilroy Improv* Chapter 3 for more Quality fun!**

 **Let's apply**

Try the scene or monologue applications with each quality unveiled and then with varying degrees of veiling. Then apply them transforming from one to another.

 **Cookie Flyback**

Remember to Flyback often. Experience without self-reflection yields slow growth, if any. Good Flybacks will reduce the number of times you get to do it, while multiplying the growth factor of each application. This is efficient use of energy—a key ingredient in making your training a peak process.

Try blocking and sequences of activities with your text using all four QoMs.

As you advance in skill with these tools and begin to interact, keep in mind, it's great to have a polar QoM in a partner to keep tension strong. Changing QoMs in key moments is a wonderful way to create significance for that moment.

And the best way to master these is through your POAs, three times daily, practicing, observing and applying (See POA sheet on page 288).

Next up ... Archetypal Gestures! Would you like to awaken the character's needs in your body? Archetypal Gestures will do that for you! We will want to be well warmed up for our next set of tools as it is possibly our most physically active sequence!

# 4
# Archetypal Gestures

> Help, I can't "do" my objective!
>
> I know what it is, but it doesn't help me act.
>
> What do I do with my hands?

Have you ever watched an actor do a scene or monologue and wondered what their character wanted? Have you ever been frustrated because you can't seem to connect the character's objective with your body and voice? Somehow, what the character wants and needs isn't coming through, even though you know precisely what it is intellectually. Have you ever struggled with what to do with your hands?

Would you like to learn how to activate the character's urgent objectives in your actor's body in one breath? If so, Archetypal Gestures (AG) are here to deliver the goods!

## Learning Archetypal Gestures (#4)

How do you learn the AGs and develop skills with them?

Let's jump right into an improvisation (improv) to help us grasp this next set of tools.

 Let's play get on the bus

Create a hallway formation with two lines facing each other, pairing people up with someone across the hall from them. If an uneven number exists, create a threesome with the extra person on the left side of the hallway, which will be Group A.

## The given circumstances

Imagine the empty space between the two rows, which is now a dangerous six-lane street busy with speeding traffic. A school bus is at the end of the street on the children's side (Group A). In Group B is one single parent for one or two children.

- Circumstances for Group B, the parent: You are on the other side of this very busy road from your child. You must coax the child onto the bus quickly and get to work. If you are late, you will be fired, and because you are already about to be evicted, nearly unable to care for the child, social services will take your child from you.

DOI: 10.4324/9781003512745-7

The Parent's Task: Get your child(ren) on the bus fast, without being able to cross the street or letting them run into the street and get hit.

- Circumstances for Group A, the children: You are four years old and have never been on a bus. You want your parent (Mom, Dad, Grandma), and you won't get on the bus, but maybe you fake out whoever is there and almost get on?

Parents, You have two minutes! Action!

And cut! Release and clear the traffic back up to the sphere of images.

##  Journal/Discuss/Flyback

*What did your parents want to actually do had you been allowed to cross the street? What did the children do in their refusal? What movements were being done by the parents or the children in response to trying to get them on the bus? Parents, how much of your body was trying to get the child on the bus? Children, how much of your body was avoiding the bus?*

Watch each other's emphatic body language as you Flyback and share observations. Notice how parents wanted to *push* their child, *lift* the child, *drag* the child, *reach* the child, *hug*, or *wrap* their arms around the child. The hands of the players will be doing mini versions of what they wanted to do but couldn't. Also, note that the parent's emotions rise and fall with the success or failure of achieving their objective.

*How many different tactics did the parents use? What were the children doing? Smashing things, pulling away, reaching out?*

## Discussion

These movements are innate actions humans do across the world. They are even done in the womb—the child pushes, wraps their arms together, sucks their thumb. Shortly after emerging, the child will reach, gather, and pull your hair and throw a pacifier after pushing it into their mouth.

These movements are primal survival functions we can call gestures.

Gestures underlie all communication. You can see this when people talk. Your mind gets an image of how you want your energy to move and how you want to affect your listener's energy. It translates that into words, and often, you will do subtle movements that indicate these underlying intentions even before the words flow out. If you want to get person B out of a rut, your hands might be doing a small pulling movement. If they want you to calm down, they may do a small pressing down with their hands.

We call these body-language actions emphatic gestures. They emphasize our intention/objective/aim and clarify our communication. They are realistic movements any human does and are usually appropriate for most styles of acting. To help us find what our character would be doing, we turn to discovering the largest unveiled expression of that impulse and practice it in an exaggerated size and then veil it to the perfect size for the style of the show.

> ⚛ **Axiom 4.1: Chart of Inspired Action implies Q & As for the PPEs:**
>
> X/C = What
> QoM = How
> AG = Why

If we imagine that **Expanding/Contracting** answers "what" the primary movement pattern of energy is, and the **Qualities of Movement** answer the "how" that energy expands and contracts, then the **AGs** are "why" energy expands and contracts. For example, the energy Expands in Molding **to Push** or Contracts in Flying **to Pull**. Enough chit chat! Let's get up on our feet, and we will come back for a more in-depth discussion afterward.

##  Let's play build the power of your AGs

Standing in your universal stance of readiness, imagine an urge begins to perk up inside you. It wants to do something. It wants to push something. But it cannot do it yet. It needs the help of your energy body to do the actual push. This energy body is bigger than you, and you are inside of it. It is what helps you move. In the energy body, the urge begins at a slow boil. The urge to push is getting stronger. Imagine this urge starts to boil over. You and your energy body must push soon. It's getting so powerful that if you don't push something, you will explode. Your energy body revs you back and says, "Let's Go!" Push! Push with your whole body.

Try several pushes. Flyback after each and ask

## Journal/Discuss/Flyback

*Are you using every part of your body, just like in the ball toss? Try another push and check to see if you are using PASS. Are you **preparing** in the back space (background) on an inhale? Is your **action** of pushing with your whole body on an exhale, then **sustaining** it for three seconds, continuing the exhale, and **stopping**?*

The entire movement—moving into the backspace on an inhale, gathering all the cosmic forces behind you and allowing them to push through you on your exhale, and sustaining for three counts, then releasing—ideally takes one full breath, no more, no less. If you are running out of breath before you sustain, decrease the imaginary resistance. If you have lots of breath, make it harder to push so that you slow down and run out of your last breath at the end of your sustaining.

Start each push by imagining it starts in the energy body first, and your body follows. And the energy body can sustain after you stop. It can keep pushing right through the wall.

In fact, if you have two people who can demonstrate, this can be fun and effective in communicating the idea of the energy body and the physical body. It might be clearer if the smallest person (A) and biggest person (B) in the group might volunteer for this demonstration.

Have a smaller person stand in front of a larger person. Let's imagine B is A's energy body, enveloping A's whole being. B moves just before A and does all the moves much bigger.

A starts to lean into the space behind and moves their arm above and behind them to gather the forces of the universe. B moves perhaps five steps back behind A during this time, with huge gestures of gathering the forces. Then, B begins to push forward from behind as A also begins to push forward. A reaches their full extension while B continues forcefully five steps past A, while A sustains the push in their imagination. A and B stop simultaneously. Release the energy.

We are training our imagination to lead our physical body. To do that, we start moving the energy body first in all psycho-physical exercises. Try this several times, concentrating on moving the energy body first and last.

Now, add the numbers 1-2-3-4-5 as you exhale. Start on the actual pushing gesture and sustain the count through your sustaining. Imagine the sound wave itself comes from behind you and can push through the air and move an object. Allow the throat to remain open rather than closed. Check to see if you are adding any emotion to your AG and allow that to disappear. This push is completely neutral and only seeks to move energy from behind you, through your center, to the periphery. There is no reason why it wants to and no consequence of its success or failure to do so. We are moving an abstract mass of energy rather than any sort of specific object. This keeps it distinct from mime.

Allow the face to be at ease. And while Chekhov suggests we want to do these with ease, we do need some tension in the body. We want to be able to easily play with the real tension of push.

Practice pushing against a wall or another partner, hand to hand. Notice how pushing with the heel of the hand changes the sensation of push in the groin and legs. Try pushing with your partner with fingers and no heel of the hand. Can you feel the sensation change in the lower body?

Often, when the heel of the hand is not pushing strongly, the sensation fades in the groin and lower limbs, which is where the urge to act must live. This is important to remember.

Without using a partner, try taking a step forward as you push. Now, try pushing your partner again and taking a step while doing so. Did you lose power when your leg came off the ground to move forward? This is natural because your body was no longer completely united toward the single idea of push. Your legs were focused on lift and balance.

If you want to awaken the strongest will force—the strongest urge to push—you might choose to keep your feet offset, leaning on to the back foot in your inhaled preparation, moving forward on your exhale with the pelvis, arms, and torso on the action as you push arms forward with a strong heel of the hands, transferring your weight to your front foot, keeping both feet on the ground. Keep the pelvis and Ideal Artistic Center (IAC) upright and forward pushing.

 Axiom 4.2: The AG is pure will.

**Our aim is to awaken throughout our whole being the will/the urge to push!**

The single biggest flaw in actors regarding their bodies is the disconnect between their hips/legs and their chest/head. All is lost when acting from the waist up, especially in a close-up on camera. Failure to engage the lower body leads to loss of truth and believability.

Let's try veiling the push a little bit. This time, keep your imagination on the huge archetypal push of the energy body and yet move your body only about 75% of that. So, you prepare by only going three-quarters of the way back. You push with the same force, three-quarters of the way forward, and sustain while your energy body keeps pushing fully. Try it with or without numbers, letters, or a line of dialogue.

Try this again with a 50% veil, going halfway back and pushing halfway forward with a full-energy body. See if you can keep the "push" in the voice while the volume decreases. Can you keep the push in the eyes and breath while the body's outward movement decreases?

Reduce the movement again, now to 25% showing through the thicker veil, with maybe a slight weight shift forward, a little bit of the hands and the chest.

Veil even more heavily until all you are physically moving is the breastbone centered in your chest.

Now veil again, revealing the full push through your IAC and eyes only. Speak the numbers. Speak a line like, "Hello, How are you?" Free yourself from any meaning behind them. Just push the sounds as if they mean no more than the numbers.

 Journal/Discuss/Flyback

*Are you allowing the voice to be fully influenced only by the gesture? Or are you trying to make sense of the line? Or are you making the line sound like it should since you are pushing?*

Try this entire sequence now using pull.

Perhaps you can imagine an urge to pull moves one leg forward as both arms reach out in front, gathering as they go; all the forces of the cosmos come from behind and reach further than your arms can to pull a massive force of energy through you into the space behind you. It might look a little like pulling a mime rope; however, in your imagination, it is a force of pure energy. Keep your eyes focused forward on the mass you are pulling. Here again, you can practice an actual pull with a partner, perhaps using cross-handed wrist grips. Notice that if a leg comes off the ground, you may be losing your pull-ability. Try the pull by moving your weight onto your front leg as you reach forward and grasp the mass, then pull with your pelvis, drawing the arms back as you shift the pelvis and weight onto the rear leg.

If you are losing the sensation of the urge in your lower body, try some pushes and pulls with your arms behind you in the small of your back. Does that help keep the lower body active?

 Let's improv Push and Pull

Having played with these two contrasting AGs, build your strength and understanding by doing some improvisations. Pair up with a partner, and each choose to be either pushing or pulling. Then both of you are pushing, then both pulling. Feel free to be very full bodied or gradually veil, etc. You can use the exact same given circumstances for each of the five pairs of gestures to see how the gesture affects the improvisation.

**Suggestions**

Two shoppers at a big sale.
Car mechanic and customer.
Teacher and parent at parent's conference.

 Let's apply Push and Pull

Use these suggestions for all ten AGs below. Explore two AGs at a time, improvise with them and then rehearse.

Try a monologue unveiled and gradually veiled with one gesture all the way through:

- Try different gestures for different beats, veiled and unveiled.
- Try gestures you believe you would never choose for this character.

Try a scene. For scene practice, each player chooses a gesture. It can be the same or contrasting. Do the same pattern of beginning unveiled and gradually veiling with blocking, trying polar gestures. Initially, it is not your task to respond to your partner's gesture. If you were playing in a chamber ensemble, you first would focus on how to play the music on your instrument. After you mastered the music on your own instrument, then you would focus on listening and responding with your partners.

 Cookie Flyback after each version

- Clarify with your scene partners your plan, including whether you will be responding or focusing first on allowing the gesture to free you of a preconceived idea about the scene.
- Each player in the scene should be engaged in some phase of a gesture throughout. We don't stop wanting what we want while listening to our partner. Our inner urge is still driving us toward its goal.

- If the energy of the scene gets lost when veiling, unveil by degrees until it returns and try again to keep the invisible power as you veil once more. Remember these are all muscles that will strengthen with *repetition*.
- As you move the gesture from unveiled into the invisible world, the gesture is freed of the physical limitations of the body so now you can pull ten times in one second or pull for ten hours in one pull.

 Axiom 4.3: Your invisible, veiled gestures are free of our time/space limits.

## How many AGs are there?

When Michael Chekhov taught these, he never crafted a set specific list. Some of Chekhov's students never learned these and were taught Rudolf Steiner's eurythmy gestures. Others of Chekhov's students place these as the highest priority in the training cannon. One said there were five, another thirty-seven. Here we focus on six primary AGs and four secondary AGs for a list of ten. This list is based on functionality. These ten AGs are frequently found in every text, and every gesture thinkable can ultimately be pared down to one of these. If you can analyze the beats and units of your script, you can score the objectives by stating them in "gesturable" verbs that can fail or succeed. This means that all your analysis can be psychophysically integrated and expressed through your body and voice. It prevents "heady acting." In learning the AGs, time may limit your ability to do all ten. Select the ones that most interest you and will be useful for you.

Play with each of the ten Archetypal Gestures as time permits, using the same ideas as your first exploration with push. **Your aim for doing AGs is to awaken in you the URGE to** … push, pull, lift, smash, gather, throw, penetrate, tear, drag and reach. Make up your own version, watch an online video, or follow the steps below that outline a form. There are suggestions for variations to explore along the way.

- See **OR 20.4.** for video links to see AGs.

## Is there an ideal form for each AG?

The Dartington students tended to teach the AGs by showing us the specific form, such as of push or pull described in detail above. The Hollywood students tended to teach the guidelines needed to make up your own effective AG. This way of teaching is a natural evolution for Chekhov's teaching style from having an ensemble for three years of pure training to a quick private coaching or a once-a-week group class of an ever-changing Hollywood population.

It is interesting to discover that both can lead to the exact same gesture if the guidelines are applied. The National Michael Chekhov Association (NMCA) pedagogy encourages learning some specific forms and making up some others according to the guidelines so that you experience both paths to the same aim. Some of us actors don't need to know the guidelines and may be confused by trying to remember or comprehend them. Just show me, please! Yes, learning by imitation is, in fact, how we learned in the cradle. The critical aim is that you grasp what this can do for your acting and be able to use it to inspire your acting. Any way you learn it is perfect.

Sometimes we create a gesture that stimulates us, and it doesn't fit all of the guidelines. We love when this happens mysteriously because the bottom line is that you use a tool only to get things working! If whatever you are doing inspires you, go for it. There are no NMCA police out there arresting folks for not following Lisa's law. The laws or guidelines are principles to take into consideration if what you are doing is not working. That's the time to Flyback over what you are doing and ask if you are missing an element. You will discover that the slightest adjustment of the head, a hand, a shift of weight, more energy in a wrist or change in the resistance can completely alter the effect on you, the artist.

## How do we do an AG?

Begin in an ideal universal stance. Imagine your energy body is a large sheath or aura surrounding your body in the same shape yet larger and is activated by impulses coming from your IAC. Concentrate on the image of your energy body initiating the gesture. Add the movement of your physical body. Make a full-bodied gesture as big as you can without losing your balance. Continue the gesture in your imagination for three counts after your physical body reaches its fullest expression. Then release all energy as you return to ideal universal self or hang time. Flyback. For your double stuff, ask questions such as *Was I able to stay concentrated on the image? Did I allow the image to lead me? Did I sustain the image for three counts after my body reached its maximum expression? Did I lose my balance? Did I have a clear beginning, middle, and end with a strong inhale on my preparation and exhale through my action and sustain, or did I lose my breath?*

To help understand the idea of an energy body as enveloping the physical body, have Player A be the energy body doing a push using the whole room, while Player B does the regular archetypal push. Player A begins standing behind Player B and then moving on the inhale maybe five feet into the backspace of B and pushing past B perhaps ten feet during the sustaining. Players B and A try to breathe in synchronicity and concentrate on the image together.

There are AG Guidelines that suggest what will be present in a well-done AG/ball toss/PG:

- Breath—One inhale and exhale. If you have excess breath at the end, increase the resistance.
- Body—Full use of the form, especially the pelvis, legs, and heel of the hands.
- Extreme polarity—The movement begins in the polar opposite direction of its ending.
- Effort—100% commitment of the will (key to star quality) with real tension easily done.
- PASS—Prepared, acted, sustained, and stopped with clear beginning, middle, end.

**What is BBEEP?** Breath, body, extreme, effort that is PASSed.

This NMCA acronym is designed to help you remember five questions to lead your imagination if your AG or PG is not inspiring you. Remembering this one question opens you to the five specific guidelines: "Did I BBEEP my gesture?"


## Deeper discussion

If we look deeper into the energy pattern of these emphatic gestures, we discover a larger impulse connected to a universal array of gestures shared by cultures worldwide. Hidden within that micro-emphatic gesture is a bigger one, the grandest version of an impulse to move energy in a certain way for a specific reason. The grand expression of that impulse is known as an Archetypal Gesture. If we use a macro-sized invisible Archetypal Gesture and veil it to micro-size, it becomes a naturalistic emphatic gesture. If we can understand the nature of these Archetypal Gestures by physically exercising them, we then are able to change our unconscious emphatic gestures to conscious ones.

It is exciting to discover the concept that grander invisible gestures really do underlie our intentions. Our language seeks to express images, and, in this way, we understand something beyond words. We sense the image that the words are seeking to express or in some cases, to mask. By concentrating on radiating or receiving images and allowing the voice and body to reflect this process, we can then allow the text to be spoken as the image directs. We will not need to decide through our thinking forces what to emphasize or where to pause. The success and failure of the gesture will activate our emotions, freeing us of wondering what the character should be feeling in this moment. The interplay of gestures in a scene will always keep the players "in the moment" of the characters, rather than in the moment of the actor's personality. If we want the power to be able to consciously align our energy with our character's, then we can practice these gestures in their biggest archetypal forms.

## Why?

As actors, we have personal emphatic gestures that relate to unconscious and habitual desires as well as that emphasize our immediate communication needs. Each of these subtle body language patterns masks an image that contains a grand invisible gesture.

*Do you want the audience to always see your personal habits and never the character's?*

We must be aware of this in order to allow our personal mannerisms to be altered to express the character's mannerisms. We want to fully reveal the character's objectives and psychological tactics for achieving their aim, not our own. When we train our bodies to be able to express a broad range of archetypal objectives through doing AGs, then we can choose any variation of those AGs for specific aims. They will create the specific body language unique to this character. They will fill our hands with subtle impulses which connect directly to the character's subconscious. And yes they can free our hard-wired habits.

## Gesture as subtext

Subtext literally is unspoken text below the written text that is intended to give it a different meaning. The challenge with subtext is that it is still text attempting to express an image. If the subtext of "Hello, how are you?" is "What are you doing here?" I still don't know what is really being said. There are still a multitude of meanings for that subtext that could be friendly or not so much. Subtext itself is at least one step away from the creative stimulus being sought. A gesture is clear in its intent and can be described by different words without losing any clarity of its meaning. As a directing technique, try giving the player a gesture instead of subtext.

## AG for Life

Doing AGs can be a personal bonus. Identifying our own invisible gestures will allow us to make new choices when our habitual tactics are not succeeding.

> ### Can't need help!
>
> Monique was a very talented, highly independent and self-driven athletic young woman who was working, training, auditioning, and going to grad school. I had very high hopes for her future because she responded to the training so well. Then, on this day when we were doing AGs, Monique had a very difficult time pulling, but she got push instantly. She was shocked by her inability to pull—losing balance, unable to figure out the body position, and not able to pull firmly. It was confusing to both of us. She left class with the determination to figure this out. She began practicing pulling and realized her confusion had simply been from lack of using her natural pull energy. Perhaps somewhere along the line had pull become a sign of weakness or simply useless with no one to pull? There's no need to know the final *why* the challenge existed. It simply wasn't in her piece of the pie. **Note to Self: Fixing the consequences heals the inciting incident.** The following week Monique waltzed back into class, light and easy, saying "Did you know that people will help you if ask?" She discovered that she could indeed pull support to her, and many people welcomed her doing so. She had often been exhausted from doing everything for herself. Her life was much easier to handle once she reintegrated into her piece of the pie her inherent push/pull dynamic, allowing others to support her. Many corporate and life coaches are successfully using gesture to help clients. More on this in Chapter 20.

## What is an Archetypal Gesture?

For our purposes, **archetypal means that which we know and were never taught.** It is like an invisible blueprint in the cosmos that all humanity knows intuitively. An archetype can be considered an ideal idea that contains everything necessary to define or distinguish the type. One of my mentors, Jack Colvin,[1] posited that the first expression of an archetype could be called a prototype. All prototypes and stereotypes contain the truth, the DNA, of the archetype within them. There are archetypal personalities/characters such as heroes and villains; archetypal events such as death, birth, puberty; archetypal stories such as boy meets girl; archetypal forms such as chairs, tables, and beds. All of these archetypes might be found in one story. Fairytales are a great example of this. Our goal might be thought of as to create unique prototypes of the archetypes that arise in storytelling, retaining the essence of the truth of the archetypal ideal while avoiding the cliché of stereotype. This means creating a new prototype for each role, even if you play the same archetype from story to story.

For our purposes, a **gesture is a movement plus intention.** Movement without specific intent is motion. The formula is

 Axiom 4.4: Movement + Intent = Gesture

An Archetypal Gesture is an intentional movement of archetypal scope.

## Layering skills in the AG sequence

There are so many possible ways to work with AGs and so much to learn from them that a week could be spent just on push and pull. So, we introduce different concepts to consider and priorities in a learning curve as we move further along the list. For example,

- First, we hope you understand the fundamental idea and its potential value.
- Then we work for BBEEP on the first set of tools, making sure you engage the will centers in the body such as the pelvis and heel of the hands.
- We add in basic sound. Usually, we use letters of the alphabet A to E or numbers one to five that have no meaning. We want to spread out the sounds through the entire breath, timed to begin at the start of the A of PASS. Thus, the preparation is on the inhale and the action/text is on the exhale through the sustaining.
- Then we replace those random words with "Hello how are you?" which has the same number of syllables. Our aim is to just push or pull those words with no more or less emphasis or subtext than the letters or numbers. We want to free ourselves from the meaning of the text. In effect, the invisible gesture becomes the subtext.

 Let's improv with AGs

As you explore the AGs below, add an improvisation for each pair to deepen your skill with that pair of AGs.

- See *Kilroy Improv* Chapter 4 for a smashing good time with improv for AGs, especially the speed dating game!

Let's apply AGs

Rehearse your script with each pair of AGs.

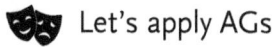 Cookie Flyback with each pair of AGs

*Did the meaning of the script change with the different AGs? Did I allow the gesture to change how the lines were expressed? Did I attach an emotion to it or was it free of my personal opinion?*

**Increase discoveries as you go**

- Basic veiling is explored with **Push and Pull**.
- With **Lift**, we explore more deeply the connection of the heel of the hands and the groin area. Any gesture can be sustained with strong energy in the heel of the hands. Any gesture can be released by sending it through to the finger tips creating for example a "lift off." What happens when the lift is sustained with strong heels of the hands up to the sky, still lifting with the energy body? How does that affect the groin energy? How does that change when the wrists release, and fingers end up pointing to the sky? Does it feel the same? Does it look to others like you are lifting now or reaching?
- We also discover that, though **Smash** seems angry, we can have a smash hit, smash the egg shells to make the omelet, and look smashing while we do it. Each AG is actually completely neutral off any emotions.
- With **Gather**, we play with changing the tempo and rhythm. Speed it up and suddenly it is snatch or steal or capture. What if you just gather with the hands molding? Maybe it becomes strangle or choke or wring. Try it just with the hands, floating. Does it protect, shield, cup? Slow it down and tilt the head left. What does it become? Repeat at the same speed and change the head to tilt right. Is this different? How so? Is left more tender and right more curious or protective? Right brain/left brain differences are discovered, deepening our understanding of the subtle yet powerful impact minor changes of form and speed can affect.
- We introduced changes of tempo and rhythm as with gather; the AGs gained more psychological impact and lost their neutrality. More on tempo/rhythm in Chapter 14.
- **Throw** in many different ways, such as two-handed overhead or a baseball. What is the difference, once again, of following the energy with our hand extended as if it is helping the energy to go further? Or following through across our body, as if it is now on its own momentum and we can affect it no more? We realize that how we sustain can be perfect for different characters.
- Think of some idioms that have "throw" in them and do the gesture that way. Throw your two cents in. Toss this idea out. Throw in the towel. Throw down the gauntlet. We see that each of these gestures is used regularly in metaphor. Find the truth that makes the metaphor last.
- What characters might be gathering or throwing? Who is gathering their wits? Who is throwing a tantrum? Who is tossing a compliment? Who is gathering clues?
- These first six gestures are often, though not necessarily, paired in polarities. If we use direction as a basis for distinguishing these gestures that are all variations of X/C and of Push/Pull, then Push sends energy from the center to the periphery on a horizontal plane. Pull draws energy from the periphery on the same plane. Lift and Smash direct the energy up and down on the vertical plane with smash coming from the periphery to the center and lift from the center to the periphery. Throw is more purely scatter, but the word throw is used clearly in Chekhov's writing. Throw/scatter disperse energy in all directions from the center. Gather collects energy from the periphery into the center.
- In **Penetrate** we find a secondary color as it is made up of a focused push into. We discover that vast arrays of archetypal characters use penetrate. Sorority girls, thieves, armies, lovers, parents trying to understand, detectives are all able to use penetrate.
- **Tear** can be two pulls apart or a pull away from. Try three different tears. One tears two things apart at the center of the chest to your sides. Try a vertical tearing of two things apart, going up and down. Now try a version where both hands reach across to an upper corner in front of you and tear away, across your

body down. Play with the variations. Identify the one you prefer. This is training us to be aware of our IAC's artistic preference so we can use it more frequently.
- **Drag** seems to be a variation of pull with a slow tempo. Here we activate the gesture through the backspace of our kinesphere. We discover and express many idioms that use drag, such as *dragging your feet* and how it differs from *dragging your heels*. We look at the stereotype of drag queen and find the archetypal truth that the drag energy must be present in order to qualify as a drag queen rather than a transvestite.
- In **Reach**, we discover the stem cell of all gesture. Like a stem cell, reach can begin and then transform into any of the other gestures. When in doubt, it is the "go to" gesture because everyone is reaching for something—love, power, money, food, sex, identity, purpose, etc. Try reaching for something you just can't get. Finally, you succeed. Notice how emotional failing and winning can be? All good gestures will be able to succeed wonderfully and fail miserably.
- Play with verbalizing the gesture to see if it increases or decreases the degree to which the gesture activates the will force. Say "I want to lift" as you lift. Say "I am lifting" or "I lift." Try the line before, during, and after. Try thinking it without speaking it. Compare the impact on yourself and note it.
- Continue to develop use of the gestures by veiling them while doing an "étude" (a study, from the French), which comprises a sequence of behavior with a clear beginning, middle, and end. Walk to a water bottle, pick it up, open it, take a sip, close it, set it down, and return to the start point. Try this same sequence with different gestures.
- Add text. Keep flying back after each round of your game.
- After playing with many gestures, create two contrasting scores of AGs on either side of a script using symbols for your AG using shorthand symbols (see Figure 4.1).

### AMCW Table 4.1 Archetypal Gesture Symbols

| Archetypal Gesture (AG) | Score Symbol |
|---|---|
| Push | →  |
| Pull | ← |
| Lift | ↑ |
| Smash | ↓ |
| Gather | ⟳ |
| Throw | ↷ |
| Penetrate | ⤙ |
| Tear | ⇄ |
| Drag | ↗ |
| Reach | → |

*Figure 4.1* AG symbol table. Use the above symbols as shorthand for quickly identifiable notes on your scripts. Alternatively, create your own system.

If Expanding/Contracting is the black and white of the artist's gestural pallet and the Qualities of Movement are the medium (clay, oil, water, pastels/laser), then the basic six AGs are the red, yellow, and blue from which all other colors can be made.

>  Axiom 4.5: All acting can be created through these three Psycho-Physical Exercises (PPEs).

## What is the difference between AGs and PGs?

- An **Archetypal Gesture** is the largest possible gesture of a primal intention. It is pure WILL with no reason (no thinking), and it is neutral (no emotional feeling of good or bad).
- An AG should charge the whole body with the urge/desire to push, pull, lift, smash, gather, throw, penetrate, tear, drag, and reach with a *universal, objective* attitude.
- When you add a reason/why (thinking) and a quality/how (feeling), an AG is no longer objective and then becomes a **Psychological Gesture** with a reason **(Thinking)** and a quality **(Feeling)**.
- The moment an AG is placed into a scene it is instantly a PG because it gains "reason" through the context of the story and quality through the feeling life of the player.
- Therefore, AGs are a training tool to develop the PGs that AGs transform into when used in a scene or monologue.
- However, our goal is to be capable of using AGs archetypically. This will help free us from limiting the use of the tool to how our everyday self uses it. Your aim includes freeing yourself of always attaching rage to smash, for example. When you succeed at this, you will discover many new opportunities to use smash.

## Summary and resources

- See OR 4.1 for lists of AGs and a gazillion synonyms and idioms

At the beginning of this section on PPEs, we had challenges that stifled our happy states. Let's review them and see how we can answer them.

> *Help! Why didn't my great idea come out right?*

Because your image got trapped! You now know how to free your images.

> *Why do all my characters seem the same?*

Doing PPEs will free your body to transform into unlimited ways of moving.

> *How is my objective supposed to change my acting?*

AGs will send impulses through your whole body, inspiring the Character's unique body language.

Having learned the three primary Psycho-Physical Exercises, you already have at least 16 possible tools that you now know how to apply to a scene or monologue. You may not be able to wait until the end of the book to start applying them in the "real" world.

- See OR 4.2. Monologue prep and OR 4.3. Scene study preparation.

## Note

1. Jack Colvin, an artist-actor known for playing Jack McGee in the Original TV show, *The Incredible Hulk*, was Chekhov's personal assistant for the last five years of Chekhov's life and mentored the author from 1993 to 2003.

# Part III

# Emotional life for Actors

"OMG! Will I feel the moment?"

"What if I don't really feel it?"

"Yikes, I will be a terrible actor!"

Have thoughts like this ever haunted you? Would you like a technique to remove the fear of "not feeling it" forever? Can you imagine your life as an actor free of ever fearing delivering emotions truthfully on cue? That's the actor's challenge that Chekhov tools can free us from—the fear of the moment. The Chekhov technique does so in a healthy way with easy steps that can be done consistently and repeatedly. No more needing to stay in the emotion for long periods. No need to have a life of suffering to be an actor. The idea that to be great, you must be a suffering artist is "oh, so 20$^{th}$ century!" Let's move to the future using our highest powers to joyously create the pain, terror, and rage as well as the joy, thrill, and satisfaction in the artistic moment rather than recall from our "been there, done that" past or substitute and project imagined horrors onto our actual loved ones or ourselves. That's not safe and not healthy.

> ⚛ Axiom P.1: We aim to render a character's emotions truthfully in a manner healthy for actor and audience.

Michael Chekhov's approach to the actor's emotional life is exquisitely simple, reliable, and transformative. We use the natural and intuitive gifts that movement and images bring to us. In our imagination, we develop our human selves to pave a pathway to joyful creativity in art and life. There are three primary, imaginative means of achieving emotional depth and expression for the character we seek to portray. They are

1. Three Sister Sensations of Equilibrium (#5 3S)
2. Qualities and Sensations (#6 Q&S)
3. Atmospheres: Overall and Personal (#7 ATMO, OA, PA)
4. Four Brothers of Art (#8 BEEF)

Let's explore each of them here.

# 5
# Three Sister Sensations of Equilibrium

## Falling yielding

 Let's play discover Falling yielding

*(Remember to activate your body and imagination as preparation for this activity.)*

Let's walk randomly through the space you are in. What if you imagine that gradually, gravity pulls you toward the ground, allowing you to fall or flop as you walk? Allowing your breath to fall, let a sound fall out with your breath as your chest falls in. Maybe you gradually speak numbers or letters, pretending that the letter falls out of your mouth. As you are moving, can you sense how each step you take can fall? Even bringing your foot up for the next step might be a fall upward. If you wish, gently fall to the floor, one body part at a time in a series of falls. Fall back up to standing. Allow an arm to fall up over your head. Let it "fall for that old trick." Let the other arm fall up and then "fall in love." What if our heart falls? Or your chin falls? Or your mind? Fall in all directions. Try some lines of dialogue imagining them falling on the ears of your audience. Play with veiling the sensation of falling, step-by-step starting with 100% unveiled (full-bodied expression), then reduce the size of the movement by 25% so 75% is unveiled. Next, veil more, softening the physical expression in the body to 50%–25%–5%–1%. Can you keep your energy body Falling at 100%, making it your secret physically while the breath reveals the energy body? Allow just one body part to reveal the fall, then another.

Release the energy and restore it to the sphere of imagination where it is always available to you for the asking.

## ✒ Journal/Discuss/Flyback

*What sensations are awakened as your energy is Falling? When have you fallen up? To the side? What inside you can fall? What physical sensations are awakened? What emotional sensations? When might you use this?*

## Play again with falling

Imagine your chest Falling, and allow it to actually sink. What does this motion awaken? We might be crestfallen, heartbroken, exhausted, sorrowful, tired, bored, depressed, or relieved. It could trigger an emotional response, an image or a desire, a feeling of age or illness. Physicalize these metaphoric phrases; picture the literal, physical pattern of energy described and move with it. Can you find the essence of Falling in the action that the following metaphors suggest?

- Falling to pieces
- Falling for that old trick
- Falling asleep, into bed
- Falling in and out of line
- Falling in love
- Falling out of favor

- Falling on your face
- Falling into a trap
- Falling in your lap
- Falling within the limits
- Falling behind or below
- Falling into ruin

Once you have completed the exercise, release the energy, and restore it to the sphere of imagination where it is always available to you for the asking.

## Floating weightlessly

 Let's play discover Floating weightlessly

Resume walking through space, now free of gravity completely. Really pretend you are Floating like a space person weightlessly as if there were no up or down, and no gravity to pull you anywhere. Allow your Floating movements to suspend themselves in hyper-slow motion. Let your breath float out of you weightlessly. Allow the sound wave to float slowly out of you. Let every syllable float at the same slow weightless speed. It may sound like a warped record; and, since we are playing with mastering energy patterns we may not use very often, being incoherent is "perfect." We can even inhale in the middle of any wor…d, or float a line of dialogue even if it feels like it's taking forever. After you feel that your whole body and imagination are safe moving this slowly and possibly weirdly, perhaps you play with veiling the sensation of floating, making it your secret, while making sure your breath and speech stay transformed by the feeling of weightlessness. At first, allow just one body part to reveal the float, then another, and another.

When you are ready, release the energy and restore it to the sphere of imagination where it is always available to you for the asking.

 Journal/Discuss/Flyback

*What sensations are awakened as your energy is Floating weightlessly? When have you floated like this? What physical sensations are awakened? What emotional sensations? When might you use this? Does moving this slowly drive you crazy?*

 Play again with Floating weightlessly

Imagine your chest Floating and allow it to actually move up or sideways. What does this motion awaken? Physicalize the following metaphoric phrases, picturing the literal physical pattern of energy described and move with it. Can you find the essence of Floating weightlessly in the action that the metaphor suggests? It could trigger an emotional response, an image, or a desire.

Head in the clouds
Spaced out
Airhead
Empty-headed

Get a rise out of you
The rising generation
Drifting in sorrow
Floating in a sea of grief

Release the energy and restore it to the sphere of imagination where it is always available to you for the asking.

We might be swelling with pride, standing in awe, suspended in shock. When you let your mind float weightlessly, it may awaken feelings of being spacey, airy, lost, stunned, stupid, dysfunctional, dissociated, or superior. To move, breathe, and speak with a sensation of Floating weightlessly sometimes activates naïveté, hopelessness, loftiness, incapacity, retardation, elevation, paralysis, inflation, expansion, rising, ascending, or meditating. All answers are the right answers and what it awakens in you is what is in your "piece of the pie." And now you can expand to many more aspects with this sensation of *weightless Floating*.

## Balancing teetering

 Let's play discover Balancing teetering

Let's find space for walking and beginning to speak or think of a steady stream of numbers or letters while you are Balancing on a very wobbly tightrope. See if you can push the edge of your security, truly almost losing balance. Have a classmate spot you if you like. Sense the inner tightness of teetering on the edge. Keep talking because you probably like to stop talking when you really almost lose it. Allow your voice to go into falsetto as you teeter. Try another image for creating the experience of struggling and Balancing. Perhaps you notice you are avoiding Falling and/or floating away. Cross one foot over the other as tightly as you can, trying to keep your ankle touching. Rise up on your toes for as long as you can, reaching your head to the sky. Keep a constant flow of sound that reveals the wobble, the struggle to get balanced. How would the syllables sound if they were sound waves struggling on a tightrope? Now add a line of dialogue. Imagine the sound wave of the words teetering on the edge. Play with veiling the sensation of balancing, making it your secret a bit at a time. Maybe we allow just one body part to reveal the struggle, such as your gut or your groin.

Release the energy and restore it to the sphere of imagination where it is always available to you for the asking.

## ✒ Journal/Discuss/Flyback

*What sensations are awakened as your energy is caught in Balancing? When have you teetered like this? What physical sensations are awakened with different body parts? What emotional sensations? Did you find yourself holding your breath? Did your voice reveal the struggling in your body, or did you try to block the voice from sounding weird? When might you use this?*

 Play again with Balancing teetering

Imagine your chest struggling for balance and allow it to tremble or shake. What does this motion awaken? Physicalize these next metaphoric phrases, picturing the literal physical pattern of energy described and move with it. Can you find the essence of trying to stabilize and struggle for balance in the action that the metaphor suggests?

- Hanging in the balance
- On the edge
- Walking on pins and needles
- Strike a balance
- The scales are still in motion
- Balance of power
- Balancing out
- Teetering
- On the brink
- Torn between two choices
- Waiting for the other shoe to drop
- Ready, Set, …

Release the energy and restore it to the sphere of imagination where it is always available to you for the asking.

Frequent responses include terror, giddiness, anticipation, excitement, eagerness, worry, aggravation, panic, apprehension, contraction, chaos, disorientation, hyperactivity, and repression. It also could be used for age, injuries, speech, and physical impediments. All answers are the right answers and what it awakens in you is what is in your "piece of the pie." Those of us who like to be in control and/or avoid conflict, might feel very uncomfortable practicing this technique. If we allow our Balancing to be colored by the opposite of what it normally awakens in us—for example, filling it with excitement rather than fear, we expand our piece of the pie as artists. We will be able to have fun inducing these once-scary states of energy inside us with a new ease.

## Deeper discussion

The Three Sister Sensations of Falling, Floating, and Balancing (3S) can create almost any emotional, physical, or psychological condition. Mastering these techniques, especially through the Ideal Artistic Center (IAC), can be a rapid and reliable way to connect to feelings and to radiate the sense of a deep connection.

The fundamental concept of the Three Sister Sensations of Falling, Floating, and Balancing describes the relationship of an object to gravity. Gravity is the law of physics that affects the human being most powerfully and continuously. We are speaking about the nature of equilibrium, the search for stability. In the three-dimensional world, any object can be identified either as Falling, Floating, or Balancing. This includes our bodies, our breath, and our eyes. Likewise, intangible energies such as our thoughts, feelings, desires, spirit, centers of energy, and Personal Atmospheres can be described with these three sensations. Our basic breathing pattern as well as our walk can be described as a sequence of Falling, Floating, and Balancing.

By mastering the potential to move freely with these three sensations, we can then allow images of them to inspire us in several different applications that are effective by veiling or unveiling in any style, medium, or genre of performance.

## What is Falling?

One could say that if the energy is yielding to a gravitational pull in a specific direction, there is a sensation of Falling. Usually, this falling is in a downward direction. To experience this fact, simply raise one arm up, and release all tension. The arm falls down. The breath falls in an exhale from the lungs. When exploring Falling, we can exaggerate the Falling exhale with breathiness in our words, really letting the air audibly "fall out." This unveiled breathiness will help us keep our sound filled with a sensation of Falling, transforming the words even when they remain strongly veiled.

Have you ever fallen up a flight of stairs? If we want to choose the broadest interpretation possible, we will consider that things can fall in any direction. The key distinction here is that there is a yielding to the gravitational pull of the Earth, but, if downward was the only option, the Moon would not pull the tides with its gravity. In this tool of Falling, we are yielding, giving into the pull of gravity and therefore making no effort to "not fall."

## What is Floating?

If Falling is sinking into the pull of gravity, Floating is a sense of freedom from that gravitational pull and is directionless. The breath of Floating is the inhale.

Floating in the three sisters concept is different from the "Flowing" quality of movement. The easiest way to clarify the difference is to note that the four kinds or Qualities of Movement correlate to the four basic elements of earth, water, air, and fire. An expanded interpretation of the "Flowing" Quality of Movement could include any kind of water-like movement from, for example, a floating lily in a pond to a flowing waterfall. The element of water is used as an image that activates a degree of resistance to movement. Within the Three Sisters Sensations of Equilibrium, Floating refers to the sensation of no resistance at all. There is nothing to resist, there is weightlessness, suspension, detachment, or levity (from Latin, *levitas*, lightness or the opposite of gravity from which we get the concept of levitation; source, etymonline.com). Working with extreme slowness will help distinguish this from the movement of water. In today's world of fast talking, fast-paced video games, and an overall need for speed, moving in hyper slow motion is rarely in our piece of the pie. The artist who can't slow down their speech and movement will lose a great deal of expressivity. All your characters will move and speak at a similar fast pace, making it hard for audiences to hear or follow. Training our brain, breath, and body to slow down is a health practice with extensive science to back it up. Both your health and your creativity will strengthen when you train like a Zen master to float in stillness comfortably. It is free of tension.

## What is Balancing?

Balancing (the active attempt to become balanced) is the urge to attain or sustain equilibrium of opposing forces. It is teetering. The energy is willfully engaged in the struggle against gravity and levity—to not fall, to not float away. Yielding to gravity is encompassed by the term "**Falling**." Trying to stop or break the fall is encompassed by the term "**Balancing**." The state is imbalance, unbalance, and instability. One tries not to topple or drift. The breath of balancing is held. It is a very highly charged state of energy that, like a tightrope walker, is most riveting in a chaotic struggle for control. It provides strong contrast to Floating weightlessly and to Falling yieldingly.

For our artistic purposes it is important to distinguish between balanced and Balancing. Balanced (to be in a state of balance) suggests that the forces on either side of the center of gravity are equal, producing stability. This condition is one to be desired as a human being since it suggests freedom from conflict. In the Chekhov technique we describe this condition as a feeling of ease. However, the nature of storytelling is centered in conflict. As such, only in brief moments would **balanced** be the ideal choice of sensation without losing the interest of our audience. Balancing as an active process will be infinitely more useful to the actor.

To veil this tool, sit on the edge of a chair. Look straight ahead while trying to touch the ceiling with the fontanel of your head and extend your arms wide. Picture that your chair is on a tight rope, and you are pulling everything straight up through your spine and balancing by tightening your gluteus muscles. You are inwardly trembling with the struggle. This is one example of veiling Balancing. What does the image awaken? Perhaps, you are "sitting on the edge of your seat." We might think of your torso as the fulcrum of a scale with arms. That fulcrum can be as thin as a knife blade, but it will hold up the arms only if the balance is perfect. To do so, it must maintain an upright tension. Now try walking "normally" across the floor but with the secret image that you are on a tightrope.

## ⸎ Let's improv 3S

Now is a great time to build your skills with the Three Sisters set of tools. One of my absolute favorite improvs is "callers," where two artists are playing out an established scenario such as "two new roommates moving in with each other." Assign each artist a partner who will prompt them from the edge of the stage, "calling" one of the three tools. The artist must instantly shift into the tool called. The callers must speak loudly so their artist can hear them. The artists try to keep the scene going as they morph from Falling to Balancing to Floating based on their prompt from their partner. Start playing very unveiled. As you get the hang of it in this very exaggerated form, the callers can also prompt whether to veil more or less.

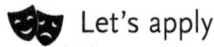 Let's apply

Play with the Three Sisters in your scene or monologue. Begin by applying just one of the three tools at a time for an entire section in a fully unveiled expression. In the learning phase of this sequence, our prime aim is to allow the images of the tool to inspire tempo, rhythm, subtext, tone, breathing patterns, sound, and movement. We are not yet ready to respond to what the other actor is doing. Whether applying solo or with partners, start by speaking your intention out loud. "I will be focusing on unveiled Falling for this rehearsal." This helps you make clear choices before you start rather than randomly picking things as you go.

 Journal/Discuss/Flyback

Flyback at the end of the section, considering whether you met your aims, and then declare a new focus: "I will now focus on transitioning smoothly from Balancing to Floating to Falling using a 50% veil." Practicing Floating at the extraordinarily slow tempo will take lots of concentration, patience and focus. If practicing with a partner, both of you are always in one state or another and don't need to be matching, contrasting, or reacting to each other. As you develop the skills to consistently meet the prime aim, veiled or unveiled, try improvising the scene at 50% veiled while responding to the other character. If they fall, do you try to help them float? If they are struggling for balance, do you also struggle?

> ### Homeplay
>
> Do some practicing, observing, and applying (POA) observing these Three Sister Sensations at play in the universe to garner a vivid knowledge of the variety of states and conditions that can be expressed through them.

 Let's improv they walk in

Now that you have applied these tools in a variety of ways, let's practice strong veiling so that your body moves subtly, showing 5%–10% of the powerful energy you are actually using in very natural motion. Finding your creative space, float your head to a doorway across the room. Imagine someone enters. As they do, your heart begins to float. They slowly walk across the room, and your gut begins to balance; now your hands struggle for Balance. As they come nearer to you, the struggle travels to your left lung. When you can feel them breathing, your balancing releases and your armpits float … your inner thighs float … your eyes float. The person turns away and your jaw falls gently … then your heart falls … your breath falls … your left ear falls … right big toe falls. As they walk away toward the door, your tongue struggles for balance … your elbows are Balancing … a hand falls. They turn and smile at you. Your navel floats … your lips float … your eyes float with them as they disappear through the door …

Release and gather that image and send it up into the unlimited I-sphere enveloping the Earth's ozone layer.

### Journal/Discuss/Flyback

*What was the story that just happened? What emotions were there? What did you want to say or do? How did you feel? What would an audience have thought was happening here?*

An audience will see a story in this étude. They may project upon the stage an emotional heightening, anticipation, hope, anxiety, excitement, yearning, abandonment, depression, disappointment, relief, etc.

Yet, all we did was imagine Falling, Balancing, and Floating with various body parts. This is repeatable take after take and rehearsal after rehearsal. We needed no memory of anything from our past or present. We are completely living in the moment, allowing images, sensations and movements to play us. We don't need to add anything to the objective tool; there's no need to tell the audience what we are feeling.

The actor allows the audience to color the work as the audience sees it and accomplishes this very simply by moving and breathing with the tools. It may awaken many images in the actor; and the most important part of any tool is that, regardless of how it impacts the performer, the audience will have an active response. This use of the Three Sisters for activating emotional truth is but one of three ways to use it.

## Three applications for 3S

 Axiom 5.1: Three Sister Sensations are effective in three ways: for emotional truth, characterization, and transitional gestures.

The primary use is for emotional truth, as we have been exploring. Employing one or more of these can awaken any emotional state. And they can be localized to a body part.

Secondarily, these Three Sister Sensations can be a defining character trait in the same way that thinking, feeling, willing, and Personal Atmospheres can be predominant traits, as you will see in later chapters.

Perhaps Lady Macbeth is a balancer and Ophelia is a floater. Maybe Hamlet is a balancer one day and a floater the next, and then a faller. Goneril and Reagan can be contrasted by choosing Falling versus Balancing Personal Atmospheres.

In the famous film, *The Wizard of Oz*, one could say the Tin Man is Balancing in search of his feeling heart, the Scarecrow is Floating in search of his thinking, and the Cowardly Lion is Falling in search of courageous will. The Good Witch and Scarecrow are Floating, the Wicked Witch and Tin Man are Balancing and Dorothy and the Lion are Falling. With the help of the man behind the curtain, they achieve balance.

In the famous television show, *Seinfeld*, Jason Alexander's character, George, could be called a Falling character. Jerry might be a floater, and Kramer would be the Balancing character. In *Friends*, Ross and Rachel are hapless fallers, Monica and Chandler are balancers, and Phoebe and Joey are floaters.

Additionally, the arc of a character can be expressed by transforming the Personal Atmosphere from one "sister" to another. The drug addict begins as a floater, goes through detox as a faller and gets sober in a tender balance.

Thirdly, let us explore the Three Sisters as transitional gestures.

When characters reach, push, pull, lift, etc., there is a moment where they do not know whether or not their effort has succeeded. Until they do, they can sustain in a sensation of "hanging in the balance." Once they know the result, there is an inner and/or outer reaction. There must be a visible and invisible movement to connect the initial effort with the next movement. If the initial action has failed, an increased effort of the same gesture or changing to a more effective gesture will follow. One of the Three Sisters can be the ideal transitional tool between them. This is because the tool is objective, with no positive or negative quality, and can be applied and then given an emotional color. If the gesture is a reach, for example, the movement can be falling away from the failed reach in frustration, floating away in confusion, or balancing away in fear or defeat until the character decides on (yes, the character decides! More exploration of that in Chapter 12), prepares, and executes the next gesture. Once again, the character will be hanging in the balance to see if they have won or lost. With a victorious win, the transitions can also be any of the Three Sister Sensations: Falling in relief, Balancing in excitement, Floating in joy, etc. until the next gesture is determined.

Chekhov uses Horatio's speech to the ghost of Hamlet's father to demonstrate a Psychological Gesture (PG) of reaching.[1] The reaching arm extends over seven lines. By leading our imagination with questions, this set of tools can provide many answers. Are there seven different reaches, or is it one reach that is sustained inwardly gaining momentum? If it is a matter of seven different reaches, what segues or transitions to and from the gestures? For instance, to "reach" and then "reach again" requires withdrawing the arm after the first reach. How? Try the 3S to connect the reaching gestures with the two different reactions Chekhov suggests for Horatio. It is an excellent exercise to witness the possible impact the three sisters as transitions can offer the actor.

- See *Kilroy Improv,* **Chapter 6** to fall in love with the 3S!
- See **OR 5.1** for the Three Sister Sensations origin and video link to performance.

## Note

1  Chekhov, Michael. *On the Technique of Acting,* Harper, 1991, 66–73.

# 6
# Qualities and Sensations

## Qualities

 Let's play Qualities

Finding your creative space in the room, gaze at your hands. Start with a quality of caution in your fingers. Begin to move them very cautiously. Now, cautiously add in the whole hand. Now add the elbows, and then the arms as if caution were creeping into your whole body. Cautiously look all around you: in front, behind, to one side and the other, above, and below you. Shift your weight, lifting your foot cautiously. Walk cautiously. Go faster, cautiously faster. Freeze, cautiously looking, only moving your eyes. Breathe the breath of caution. Speak a line. Look at your hands.

Begin to move your fingers with a color of pink. Now, add pink to the whole hand. You don't need to know what pink means; just pretend you do. Now add the elbows, and then the arms, as if pink were filling your whole body. Pinkly look around behind you. Walk pinkly. Go faster, pinkly faster. Freeze, pinkly looking, only moving your eyes. Breathe the breath of pink. Speak the same line.

Now, move with a quality of blackness. Now, add blackness to the whole hand. You don't need to know what black means; just pretend you do. Now add the elbows, and then the arms, as if black were filling your whole body. Blackly look around behind you. Walk blackly. Go faster, blackly faster. Freeze blackly looking, only moving your eyes. Breathe the breath of blackness. Speak the same line.

Move your hands with a color of anger. Angry fingers, wrists, and elbows. Angry breath. Angry feet. Breathe the breath of anger. Go faster angrily. Slow down angrily. Freeze angrily. Speak the same line.

Look at your hands as the quality of anger shifts to eroticism and lust. Now, add lustiness to the whole hand. Now add the elbows and then the arms, as if lust were filling your entire body. Lustily, look around behind you. Walk Lustily. Go faster, lustily faster. Freeze, lustily looking, only moving your eyes. Breathe the breath of lust. Speak the same line.

Lust falls into the color of grief and sadness. Streams of grief flow into your fingers, sadly touching one another, pouring into your forearms, into your armpits. Long streams of sad sighs escape your lungs. Exhale sadly for so long you can hardly breathe. Your inhales get stuck in your throat in short, sad spurts, which are not enough to help as the next long exhale sighs sadly out of you. Your feet step sadly across the floor, and your chest sinks sadly with a grieving heart as you exhale long, long breaths and inhale short, staccato, incomplete breaths. Try to speak the line through the long, sad exhale and during the truncated inhales.

Look at your hands and move them with silliness. Reverse your breathing with long inhales and short exhales. Move your butt with silliness. Move your toes and feet sillily. Look around the room with silly eyes. Speak the same line. Shake it out!!!

Release the energy and restore it to the sphere of imagination where it is always available to you for the asking.

## Discussion of Qualities and Sensations (#6)

When we move with a Quality (caution, let's say), the Quality awakens a Sensation (danger), which may coax a feeling (fear). The essential task is for our whole being to be filled with the Quality. The rest takes care of itself as we shall see.

>  Axiom 6.1: Move with a Quality to awaken a Sensation that MAY lead to a Feeling.

We can use either the word "quality" or "color" to describe "how" you move and breathe. The character must breathe as any human does, filled with the psychological conditions of the moment. Every primal feeling has a breathing pattern to it, which, even when technically executed with total commitment, will induce movement and speech patterns identical to those of a "real or personal" feeling. This approach offers a reliable, repeatable, and consistently performable skill to support your talent. Remember, techniques such as these are to be used when inspiration fails to provide the desired performance.

It's useful to start moving with the Quality in your hands first due to their exceptional sensitivity which science verifies: "Each hand has about 100,000 nerves, and each of its five fingertips has over 3,000 mechanoreceptive nerve endings."[1]

Let's look for a moment at the words "emotion" and "feeling." Many people find it useful to think of feelings as a sense inside of us and emotions as energy in motion (E-motion) traveling through the body. This can be a useful idea for us. It is an idea used for millennia in Eastern traditions.[2] Some contemporary psychologists refer to emotions as a state that grows into feelings when the mind gives context to the state. In any case, they are considered two different things. As professional artists, we can awaken feelings in audiences by expressing emotions.

When training, there are many universal emotional states that an actor can choose to master. Just about every emotion will be one or a combination of the following: all springing out of the presence or absence of love with fear as love's polar opposite:

- Love/joy/happiness/peace/contentment
- Awe/wonder/amazement/surprise
- Lust/desire/eroticism/yearning/excitation
- Sadness/grief/remorse
- Anger/rage/disgust
- Apathy/boredom/exhaustion/relief
- Fear/anxiety/anticipation/shame

Each of these will have its own

- Breathing pattern, with differences in depth of the inhale/exhale, length and tempo of the inhale/exhale, length of hold between inhale and exhale, and rhythm of the breath
- Intuitive center in the body, perhaps in an organ
- Tempo/rhythm of the movement
- Variables of the size and nuance of the expression
- Speech patterns and pitches affected by the breath

Through the practice of the primal emotional qualities in the largest, most childish, unrestrained physical expression, actors eliminate from themselves any subconscious or physical fears of expressing these feelings.

In addition to emotions, Qualities can be inspired by almost anything, including colors, textures, animals, elements of nature, temperature, tempo, and rhythm.

Sensations radiate from within, then through the body outward, and begin when you ask yourself to move with the quality/color. Actors need only invite the pure objective quality when acting. Audiences will see your movement as colored by your character's emotions. Moving and breathing the Quality assures that the actors will look and sound like they are having a feeling even if they are not, in fact, feeling the character's emotions. This approach to performance usually allows the audience to access and colorize their own feelings more fully. Ultimately, who is it that needs to *feel* the moment?

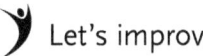 Let's improv

You can play this solo or with a group or several groups simultaneously. Each player chooses three random props. Select a different Quality for each of your three pops, either from a list of possible qualities or assigned to you by a partner. The location is a store. Pretend you are going to purchase these props, and play out the improv, switching qualities as you deal with each prop. One person could be a store clerk who also has to change qualities with each prop they sell.

Returning to the letter étude is always intriguing. Choose three to five contrasting qualities to apply as you receive, open, read and close the letter.

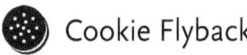 Cookie Flyback

*Flyback to identify what worked overall.*

*How could you double stuff it for next time? And what was your favorite moment?*

 Let's apply

Play with Q&S in your scene or monologue. Begin by applying one at a time for an entire section in a fully unveiled expression. Create an étude—a short sequence of physical actions with a clear beginning, middle, and end. For example, walk to a chair, turn and sit, pick up a book, open it for a moment, then close the book, set it down, rise, and return to your starting point. Work silently. Gradually add a line of monologue or exchange a few lines of dialogue. In the learning curve of this sequence, our prime aim is to allow the images you create using the tool to inspire tempo, rhythm, subtext, tone, breathing patterns, sound, and movement. We are not yet ready to respond to a partner. Whether applying solo or with partners, start by speaking your intention out loud. "I will be focusing on a quality of awe for this rehearsal." This helps you make clear choices before you start rather than randomly picking things as you go. Flyback at the end of the section, considering whether you met your aims, and then declare a new focus: "I will now focus on moving with a quality of sandpaper gradually turning into purple using a 50% veil." If practicing with a partner, both of you are always in one quality or another and don't need to be matching, contrasting, or reacting to each other. As you develop the skills to consistently meet the prime aim, veiled or unveiled, try improvising the scene at 50% veiled while responding to the other character. Release and restore your images to the sphere.

✏ Journal/Discuss/Flyback

*Does the Q&S of your partner trigger a change in your Quality?*

### Homeplay

Observe the natural breathing patterns people use in life and notice how these patterns change as people shift from one state to another. Try to observe some babies and young children. Practice moving with different colors and Qualities as you go through your day. Baptize them with names.

### Journal/Discuss/Flyback

*How are you feeling about feelings? Do you feel more confident?*

- See **Kilroy Improv Chapter 7** for more sensational quality fun!

### Notes

1. https://www.secondmedic.com/blogs/which-part-of-the-body-has-the-most-nerve-endings
2. The Hand in the Brain By Til Luchau [The Somatic Edge] https://www.abmp.com/textonlymags/article.php?article=2244#:~:text=Your%20hands%20are%20truly%20sense,are%20finely%20attuned%20to%20pressure

# 7
# Atmospheres: Overall and Personal

Did you ever see a show that just lingered in your soul?

Even today, when you think of it, does something stir in you?

Do you savor the memory of having seen it?

This is the kind of storytelling the actor of the future must deliver to our audiences. The secret here is in the Atmosphere.

## Overall Atmospheres (#7) discovery

 Let's play crossing thresholds into Atmospheres

Let's everyone spread evenly spaced around the room's periphery. Imagine a threshold at your feet: a big circle or perhaps a rectangle. On the outside of this threshold in the periphery where you are standing is this room, this space now. Beyond the threshold is a whole new Atmosphere, a different vibe or place.

 Engage your goblet

If you wish, tap the light-filled awareness in your Ideal Artistic Center (IAC), inhaling the air in the room. Allow the radiant light from your center to radiate down through your core, into your legs, and into the ground below, penetrating deep into the Earth and meeting its fiery core. This process anchors you to your foundation. Allow that radiant light to also stream upward through your head, through the ceiling, through the roof, up into the sky, and through the Earth's ozone layer. Imagine that there it bursts into a sphere of images. This sphere contains images of everything: stories, characters, historical and fantasy, past, present, and future. It crosses dimensions and space. It is like your own super cloud containing all the information you want to download into your creative being. Your IAC is your own personal search engine.

Ask your IAC to lead you to the Overall Atmosphere (OA) of a cemetery at midnight. Inhale that Atmosphere deeply and exhale it across the threshold into the space. Imagine the molecules of that cemetery pouring into the space and activating all the other molecules. Wait a few moments for the entire space to be filled with the OA of the cemetery at midnight. Gently extend one hand across the threshold into the Cemetery.

Inwardly ask, Is there a difference in the air across this threshold? Is it colder? Is the space darker? How might I describe it?

DOI: 10.4324/9781003512745-11

Withdraw your hand and pause. Step across the threshold, immersing your whole being in this new OA. Pause for a moment, allowing the molecules of the cemetery to permeate every pore of your skin. Breathe this OA into your lungs, filling you with cemetery air. Imagine that you begin to walk through this cemetery, moved by these elements of the air, in harmony with them. Explore this new OA. Notice that your shoe has come untied. Find the best way to tie it in this OA. Continue through the cemetery and exit at any point on the threshold. The moment you step across the threshold, you are instantly in the room, in the present.

Release and restore: When everyone is out of the OA of the cemetery, imagine with a grand gesture that you can gather the whole OA up in your collective arms and send it back up to the sphere of images from whence it came, knowing that this sphere is always available to you. You can re-access it whenever you wish.

 Journal/Discuss/Flyback

*What did you feel when you were in the cemetery? What was your experience?*

 Engage your goblet

Reground yourself. Allow the radiant light from your center to radiate down through your core, into your legs, and into the ground below, penetrating deep into the Earth and meeting its fiery core. This process anchors you to your foundation. Allow that radiant light to also stream upward through your head, through the ceiling, through the roof, up into the sky, and through the Earth's ozone layer. Imagine that it bursts into your sphere of images.

Ask your IAC to lead you to the Atmosphere of a somber funeral. Inhale that Atmosphere deeply and exhale it across the threshold into the space. Imagine the molecules of that funeral pour into the space and activate all the other molecules. Wait for a few moments for the entire space to be filled with the Overall Atmosphere (OA) of the funeral. Gently extend one hand across the threshold into the funeral.

 Journal/Discuss/Flyback

*Can you feel a difference in the air? Does your hand, for example, feel a change in the air across the threshold? What is it? Is it different from the somber funeral and the cemetery? How might you describe it?*

Withdraw your hand and pause. Step across the threshold, immersing your whole being in this new OA. Pause for a moment, allowing the molecules of the funeral to permeate every pore of your skin. Breathe this OA into your lungs, filling you with funeral fragrance. Imagine that you begin to walk through this OA, moved by these elements of the air, in harmony with them. Explore this new OA. Notice that your shoe has come untied. Find the best way to tie it in this OA. Continue through the funeral and exit at any point on the threshold. The moment you step across the threshold, you are instantly in the room, in the present. When everyone is out of the OA of the somber funeral, imagine with a grand gesture that you can gather the whole OA up in your collective arms and send it back up to the sphere of images from whence it came, knowing that you can access that again whenever you wish.

 Journal/Discuss/Flyback

*What did you feel when you were at the funeral? What was your experience? How did you tie your shoe differently here than in the cemetery?*

Engage your goblet

Once more, ground yourself. Allow the radiant light from your center to radiate down through your core, into your legs, and into the ground below, penetrating deep into the Earth and meeting its fiery core. Allow that radiant light to also stream upward through your head, through the ceiling, through the roof, up into the sky, and through the Earth's ozone layer. Imagine that it bursts into your sphere of images. Ask your IAC to lead you to the OA of a bustling shopping mall on a holiday, Friday of a special weekend, or other hectic, exciting time for shopping. Inhale that Atmosphere deeply and exhale it across the threshold into the space. Imagine the molecules of that shopping mall pouring into the space and activating all the other molecules. Wait a few moments for the entire space to be filled with the OA of the shopping mall. Gently extend one hand across the threshold into the shopping mall.

Inwardly ask, *Is there a difference in the shopping mall air from the cemetery or the somber funeral air? If so, how might I describe it?*

Withdraw your hand and pause. Step across the threshold, immersing your whole being in this new OA. Pause for a moment, allowing the molecules of the shopping mall to permeate every pore of your skin. Breathe this OA into your lungs, filling you with shopping mall air. Imagine that you begin to walk through this hustle and bustle, moved by these elements of the air, in harmony with them. Explore this new OA. Notice that your shoe has come untied. Find the best way to tie it in this OA. Continue through the shopping mall and exit at any point on the threshold. The moment you step across the threshold, you are instantly in the room, in the present. When everyone is out of the OA of the shopping mall, imagine with a grand gesture that you can gather the whole OA up in your collective arms and send it back up to the sphere of images from whence it came, knowing that sphere is always available to you. You can access that again whenever you wish.

 Journal/Discuss/Flyback

*What did you feel when you were in the bustling shopping mall? What was your experience? How did you tie your shoe differently here from when in the cemetery or at the funeral?*

### Let's discuss Overall Atmospheres (#7)

How are we changing the Atmospheres?

Let's try this little experiment. Pick up an object that, when dropped to the floor, will make a sharp noise but won't break when you do. (If in a group, have one person in front of the group hold the object.) Now, let's imagine you are sleeping late at night. (Drop the noisy object.) You are startled awake. Take a few breaths in this state. Then, in your imagination, look over to notice it was simply a thing that fell. And release the image to your creative sphere.

 Journal/Discuss/Flyback

*What happened to the Atmosphere in your imagination? Did the Atmosphere change with the noise? Did it change again when you saw that it was nothing? And, has the OA in the very room you are doing this exercise in right now changed? Even though you knew there was no real danger? If you knew in reality that this was just an exercise and what the dropped object was, and even as you watched it fall or dropped it yourself, the OA still changed, what was the cause?*

It was the images of the potential danger that a loud, startling noise might bring with it that changed the Atmosphere (ATMO). Simply put, your mind changed the air around you. That is, the vibration of the air literally changed. How did your perception of the surrounding environment make the change?

With every deep breath, we exhale about $4.93 \times 10^{22}$ molecules.[1] They vibrate at different rates depending on the images we last held in our imagination. As the molecules enter the mass of air around us, they activate their neighboring molecules and are, in turn, inhaled by us. This science gives us another way to play, which might help us awaken an ever more visceral response to ATMOs.

 Let's play molecules

Finding your own artistic space anywhere in the room, let's revisit the cemetery at midnight, imagining you are now a molecule of the air there. Once more, start by moving our hands like we did with Qualities and Sensations (Q&S). Notice your fingers becoming the molecules of cemetery air, revealing what the energy is doing. What if we add a sound effect? Now, allow your whole body to be a large abstract molecule of the cemetery air moving through the space. We can call this "gesturizing" the Atmosphere. Each person may express as their own creative molecule and permeate the space with their gestures and sounds. Use your legs and body as non-human structures in large, abstract movements, playing off your colleagues. Imagine a human enters your cemetery. What do you want to do to them? What is your gesture? Do you give them chills? Do you haunt them? Play for a few minutes and then step across the threshold, transforming into a human as you do and leaving the molecules of the cemetery inside the threshold. Pause for a moment, gazing across the threshold, imagining it is still filled with all that activity. Now cross the threshold as a human and imagine yourself inhaling that ATMO as if it is permeating every pore of your skin from the outside. If you have a group, split the group into halves with some as molecules and others as humans who can only sense them. Switch to give all participants a chance to be a gesturizing molecule and a human impacted by the molecules. When ready to pause, peel off any remaining energies from the body, gather them in the space, and send them back up to the unlimited I-sphere.

If time permits, discover more abstract OAs such as champagne bubbles, green, hopscotch, impending doom, pink, and eager anticipation. Always conclude your discovery explorations with a positive uplifting tool.

### Discussion: Why is Atmosphere important?

Can you remember a show from long ago that still sparkles in your memory and makes you reminisce about how good it was? What likely distinguishes it as so much more powerful than other shows was Atmosphere. Do you want to have powerful connections with your partners and your audience? If so, this is the most powerful tool for uniting with the soul of the performance.

 Axiom 7.1: Atmosphere is the soul of the story.

Imagine the play as if it is a living being. The body of the performance is everything that you see and hear, the mise en scene. The spirit of the performance is what lives in the ideas of the play as conveyed to your audience. The Atmosphere is the very soul of the performance that bridges the body and the spirit. It is literally the vibration of the air inhaled and exhaled by cast, audience, and crew. No amount of music, lighting, and set decor can substitute for the actors' power of preparing, creating, and transforming the Atmospheres of the story. The failure to create powerful ATMOs is perhaps the single greatest weakness in performances today, whether on stage or screen. The need for the actor to understand the concept of ATMOs and be facile at creating them is increasing as technology removes actual set pieces in favor of projections on stage, and filming on green screens where the set will be digitized later.

The terms *Overall*, *objective*, or *general* Atmosphere (OA or GA) are used interchangeably to identify the quality of energy in the air which affects everyone and everything in the place.

This is Chekhov's alternate approach to sensorial imaging of individual elements of the location. In the traditional "US method" approach, the actor is encouraged to have highly detailed images of all elements of the space, so that they can behave truthfully in the given environment. This can encumber actors if it means expending too much concentration trying to visualize the individual components, while trying to stay in character, in the moment, to remain connected to an objective, to remember lines, and to do the blocking. It is difficult for actors to act that the chairs are steel versus leather, and the table is oak versus glass, etc., and for that to make a difference in how they act as, for example, the intense business negotiation of the scene begins.

The gift of OA is in its simplicity and unity. It is one image arising from how the individual elements unite to create a feeling of the space. When invited to explore it, we can rapidly sense that the energy in a conference room comprised of glass and steel might feel colder than one of oak and leather. This coldness instantly inspires a different kind of physical movement than the warmth of oak and leather.

Atmosphere is the aggregate effect that the elements of the place have in combination with the events happening in the space. Every element is in fact a form of energy in motion, regardless of whether or not we can see it; and it gives off molecular energy.

OA unites all of the elements that factor into the feel of a place in one tool, one image for the actor to respond to and integrate. This integration into a singular field of focus awakens the actor's peak performance.

When the business negotiation (or other objective of the scene) goes well, the glass and steel chairs will still be there, and yet an OA of warmth will have appeared. The opening OA of the conference room scene might be *chilled anxiety*. The successful business negotiation is the event that changes the OA to *victorious warmth*.

 Axiom 7.2: Place + event = Overall Atmosphere.

Why are OAs so essential?

Atmospheres are the fastest means to uniting a cast with an audience; and if strong, they can linger in the audience longer than anything else in the performance. Every exposure the audience has to any element of production before the show begins contributes to building anticipation of the Atmospheres they want to experience. Every subsequent moment from the opening of the show through to the exit from the theater contributes to the Atmosphere of the event.

 Axiom 7.3: Only one Overall Atmosphere can exist.

Everyone shares the OA, and only one OA exists at a time. When two conflicting OAs collide, a third will form until one of the first two dominates the other two or it transforms into another altogether.

Awareness of Atmospheres awakens your feelings as an actor. The Atmosphere forms in the space around you and is created by your imagination. Once produced or materialized, it influences you from the outside. (See Figure 7.1.) Rehearse several times just for Atmospheres and their transitions.

*Figure 7.1* The Overall Atmosphere fills the space and affects all characters from the periphery. The Personal Atmosphere is specific to each character.

## Baptizing Atmospheres

When we give a name to something, we can be said to be baptizing it. Michael Chekhov chose words very carefully to give them richer meaning for the actor. In choosing to name this process *baptizing*, we are reminded of how the origins of our art are sacred.

Find one to three words that trigger your imagination to describe the OA. Choose juicy words that activate and excite your creativity. The more specific we can be in word choice, the more we can gesturize it, the more powerfully the image will radiate. For example, to baptize an Atmosphere as "tension" is very generic—as there is tension in a dentist office, in a lottery drawing, in a singles bar, and in the oval office. To modify it will heighten its affect. Consider oddly combining adjectives, adverbs, nouns, gerunds, or verbs: e.g., fracturing tension, curious relief, romantic awe, orange sizzling, tender eggshells, desperate confessing, tense side-splitting. It may not make grammatical sense and yet it can serve us powerfully.

We can choose a metaphor for a whole monologue, scene, or play. Here is an example of using images from nature as an evolving sequence: pre-storm stillness, distant thunder, gusting chill, lightning crack, soft drizzling, torrential downpour, hellacious hail, disarrayed aftermath, blossoming joy.

- See **OR 7.1** Deeper OA: Archetypes of Atmosphere lists

> ### Homeplay
>
> Practice observing and baptizing Atmospheres in your life, giving them juicy names, so that baptizing will come easily for your scripts. As you are building up your skill with this tool, you will discover that the POA techniques are highly effective.

### 🎭 Let's apply

At first, choose one random OA that you have played with to see if you can allow it to transform your monologue with an étude or scene with blocking.

Try two more contrasting OAs that don't relate to the actual story.

Play with starting in a random OA and changing to two different ones over the arc of the script until you are confident that you are allowing the OA to move you through the scene, inspiring different patterns of speech and blocking.

Experiment with instant changes or slow transitions. For example, begin in *midnight graveyard*, transition instantly into *frenzied shopping mall*, gradually transition into *bright yellow*. If your OAs are not stimulating a response, try unveiling and gesturizing them as molecules to charge the space and saying the lines as molecules.

If this all sounds like exaggerated nonsense—perfect!

Then, try the scene once more in the veiled OAs. Check in to be sure you are not indicating or acting out the OA as a scenario. For example, if you applied "sunny beach" to the conference room scene, you would avoid activities like putting on sunscreen. What we are creating is the same "vibe" as a sunny beach, while doing the same blocking and dialogue.

 *Journal/Discuss/Flyback*

*What did you like overall about how you played with OAs? Did the OAs sustain and influence you? Did you have some favorite surprising moments?*

Moving forward, hopefully you have read the entire script for your monologue or scene. Now, within the context of the whole story, find the three most important events that happen in your section. For a scene, choose with your partner the same OAs. If working alone on a scene, for example for an audition, you decide. Can you sense where the OAs change in relation to these events? Baptize the opening OA, a middle OA, and the ending OA. How polar opposite can you make the beginning and the end? Try several different combinations of OAs. Choose some that you are sure are inappropriate to the logic of the scene just to be sure you are letting the OA lead your inspiration. Rehearse several times just for Atmospheres and their transitions.

Rehearse the script as gesturized molecules and then veil some rehearsals. Remember, all characters in a scene are affected by the Overall objective Atmospheres, although how they respond will be distinct to each character. For example, in an OA of a sunny beach, the lifeguard, the bathers and the little child who plays in the waves all share the OA, while each has their own response based on who they are and what they are doing, etc. When someone cries for help, the OA changes, the lifeguard responds specifically as their character does, the parent responds according to their character.

## OA in life

As humans, we expend a tremendous effort on being comfortable in certain Atmospheres and avoiding undesirable ones. Clothing, decor, music, hanging out with certain people in favorite restaurants—these are all choices we make to be enveloped in Atmospheres we like. Keep in mind that we have the ability to transform OAs with our mind. We can warm a cold space and bring lightness and ease everywhere we go. Often, all we need is to choose to do so. We can develop an awareness of what OAs we like to be in, which ones we avoid when possible, and how we react when we have to be in unpleasant OAs. We can become the event that transforms an awkward Atmosphere into a happier one.

 *Journal/Discuss/Flyback*

*Ask, "Do I leave un-fun OAs, try to transform them into something more pleasant, tolerate them patiently or…?" Observe and note how others near you react differently or similarly to you. Your characters may react very differently.*

Knowing yourself, understanding your own personality, helps you know how you are similar to your character. Your similarities require no further attention from you because they are already perfect. When acting the Michael Chekhov way, attention goes to playing the differences. It's more fun than playing ourselves over and over.

- See *Kilroy Improv* **Chapter 12 for more OA play.**

## Personal Atmospheres

PA Discovery

 Let's play body bubble

Find your own creative space in the room, allowing enough distance from others to be able to rotate with your arms extended. Now, using your palms, pretend you feel the outer lining of your kinesphere, in other words, your auric energy field. Define it clearly above you, around you, and below you. Now begin to walk with it, knowing it goes with you everywhere you go. See if you can sense the auric energy shift as you get within arm's reach of the person or thing. This is your Personal Atmosphere, also called your bubble or personal space.

### Journal/Discuss/Flyback

*Can you feel when someone else is in your energy field? Are there people who you enjoy having in your aura? Are there people who make you less comfortable when they are in your bubble?*

Pause. We just recognized our unique personal bubble or Personal Atmosphere; and now, we are going to change our PA to our character's PA.

 Engage your goblet

Let's begin by activating our IAC, inhaling from the sphere of images a PA of condescension. Exhale the condescension into a bubble in front of you. If you like, create an opening in your PA, as if you can open a curtain, step out of your Personal Atmosphere, then step into the character's PA. Now, let's fill the bubble with a strong Atmosphere of condescension. Pretend that you can inhale the condescension inside this character's kinesphere and as you exhale, imagine painting the inside of your character's aura with condescension. Every molecule in your new aura condescends on everyone else. Maybe you paint with large condescending gestures, like pushing down or self-elevating? Now, walk again through the room, allowing your new PA to carry you. When you have filled the bubble, allow it to do the work. All you need to do is respond to its influence on you. Once again, notice that your shoe is untied, and you must tie it. Greet people. How do these activities change with this PA? Play with this for a few minutes, sustaining the air of condescension everywhere you go.

Release and restore: Now, peel off this PA and pack it up. Send this bubble back up to the sphere of images. Step back into your own PA and restore it fully, or continue with a new PA.

**Engage your goblet**

Pretend that you can inhale shyness and, as you exhale, can paint the inside of your character's aura with shyness. Every molecule in your new aura shies away from everyone else. Maybe you paint your PA by filling it with gestures, like pulling into or Contracting away? Now, inhale the shyness and walk again through the room, allowing your new bubble to carry you. Once again, notice that your shoe is untied, and you must tie it. Greet people. How is this new PA changing how you do these activities? Play with this for a few minutes. Now, peel off this PA of shyness and pack it up. Send it back up to the sphere of images. Step back into your own PA and restore it fully or continue with a new PA.

 **Engage your goblet**

Pretend that you can inhale curiosity, and as you exhale, can paint the inside of your character's aura with curiosity. Every molecule in your new aura, curiosity, investigates everyone else. Maybe you paint your PA by filling it with gestures, like poking into or peeking? Now, inhale the curiosity and walk again through the room, allowing your new PA to carry you. Once again, notice that your shoe is untied, and you must tie it. Greet people. Play with this for a few minutes. Now, peel off this PA and pack it up. Send it back up to the sphere of images. Step back into your own PA and restore it fully or continue with a new PA.

Play with as many different PAs as time permits. For ideas, see the list below.

 **Journal/Discuss/Flyback**

*Flyback on your experience with Personal Atmospheres, did you feel like this character had a different personality than you do? Did "how" you did the same stage business change? Can you imagine how this might help you play characters different from your usual type?*

## Let's combine OAs and PAs

 **Let's play clashing ATMOs**

Cross the threshold of the playing space to the periphery of the room.

 **Engage your goblet**

After centering and grounding in your IAC, inhale your OA of the cemetery from the I-sphere of images. Once it is established in the space, inhale and create your condescending PA, bringing it straight down on top of you. If you want to refresh your gestures to empower the PA, please do. When you are ready, cross the threshold with your condescending bubble and explore the cemetery from this PA's perspective.

Gradually allow the OA of cemetery to morph into the hustle and bustle of the bustling shopping mall. Keep the PA of condescension. Now let the PA of condescension morph into a PA of shyness in the mall. Now, let the mall morph into the wedding chapel while you maintain the PA of shyness. Then, let your PA morph into curiosity.

Play with morphing the OAs and PA as time permits so that you can see how the two tools offer different experiences for the artist. Always conclude with a happy combination of OA and PA and then clear the images to the sphere and restore your own PA.

## Discussion

When Mr. Chekhov was disseminating his work, the concept of a field of energy embodying each person was still considered taboo. It has been an accepted concept in eastern medicine for thousands of years. We now have instruments that can photograph this "aura" that we carry with us everywhere.[2] In *To the Actor*, published in 1953, Chekhov could not use the word, *aura*, so he uses Personal Atmosphere instead. In *On the Technique of Acting*, the 1942 manuscript, Chekhov does actually use the term *aura*. Chekhov also called it a subjective or individual ATMO. However, for simplicity, we will refer to this as a Personal Atmosphere. There are several aspects notable about a PA:

- It goes everywhere the character goes, regardless of the OA.
- It is not a mood that changes with short-term objectives being met or not met. It is not a short-term emotion or sensation.
- It tends to be long term and may or may not transform over the arc of the story. In Dickens's *A Christmas Carol*, Scrooge's PA transforms, while his nephew's PA remains the same.
- Two conflicting Personal Atmospheres can co-exist and create dynamic story telling.
- Likewise, a PA in conflict with an OA can create great drama and comedy. This is the classic "fish out of water" scenario.
    - **The fish is the PA, and the water is the OA.**
- In TV series, the PAs of the series regulars usually stay the same because their contrasting natures create the source of conflict.

A PA is an "air" or "essence," which, as we have seen in practice, tends to be filled to one degree or another; and, it often can be described using "-ness", "-tion", "-ity", "-ism," etc.

| | | |
|---|---|---|
| Pretentiousness | Futility | Optimism |
| Humility/humbleness | Authority | Pessimism |
| Meekness | Gentility | Hedonism |
| Condescension | Stupidity | Narcissism |
| Depression | Superiority | Opportunism |
| Erudition | Causticity | Perfectionism |

 **Let's apply**

At first, choose one random Personal Atmosphere to see if you can allow it to transform your monologue with an étude or scene with blocking.

 **Engage your goblet**

Begin by creating your bubble and filling it with the essence of the PA. Then begin your rehearsal. Flyback following each run. Try two more contrasting PAs that don't relate to the actual story. Play until you are confident that you are allowing the PA to move you through the scene, inspiring different patterns of speech and blocking. If your PAs are not stimulating a response, try unveiling and gesturizing them as molecules to charge the space and saying the lines as molecules. If it sounds like exaggerated nonsense—perfect! Then try the scene once more in the veiled PA. Release and restore.

Now, in context to the whole story, can you sense the role your character plays in the plot of the story? What do other characters say about your character? Are you a hero in the story or perhaps the villain? What kind of character must you be for the story to make sense? Does your PA stay the same throughout, or does your personality change over the arc of the story? Take a moment to ground yourself and imagine through your IAC, traveling up to the sphere of images and entering the world of the story. Perhaps you chat with your character and ask it to show you its PA. You can even pretend to get an answer regardless of whether or not you do. Feel free to make it up. When you have some ideas, try them with full commitment so they have a chance. After you Flyback, discard them if they don't feel right and try another. It's a little like Goldilocks —you might need to try several until you find the perfect fit.

>  Axiom 7.4: Every "No, thank you," turns you toward a "Yes!"

Discovering that a certain tool doesn't work can be very helpful. Most good scientists will test an idea and, if it doesn't deliver the results they had hoped for, will consider it as getting them one step closer to a better idea. Let's enjoy the exploration and keep developing the ability to Flyback with the cookie process so that we cultivate more and more skill for identifying what is working and what is not and how to "double stuff" for juicier choices next time.

Try both gesturized and veiled rehearsals. Remember you carry your Personal Atmosphere throughout the story.

##  Let's improv OA and PA combos

Create an Overall Atmosphere of an empty chapel. Enter and experience it as yourself.

Now, adopt a Personal Atmosphere and again enter the empty chapel. Try two more PAs in the same chapel OA. How is this experience different?

## Two OAs collide
 Let's play wedding and funeral

If playing with a group, divide in half with Group A stepping outside the door. Group A creates and carries in an OA of grievous funeral, merging into the chapel. Meanwhile, Group B gathers together at the opposite end of the space and creates an Overall Atmosphere of joyous wedding chapel. Group B begins to approach the exit just as Group A enters. What impulses arise as you approach the other group? Do you want to release yours and adopt their OA? Do you try to maintain your OA and envelop them in your OA? Follow your impulses, responding to the clash of the OAs. Continue to pass through until the wedding party exits the space. Release and clear the OAs to the sphere of imagination.

##  Journal/Discuss/Flyback

*What happened to the OA when the groups met? How did the two colliding OAs interact? Was there a new OA? If so, what would you call this new OA? How does this collision affect the emotional life of the characters?*

Usually, one of the two OAs will overpower the other. For instance, the funeral OA possibly overrides the wedding. Or the struggle itself may activate a third OA which is neither wedding nor funeral. This third OA may disappear, and the original ones may reappear as the groups separate.

## Continuing to increase the layers

Let's play the game again, switching groups so that A is now the joyful wedding party and B is the somber funeral party. Decide which group is already inside the Chapel. Let's up the challenge by having each individual select a Personal Atmosphere or return to an earlier one. These can also be assigned, for instance, "You are the efficient funeral director; you three embody an affectionate, jealous, or stoic family member of the loved one; you play the rude floral delivery person…" and so on. Now you are playing with your own PA, aiming to keep it consistent while creating and entering into conflicting OAs. As you do so, depending on who you are in the scenario, you may also want to use Qualities and Sensations or Three Sisters of Equilibrium (3S) to express your character's response to the events. Release and restore when done.

## ✎ Journal/Discuss/Flyback

*How is this different? Overall, what did you like about what you did? Were you able to retain both your PA and the evolving OA?*

*Can you think of other situations where conflicting PAs meet? See if you can imagine how that would play out. Did you have a favorite moment? What would you do differently next time?*

---

### Homeplay

Observe life to find more examples of OAs that collide and transform. Create a list of these. As you jot each down, pause for a moment to imagine how the improvisation above might be using your newly discovered examples from life.

---

To help you understand the distinctions between OA and PA, we have laid out a comparison of the two Atmospheres in a table. (See Figure 7.2.)

## Review of key concepts

1. Atmospheres, Overall and Personal always exist. Look for them if they're not given.
2. They are our strongest intangible means of expression.
3. Be careful not to confuse Personal Atmosphere with the character's moods, feelings, or emotions. For example, a character can have a Personal Atmosphere of shyness that remains as they shift from happy to angry.
4. Awaken awareness of the objective Atmosphere while in your subjective Atmosphere.
5. Baptize the desired Atmosphere in the most specific words. This will give your imagination the strongest stimulus. Notate your scripts with the choices you've made. Rehearse and change them when they don't work.
6. Keep observing real-life Atmospheres and define them clearly. This act of observing and defining is an exercise that, with repetition, will develop in you the facility to quickly recognize and create Atmospheres for yourself. You will develop an inventory of ATMOs that can replace or supplement sense memory and effective memory recall. Choose what works!

Atmospheres: Overall and Personal    111

## Atmosphere Comparison Chart (OA vs. PA)

| Atmosphere Perspective | Overall Atmosphere (OA) aka, General or Objective | Personal Atmosphere (PA) aka, Individual or Subjective |
|---|---|---|
| Answer for each: "What is ..." | | |
| Direction of influence on character | From outside | From within the sphere of character |
| Source | Place or event | Character's aura (created by author, director, & actor) |
| Location | Fixed to a place or event | Moves within an OA with the character |
| Variability | Changes with scenes & dramatic events (OA of quiet lake returns when accident clears) | Can change temporarily or permanently |
| Possession | Shared by all | Remains with the character |
| Impact of contrasting atmospheres | Dominant atmosphere overpowers another ATM OR a third will develop | Can co-exist, creates dramatic conflict |

*Figure 7.2* This chart clarifies the differences between the two kinds of Atmospheres. The first column might be understood to ask, *"What is the ..."* The middle column answers for the Overall Atmosphere and the third column answers for the Personal Atmosphere.

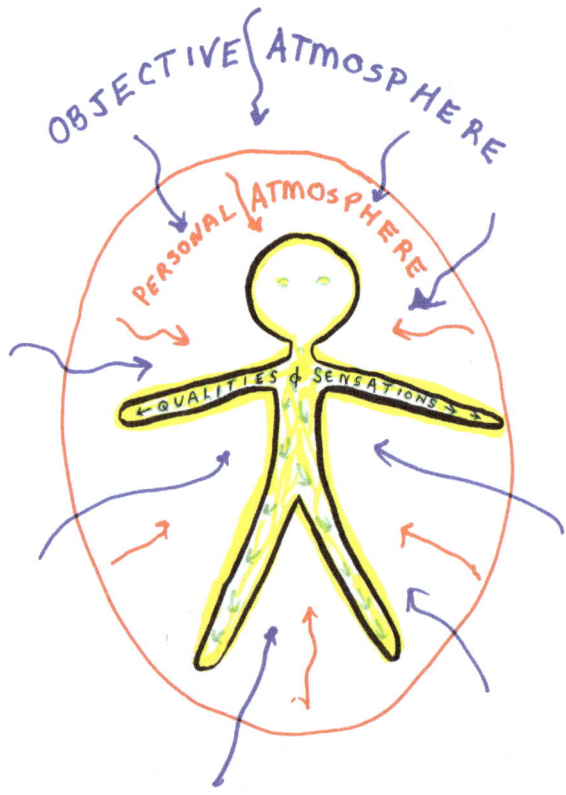

*Figure 7.3* We receive OAs and PAs into us and radiate Q&S through our movement, outward. Rehearse each tool independently. Your higher self unites them.

7. Awareness of what you carry in your Personal Atmosphere will help you understand how people want to cast you. If your body looks like a certain type that is unlike who you are, building the skill to turn on that type through PAs will increase your castability.
8. Overall objective, general Atmospheres are consciously created with your imagination, and then received by you from the present space around you, flowing from periphery to the center. Personal, subjective, individual ATMOs are carried in an auric bubble around the character wherever they go and flow from the periphery of the kinesphere to the center. Qualities and Sensations flow from the center to the periphery (see Figure 7.3).

**Want to deepen your sensational feeling life skills?**

- See **OR 7.2 Sphere of Emotions advanced game merging multiple tools.**
- See *Kilroy Improv* **Chapter 12 for more PA play.**

## Notes

1. Brown, Theodore L., LeMay, H. Eugene Jr., Bursten, Bruce E., Murphy, Catherine J., Woodward, Patrick M., Stoltzfus, Matthew W., Lufaso, Michael W. *Chemistry Central Science*, Pearson Higher Education, 2013.
2. Coggins, Guy, Founder of Auraphoto.com, Aura Imaging Photography.

# 8
# The Four Brothers of Art

## The feeling life of the artist

We began with the Psycho-Physical Exercises (PPEs) of Expanding/Contracting (X/C), Qualities of Movement (QoM) of Molding, Flowing, Flying, Radiating (MFFR) and the Archetypal Gestures (AG). By building a receptive body, we can now express anything imaginable. And we'll never worry about whether we will feel the moment because we've added the tools of the Three Sister Sensations (3S), Qualities and Sensations (Q&S), and Overall and Personal Atmospheres (OA and PA) to inspire truthful artistic feelings for the character using the fun and pain-free Michael Chekhov way. But maybe you are not quite convinced to let go of suffering.

## The TED-E Talk

So, let's take a deeper dive into this whole question of how important kindness is to the evolution of humanity. Here, I am speaking about how we treat ourselves and each other and how we are treated. Chekhov was known for his gentleness in the classroom, which has grown in importance over time. One thing he was not gentle about was when actors abused themselves during their work. In *Acting the Michael Chekhov Way*, there is no tolerance for unkindness and abuse of self or other.

For over a century, actors have been damaging themselves, destroying their immune systems and their mental health to deliver so-called "emotional truth." We hope that having now experienced many ways to create artistic feelings, you feel free and confident to choose this path. We must, however, share with you what may be startling realities of the dangers that lie elsewhere in search of feeling the moment.

If you have seen a TED Talk, you might notice that having a horror story from which to recover helps the speaker prove the value of their message. So, in a few paragraphs, you will get a touch of mine. And the fact that I am writing this, of course, proves that I survived.

We will discover why Chekhov offers these tools as safer and healthier artistic alternatives to three specific approaches that are currently popular: recall, substitution, and moment-to-moment.

The Institute of HeartMath Research has shown since the 1990s that thinking of negative things causes incoherence, damaging your health and impairing performance. Conversely, positivity creates coherence and boosts your performance.[1] (See Figure 8.1.)

It is common knowledge in the 21st century that stress is the precursor to our most frequent health problems. It's psychosomatic. Our soma (body) responds to our psyche. Fortunately, managing stress is built into the Four Brothers of Art, which we will discover very soon. They help save my physical and mental health every day.

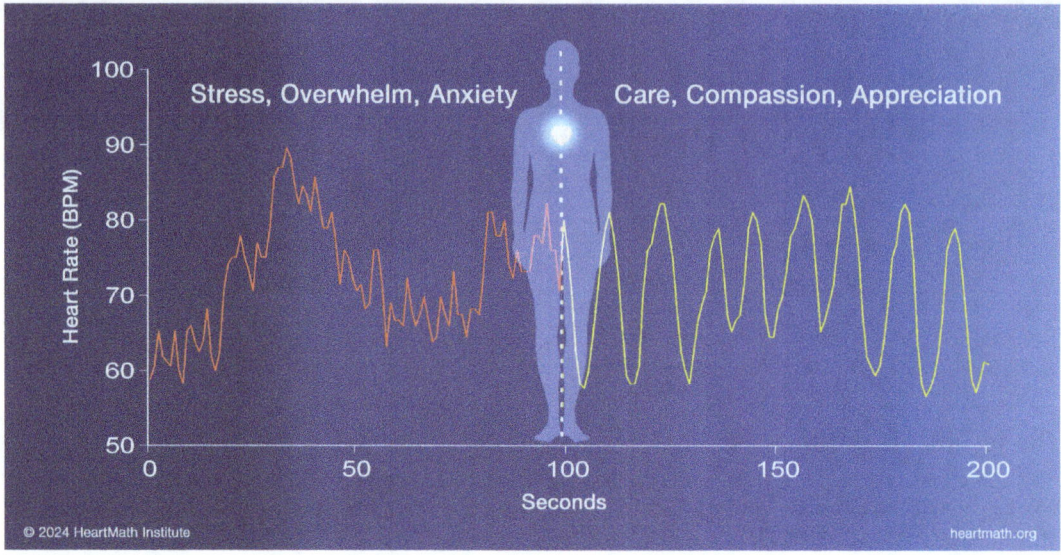

*Figure 8.1* Stress to appreciation: Incoherence (left) from stress impairs performance. Coherence (right) promotes optimal performance.

Image courtesy of the HeartMath® Institute—www.heartmath.org.

---

### Fear of being unloved

When I was in college, I thought I had to have pain and suffering to be able to act.

People told me so, and I believed them when they said I had to use my own life to create truthful acting.

I was so insulted when a doctor told me that the sharp, excruciating pains in my stomach, which brought me repeatedly to the hospital, where they found nothing wrong, were the result of stress from living with an abusive alcoholic. Who would imagine that recovering from multiple assaults, or that the terror of anticipation of the next, could trigger such stress? Not I, clearly. The idea that I could allow stress to cause real bodily symptoms meant I was shamefully weak. The doctor prescribed valium, which I refused to take, and I managed to stop the pain but not my assailant.

And why did I allow myself to stay with such a dangerous person—for four years? Well, it wasn't so different from the cruelty in my theater department. It certainly gave me lots of memories to use for conjuring up fear, grief, and pain. And when he was sober, he treated me like a goddess. I will spare you the rest of the gory details. Suffice it to say, I had memories and anticipated future moments to recall for acting. What I didn't know was the truth of Axiom 8.1.

---

 Axiom 8.1: LOVE is the most creative power.

That "artists need pain to create" is a LIE!

## Memory

Try for a moment to recall what you were wearing five days ago? Where did your eyes go when you tried to recall? Where did your energy go? Most likely, your eyes disconnected from the present and shifted right or left as your energy went up and back. This is natural neurolinguistic programing. By definition, when you recall, you are not present, not in this moment. An easy example we all know is that audiences feel this disconnect distinctly when an actor tries to remember a line.

In addition to recall dissociating us from the present, memory is a fickle creature that morphs. It is a kind of imagination all by itself and one that we have little control of.

Memory changes and can inspire you one day and leave you dry the next. In fact, when we go to a transactional counselor to get psychological help, we recall memories there so that we can heal and release our pain. Our "what for" is "for healing."

Memories, after being recalled, restore to our deep recesses now mixed with the energies of the "transaction." In counseling, they now carry the new information and perspectives of an aware you. And we are carefully cared for by a professional, in private, who will follow up. This is the opposite case in acting. Usually, our "what for" is to increase dark feelings, and it is being done in public with no professional follow up care for what is unleashed.

Making it worse, if our memories are not powerful enough to cause the effect we are seeking, we feel untalented, that we have no business being an actor. Some teachers and peers in fact yell this at us. Suddenly our lifelong dream of expressing ourselves as artists is crumbling inside us.

Now your painful memory restores itself with the added pain of failing at something you have loved since before birth. If your memory does succeed in triggering your pain as you hoped, and you are affirmed that using recall proves you are talented, your memory restores with mixed messages. "Is this still a bad memory since it served me well? Will it work again? Is it good to have bad memories? Do I need to make more bad memories since this is now used up? Did I disrespect my memories and my personal life?" Our memories are sacred. Our mental health is a matter of private concern with properly trained professionals.

Another challenge actors face when reexperiencing emotions is whether what is happening inside the actor ever reaches the audience. If you have watched actors working with this recall of personal memories and crying tears or raging, you may find yourself thinking, "Wow! They are doing really good work, digging deep." But are you feeling what they are feeling or are you feeling perhaps compassionate? And that by itself is a problem. If you are watching them and thinking about how well the actor is using a technique, you are not having an audience experience. It is the actor's job to radiate images to the audience so that the audience goes on their own journey. To do that, we allow our highest universal self to become the source of our images for our art.

Working from the lower ego, AKA your piece of the pie, makes the work accessible to only those whose piece of pie overlaps yours. The Three Sister Sensations, Qualities and Sensations, and Overall/Personal Atmospheres work through the grand archetypes to which all humans can relate. We access them through imagination that brings our energy forward, naturally including the audience rather than back to the past. We can step into these images and out without inadvertently triggering uncontrollable emotions from the past. And it is unlimited in scope.

Every particle of your body is energy recycled from the foods you've eaten and the air you have breathed. Those molecules have been many things and must have intelligence of some kind because somehow, they know where to go next! What if your energy body has experienced everything possible and has a miraculous way of knowing all there is about humanity?

Scientist Carl Sagan in *Cosmos*[2] says,

> The nitrogen in our DNA, the calcium in our teeth, the iron in our blood, the carbon in our apple pies were made in the interiors of collapsing stars. We are made of star stuff.

We don't need to believe this for real. If we pretend it's true, we already have the talent to portray every human condition in existence. The rest is building the skill sets to express them and making responsible choices of which to play when.

Our central message here is that it is a lie to believe you need pain, that you need to suffer for your art. We can create more powerfully, more healthily when we use our love, our higher self, our imagination, movement, and inspiration to lead us. When we act from our everyday self, in Chekhov terms, the lower self and its pain from our "piece of the pie," our energy goes inward. Our love of who "I am" is needed to fulfill our natural desperation for approval and connection.

In college, I had abandoned my own value. I needed to put the oxygen mask of loving respect on my self first. When I would use memory to activate my emotions, I cried and blubbered incoherently and triggered asthma on the stage, and it wouldn't stop when I was trying to do the next scene. With Chekhov teaching me to use my imagination, I was able to perform with freedom and power on stage. In life, I was able to gain understanding and inner strength to escape a bad relationship and find healing and a very loving spouse.

- **See OR 8.1** for how to Chekhovize a memory when only memory feels true for you.

## Substitution

The concept of substitution generally calls for us to find a present-versus-past condition in our own lives that is parallel to what the character's condition is; and then in our minds, we would substitute that for the story's given circumstances. You would imagine for example that you are in fact talking to your real mom instead of the character in the story. With this process, you might trigger truthful responses in your everyday self that would happen if your mom responded to you as this character does. If this character rejects your character, you respond as if your mom is rejecting you, and if the character exits and dies off stage, leaving your character feeling guilty, are you supposed to imagine this actually happening to your mom? NOOOOOO! Don't do it.

Some teachers ask you to imagine your worst nightmare coming true. THAT IS ABUSE! And how terrible would it be if something did happen to them? Once again, substitution is asking us to abuse our personal lives and relationship needs to activate "real" angst in us. Please trust that you have an unlimited imagination that can pretend the story of the script is real and you can transform into the reality of that fantasy. Maybe take a moment and read that last line again.

Later, in SynthAnalysis™ (SA), we will be learning more powerful activation tools for connecting with the story of the play. As they say, IT'S ACTING! And an audience has agreed to sit and watch you ACT! PS, they know it is a show. You are playing; they are paying.

## The mask and the moment

Some techniques ask us to respond only to what our partner gives us, having removed our social filter. They want a gut response. Acting is reacting in the moment to what your partner gives you. Developing the ability to remove your social filters and say or do anything your lower ego impulses lead you to can be helpful in understanding the nature of impulse and will. Taking it into an entire approach to acting, however, has its challenges. First, our characters don't generally act without a social filter. Meaning it is neurotypical to have social filters. A person with no social filter is often perceived as neurodiverse. In today's society there are more opportunities to act characters who have no social filters than in days past. And we now have more opportunities for neurodiverse artists to perform. However, the majority of people and characters wear a social mask that allows them to relate to their lover differently than to their parents or baby sibling.

All of this masking is a perfectly healthy way to manage our personalities. While acting, we want our characters to have the social masks they would or would not have. We don't want them to have the same unfiltered responses that our lower ego has. We would then only be "revealing" our lower selves and not acting. Also, many characters intentionally disguise their true inner feelings such as spies, criminals, con artists, politicians, doctors, or lawyers. Insecure characters compensate with bravado like the Lion in *The Wizard of Oz*. So playing what we "truly" feel doesn't always serve the story.

A second challenge is that relying solely on your partner to respond to means you can only be as good as what you get. You can't do a monologue or act on camera with an "X" as your eyeline. You won't audition well if the reader isn't a good actor. Taking direction well will be unlikely. And all of your acting will have the sameness of your everyday lower ego.

With Chekhov, we train to be in the moment from the character's point of view. We train to respond as the character in what we call "communion with" many partners: the author, the director, our higher self's imagination, our body, the mise en scene,[3] and the other characters in our scene. So first we train our body and imagination to partner with the higher self and then we can respond to imaginary bodies, invisible atmospheres, props, scenery, and the story's characters as easily as we respond to a scene partner. These will be unique to every role we play. We can act in the moment, in any situation, revealing and masking the impulses of the character as appropriate to the story, style, and direction we are given.

## Further dangers

There are a few other misunderstandings in popular thoughts about acting that do a disservice to the profession.

Have you ever worried about finding the character again and so you tried to stay in it, out in public? If so, was it exhausting?

*TRUE OR FALSE?*

Stanislavsky said, "You must stay in character throughout the production of a story."

FALSE: Nowhere in the canon of Stanislavsky's notes does it say that. Michael Chekhov talks of how Stanislavsky would be backstage talking to the stage manager up until his cue and then do a few gestures and step on the stage.

Staying in character depletes the energy resources of the artist, makes everyone uncomfortable and is based in the actor's fear that they cannot regain access to the character. People like Jack Nicholson and Meryl Streep show us again and again that we can turn it on and off. They work from the love of acting rather than the fear. And we love them back even when they play evil characters.

*TRUE OR FALSE?*

It takes time to justify a change in my emotions.

FALSE: Watch an infant or two-year-old. They seem to switch emotions without any biological justification and do so instantly.

*TRUE OR FALSE?*

Using Chekhov techniques like Atmosphere (ATMO), Q&S, or 3S will never awaken memories.

FALSE: Sometimes Chekhov's imaginative movement tools do awaken memories. When that happens, we simply acknowledge them and let them continue to pass by. We allow the memory to be, and we focus our attention and movement on the tool. This way, we honor and protect the subjective memory from abuse, and we rely on the objective technique as our start point leading us to the character's experience. Where attention goes …

I went through many years of being humiliated by acting teachers in the name of "truth" and am so committed to reversing a century of misinformation that I wrote a book about it. The main title is a quote from Stanislavsky's private notes where he was concerned that his method would become the "murder of talent." We have a brilliant actor, Daniel Day Lewis, who retired from exhaustion. We have lost Heath Ledger and Philip Seymour Hoffman and too many more listed in that book. Let's not be them.

What appears in the text box is an excerpt from the Amazon best seller, *Murder of Talent: How Pop Culture is Killing "IT"*, by this author.

> ### Confessions about feelings
>
> The fundamental scientific truth is that no one needs to recall anything to achieve an emotional state. The body can be led to creating the energetic patterns of an emotion through many means. And there is no scientific requirement for a certain length of time to pass before a feeling changes. Instantaneous change happens all of the time, in real life, to everyone.
>
> If I called you up right now and said you have won a million dollars, would you say, "Excuse me—I need a moment to transition"?
>
> If I were to announce to you your Oscar nomination, would you say, "Hang on—I will need to remember what that feels like; let me conjure up my feelings from the last time I won one"? (Or won the school play contest? Or the swim meet?)
>
> No, you wouldn't. If your best friend is diagnosed with cancer, you don't need a moment to transition. We respond instantly, and then we react inwardly or outwardly depending on who, what, where and how we are.
>
> Have you ever felt something and shared it with someone, and they were totally surprised that you felt that? They had no idea you were feeling that? Were your feelings real? Yes, of course they were. Did they show up to others? Not always.
>
> That's another big issue for the actor in conjuring up these memories or feelings in any way. That mask I have spoken of can hide your true feelings. So just because a memory may trigger an emotional state, that doesn't mean it's going to show itself to anyone.
>
> People have one way to know what your feelings are, and that is through movement of your energy. Molecules carrying your emotions inspire different qualities in your movement. What movement? What if I am standing still? Think more grandly about the concept of movement. What moves? Your breath, for one—your energy that radiates from you or that you draw into you, little micro-mannerisms, subtle shifts in weight, etc.—all of these happen no matter how still you may be.
>
> These are a gold mine for the actor, and a path to consistently free access—a healthy path of free access for everyone, independent of memory. You can move with a quality of sadness in your hand as you open a letter and place the envelope on the desk. You can move your breath with the same archetypal breathing pattern that sadness induces—and your voice will move into space, sounding sadly. Your chest will heave with grief, and when all those body parts move in harmony with that sadness, you will most likely have triggered a powerful sensation of sadness within. AND if you haven't, you look like you have and you sound like you have—and that's the actor's job at minimum.
>
> Actors live in terror of not feeling the moment. Look at this drawing I have begun. (See Figure 8.2.)
>
> Now look at Figure 8.3 and describe what the teddy bear is feeling.

The Four Brothers of Art 119

*Figure 8.2* What does it look like I am drawing? Yes, it is a teddy bear.

*Figure 8.3* What is the bear feeling?

Perhaps you say the bear is feeling sad, depressed, and unhappy.

Okay. Now tell me what this next teddy bear is feeling. (See Figure 8.4.)

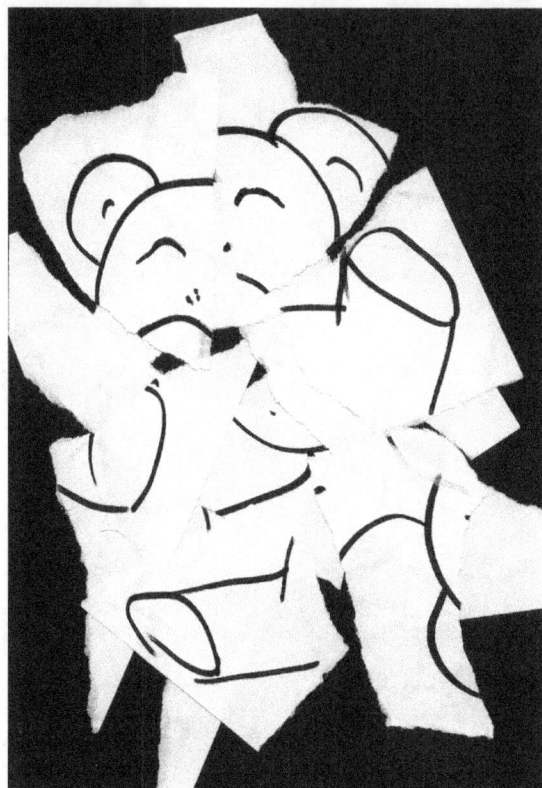

*Figure 8.4* Torn teddy.

OUCH! He's been murdered! Torn to shreds!

Actually, he is feeling nothing. In Figure 8.4, he is feeling nothing. **He is magic marker on paper! He feels nothing!** Nor does he need to FEEL anything, ever. So, who is feeling something? You, the audience, feel sad for him. It is you, the audience, who must feel something. The actor is not required to feel anything—just like the ink and paper need no feeling to evoke powerful responses in others.

What I am saying may seem like sacrilege to many, especially when actors spend a fortune in cash and angst trying to solve the problem of feeling something truthfully. It is a massive misconception, verified as such by the very nature of all art—and in particular, animation. Bambi and Nemo are dots on cellophane, or pixels generated by a computer—and they feel nothing. WE feel their pain and their joy.

I know it's a bit like saying that there is no Santa—a violation of a sacred social agreement to promote and sustain a lie for the sake of commerce.

If the artist were required to feel in order for the audience to feel, the *Winged Victory of Samothrace* would not be lifting the spirit of its Louvre viewer to soaring heights. The *Mona Lisa* would not be enigmatically enticing conversation, centuries after being painted. Animation would be dead. Stuffed animals would not exist. Stories would not exist either. The words on the pages of *A Tale of Two Cities* and *Fifty Shades of Grey* are not feeling anything more than any given piece of paper and ink feels. Daffodils and ocean waves are not feeling a thing while they awaken our senses.

It is the FORM of the art that activates the state inside the viewer, the witness, the audience. The artist, the actor feels the exhilaration of creating the ideal form that invites you, the spectator, to participate with your own life, with your own thoughts, feelings and desires.

**When an actor does all the feeling for you, the spectator,**

**they have very little to bring to the union of artist and audience.**

**You also have very little to receive.**

## What's next?

What about your life as an artist? Isn't there more to being an artist than just crying, laughing, and raging on cue? Of course there is. As actors, we spend most of our lives seeking the opportunities to act. As the lead on a film set, we may be acting for only one hour of twelve in the day. On Broadway, we may be acting for only two hours. And yet, we are artists all day and night, 24/7. Mr. Chekhov recognized this, calling it Continuous Acting and gives us four distinct tools to create our lives as works of art. What if you could...

 Axiom 8.2: Live every day as a "little piece of art."

You can if you frame your life with these:

## The Four Brothers of Art (#8)

All four of these brothers will be described in the subsequent sections. To start, we have our leading questions: *Do you get nervous? Perhaps a touch of stage fright? Maybe a full-blown panic attack? Are you worried that if you don't relax everything will be a disaster? Do you yell silently at yourself, "Relax!!!! Relax already. Why are you shaking? What are you scared of?"* Have you faithfully done your relaxation techniques and then 30 seconds before you go to act, your nerves go crazy ... again? If so, you are missing this next tool.

## Feeling of Ease

*Before beginning this discovery, be sure to be sufficiently warmly activated in body and imagination and place the safety of yourself, your colleagues, and the space as your number one priority.*

 Let's play discover a Feeling of Ease

Select a chair that you can manipulate. If a chair is not available, try a stick, stool, or some other sturdy object. If the chair is too heavy to lift, explore spinning and rolling it on the floor. Find the creative space in the room that is calling to you, allowing ample space to avoid collision.

Begin moving the chair as if it is light and easy to do so. If it feels heavy, imagine fooling everyone watching into thinking it is really light as a feather. Dance with the chair as your partner with a continuous flow of abstract movements. Press the edges of an envelope of possibilities to see if you can do some unknown moves with a feeling of ease. Ease is what we are practicing. Spend a minute or two just playing easily.

Being unique or creative is of no value to us at this point as all our focus is on doing challenging things easily. Pretend everything is really easy to do and of course, that you are doing it all perfectly regardless of whether it is unique.

 Journal/Discuss/Flyback

*Where are you tense? What habits of tension-holding are you discovering? Are your shoulders moving easily? Is your jaw tight? Are you doing anything with your lips that shows tension or concentration? Are you trying to do unique things no one else is doing?*

Now add to your discovery some sound, a hum or a "la-te-da" while moving the chair with ease. Perhaps you can continue for about five minutes or so and then form groups of three. Take turns in the group, pausing to watch each other. Allow the sound to come and go. What do you observe of your colleagues? Of yourself?

 Journal/Discuss/Flyback

*Where is the tension? What are the habitual expressions of tension? How is the breathing? Do things change when you are humming? If so, how? What was your experience? What differences happened when humming and not humming? What body parts tend to reveal what was not easy? How does your breath affect your feeling of ease? Why do we want ease?*

Resume and play until all have had a chance to explore and witness. Bring everyone to a closing pose. Release.

 Cookie Flyback

Flyback with your partners for one minute each. Begin by sharing your self-observations with your partners.

*What did you like about your overall experience? What do you want to work on? What was your favorite moment?*

Partners, use the same cookie structure discussed earlier to support you by affirming what you did well, helping you discover perhaps something you missed and recognize a favorite moment, in one minute or less.

## Feeling of Ease discussion

Ease is Chekhov's alternative to relaxation exercises. Why is relaxation so important to the artist? Because tension may block our creative expression? Because the audience doesn't want to watch tense actors? True. But does relaxing achieve these aims?

## Discover ease again

Right now, relax as much as you possibly can. You can relax on the floor if you like. Relax in whatever way you know how. You can make sounds, change positions, whatever you like.

Now, look around the room. Imagine being in the audience watching this.

How much would you pay to watch this relaxing performance?
As a performer, how ready are you to spring into a peak performance?
What level is your energy on?
Is this really where you want to begin your role?

Most likely, the essential answer here is that we don't want to be relaxed, per se. It looks boring and lifeless. Relaxing is designed to diffuse tense energy by diffusing all energy; however, it isn't something you can actually do. It is a result. To move, breathe, and speak with a feeling of ease is an active task, unlike "to relax," which is passive and in fact results from an action or sequence of actions.

## ✒ Journal/Discuss/Flyback

*When you were guided to relax in class, what did you do?*

You moved, you adjusted, and you exhaled to allow your body to give into or fall into a relaxed state. The word relax is not a doable command.

Pretend you are extremely tense, and that tension inside is making one of your hands tremble and shake. Try to stop it, using the other hand. Yell at it to stop. What happens?

Both hands start shaking. The tension travels into your whole body. **Where attention goes, energy grows.**

Now, let go of the trembling hand. Continue the tremble and start moving the other hand easily through the space, breathing easily with it. Place all your attention and focus on the flowing, easily moving hand.

## ✒ Journal/Discuss/Flyback

*What happens to the tremble? To the tension? Notice how the trembling hand wants to join the flow? That the only way the tremble will continue is if you split your focus and force it to shake? If you place 100% of your attention on the easy moving hand, the trembling will fade from the other hand as it seeks to join in the easy movement. Why? Because*

**Where attention goes energy grows!**

Let's talk now about what it is that is making the tremble in the first place.

- What is the chemical that makes us tremble? Adrenalin.
- Why is it here? What is the function? To assist us when in danger since our time in the caves.
- What does adrenalin do for us? Gives us superhuman capabilities like lifting cars off babies.
- If it is divinely gifted into the human being to help us, then why do we want to stop it? Because it could mess us up.
- Are there any other times when adrenalin comes to us? When we are excited.
- What is the difference between adrenalin for fear and adrenalin for excitement? Nothing, adrenalin is adrenalin.
- Where then is the difference? In our minds. And we can change our minds to reframe the experience of feeling adrenaline as negativity to one of positivity. It's here to help us.

Try this. Pretend you are two years old and very active in your whole body. Say, *"I'm scared."* Now say, *"I'm excited!"* Which position seems best for springing into a peak performance?

Audiences come to you to inhale your energy. They will pay five hundred dollars a ticket and more if you give them enough of it. They won't pay five cents for your relaxation.

> ### How is St. Joan, BTW!
>
> Emmy winner Sharon Gless told me this story when she was studying with George Shdanoff, Chekhov's co-director of his school and one of my teachers. They were doing a scene showcase, and she came to him before the curtain went up and said, "George, I feel nervous!" He said, "The audience doesn't care how you feel. They want to know how St. Joan feels."
>
> Let's keep our nerves from infecting the audience. It makes them worry for us and takes them out of St. Joan's story.

If adrenalin is indeed helpful to us, then when you feel it, what can you do? Call it excitement and know it is there to help you. Put all your focus on moving with a Feeling of Ease. The Feeling of Ease is so cool because it is 100% fakeable. Practice pretending you are really at ease and most people will think you are. Focus on unease and you and they will feel that. Eventually unease, lack-of-ease, may lead to dis-ease. Use your life as a playground for developing a Feeling of Ease. Whenever things are making you feel uneasy, just ask yourself to move and breathe with ease, especially during tests, traffic, and social environments. Getting stressed over things does little to resolve them and can lead to poor choices. "Making friends with" is a Feeling-of-Ease building concept we learned in Chapter 1. Since we are always artists, we can always practice these tools in life.

A Feeling of Ease can be accompanied by a feeling of lightness. Lightness and Ease are always present in great acting, even when the character is heavy or violent. All that the artist does can be done with lightness and ease.

> ### Bridges blessed with ease
>
> Dorothy Bridges, mother of Jeff and Beau Bridges, shared with me a story of how she was in deep grief after she lost a child. Lloyd, her husband, took her to Michael Chekhov's class to help her get over her grief. The class was on the Feeling of Ease in the home of Akim Tamiroff.
>
> Each player was to get up from their seat, walk to the fireplace mantle and move a vase from one point to another, with a Feeling of Ease. Unable to get over her nervousness, Dorothy kept passing on her turn, until finally she was the only one left. Chekhov stood up, invited her to stand, and, opening his arms, said, "Dorothy, just come to me, dear." It is natural to have compassion when you yourself are at ease.

## Let's improv

Play with some improvisations where you must do difficult things and make them look easy.

## Let's apply a Feeling of Ease

Play with ease in your scene or monologue. Try difficult tasks, focusing on a Feeling of Ease. Speak all your lines as if remembering them is easy. Sing them with ease.

When you can't shift yourself into moving with ease, ask "What makes me UN-easy?" Perhaps it is because something isn't the way it is supposed to be. That suggests we are missing this next tool.

## Feeling of Form

 Let's play discover the Feeling of Form

Return with your chair to the special space in the room where creativity beckons you. Retaining your growing Feeling of Ease, focus now on the forms you and your partner, the chair, are creating in the space. Practice clear, abstract movement sequences with a random pause in them. During the pause, sense the form you and your chair have created. Imagine, like a flying drone camera, you can see it from all angles. Practice awareness of every body part in relation to the form. The audience sees every part and thinks it means something. What story is this form revealing? Make a shift in the form, perhaps a tiny change in where your foot is pointing. Maybe a little finger moves. How does the story change? Continue exploring forms with the chair and check in occasionally on whether you are moving with ease. Keep the forms abstract and free of conscious storytelling. Discover what the story might have been after the move in the pause.

### Discussion: What is form?

Form is what I call "the primary communicating factor." It tells us what something is. From the moment we are born, we start exploring things and determining whether "Yes, we like them" or "No, we don't." The infant touches an object, says yes, and then what? They hold it, shake it, and listen to it. They put it in their mouth. They sensorially explore it and decide what they do and don't want to do with it, moment to moment. They enter that data into their memory bank that grows bigger every day. Each form that appears in their world is cross-referenced against this database and immediately categorized as a y *(Yes)* or n *(No)*, a p *(Plus)* or m *(Minus)*, or "I don't know yet."

Identifying the form gives us an idea of how to relate to it. Forms in relation to other forms change the meaning, giving context.

Let's say you are standing in your own space with your hands at waist level, holding the edges of an imaginary bowl about eight to ten inches across. Not knowing that what is in your hands is a bowl, what might someone think you are doing? Walk up directly behind a colleague who is sitting nearby, keeping your hands in the same place at your waist level, fingers wrapping around. What does it look like you are about to do? Will you choke or massage or…?

The meaning of the form is altered by relationship.

### Your body as a form

The form of your body is the most important form affecting your career. You may not be happy with what I am suggesting here. No matter how progressive we want the industry to be, people will first try to cast you based on your physical form—your appearance. Please don't shoot me—I am just the messenger. The appearance of your age, gender, weight, height, features, ethnicity, and hairstyle communicates something to the audience. Casting is often about finding the right forms to communicate the intended message to the audience. Are you frustrated about type casting? Are you angry about being called a "character actor" because it means you won't be considered for a leading role? Or do you wish you were more of a character and bored with playing the same lead type repeatedly because you have that look? Are you willing to re-form your opinions here if doing so will help you get more work?

When you fail to understand or appreciate a form, you lose your feeling of ease when dealing with that form.

 **Axiom 8.3: Limitations of form are springboards to creativity.**

When Chekhov felt frustrated by the limits of film work, he chose to embrace the form rather than fight it. He used the short, out-of-sequence rhythm to create a "little piece of art." Everywhere you encounter challenges with the form of something—your small budget on a production, losing a castmate, not liking the direction— ask yourself, "How can I create with the forms I do have?"

### Journal/Discuss/Flyback

*Do you appreciate the form of your body? Of your resume? Of your opportunities? Of your lifestyle? Are you willing to feel at ease with these forms? Can you make friends with the forms in your life? Are you as at ease with Shakespeare as with a commercial or a soap opera? Which forms entice you and which scare you? Are you willing to make friends with different forms?*

The Form of the material, the playing space, the medium, the style, the era, are all forms that you can embrace artistically. If you cultivate a powerful Feeling of Form, you will have the ability to work within the dimensions of a variety of forms instinctively.

Form in<u>form</u>s us. It informs our per<u>form</u>ance. When we trans<u>form</u>, the audience trans<u>form</u>s. We TIP the scales to <u>form</u> a better world.

 **Axiom 8.4: When we Transform, we Inform and Perform (TIP).**

###  Let's play spinning forms

Did you ever play spinning statues as a youngster—where a partner spins you around and lets go and you freeze into a statue and then come alive pretending to be whatever that form inspired? The creativity of such childhood games can be remarkable. Try playing a few rounds of spinning statues. Once the actor is in their finished form, after a few moments' pause, the sculptor can wave a wand and bring them to life. In the pause, the actor senses their form and what it is awakening within them. Then, they bring it to life. This can be done as a solo character or in partnership with another sculptor/actor team.

For a less physically dynamic version, eliminate the spin and have the artist sculpt the actor into a form. You can use an agreed-upon gentle touch to safe areas or a gentle extended object as a wand. For example, moving a partner with a long, foam pool noodle allows distance and gentleness while being amusingly fun.

This game is a rare moment where the form comes from another person's actions and the actor who has been spun/sculpted creates from their own inner response to the form. Perhaps this is like the form of the director/actor relationship?

Let's play advancing the game of chairs

- Create a new form via spinning or sculpting, pause, and ignite the action. Now add a chair into the sculpture.
- Allow two sculpted actors and two chairs to improvise a conversation.
- Change the form with rules such as one actor, and only one can and must always be seated, or one hand must be on the chair, or the chair must be moved after one sits, etc.
- Define the form of sound to be used: e.g. silence, nonverbal, three-word maximum.
- Play with time as form: One minute from start to finish. Increase to two. Find an ending form.

## What do we discover?

The form of our physical body creates its own images, triggers sensations, and can inspire us. The form of the set, the dialogue, the costumes, sound, and lights trigger images in the audience and in the artist. Can we work with a Feeling of the Form?

Some think this idea of moving our bodies and discovering inspiration is somehow an inartistic process. They label it outside-in acting, as if that is a negative or untalented way of accessing inspiration. They imply it is not a truthful or valid approach. Yet we just experienced the actors being inspired by a form given to them from another and from a random pause came an inner impulse that then travels (transforms?) into motion.

It is not possible to move only from the outside as all motion begins with an inner impulse that travels instantaneously through our whole being. Our entire form is interwoven with our thoughts, feelings, and will impulses, flowing from the periphery to the center, the center to the periphery. The 20th-century paradigm that acting techniques are either internal or external, and that internal is the only truthful path, is no longer scientifically justifiable. When a human being witnesses an external form, there is an inner response. Fashion and architecture thrive on this truth. The extravagant production values called upon for stage, music venues, et al. are more and more necessary "forms" when the artist can't deliver enough to draw the ticket buyers. The Chekhov artist using these principles will always outshine the external forms of the mise en scene.

The growth of animation gives evidence that audiences can watch the form of a digital creation and attach emotional activity to it, just as people have done with stuffed animals, paintings, and sculptures for millennia. For the artist of today to compete in the world of artificial creation, we must train our forms to the highest level of sensitivity to all stimulus and then equally excel at expressivity in a way only human artists can do. A Feeling of Form is essential in all great works of art.

Now we have addressed Form as one of the Four Brothers of Art (Beauty, Ease, Entirety, and Form: BEEF) and here we are going to look more specifically at **how to create** dynamic artistic forms.

## Blocking as Form: Who goes where and does what when?

Do you ever wish you could figure out the best place to be on the stage without needing a director to tell you? For directing, wouldn't it be wonderful to have actors who easily find the right place—are in the right position on the stage to communicate the perfect message to the audience? And creating dynamic stage pictures in the process? When a director asks, "Can you show me something?" would you like to have something creatively coherent to suggest? This is the promise of knowing the artistic principles of the Japanese Rock Garden (RG) and the psychology of the stage. (See Figure 8.5.)

*Figure 8.5* Japanese rock garden with multidimensional elements in height and form. (Photo by Author. Japan, 1986.)

## Composition of the stage is an aspect of the Feeling of Form

Inspired by the principles of the Japanese Rock Garden (RG), everyone is in a different relationship to depth, frontal plane, height from floor, distance from ceiling, walls, or audience, unless they are exactly symmetrical as support stones or in the background. The one closest to downstage audience is lowest to the floor, furthest upstage is highest. There are often spiral shapes and twists in the forms.

1. Focal Point (theme stone)
2. Support stone(s)
3. Counter point (anti-theme)
4. Connecting stone
5. Background stone(s)

The RG form is given briefly here so that we can begin to apply it in improvisations. We will go more in depth with the psychology of the stage and harmonious groupings (HGs) for rehearsal techniques in the SynthAnalysis™ in Chapter 19.

### ⟩ Let's improv RGs!

Choose two contrasting themes, such as victory/defeat. Start with one person entering the space and creating a form as Focal Point 1 (FP1), the theme stone of victory. Gradually other players enter and continue improvising the form until you are happy with a clear harmonious grouping. Remember the forms. Release and start the next form.

Use the same process to create a second RG with a contrasting theme. Have the players go in a different order. Remember the form.

Morph from the final form back into the original form in a series of five movements that each lasts about five seconds. Try to create interesting dynamics possibly with twists for each of the suspended moments while retaining the evolution from one theme to its contracting theme.

Release and Flyback. Repeat in smaller or larger playing area and different themes. Avoid directing and cultivate your sense of form for the whole.

 Let's apply

Planning where we are going to move and when is part of a Feeling of Form called blocking. Try your scene or monologue now, focusing on the form of your blocking. Maintaining our Feeling of Ease, let's do both some logical actions that fit the material and then some forms that are in contrast and don't make sense.

**For a monologue:** Rehearse your material with one chair. Create a sequence of movements where you approach the chair, sit in some way and do an activity, then rise and return where you began. Once you have your sequence designed, say your monologue as you move through it. Try it with three variations.

**For a scene:** Rehearse your material with one chair. Create a sequence of movements where you and your partner each use the chair at some point. Play with the ideal form as it might suit the scene. Add a second chair where only one can be seated at any given moment.

**Style** is also part of Form. Try your material in different styles: classical, melodrama, musical theater, opera, tragedy, sit-com.

Stressed when things aren't finished? Calling back that friend to say goodbye because the phone cut off before you could? Server removes your plate before the last bite? Can't think of that person's name when telling a story to Bob? Bingo, you remember a day later and call Bob to tell him! What is all of this about? Loss of ease because the form is missing this next tool.

## Feeling of Entirety (wholeness)

 Let's play discover Entirety/wholeness

Find your creative space with your chair. While retaining your new ease and form skills, let's explore a feeling of the whole, the entirety. Working solo, create a whole sequence with a very clear beginning, middle, and end. Hold the end for three seconds, sustaining the movement. Create another. Perhaps the whole sequence takes three seconds. No story is necessary as we know that whatever form is held will contain its own story and be perfect. Keep checking that your whole body is in a full stop when you stop. Wiggling fingers, toes, or wagging heads violates the feeling of the whole in a pause. Commit fully to your sequence without knowing what it will be. Stop suddenly. Surprise yourself as you easily create a clear, unhesitating form.

Aim to complete about 20 sets of moves with a clear beginning, middle, and end. If time permits, find one or two partners to witness several sequences of you using an approach, a movement with the chair, and a return to your start point. Working in teams of two or three, watching each other, can help. At this point, try to do one very clear sequence and then Flyback.

Flyback on yourself first and then receive support from your witnesses.

✒ Journal/Discuss/Flyback

*What did I like overall? Did I fully commit to my beginning? Was there any hesitation, a double start? Was I clear that I had ended? Did I have a false ending? What else did I notice? What was my favorite moment?*

✒ Journal/Discuss/Flyback

*Observers share where they thought the exact moment of the beginning and ending were. Gracefully share any differences or affirm the artist's self-evaluation.*

## Discussion

Nature seeks wholeness of the form and a Feeling of Entirety in such an aggressive manner that there are sometimes violent reactions when "completeness" is absent. Consider the consequences of violating the wholeness of an atom, as an example. What about the action of a cancerous cell whose unmated ion drives it to strip its neighbor in its search for wholeness? The now famous "You complete me," line is another example of our human need for feeling of entirety.

Unfinished forms are uneasy, malformed, and often just plain "ugly." Think of how it feels to lose contact with someone in mid-sentence. What happens when you misplace something important? How much of your body is affected by that paper cut? How clever is the editing and storytelling of a TV series that always leaves us "hanging" so we will come back for more? Where in the dramatic structure of the play is the writer using our human longing for wholeness and completion to keep us engaged? How much satisfaction comes from finishing a big project? How much stress comes from an unaddressed "to-do" list?

Messy or missing pieces in the form of our daily life make us uneasy, often unwittingly depleting our energy and nagging at our focus. Using awareness, you can restore ease that is triggered by perceived incompletion. You have the power to redefine what is and isn't entirely whole. A clear beginning, middle, and end can often be formed through awareness and concentration, making something that formerly felt incomplete into a whole. For example, you can decide that forgetting that name was "perfect" because it offers you the amusing opportunity to reconnect with Bob and share a laugh. You can find acceptance for the form of your "to-do" list just as it is.

Scan your acting practices and your life for unfinished, incomplete forms and see whether you can see them as whole right now. Notice how doing so can free up some energy.

✒ Journal/Discuss/Flyback

*Are you engaging your whole body? Are your feet connected to your fingertips? Does your speech reflect the nuances of today's performance, or are your lines sounding the same despite variations in your physical form? Are you waiting for "the other shoe to drop" somewhere in your life?*

By now, however, having discovered that full-bodied acting awakens your entire being, you will easily begin to see how disconnected body parts, especially the legs, cause the feeling of truthful acting to disappear. This is a lack of Entirety in the actor's form. Sometimes we are afraid to use our whole form because we might look like bad actors. Remember that veiling will help us reveal just the right amount to fit the form, like Hamlet says.

## Off-stage

A big project not getting done? When you make a big activity into a series of steps, see if you can look at each step in its own Entirety. This process is identifying the smaller parts in the whole as whole parts in themselves. Those smaller parts, like atoms that make up molecules that make up the larger forms are like holograms, containing the larger whole in every part.

**What is felt as incomplete is a *form*. Feelings of *Ease* awaken with a Feeling of *Entirety/wholeness* of the Form.**

 Let's apply

Practice your material from beginning to end with a Feeling of Ease, Form, and Entirety. Add in your entrance and exit so you feel yourself as if off stage or standing by on a set, crossing the threshold onto the stage or hearing "Action!" and then delivering your performance, sustaining the final moment, and exiting or "cutting" the scene to complete it.

But what if the darn form is complete and you still feel uneasy? Perhaps it's because you think it is ugly! You are missing this next tool.

## Feeling of Beauty

 Let's play discover Feeling of Beauty

Take a deep inhale and, with your chair, find a spot in the space that welcomes your creativity. If someone else goes to the same spot, it will simply be a guidepost to help you find another perfect spot.

With that sense of ease and form, use your entire being to explore the Beauty of your chair and the forms you and it co-create. What if everything you discover, you think is beautiful, especially that amazing sculptured green gum wedged underneath the seat? The rusty screw and the torn leather make for beautiful contrast. The line of the chair and how it supports your back is awesome. It smells wonderful. It wobbles in an upbeat rhythm. It feels rugged to the touch. The chrome is a mirror.

Take about five minutes to focus all your senses fully on everything about this chair. When you come to a pause, sustain it for a few moments.

### Journal/Discuss/Flyback

*What sensations are within me right now? What atmosphere is filling the room? What images have arisen? If with a group, call out some of the feelings, sensations and atmospheres that are present. If alone, speak them gently into the space. Perhaps peace, vitality, tenderness, richness, empowerment, and appreciation are present. What else?*

**Inhale and breathe this Beauty.**

>  Axiom 8.5: Your ability to choose to view the Beauty in the world is a moment-to-moment choice available at any time.

### Journal/Discuss/Flyback

*What if I chose to see my life as beautiful, as is, no matter what? What if we all chose beauty? How would our lives change?*

## Discussion

It is distinctly a choice you can make—to perceive Beauty around you everywhere. Every thought you hold in your head that yearns to draw you into judgment means you can judge things to be ugly or beautiful. It would be amazing to step out of judgment altogether and invite wonder in its place. When we behold Beauty, we instantly experience ease and peace. Invite curiosity in place of judgement to awaken interest in place of disgust. What we behold as beautiful is the form and its entirety.

Think of how the ensemble's perception of Beauty in the chairs in five minutes transformed the very atmosphere we were breathing. This is the power that a Feeling of Beauty can bring to this world.

The Feeling of Beauty can be cultivated through a strong will to dismiss thoughts of ugliness. One can search to find the lesson in a painful event and then find that way to focus on the beauty. Since energy follows thought, the more you focus on beauty, the more beauty reveals itself to you, the more peace you dwell in, the more peace you radiate to the world.

Every great performance, even a boxing match, has Beauty. This invitation to seek Beauty appears in many ancient spiritual traditions. Here, Chekhov offers it to us as a pathway to inspiration and a practical tool for managing life as an artist. Use it to find Beauty in someone unpleasant and scary to you. Use it when the situation feels hopeless or lost. When you live with this Feeling of Beauty, the world responds in kind. You become a magnet drawing like-hearted people into your world who want to co-create with you.

 ## Let's apply a Feeling of Beauty

Rehearse your material for a Feeling of Beauty. We may not know what that means and yet we can ask our creative self to do this and allow it to show us what that means. Can we find beauty in the ugly actions of our character? Maybe we can find beauty in a moment of improvisation after dropping a line?

 ## Let's play uniting the Four Brothers with chairs

Playing with chairs can escalate in degree of difficulty and be used to create greater awareness of these for feelings of beauty, ease, entirety, and form. Keep in mind the principles of the Japanese rock garden, especially the ideas of levels. Imagine you have an audience. Where are they? Is it a proscenium stage or in the round? In the round, the center point is upstage and therefore highest, and the perimeters are lowest.

Begin solo in a sequence of clear beginnings, middles, ends. Continue and add a partner or two, playing for a few minutes; find the pauses with no one as the leader. Become aware of another partnership, and pair up into quartets. With no leader, find the rhythm and sense of whole in your group and in the space. Gradually merge the quartet with another, and so on, until the entire ensemble is working as one entire organism. Allow the organism to find the rhythm of moving simultaneously for about three to five counts, then sustaining an absolute pause, and then discovering the impulse to move again. Bring the entire common movement sequence into a grand finale harmonious grouping where everyone stops moving at exactly the same moment, easily, in a beautiful form.

## ✒ Journal/Discuss/Flyback

*Did you maintain your Feelings of Ease? Form? Beauty? Entirety? Did you experience the middle and the periphery? Did you try to be the leader? Did you sense the whole? Did you make someone else the leader?*

##  Let's play strengthening the BEEF and QoMs

Play again, adding in the four QoMs of Molding, Flowing, Flying, and Radiating, with or without the chairs.

- See *Kilroy Improv* Chapter 2. **Where's there's more BEEF with** dancing puppets and costume relay!

## Deeper discussion

These four artistic feelings are known in Chekhov as the Four Brothers of Art. They are a family absolutely related to each other. When Ease is lost, it is often because there is a judgment on the Form as ugly or incomplete. Seeing the Beauty of the Form as whole brings Ease as your reward. Ease instantly appears when we appreciate the Beauty or Entirety of a Form.

In addition to training us to be able to render feelings truthfully in the given style and circumstance, the Four Brothers of Art can be said to frame the entire system as a means of human development. Use of them will generate perceptions and skills as a human being that will lead to high productivity and rewarding experiences in life and in art.

Cultivating these four Feelings of Ease, Form, Beauty and Entirety/wholeness awakens the higher ego and prepares the lower ego to heal and restore itself toward centeredness. From a point of centeredness, we are more inclined to attain a state of inspiration.

Embodying this family of feelings is decidedly a choice we can make in perception and a guideline in conscious, creative play. By this I mean, we can choose to perceive Beauty or wholeness of Form and choose to walk, talk, and breathe with a Feeling of Ease. And, if we consciously choose to remember to apply these, we can make strong, deeply creative, unique, and coherent artistic decisions. Our Radiation and magnetism will draw people toward us which will lead us to fruitful relationships and increased work opportunities.

Chekhov believed that all great art, all peak performances contained four feelings:

---

 **Axiom 8.6:**

Beauty

Ease

Entirety (wholeness)

Form

**Where's the BEEF?**

---

When things go wacky and you are, as Chekhov would say, *not happy* on the stage or in life, Flyback over what you have just done and check inside yourself and ask: Where's the BEEF?

Then choose to find it as it is always there when you ask for it to be revealed.

The Four Brothers are part of the intangibles Michael Chekhov refers to in Guiding Principle #3. (GP3). Understanding the practical impact resulting from BEEF will support GP5.

For deepening your skills with the Four Brothers perform the practicing, observing, and applying (POA) homeplay.

> ### Homeplay: POA
>
> The BEEF takes time to digest! Gift yourself some time to dig deeply into how each of these four feelings is existing or missing from your worldview. Select one to focus on for a week. Make sticky notes for your mirror. Send yourself a recurring text to remind you, e.g. EASE! Remember, it is fakeable. You've heard of "Fake it 'til you make it," right? Ask a friend to do it with you and check in to ask how their ease is. You might even give yourself a 10-point scale. I am at a 10—totally at ease. I am at a 0—totally uneasy or fully dis-eased. Repeatedly shift to moving, breathing, and pretending you have level 10 ease. See if it gets easier with practice! Spend some time reflecting on your life, journal as you wish, discovering where you might benefit from bringing more BEEF to it. Are there relationships, tasks, home maintenance, assignments, dreams that might be supported by your BEEF?

## Discover Palaces

Our National Michael Chekhov Association (NMCA) co-founder, Mala Powers, brought an improvisation called Palaces forward from her private work with Chekhov. A palace is an unlimited space with many areas—not necessarily a brick-and-mortar castle or any specific or real, known architecture. It's a magical space that may morph before your very eyes. Anywhere you turn might offer a new doorway, matrix, or portal to another dimension or manifestation within the grand Palace of your imagination.

We can explore our Palace from our artistic self or as a character.

- When entering the palace as the character, we can discover fascinating elements we might not ever "think" of, deepening our connection with the soul and spirit of the character. Some artists find it more enriching than writing a character biography.
- When entering as ourselves, we can discover a wealth of riches pouring in from our unlimited imagination.

Palaces are given a name to define their theme or quality. In keeping with the sacred origins of our gifts, Chekhov called giving a name, *baptizing*, as we do with Atmospheres. Mala's favorite palace was the **Palace of Beauty**. Would you like to try it? You can work with a group or alone. Each person enters their own palace and doesn't interact with the others. It's your private world. Allow about 20 minutes in the palace, plus time to Flyback.

 ## Let's play Palace of Beauty

Come gather at one end of the room. Imagine a threshold at your feet. Whether solo or with others, pretend that you can inhale a magical palace of beauty from your creative sphere of imagination. Now exhale the image across the threshold. Allow the power of your creative breath a moment to fill the atmosphere. Sense into the palace and when ready, step across this threshold and instantly enter any image that appears. Like entering a matrix of Beauty, you can look in any direction and discover a portal to a whole new world of beauty. Perhaps in the far corner is a waterfall; another spot is Shakespeare's Globe Theatre; another is a loved one. You are safe to experience your own palace without interacting with other players. You may enter the imaginary world as part of it or observe it, as you wish, in silence or improvising sound and speech. Try some of both and move into at least three different portals avoiding stagnation. Allow yourself to go blank if that happens. Ask what else is Beauty? Remember, not everyone "sees" in their imagination. Try using all your senses. When you feel ready, step back across the threshold. Gaze into your palace for a few moments. Then release the palace by gathering it up and sending it back into the sphere of imagination.

By allowing 20 minutes or so for this experience, you have plenty of time to explore. If needed, step out at any time and reenter if you wish.

## ✒ Journal/Discuss/Flyback

Flyback following the experience, allowing as much time as you took in the palace for it to resonate afterward.

*What did you discover about beauty? About yourself? What else? Were you amazed at how fertile your imagination is? Could you make things up if nothing seemed to appear for you?*

My experience with this has been that, during the exploration, we artists may penetrate deeply into this Palace of Beauty and may want to share or keep to ourselves. Sometimes it is quite emotional, often quite surprising, and different each time we do it. If we don't feel like anything is happening, pretend that it is. Trust and play. This one is good to do with someone around with whom to Flyback afterward.

Palaces can be done with any theme, quality, vice, or virtue. Palaces of ancestors, future offspring, broken dreams, wonder, longings and yearnings, grief, joys, jealousies, pain, fantasies, fears, and angers are just some of the themes. As always, conclude your palace playtime with an upbeat and positive palace and allot/allow sufficient Flyback time.

Another Mala Powers Beauty favorite was the following blessing from Navajo culture, which she would read as we moved through the space. Sometimes we would echo her like a call and response.

**Walking In Beauty (Navajo way blessing ceremony closing)**

Today I will walk out, today everything unnecessary will leave me,

I will be as I was before, I will have a cool breeze over my body.

I will have a light body, I will be happy forever,

nothing will hinder me.

I walk with beauty before me. I walk with beauty behind me.

I walk with beauty below me. I walk with beauty above me.

I walk with beauty around me. My words will be beautiful.

In beauty all day long may I walk.

Through the returning seasons, may I walk.

On the trail marked with pollen may I walk.

With dew about my feet, may I walk.

With beauty before me may I walk.

With beauty behind me may I walk.

With beauty below me may I walk.

With beauty above me may I walk.

With beauty all around me may I walk.

In old age wandering on a trail of beauty, lively, may I walk.

In old age wandering on a trail of beauty, living again, may I walk.

My words will be beautiful.

## Deeper BEEF homeplay

As we work our way around the Chart of Inspired Action, we have, with the Four Brothers of Art, an artistic frame or lens through which we can explore what we have already covered. Re-examine the PPEs and emotional tools with BEEF. This will deepen your connection to the Guiding Principles from the introduction chapter. Below are just a few of the possibilities:

*Practice X/C several times with different tempos and rhythms choosing one of the Four Brothers to lead your exploration.*

 Journal/Discuss/Flyback

*How can my Feeling of Beauty inspire my X/C? How does my changing form impact the psychological impact of Contracting versus Expanding? Are there any parts of the entire range of motion where I feel more or less ease?*

 Let's play Expanding the BEEF

Practice the Qualities of Movement (QoM/MFFR) with similar questions. Combine X/C with MFFR checking in on your BEEF. Can you create a clear beginning, middle, and end of your practice? Of each section? Are you clear on the Form? How different is Form in relation to Radiating versus Molding? Continue this theme by exploring the relationship between BEEF and the AGs, 3Sis, Q/S, ATMOs.

If there's a basic tool that you struggle with, where BEEF is missing, you probably won't use it in your repertoire. This is reflected in Guiding Principle #5.

## BEEF on the set

Anne was cast in a cable show and expected to wear shear lingerie. Anne was very self-conscious of her stunning figure. She was playing a sensual character appearing on a TV monitor. It would shoot in Brussels in three days. She faced multiple challenges. She was hired for 13 episodes; only three were written. The other ten scripts would be finished while she was there. In the few hours we had before she flew from Hollywood to Brussels, I taught her Chekhov's "making friends with..." technique for a Feeling of Ease. In this exercise, you literally say "Hi" to the floor, walls, wardrobe, props, etc. with the intent to establish a friendship. Thus, instead of being intimidated by being only in lingerie, in the cold warehouse, perched atop the wobbly scaffold, pressured by 75 pairs of eyes, jet lag, surprise scripts, etc. she "made friends" with everyone and everything. She had a delightful time. Everyone pitched in to help her stay warm, hydrated, and ready to deliver. She had a Feeling of Ease and Beauty about the shoot and was hired for another season. By focusing on just one single tool, she opened herself to a peak experience.

## With so many Chekhov tools, how do I easily choose what to use?

Great builders will go repeatedly to the tools they rely on the most: hammer, screwdriver, wrench, and saw. With those nearly everything can be fixed.

 Axiom 8.7: 80/20 Rule—80% of your success comes from 20% of your best effort.

The 80/20 rule is known as the Pareto Principle.[4] If you are lucky enough to be auditioning or performing while training, use your favorite tools first. If you have 20 tools, 80% of your success will come from using your four favorites one at a time. You're leaving the rest barely touched because you don't understand how to use them well. One day you will feel ready to pick up one of those abandoned tools and discover it gets the job done faster and better. For now, let's say you have five hours to prepare. Try spending 80% (four hours) of your preparation with the favs. Next, for 20% of the time (one hour), try something new. Then use whichever inspires your confidence and creativity. Gradually, you will expand the number of tools you think of as your favorites and meanwhile you will deliver the best you have right now. Only when you know what a tool will do for you, will you want to master it (Axiom 0.6. GP5).

If you like to make daily to-do lists, consider a maximum of ten items. Prioritize them and focus 80% of your efforts on the top two and 20% on the next eight. You will be amazed at how satisfying it can be when you choose wisely the top priorities. We will speak more of this later when we explore Focal Points.

Keep in mind the image within the holographic Chart of Inspired Action, and that each part contains the whole. Focus on one tool at a time when you are working, to allow the energy to grow where your focus goes.

## Summary of Part III

When we began exploring Part III, Emotional life for actors, we had a few concerns. Here are those challenges and what we know now:

"OMG! Will I feel the moment?"

Maybe we will, maybe not. But we now know how to activate e-motion throughout our whole body and our breath so no worries.

"What if I don't really feel it?"

Perfect! We now know the most important person we want to feel it is our audience.

"Yikes, I will be a terrible actor!"

With BEEF as a way of life and 3S, QoM, OA/PA for your characters, you will be able to live life as a consummate professional artist, happily delivering truthful emotional life on cue, time after time.

## Notes

1. https://www.heartmath.org/assets/uploads/ 2024/09/blog-todays-stress-is-different.jpg
2. Sagan, Carl, *Cosmos*, Mass Market Paperback, Random House, 2002.
3. Mise en scene (pronounced "meez on sen") a French word which includes everything that the audience sees and hears as part of the production: lights, actors, costumes, sound, set, props, media, and their composition. In *Acting the Michael Chekhov Way*, we consider it the physical body of the show.
4. Pareto, Vilfredo, *Cours d'Économie Politique*. F. Rouge (Lausanne) & F. Pichon, Paris, 1896–1897.

# Part IV
# Esthetics

We aspire to be more than actors. We are creative artists. As such, in the Michael Chekhov Way, we are inspired to cultivate a deep awareness of the intangible aspects of art which define performance as a genre. Performance relies, first and foremost, upon the relationship between an artist and an audience. And thus the concept of Ensemble finds its place, (#9) on the Chart of Inspired Acting, by the very definition of Performance needing at least one person to watch and one person to perform. To cultivate refined esthetics is an essential element of training to elevate the artist above the functional actor. Through a feeling of Ensemble we make deep contact with our highest selves, our partners, our author, our director, and our audience, and are thereby able to create an essential event in our culture. How to build this capacity is discussed in Chapter 9.

Truth is an intriguing esthetic that challenges definition when it comes to art and nonetheless all great art bears truth within it. We recognize the truth of a work of art by an inner sense that resonates within us. Unlike mathematics where two plus two equals four, artistic truth is always relative to its context. As an artist, developing your inner sense for truth will serve you for your life time, inspiring the courage to keep exploring and the wisdom for sensing which choice is a jewel. When Truth has radiated throughout your performance, it produces a rich satisfaction in "knowing." Our aim in Chapter 10 is to encourage your pursuit of knowing Truth.

Style is a Feeling of Form that is true for this performance. Chekhov suggests that every single show has its own unique style. To find the style for this particular story that rings true and is shared by the ensemble of artist, director, designers, authors, and technicians that is radiated to the audience is a sublime esthetic to achieve. Our aim in Chapter 11 is to have you fall in love with the esthetics of all styles so that you can render them truthfully in concert with your colleagues.

Having developed the foundations in Concentration and Imagination in Part I, we trained our bodies and imaginations to work together to convey what, how, and why a character moves in Part II, Psycho-Physical Bodybuilding for Actors.

In Part III, Emotional Life for Actors, with our training in the feeling life of the character and the artist, we can now express any color, quality, or emotion within ourselves, radiating outward or from around us, receiving from the periphery. We use a healthy, safe, and reliable process deliverable on cue. We have BEEF as an artistic frame for our entire life, approach to career, and performance. Mastery of these tools alone will serve most actors safely, successfully playing themselves in today's predominant slice-of-life acting.

Part IV is for those with a deep sense of artistic integrity who yearn for transformation, and desire to lift the work of acting into a high art. For this, we need a noble sensibility of truth that goes beyond ordinary life. It needs to be shared by the entire ensemble via a distinct style. Are you ready to discover how?

# 9
# Ensemble

How wonderful would it be to have a tight-knit artistic family you trust?

What would it be like to know everyone has your back and you share a common vision?

How do artists get invited into projects, even before the public audition?

Ensemble (#9) earns its place on the Chart of Inspired Action because we live in an ensemble continuously. It is an extension of the feeling of entirety. We can open the doorway to inspiration through our focus on each part of the whole. With a strong ensemble, we can feel safe to be brave. With Chekhov, ensemble is contact or communion with more than our colleagues. From the start, our exercises cultivate a sense of ensemble, especially with the ball toss and chairs. Time to take it to a new level.

 Let's play Ensemble (#9): Impulse moves

If you have one or more partners with whom to play, gather into a group in the center of the space, all facing one direction. Without words or gestures, decide as a group whether you will walk, bend, or sit, moving forward, backward, right, left, or down. Try to make three definite moves in perfect harmony. Following this effort, Flyback as an ensemble with each participant contributing a maximum of three words to any of the below prompts.

## Journal/Discuss/Flyback

*What happened? Did you feel safe enough to be brave and make a clear move? What would it take to have more courage to "go for it?"*

Now, start again. However, this time, begin in a circle facing each other. In silence, make contact with your eyes; listen with your body and with your breath; and imagine opening your heart and listening from there too. When you sense the rhythm of the ensemble is harmonized, turn so all are facing the same direction and begin three more movements, maintaining continuous contact with the whole ensemble. Try this several times, adding or changing the options for moving. Flyback to one or more of the prompts below with a three-word limit per artist.

DOI: 10.4324/9781003512745-14

## ✒ Journal/Discuss/Flyback

*Did the second version, starting with eye contact, improve the harmony? How were you deciding which move to do? What clues were you radiating and receiving?*

When you succeed in three cohesive movements, continue improvising more sequences. Try increasing the tempo while keeping precise in the movements. Add geometric options to the ensemble. For example, square, circle, spiral, rectangle, triangle, oval. Choose a starting formation, for example, evenly spaced throughout the room. See if the group can arrive at one of the geometric forms at precisely the same moment with no unnecessary steps.

These kinds of games can be played throughout a semester or rehearsal period, so the ensemble continues to meet greater and greater challenges and precision. Cookie Flyback with up to a one minute time frame per artist.

 Journal/Discuss/Flyback

*Did the ensemble improve over the sequence? Are you trusting your instinct? Are you hesitating until you feel assured by one specific person? Are you trying to lead unconsciously? What did you like overall? What would you do differently? What was your favorite moment?*

 Let's play orchestra

Choose an instrument: clarinet, saxophone, various drums, xylophone, piano, viola, oboe, chimes, base, harp, triangle, etc. Select one conductor. Allow the players to "tune up" their instruments by miming and developing a nonverbal sound. When ready, with no words, the conductor begins through gestures, to invite each section to join, to grow louder (crescendo) or get softer (diminuendo), to increase or decrease the tempo and/or rhythm. The players seek to listen and harmonize, to take center stage when indicated, and to soften and support when guided. Eventually this orchestra can transform into a marching band, traveling in different formations through the space. Ideally the conductor merges with the orchestra and the group follows the ensemble impulse.

## ✒ Journal/Discuss/Flyback

*(If time is limited, choose one-sentence responses or three-word responses.)*

*How was it? What worked overall? Did you fall into a known melody? What would you do differently next time? Could it be done without an orchestra leader? What was your favorite moment? Were you ever trying to fix or correct another player in your mind? Were you listening and appreciating everyone's contribution?*

## Audience as Ensemble

It only takes two things to act. Someone to do it and someone to watch it. Without an audience, the artist is unemployed! At some point, the artist discovers the next step on their journey is to share their creativity with an audience. Whether that is one friend or family member, colleagues in a class, or an unknown number of invisible online witnesses, you have now learned enough tools to put them to the test. If you have colleagues also acting the Michael Chekhov way, invite them to join you and create a way to share your experiments in a work-in-progress (WiP) presentation for an invited audience. This also can be a mid-term project or evaluated event presented following the PPEs, the emotional life or when the challenges seem perfectly timed.

- See **OR 9.1 for** Works-in-Progress Presentation, Monologue Rehearsal and Scene Study Tips with suggested ways to create an ensemble presentation of monologues or scenes with video link to example. OR 9.1 contains two contrasting scores of a monologue and a scene.
- See **OR 9.2** for Monologue/Scene Grading Rubrics

## Where we've been and where we're going

Having discovered and practiced the psychophysical exercises (PPE-X/C, MFFR, AG), you are restoring to your expressivity the energy patterns needed to convey any image that you access. With the exploration of the emotional life of the character (3S, Q&S, OA, PA), you now have a consistent, reliable and safe pathway to expressing the emotional life of the character. And with the Four Brothers of Art (BEEF), you have a clear call to cultivate the highest aspects of yourself to live as a creative artist. For many acting jobs, these skills are the only ones you need to deliver as promised. You can consistently connect to your Objectives and emotions. Now comes the matter of finding jobs.

What's the biggest cliché about how to get work in the entertainment industry?

Frequent answers are

- Sex
- Nepotism
- It's who ya know

And how do you feel about that?

If you want to respect your body, have no relatives to connect you, and "ya don't know" any power people, this might just cause our inner two-year-old artist to throw a depressed hissy fit!

Is it fair that it is this way?

NO!!! But wait …

If you were directing a show, who are the first people you would hire? Would you choose a show without having any idea who might play the characters? If two actors seem fine for the same part and you like one of them from having a connection to them before, who will you hire?

Another question: What if your last name was Streep, Redford, or De Niro? Would you have the same objections to how jobs are gotten?

The reality is often that we ourselves would be doing the same thing if we had the power. Our objection is not to *how* jobs are gotten but to *our personal relationship to that fact*. However, the power is not in who you know—no matter how you "know" them. The truth is found in Axiom 9.1.

 **Axiom 9.1:** "It's who knows YOU and likes you."

Because if they don't know you, they can't hire you, and if they know you and don't like you, they won't hire you. Ultimately the industry runs on relationships, just like most every aspect of our socio-economic sphere.

Our job is to become the kind of artist that people like to work with. Someone well prepared, skilled, easy to be around, on time, reliable, creative. Someone they can trust the success of their show with. Someone they like because they trust you to care for their project. Someone who works well in an ensemble.

Ensemble-oriented artists will place the project in high priority. They have an interest, awareness of, and commitment to the well-being of the larger whole without compromising their own safety and ethics. They have clear, realistic boundaries and follow the appropriate channels for maintaining them. If you wish to be honored as an artist, discard sex from the list of ways to get jobs.

Every participant either strengthens or weakens the ensemble. We become a plus or a minus. A later discussion of SynthAnalysis™ (SA) uses this concept in the plus or minus section, where our characters often fail and thus create the conflicts within, between, and around themselves that make great storytelling.

However, as artists, we want to "keep the drama onstage" and know that those who strengthen the group will be referred, recommended, sought out in the industry. No matter where you are, at this instant, on the scale of "being known and liked," take note that each person you meet, the pizza deliverer, a classmate beside you, a student director may all be your next step in your career. We are not suggesting that you put on an act to get people to like you. No. The idea here is that if you engage the Beauty, Ease, Entirety, and Form principles in your life and work, people will want you to be part of their Ensemble. Building trust builds likability. When you trust yourself to be this kind of artist, others will also trust you. When you trust the writer, your whole being will commit more fully to the story. When you trust the director, you can give freely, take risks, knowing they will guide you.

The nature of Ensemble as a tool in *Acting the Michael Chekhov Way* has expanded applications going beyond relationships with people. It begins with making a connection through the act of concentration. When we focus very strongly on something, whether it is physically present such as your chair when moving with a Feeling of Beauty, or an invisible image, our energy begins to merge with that point of concentration. We are making **contact**, another term used frequently by Chekhov. **Continuous contact**, sustaining this focus, is a means of cultivating the **Five Communions** that developed from Stanislavsky's communication ideas. Jack Colvin brought these forward, stating that Michael Chekhov added the higher ego.

The Five Communions are with

1. The author/script as it stimulates our images
2. Our colleagues—the players, the mise en scene/costumes/sound/lights/the space
3. The audience with whom we are Radiating and Receiving
4. The director whose vision unites the above
5. Our higher ego that communes with us and unites the original images through the author, our colleagues, and our director with our audience

Michael Chekhov's Love Lecture, in *To the Director and Playwright*[1] and the audio series, outlines many tips for creating strong ensemble friendliness. True friends support us and have our backs. They are lovingly honest with us and allow us to "let down our guard" and be our true selves. Your true artist self deserves this kind of community.

What if someone in your Ensemble is irritating, perhaps scaring you by forgetting lines? Maybe you feel unfriendly toward wardrobe? Or maybe to your body because it isn't the way you wish it was. Perhaps the set, or even the author's words, aren't to your liking. "I can never remember that line right!!!" Fall in love with the problem and use your Beauty, Ease, Entirety, and Form (BEEF) by finding one small aspect that you can appreciate about them and focus upon that. Perhaps they have nice eyebrows?

Most unfriendliness comes from fear and misunderstanding. Seek to solve your fears with communication in the proper channels and build your skills of concentration by insisting that your mind find and focus on the Beauty.

As a human being and as an artist, we are most likely to be engaged in inspired action when we are in a harmonious or favorable relationship with our ensemble. Making friends with the space is an example of contact that transforms your relationship into one of ensemble with it.

The Ball Toss is another ensemble building process that is especially fun for opening the gathering. For closing a gathering, here is one of the most enjoyed Chekhov activities:

##  Let's play the Golden Hoop

When playing solo, this process can still be done by imagining your communions: the author, your director, your scene partners, the audience, and your higher self.

Gather your colleagues, present and unseen, to form a perfect circle and take hands if this is agreeable with the group. If it is best not to make direct contact, spread open the circle to allow your energy-light body hands to radiate to each other.

As we reach to each other, extending our right palm face down to the right, we grasp that neighbor's left hand; extending our left palm face up to the left, we allow our other neighbor to grasp our hand.

As we engage the hands, imagine from your Ideal Artistic Center (IAC) in your chest that your heart is opening itself and radiating a golden wish for goodwill. We do not know what the highest good is for anyone, but we can radiate a wish for it to manifest. That radiant wish is flowing from your heart, across your chest, down your right arm, and into the palm of the person to your right.

At the very same moment, you are receiving this radiant goodwill into your left palm from your colleague to your left. It radiates up your arm and across your chest into your heart and IAC. In this moment, the entire circle is radiating one continuous flowing Golden Hoop of radiant goodwill.

With your eyes, try to connect with everyone in the circle. Allow the flow of energy to build in its power for a few moments. When the whole group senses the moment, release hands, imagine that the golden energy grows even stronger and now forms one large hoop at the base of our feet that the ensemble can radiate deep into the heart of the Earth.

Sense the journey of the Golden Hoop as it passes through each successive layer of the planet to its center, healing and cleansing as it goes. As this happens, the radiant good will of our hearts is connecting with the heart of the Earth. This heart is a fiery golden core of energy. Imagine the Earth receives our wish for her highest good and adds to the Golden Hoop her wish for our highest good. Imagine she sends the hoop back to us, through each layer of her body, until it comes through the ground and is at our feet once again.

When the ensemble senses that the Golden Hoop has arrived, reach down as an ensemble and raise the hoop above your heads. Pause for a moment here, and then lower it just a bit and toss it through the ceiling, allowing that wish for the highest good to be shared with all of creation. Sustain the moment of releasing the throw, radiating upward. Then complete the exercise, allowing the arms to fall to your side as the ensemble senses.

## Golden Hoop discussion

When used before a performance, we imagine the audience to be held in the goodwill of the hoop. It brings the whole cast and crew together for centering, clarifies the ensemble's intent to share a great story, and usually happens just before calling "places."

Because energy grows where thought goes, it doesn't really matter whether we are actually making a real effect. The intention of the group as it is focused on the hoop brings greater ensemble feel, confidence and ease. It has happened that sensitive people in the audience have asked whether the cast "did something" to them just before the show started.

The Golden Hoop frequently becomes a deeply respected ritual and as such is apropos since theatre is an outgrowth of ritual. When we share in ritual, Rhythm, Concentration, and Will force are engaged, strengthening the etheric body (also known as light body, energy body, Chi, Qi, and Prana) of the individual, the group, and the planet itself. It is a life-generating ensemble act that strengthens and heals. How cool is it to know that if you choose to do this, you are joining with Chekhov artists across the world to elevate our collective light!

The original process is specifically an "opening of the heart" exercise for radiating good will. We are activating our own Will force to direct heart-centered appreciation. This is love as an action. In Chekhov's *On Theatre and the Art of Acting* audio series, he speaks of love as an active verb. Although saying love is confusing for many people, he tells us not that we *should* love, but rather that we *DO* love already. If we recognize that we do love, we can nurture its power, transforming it into a very practical tool for the artist.

This exercise would fall into the category of cultivating that higher ego of which he speaks, as it builds our capacity to love, to concentrate, to radiate. Using the words "send or radiate good will" is generally a non-religious, generically acceptable, non-sentimental way of phrasing that leads to Chekhov's intent for the exercise. It is important that we detach from what we personally think would be good for someone and stay purely in the radiating of our own wish that goodness of the highest nature flows to each person and then is offered to all of creation.

In another variation, National Michael Chekhov Association (NMCA)-certified teacher Kevin Marshall, University of Florida, Gainesville, had his *Who's Afraid of Virginia Woolf* cast fill the hoop with all their preparatory energies, images, and wishes for the production on final dress rehearsal and send the hoop up to hover just above them where it radiated through the run of the show. From there, they could reach into it at any moment during the run to help them. At the end of the run they released the hoop, filled with all of the magic it has acquired, to all of creation.

If you as a learner are constantly under heavy pressure to deliver academically, appearing silly or stupid might feel socially dangerous. What if we create a shield to protect us from judgement, allowing us the safety to be bravely creative? NMCA-certified teacher Jeff Thomakos, InspiredActing.Org, introduces the idea of opening a class by "bringing down the hoop." He acknowledges that it might be kind of weird at first, and invites us to play along.

 Let's play bringing down the Golden Hoop

Imagine the golden forces emanating from a pin point far into the universe that expands, forming a protective ring around the perimeter of the classroom. Watching it come closer and closer, we reach up and lower it to the ground in front of us, then we pass through this shimmering veil of light, to the inside of it. Now we can turn and face the walls and expand the dome to include the entire space. We are shielded in safety and free to play fully with no repercussions. What happens in the Golden Hoop stays in the Golden Hoop.

## Discussion

It doesn't take long before the class will insist on "bringing down the hoop" if Jeff by chance forgets. At the end of class, reverse the process. Be creative and courageous and the rewards will flow to you.

When it is used to close a class, I like to suggest we radiate appreciation for the creativity of each person and the ensemble and include those who would have like to have joined us or who were with us and had to depart early.

## For daily life

We are part of a larger whole and are always in relation to that whole. Each human, object, atmosphere or event is part of our Ensemble, and each element of our Ensemble can work for, against, or neutrally in relationship to us. Ultimately, live the golden rule. We must be the human beings with whom we want to be in Ensemble. The world can feel quite isolating and, whether we are stopped at a light or getting a cup of coffee, our willingness to contact warmth can make someone's day.

## Note

1   Chekhov, Michael, *To the Director and Playwright*, Compiled by Charles Lenard: Limelight Editions, 1984.

# 10
# Truth

Am I good enough? What do I think I am doing?<br>
What is truth anyway?<br>
Do I need to just be me to be truthful?

With each tool we discover, we sense more deeply how every element of the Chart of Inspired Action (Figure P.1) awakens and weaves seamlessly into the other. Let's start this exploration by connecting truth to ensemble.

 **Let's play pre-show Golden Hoop of Truth**

Whether solo or in a group, pretend you are backstage, and you can expect that in about two minutes, a stage manager will give your five-minute warning. You form a circle and make contact, opening your hearts to each other. Now, you imagine your hoop contains the entire audience in its center. Inhale this image and exhale it into the atmosphere.

Next, envision that each story we reveal has its own truth to be co-created in communion with our spectators. We are actively preparing the space for them to cross the threshold into a true experience. Our love for doing this awakens our super consciousness, our higher ego.

Holding this single point of focus in your Ideal Artistic Center (IAC), you warm up your imagination. A surge of excitement awakens your truth for being an artist, reminding you of the deep legacy you are carrying forward and activating the immediate call to action you are bringing to your audience today. You sense how this truth empowers you and strengthens your feeling of ease. You bear a true commitment to transform their lives through your love. Your truth frees you from any blocks and worries. Now, you send that Golden Hoop of truth up into the universe with a mighty, joyous lift. The stage manager calls, "Five Minutes," and with excitement, you whisper "Thank you, Five!"

✒ **Journal/Discuss/Flyback**

*In what ways might doing the above pre-show Golden Hoop with truth as a focal point be helpful?*

Everyone is always looking for truth in a performance. The tricky thing is that no one actually can define what truth really is. Though we seem to know in our gut when it is absent and that it is essential. Truth sparkles like a diamond, and its absence is like coal.

DOI: 10.4324/9781003512745-15

>  **Axiom 10.1:** No truth, no atmosphere. No atmosphere, no truth.

Atmosphere, as the soul of the story, unites us with the audience. When truth disappears, the audience feels the Atmosphere (ATMO) collapse and they often sink back in their chairs. Some find themselves watching from their intellect, while others start fidgeting, coughing, and adjusting their bodies.

How does truth die? Maybe an actor drops their line and no one else helps, or a prop breaks and the cast doesn't deal with it well. Maybe the actors are in completely different styles. Perhaps the tempo is slow and so it isn't truly funny. Or the script just doesn't "ring true." Maybe the show is miscast. Or perhaps it was advertised as something it isn't.

> ### Hello, Cabbage
>
> I saw a wonderful production of *Hello, Dolly* with a live orchestra at a theater festival. The stage had a three-foot-wide runway thrusting into the audience with an orchestra pit in between the runway and the apron of the stage. The opening number was a robust spectacle with a large chorus dressed in brightly colored tropical outfits with fruits and vegetables in their headdresses and on platters, singing and dancing on the runway between the orchestra and the audience. As they made their exit, a head of cabbage rolled off a platter and sat on the runway, just right of center, between the audience and the conductor. Actors walked around it, danced around it. It sat there for the entire rest of the act. Not one person acknowledged the truth of this situation. The audience's truth: Hello, Cabbage, the star of the first act. It took us completely out of the art and put us into stress.

How fragile this ephemeral truth is. How can we prepare a fertile field for it to flourish? Perhaps exploring the myriad of facets this Diamond of Truth has will help us.

Truth of the cabbage story reminds us that audiences agree to "suspend their disbelief" and pretend to have belief in the world of the story as their "truth" during the performance. Anything that happens to shatter that truth sends the audience back into the real world and, in effect, violates our promise to them. Let's look at nine *facets of truth* we are held responsible for by the spectator.

> ### Homeplay/Discussion
>
> Following the contemplation of each of the following nine Truth Diamonds, watch one or more performances. *Ask whether the productions reflected all nine facets. Where did they succeed, making the story sparkle? Describe some examples for each of the nine facets. Where did truth disappear? How might the story have been polished? Is there a correlation between the popularity of a show and its relationship to truth?*[1]

## Nine facets of the Diamond of Truth

1. **Stylistic Truth:** Among the first impressions we make on an audience is via the style of the show.
    a) Is it in the overall genre of drama, comedy, tragedy or farce? The truth of these genres is centered in atmospheres of the mise en scene (the acting plus all production elements). Truthful marketing makes it clear to potential spectators what to expect and inspires them to attend. Delivering something different from the promise advertised becomes a lie.

b) Is it contemporary, classical, avant garde, experimental, story theater, etc.? Each of the many styles has its own set of "acting truths" that can be defined in terms of the degree of Veiling, Tempo/Rhythm and Qualities of Movement. The truth of Shakespeare is different from the truth of Lauren Gunderson. And as with genre, the mise en scene also ideally meets a threshold of truth apropos of the Style.

2. **Historical Truth, Cultural Truth, National Truth:** The storyteller can choose a relationship to factual truths of history, culture, and nation. Historical fiction for example can choose to have anachronisms manifesting in the text, the style of acting, or in the mise en scene; or it can remain accurate to these facts. The choice becomes a style demanding its own truth.

3. **Truth of the given circumstances:** Here we are interested in the fictional "truths" of the story as written. Each writer and director creates a fictional world which has its own truths. Even in video games such as *Dungeons and Dragons* or in comic book mythologies there are sets of truths about how those fictional worlds function; and these truths, when met, carry the spectator on the particular journey intended. Fans will be quick to call out violations of the "rules." Characters in stories must respond in the way the writer has intended in order for the truth of the story to unfold. Scrooge must be rude and disagreeable in the beginning of *A Christmas Carol* in order for the truth of the message to work.

4. **Truth of the character:** In *Acting the Michael Chekhov Way*, the character is imagined having an independent, real existence in our I-sphere outside the Earth's ozone layer. The artist prepares to receive and express this character truthfully to the image intended by the writer. If the ego of the artist imposes itself onto the character, the truth of the character will fail to materialize. The personality of the actor will displace the true character. The truthful performance manifests when creative individuality merges with the independently existing image of the character and is conveyed through the artist's physical life within the given style as directed. This is unique to each role.

5. **Truth of the relationship:** Each character has a relationship to every other character, and they serve as positive or negative forces to each other. Depending on the style, subtle or bold expressions of who is our friend and who is our enemy must have a feeling—a truth—for the story to unfold. We call this the plus or minus of a character. We will explore this more later.

6. **Individual Truth:** Are you being true to your creative individuality? Contemplate these thoughts: When I am trying to do it the way I think they want it, am I true to my creative individuality? I am making a fear-based decision. Is that who I truly am? When my images don't come out the way I aimed, my movements and speech are not true to my artistic self. When I am trying to impress rather than express, I am not true. When I push, or try to wake up my audience, I am judging them and not true to my artist. Do I believe I am a creative artist?

Being true to your creator-self is different from being selfish and insisting on doing things your own way. The truth we want to live is the one that we would choose if we had complete freedom from fear or danger, a need for approval or economic support, etc. Would I take this part if I didn't need the …? In the context of the story, the direction, and the production, is this the highest truth of how the character is for me to play?

7. **Personal Truth:** To know the truth of who we are becomes essential to understanding how to play the character truthfully. The truth we want includes knowing how others perceive us. Who am I and how do I differ from the character? This will be developed in Chapter 12 on transformational characterization. Here's the basic concept: If I am cast in a role because I am similar to that character, I already have most of the character present and I have no need to add those qualities. What if I think I have clear authority, but my body language doesn't show it? My authoritative character will be too weak for the audience to believe. This is where repetition of the psycho-physical exercises and journaling will help us to "know thyself" and deepen our feeling of truth.

This self-knowledge can be very helpful in life. And sometimes, we benefit from an outside eye.

> ### Sugary sweet
>
> When, in 1994, I was serving as president of the Michael Chekhov Studio in Los Angeles, newly formed with Jack Colvin and Mala Powers, I really wanted Dan, an influential friend of Jack's, to "like" me. Every time he came to an event, I went out of my way to welcome him, trying to include him in ideas, conversations, or appreciations. I wanted him to be a regular participant, which would perhaps prove to others that I was a worthy leader. The nicer I was, the more distant he became.
>
> One day, I asked Jack why Dan didn't like me. "Yes, I asked him about that," Jack replied with curiosity.
>
> I complained, "especially when I am so sweet and attentive to him."
>
> "Aha!" said Jack. "That's the problem. He doesn't trust you." Jack explained, "Lisa, you are sweet. So when you "try to be sweet," it's like putting sugar on top of a powdered sugar, chocolate-coated strawberry. You are so sugary sweet from Dan's view that the truth disappears, making you seem manipulative, excessive and fake."
>
> And I had been. I had been socially acting out of fear rather than trust. Thank you, Jack and Dan. Lesson learned.

8. **Truth of reality vs pretend:** In the animal world, safety mechanisms are best suited to the individual needs of each species: The lion fights, the deer flees, the turtle folds, and the chameleon freezes. Humans do any or all of these in response to danger. We could call this a metaframe that operates on the unconscious level. Which do you do?

   There is another metaframe for humans about safety and perception of reality versus fantasy/pretend that is useful to know about. This affects our personal experience of truth at the deepest level. Where we feel safest in a world of fantasy/pretend or in the world of reality will determine our confidence in performance. Our innate *star* quality that we experienced in the goblet exploration (Chapter 1, Figures 1.3–1.5) will be activated when we work through the artistic process that anchors us in our safety zone.

   Creativity is often associated with expanded imaginations that venture into fantasy. Many of us are safest, creating our truest art when we are living in our fantasy world. For us, to draw upon what is "true" in everyday life kills our creativity. For others, we need to feel that what we are acting is "really" reality.

   Most other popular acting trainings focus on reality-based approaches, leaving millions of imaginative artists struggling in their danger zone trying to "be real." *Acting the Michael Chekhov Way* works for both pretend and reality fans. If we have ever had a peak performance moment, we know deep within that a higher self really came through. When we understand the higher self is an unlimited part of the real you, those of us safer in reality know that we can draw upon this truth: "We are really doing. We are really Pushing or Expanding, right now."

   When we are safer in fantasy/pretend, we shine when we imagine we are Pushing or Expanding. Yes, it is subtle; and yet, it is a completely transformative concept that lights up our *star* quality when we know ourselves and where we are truthfully safest. For more details on this concept, see Chapter 6, Reality vs Pretend: How to Surmount Collisions in Search of Truth, by Lisa Loving Dalton in *Michael Chekhov and Sanford Meisner, Collisions and Convergence in Actor Training* by NMCA-certified teacher, Anjalee Deshpande Hutchinson, Routledge, 2021.

9. **Truth of the mise en scene:** Everything that an audience sees and hears has happened. Yes, the cabbage upstaged the entire cast. Live performance thrives on the immediacy of what is really happening in the space, the atmosphere. This is a truth that needs to be reckoned with. If our outdoor theater is in an airport pathway, we artistically plan on how to handle being drowned out by the noise of that setting. If an actor misses their cue, can we deal with that truth artistically? If the theater has a pillar built into the stage, we can't just pretend it isn't there. When we use the pillar to our creative advantage, we delight the audience with the truth of that. In improvisation, when we take a "Yes, and …" approach, we are accepting what has been established as truth in that moment.

## Conclusion of Truth

A Feeling of Truth must always be present, and Michael Chekhov invites us to recognize that Truth is relative to Form. There is a higher truth that transcends the imitation of life. This allows for a multitude of styles. Realism is one very small part of the storytelling art. If one limits oneself to speaking and moving on the stage or on camera exactly as one would in everyday life, your performance generally fails to meet the truth of art which is a heightened spiritual act. "Everyday" actors tend to make themselves smaller, shutting down their charisma, and collapsing the atmospheres, both overall and personal.

To counteract this, Chekhov was a big fan of studying and working with fairy tales and mythology as ways to develop a sense of artistic and human **Truth**. These tales evolve through the culture as a means of communicating archetypal truths to their societies. Exploring these can help one develop the understanding of humanity, of our deepest concerns, challenges, hopes, and dreams as we discover universal truths that span the ages.

Clowning is another pathway into exploring truth. The foundations of pure and simple truths become quickly evident in this art and will be developed in a future book, *Applying the Michael Chekhov Way*.

When a Feeling of **Truth** is missing, it is often due to a lack of Entirety. Remember the actor who is "over the top" and not believable in Figure 0.3? This can occur because the actor's energy is focused on the upper portion of the body. The legs are unable to engage the character's objective because all they can do is focus on keeping the actor from literally falling forward. Lack of commitment produces a lack of **Truth**. You must always commit 100% of your body to your choices.

Additionally, there are tasks an actor must engage in to be a professional. These tasks include auditions, headshots, networking, and marketing. What if you are able to approach these often-dreaded tasks as simply another style of performance? We can find the Truth needed to be effective with a full commitment to enjoying these parts of the business by falling in love with them as artistic expressions of our creative individuality. Developing a Feeling of Ease with a variety of styles expands the actor's repertoire and employability. Using **Truth** to create your marketing is similar to accurate marketing of a show. A fresh, up-to-date headshot for example will be appreciated for its truthfulness when you walk in the door.

Perhaps your IAC has access to a master marketing character to help you with this. Look for the future *Applying the Michael Chekhov Way* with chapters on specific styles such as classical, sit-com, headshotology, networking, and more.

In summary, here are some responses to our Truth concerns:

- What do I think I am doing?

    Whatever it is, commit 100% to it. Check to see if your legs are engaged. Are you judging something?

- Am I good enough?

    The Truth is you were born for this, and the rest is skill development.

- What is **Truth** for an actor anyway?

    An event that is undeniably experienced in the moment as happening.

- Do I need to just be me to be truthful?

    If by *me* you include your whole higher self, your artistic frame, and your radiant starlight beingness, then yes. If you mean mumbling, acting as if you are not acting, and shutting down your charisma, then no, that wouldn't be true to your artist self.

How can I be truthful in Shakespeare or situation comedy? Go deeper into Style!

## Note

1  Viewing and responding to a production based on the nine Diamonds of Truths could be an assessable activity as part of an evaluated course.

# 11
# Style

Pop quiz!

Don't worry, dear fellow actors and readers, it's only three questions long:

> How many shows on Broadway or in London's West End are acted in the Style of realism?
>
> How often do film actors play non-realistic characters?
>
> How much work can an actor get if they only do naturalism?

That wasn't so bad, was it? Now, keep your questions and answers in mind as we proceed.

 Let's play Style (#11) Truth and consequences!

Grab some colorful markers, chalk, and crayons and find a blank flip chart, drawing board, journal, or paper bag! If you have an ensemble, share the art space and get ready to jot down notes, draw pictures, write words and phrases. Randomly place on the drawing surface anything that comes up reflecting your TRUTHFUL response to the following:

*How do you feel about Style? About doing Shakespeare, Greek tragedy, clown, French restoration, Ibsen, story theater? Acting like an animal, alien, or superhero? What comes up when you think about "being a classical actor" or doing a Style other than naturalistic acting? Is there anything that worries you or you don't like about it?*

Allow this process to be impulsive and random, overlapping with the next step. And, if you are playing with an ensemble, feel free to jostle for access to the board and markers. Unleash your opinions; repeat others if you agree—delightful or ugly, excited or scared—just go for it! Go for your truth now.

As the images accumulate, call out what you have written or see (especially if you're playing solo) and begin to "gesturize" or express the images with full-bodied movement and sound, uncensored, like a two-year-old might. Perhaps a rant emerges. Have fun letting it out. Maybe more comes up as you physicalize your inner reactions with exaggeration. Add it to the drawing board.

After you think you have vented everything, pause for a moment and tap your Ideal Artistic Center (IAC) and ask, "What else?" Listen with your heart and see if something else comes up, and add that to the images and express it in sound and movement. Try one more round of connecting with the IAC to see if there is anything else lingering deep down. Listen to your highest self, your inner child, your inner star. "What else?" Add any final images that arise and incorporate them into sound and movement. When done, release. Inhale and exhale as you step back to flyover what has emerged. Snap a picture if you want.

WARNING: If you have any concerns about Style and you read the above exercise without doing it, go back and do it now. Do not pass Go or you may be in Style jail for life. Unless you understand what the "icky"

DOI: 10.4324/9781003512745-16

Style 155

ingredients are of your piece of the pie (Figure 1.2) in relation to Style, you won't be able to transform them into yummy stuff and find your truth in performance.

Perhaps you think you can get by with a little last-minute help. Danger! Danger! We will need more than a brief visit from a dramaturge and a Style consultant. Yes, we need them to make clear the period's body language, the era's deportment, the etiquette and protocols that must be understood, as well as the effects of the wardrobe, furniture, and props on the character's physical life. Yet, if we can't integrate the information, are we doomed?

Many of today's actors just don't have adequate physical skills to hold the Style of movement and speech required to deliver anything beyond naturalism in a truly engaging way. Clearly the language is of paramount concern, yet we must not leave our speech teachers with the sole task of preparing us to inhabit the vast worlds of Style.

Do you relate to these responses in Figure 11.1?

All of our responses are valid, so let's see how training the Michael Chekhov way can help us fall in love with Style! Here are three "problems" that Style presents to us today. Lack of belief, skill, and understanding.

We need

1. The belief that period Style can have a feeling of Truth. Then, we can commit fully to the Beauty of the Form of any given Style.
2. The skills of uniting the language and the body with the period's posture, mannerisms, and movement.
3. The understanding of Style as a variation of the psycho-physical exercises (PPEs) and other tools on the Chart of Inspired Acting, which we already can do.

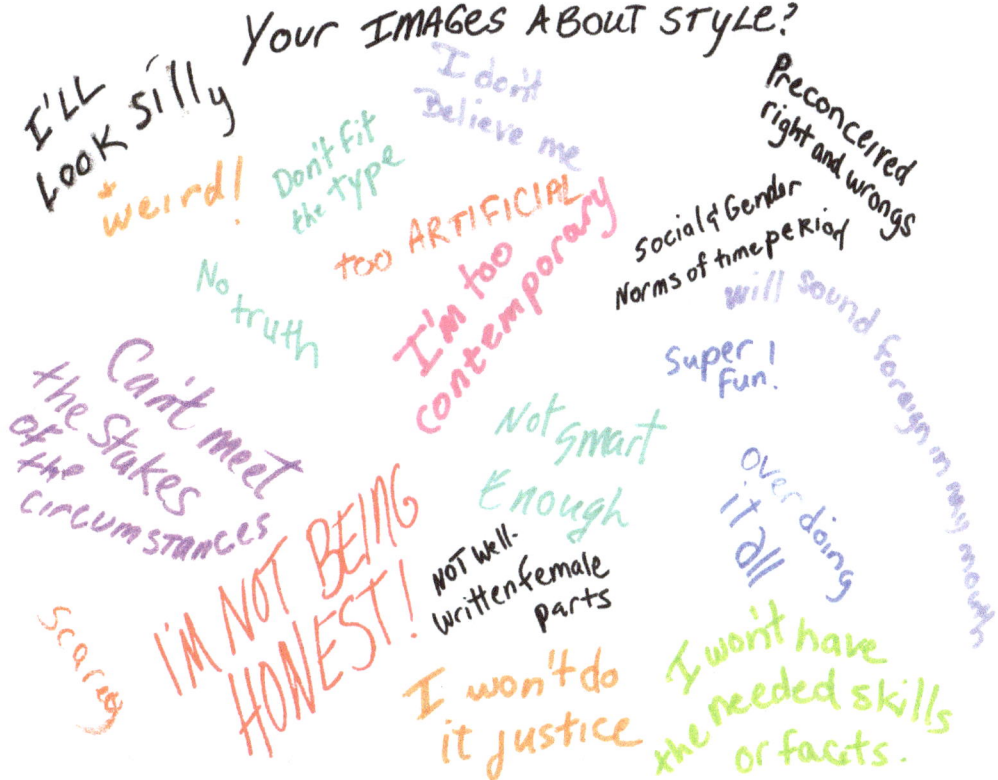

Figure 11.1 Actors' responses to "How do I feel about Style?"

## Belief

Many of us have very little early exposure to different Styles of acting, so we tend to believe all good acting is naturalism. This contributes to the fright that many of us bear toward the classic Styles. Our fears of looking stupid, feeling embarrassed, anxiety over doing it wrong, and of not being believable each has its own uniquely paralyzing power, making us feel vulnerable. These sensations of inadequacy literally live in the biology of the body. No amount of talking will alleviate them. All the skill sets in the world won't help us feel safe playing a stylized character if we don't believe in the possibility of a Truth beyond naturalism. Without belief, skills we may build will fail to be sustained. It is probably clear to our intellect that what is true in Greek tragedy is not true in some of the most produced plays of the 2020s, such as *She Kills Monsters* by Qui Nguyen or *Clyde's* by Lynn Nottage.

 **Axiom 11.1: Truth is relative to Style.**

Chekhov's approach is capable of helping build trust into our bodies through experiential processes with its playful, judgment-free approach. When we develop confidence in our ability to play Style truthfully, we expand our range of castability. It is a fact that you are rarely cast in a *Star Trek* show without Shakespearian credits on your resume. Your chances of playing a non-human are pretty high in both film and stage. Time to fall in love with Style!

## The artist's attitude

Michael Chekhov references the need for artists to be aware of their attitudes toward their characters. I extend that to the entire premise of Style. Because many artists fear Style, we are looking to employ Chekhov's idea of "falling in love with the problem." Remember, right now it is more important to cultivate the fun, joy, and eagerness that leads to confidence than to become masters of Style today. The following are steps toward that aim.

 **Let's energize with Expanding/Contracting (X/C) and Molding, Flowing, Flying, and Radiating (MFFR)**

Getting up on our feet, let's energize our imagination and body, moving in large Expanding abstract gestures. Allow random sounds to radiate into space. Now, imagine the pulse of creation drawing you into your IAC, Contracting with tightening, hardening, and darkening robust energy into a small ball on the floor or perhaps in a chair. From there, allow the pulse to reverse, begin Expanding through Earth-like resistance, Molding your gestures in the space. Gradually morph through Flowing, Flying, and Radiating with various moments of Expanding and Contracting. Arrive at a beautiful, expanded, radiant form and sustain the final moment. Hold for three counts and release to your ideal universal self, moving in silence to the periphery of the space. Turn into the center of the room and imagine a threshold before you.

 **Let's ground our sun-like centered energy, radiating into the Earth**

Allow it to travel upward through the ceiling, sky, and Earth's ozone layer, into the unlimited sphere of imagination. Inhale the Atmosphere (ATMO) of a popular shopping mall and exhale it across the threshold before you.

## 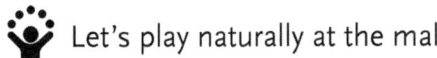 Let's play naturally at the mall

Cross the threshold as a realistic everyday person, improvising your typical mall activities for several minutes. Interact with real or imagined people and things. Allow yourself to be natural like you really are at the mall. Then cross the threshold out of the mall.

If solo, turn and gaze across the threshold, imagining you can watch the "video replay" of what you did. You could even video yourself and watch the actual replay.

If in an ensemble, you might have half the group cross the threshold and the other half observe and then switch.

Gather the image and send it back up to your unlimited sphere of imagination.

## ✒ Journal/Discuss/Flyback

*Now, let's Flyback, using the language of the PPEs. Let's call the Style in which this improv was done, "naturalism." What was the range of Expanding/Contracting for most people? For example, if we use a 0–10 scale, where were most people? Remember that this is one way to "score" the scene with X/C. (This identifies the pattern of the movement.) Keep this as a separate question from the "Quality or Sensations" observed. For example, 10 is super expanded to the absolute physical maximum and could be any emotion from rage to boredom to joy. Look now only for the degree of X/C that was visible from the audience's perspective. Perhaps most artists were in the average range of the scale, hovering from 4–6.*

*What Qualities of Movement (QoM) were most common? Molding, Flowing, Flying, Radiating?*

*What Qualities and Sensations (Q&Ss) did you experience? How much of those Q&Ss were perceivable to the audience?*

*How veiled or unveiled were the artists? (How much expression were the naturalistic artists allowing to be recognizable in body and voice?) Was their behavior heavily veiled, so the audience saw very little; or was it largely unveiled so everything they were thinking, feeling, and expressing was boldly obvious?*

*How was their posture? Vocal clarity? What else could you observe about "naturalism" as a Style in the language of the Michael Chekhov way? Did you observe or experience any Archetypal Gestures (AGs) such as a Push, Lift, or Reach?*

*What patterns or tendencies live in the life of the eyes, hands, and feet?*

*How do we relate to our clothes, props, and environment in the Style of naturalism?*

*Take note right now of the contemporary energies most are embodying and the resulting Atmosphere in the room.*

##  Let's play Palace of Styles

Back to the drawing board!

Pause for a moment and imagine as many different Styles as you can think of. Jot or draw them on the board, either on the same surface or on a new sheet or board. Review the many Styles; imagine your higher self somehow knows exactly how to do them. After a few moments, step to one end of the room.

##  Goblet process

Ground, center, and welcome the Image using the Goblet process to access the I-sphere. Just like we did with Atmospheres (Chapter 7) and the Palace of Beauty (Chapter 8), imagine a threshold at your feet. On the other side is a Palace of Styles. Whether solo or in ensemble, pretend that you can inhale a magical Palace of Styles from your creative I-sphere. Exhale the image across the threshold. Imagine that you can step across this threshold and instantly enter into any Style that appears. Perhaps in the far corner is a Palace of Greek tragedy; another spot is Shakespeare's Globe Theatre; another is Moliere's French farce; then *Dungeons and Dragons* or a circus; and then there's a *Star Wars* spaceship, etc. You are free to experience any Style in any spot. We can enter into the imaginary world or observe it as we wish, in silence or improvising sound and speech. Try some of both.

Allow 15 minutes or so for this experience so you have plenty of time to explore. This is a private, no-pressure improv where the artist cannot possibly get it wrong! It can only be perfect!

After stepping back across the threshold, out of the Palace of Styles, gather the images and send them back up to your unlimited I-sphere.

##  Journal/Discuss/Flyback

*Overall what did you like? Did you have fun? Did your X/C and MFFR change in different places? Your voice, posture, size of gestures? What changes happened? Did you observe anyone else?*

*From your imagination of what the audience experienced, what did you notice?*

*We can ask all of the same questions we did of "naturalism."*

*What patterns or tendencies were living in the eyes, hands, and feet?*

*How do we relate to our clothes, props and environment in this or that Style?*

My experience with this has been that during the exploration, we seem to unconsciously transform out of our contemporary stances and embody the frames of skillfully trained artists. Our degree of veiling varies, the expressivity gains clarity, and our feeling of truth lives. It is fun to observe this in action.

Let's glance back at the original responses to how we felt about Style.

*Do you feel more intrigued and excited about acting in Style? Can you feel a greater sense of Beauty for the process and Ease about the possibilities of acting truthfully beyond naturalism? Do you have more confidence that you can at the very least, pretend to do the Style, even if you don't really know how?*

## Posture

Have you noticed that a lot of us are essentially collapsed through the core, having been slumped over a small screen much of our lives? This collapsed core is usually accompanied by limited lung capacity, minimal breath support, and excessive curvature in our spines and shoulders. The sense of uprightness needed in many Styles seems unattainable. We lack the stamina needed to sustain an upright Style throughout the play or to craft convincing characterizations of power. We are, at best, relegated to playing only low status characters. The literal physical inability to open and lift the torso must be dealt with through deep extended training. Luckily for us, this is precisely what the PPEs are already doing for us.

Michael Chekhov's tools of Expanding and Contracting are an excellent starting point for building both your physical capability and your psychological safety as an artist. Let's put a spin on them.

## 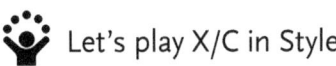 Let's play X/C in Style

Following our Goblet process of engaging the IAC and imagination, improvise X/C using a variety of images from the hierarchies of plants, insects, animals, landscapes, humans, etc. If preparing for a particular Style—Greek or Elizabethan for example—use images from that era. Expand as a Greek god or king; contract as a lowly servant or slave. Expand into a lion, contract into a mouse. Expand into an oak, contract into an acorn. Expand or contract into a superhero. Try adding a line or two of text through the movement. Keep the movements growing rather than leveled off. Avoid just "being an oak or an acorn." **The body moving simultaneously with the moving image is the active principle.** When you have finished exploring, cross out of the palace, gather the images and send them back up to your I-sphere.

## The impact

Repetition of Expanding/Contracting energy with a variety of images will begin to dissociate from us any limiting beliefs about our own ability to be big or to be small. We will begin to feel safe taking up a different amount of space from our everyday selves. Furthermore, it will plant the seeds of bringing images to life in our body as we gently begin to develop a stronger relationship to form.

Moving into rehearsal, it will be easier to hold an image of a giant oak than to remember to stand upright, project, and stay grounded. The image will bring many elements into one single focal point or inner object, which having done the exercises, you will automatically feel the effects in your whole body and voice.

## Mannerisms

Mannerisms of today are distinctly lacking in precision and definite form. Attitudes are relaxed and loose, floppy and sloppy. Few of us have any disciplined use of our hands and feet. Our thumbs may be our most developed appendage. Body language gestures that we use in everyday conversation are being lost to emoticons as so much communication is texted. Actors don't know what to do with their hands and have very little life in their legs. The problems of "big hands" and "dead legs" are rampant.

To awaken an awareness of the power of expressivity in the whole form, the four Qualities of Movement: Molding, Flowing, Flying, and Radiating (Chapter 3) are already helping you develop specificity and awareness of how much information comes through your hands. They also can be corresponded with the four temperaments popular in Shakespeare.

- See **OR 11.0** for how QoMs prepare us for truthful Style.

## Atmosphere

When we color ATMOs with a time period, or an era, such as Greek, Roman, French Restoration, Elizabethan, Edwardian, etc., we have a vast array of energy patterns to master. For basic eras, we can begin by imagining the architecture. If time permits, baptize a palace with the era; explore it purely through your fantasy; Flyback, and then do a little research. Gaze at photos of temples, castles, drawing rooms, and their furnishings; and then, imagine establishing a threshold for the above Atmosphere, and filling this ATMO with these images. When working on a specific show, doing this early in the rehearsal period, long before the sets are built, will help you prepare for when the scenery arrives. It will also build your imagination skills for on-camera green-screen work where no sets ever physically arrive! Building your imagination skills for unreal worlds comes in very handy for sci-fi, cartoon, animation, and other fantasy lands.

Atmospheres will intuitively expand or contract us and guide us to want to mold, float, fly, or radiate. So, having done these basic exercises, we will be free to respond confidently to whatever atmospheres are presented.

 Let's apply

Try a generic scene or monologue of 8–12 lines with three different eras.

For scene study and for rehearsals, focus on one tool at a time, allowing yourself to discover just what that tool has to offer. When we focus on Atmospheres, we create the emotional through line for the audience. Try a step-by-step layering by first focusing on the era (Greek, Elizabethan), then the genre (tragedy, farce), followed by the specific shifting Atmospheres within those that result from the plot events as determined by your SynthAnalysis (Chapter 19). This process will keep a consistency in the overall form of the production while enhancing the unique dynamics of each scene.

## Image and language

One of the most difficult challenges we meet as contemporary artists is creating multidimensional characters and experiences with heightened language. The depth of imagery usually present in the heightened language far exceeds contemporary speech. We barely understand what we are saying. It can be hard to get the rhythm demanded by the Style, leaving the words lifeless as they stumble from our mouths.

This is where the Chekhov way of using gesture can free us. Start by activating your artistry (mind/body) with X/C and MFFR.

 Body talk with the artist and the witness

Choose a section of text that is challenging for you. If you are working solo, consider doing this in front of a mirror or self-taping so you have a witness. If you are working with others, find a partner and take turns being the witness.

After the warmup, read your text out loud as the artist, and then set it down and explain what you believe the complicated parts mean in contemporary words. While standing up, freely move your hands to help describe the meaning. The witness watches the artist's body language, especially the hand gestures, no matter how small. They also notice impulses that the artist has to move in a certain direction. Afterward, *Flyback* on what happened. The artist tries to recall what movements the artist did, and the witness confirms and adds anything that may be missing from the artist's self-observation. Now find the most difficult words/images and exaggerate the body language you instinctively used, inflating it as big as possible, using the whole body and full voice. Unveil the body's expression, even acting out the image. This process can be done with single words, small as they may be—petals, if you will, or whole phrases. Be the flower come to life.

Once the section has been expanded fully, gradually keep the images living invisibly and veil to the appropriate size of the Style.

Here is an example using an excerpt of a momentous speech by Constance in Shakespeare's lesser-known *King John*, from Act III, Sc. 4 (see Figure 2.2).

> But now will canker-sorrow eat my bud
> And chase the native beauty from his cheek
> And he will look as hollow as a ghost,
> As dim and meager as an ague's fit.

Take the word "but" and find its gesture. Feel the negation in it. Move on to…

> "Now"—play with the gesture of this word alone.
> "Canker"—what movement does this word evoke?
> "Sorrow"—what does this conjure?
> "Canker-sorrow"—how do these combine?

Feel the gestures of "will," "chase," "eat," "dim," "meager," "ague," "fit," etc.

Notice the word "bud." Constance is referring to her kidnapped young son, her "bud." Can we imagine the pink cheek of her young son growing hollow as a ghost in a dark prison cell? Physicalize a beautiful young bud beginning to bloom in beauty, then captured, tortured and withering as the darkness of sorrow like a canker sore eats away the bud's petals, stems, and leaves, (the face and body of her boy). Now step into Constance's royal Imaginary Body (Chapter 12) and observe through her eyes that entire scene purely in your imagination. The vividness of the images will radiate through your speech, inspiring your emotional life, awakening the audience's empathy.

Release and restore your artistic world by gathering the images you have played and with appreciation, send them up to your unlimited I-sphere, where they will always be available to you.

Check your commitment to this imaginative play. Moving even the small or seemingly contemporary words will awaken the senses and enliven the entire being so that when veiling (making the movements more subtle), the energy will live palpably in the spoken words of the artist. The artist will be able to fill large gestures of grand Style with comfort and easily shift to more natural techniques as needed. This power will awaken belief and enthusiasm in your artistry.

Look for consonance (repetition of consonant sounds) and play just with the gesture of the alliterated letter to discover the mysteries within: "c" and "k" in canker and cheek; "ch" of chase and cheek; "m" in dim and meager; and "g" in meager and ague. Use your own gestures for the sound or work with Rudolf Steiner's eurythmy.[1]

## Genre

In storytelling, there are four "Styles," that we will refer to as genres: tragedy, drama, comedy, and farce. All of the genres are centered in three sources of conflict or evil. Evil comes from outside forces of gods and nature, between humans, or from within the character. Each genre has its own psychological *presence* associated with it and is, in effect, an archetypal atmosphere.

- See **OR 11.1** for detailed Chekhov approach to these four genres. Learn about the doppelganger, the gremlin and more!

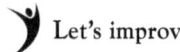 Let's improv

Try the letter etude, speed dating, or one of the previous improvs in different Styles/genres.

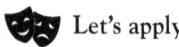 Let's apply

Try some improv and text with the four genres, using the suggested techniques.

## Radiance

The final tool I will address here in detail is that of Radiance (Chapter 13).

The Radiance to which I am now referring addresses the energy pulsing in the performer that is felt by the audience. It is the essence of "star quality." It is what engenders the metaphor of "star." Each one of us has this energy, but for some it is powerful and palpable. For others it is weak, shy, or perhaps even hidden. For some it comes out in certain moments and then hides.

Some of us hide our Radiance when asked to do a Style beyond naturalism for fear of feeling, looking, or being unnatural or foolish. Others of us come alive under the artificial or heightened Style. (See Diamond of Truth #8 on Page 151)

It is important to note that Radiance is an innate gift that is desired by the world, and desired by the artist who dares to act at all. So, building your confidence to radiate is an important task.

1. Fun and love ignite Radiance. All these exercises encourage freedom to fail, to be free and to awaken sleeping ways of expressing yourself with full abandon like a child.
2. Simple exercises such as the Staccato-Legato radiance activation (Stac-Leg 6) will awaken this energy. (See Chapters 13 and 14.)
3. This Radiance can travel from your Ideal Artistic Center in the chest out to the universe (Radiating), or you can draw this Radiance in to your IAC from the universe (Receiving). (See the Actors March in Chapter 12.)
4. There is no correlation between the direction of flow of the Radiance with the degree of power or authority. Glen Close in *Dangerous Liaisons* was a completely Receiving character. Macbeth might be receiving premonitions, Lady M may be radiating her lusty desires and then receiving her haunted guilty nightmares.

Additional Chekhov tools, such as the following, will have great effect as well.

- The actor will more consistently, rapidly, and convincingly "integrate the protocols, and populate their body language with the mannerisms of the era" (Orlandi) with the **Four Brothers of Beauty, Ease, Entirety and Form** (Chapter 8).[2]
- They will hold the authority levels and the grace of the status necessary with **Imaginary Bodies and Centers** (Chapter 12).
- **Inner and outer Tempo and Rhythm** (Chapter 14) training will build the skills to hold still, move swiftly and smoothly, or very slowly and powerfully—all traits that terrify today's non-stop hyper-speed actors.

## Conclusion

Oscar nominee Michael Chekhov was renowned for his classical and clown-like performances. The Oscar winners for lead and supporting acting who had the briefest appearances, to date, were Chekhov-trained artists Patricia Neal (1964) and Beatrice Straight (1977). In the century of Oscars, no one has won with less screen time, male or female as leading and supporting artists. And both are Tony Award winners (1947, 1953) as well. It is clear that *Acting the Michael Chekhov Way* trains you to be ready for any Style on stage or camera. Then with the help of Style specialists and dramaturgs, you can learn the specifics for any given production.

## Summary

1. Believe in your talent regardless of your skill or interest in the various Styles.
2. To expand your work options, learn Chekhov's universal skill-building tools to free your talent for all Styles, whether you feel safer in reality or in pretend.
3. Find one juicy image that unifies all the elements that are important for that Style and hold that in your imagination.

## Notes

1 Eurythmy was a required course at the Michael Chekhov Theatre Studio at Dartington Hall, UK and Ridgefield, CT, 1936–1942. It has performance and therapeutic applications. See www.EurythmyOnline.com
2 Orlandi, Janice, Period-Style Consultant, Michael Chekhov Teacher, Actors Movement Studio, New York, Interview, Oct. 2016. http://actorsmovementstudio.com. Janice Orlandi, a Chekhov-trained Style consultant, conveys the *physical dramaturgy* of the period using Chekhov's catalog of terms and tools.

# Part V

# Transformation: Characterization and Gesture

Want to win awards? Here's a tip: Transformation is the secret ingredient in most highly regarded performances. Characterization is the art of transforming our everyday selves into this one particular character for this one story. Delivering the outrageous pain, rage, or joy of a role is not artistically our aim. It is *how* you reveal this role in a way so specific to this story that it is unlike any other character/any other pain, rage, or joy of any other story. It is unlike anything you have done and unique from the way this role has been done before. In other performances of this role, the artist's objectives and actions may be the same, the motivations and emotions may not change. It is in *who* the character is and *how* they pursue objectives, execute actions, and express or repress emotions that your artistry of "characterization" shines. Every single movement that you make can be an expression of thoughts, feelings, and desires specific to your character. That's a lot of *hows* to choose from!

The many tools on the Chart of Inspired Action provide you with a nearly infinite number of ways to answer "how" does the character look, move, speak, react, think, express, gesture, walk, etc.? You have been diligently observing and recording in your practicing, observing, and applying (POA) and journaling about *how* your everyday self looks, speaks, walks, etc. Identifying, via the Michael Chekhov way, the multitude of *hows* you personally do builds your confidence to discover how you are different from any given role you play. In this difference lies your opportunity for creative expression. You create a whole new being distinct from yourself, and you do so safely and reliably.

Our primary tools for Characterization are Moveable Centers, Imaginary Bodies, and the Trinity of Psychology: Thinking, Feeling, and Willing and Archetypal Characters.

Transformation also comes with Radiating/Receiving, Tempo/Rhythm, Focal Points, and the pinnacle of *Acting the Michael Chekhov Way*: Psychological Gesture. We will cover these here in Part V. Part VI will follow by putting it all together through SynthAnalysis™ and Love.

That may be a lot to digest, but let's get the concepts up on their feet, so to speak, and see what we understand.

# 12
# Transformational characterization: Ideal Self, Centers, Imaginary Body, Trinity of Psychology—Thinking, Feeling, Willing

Bored with just being yourself?

Are you yearning to express a whole new being?

Do you seek artistic transformation as a way to transform audiences?

## The ideal you

 Let's play everyday

Let's begin walking around the space, as we do in daily life, with nothing special going on. As you walk, do you notice a part of your body that tends to draw your attention? Perhaps it seems to lead you, hold you back, or pull you to the left. It may be so subtle you are unsure whether or not there is something there. Imagine you do sense it and begin gradually to lean into it, exaggerating its impact on you. Here's an example on how this is for me.

> ### Titanium stroll
>
> From my days as a stunt woman, performing feats that no smart person would even think of attempting, like crashing into a cliff, my lower spine has suffered, let's say, "intense reorganization." It's now fused with titanium, making me bend forward a bit as I stand, walk, ride, or sit, for that matter. My left hip tightens and can create a slight limp when I do get up and move. My feet land fairly wide apart, so my walk is more like a waddle. Instead of naturally rotating, my hips and shoulders face squarely ahead, so I pull myself forward with my front foot. The movement and weight distribution are hard on my knees, which in turn causes me to favor the one side and go gently into that good night … limpingly. That's what's leading me, the center of my impulses to move around the space. For this exploration, as I exaggerate these idiosyncrasies of my everyday walk, I bend forward and limp more on my left side than I usually do. I imagine my voice emanates from there. If I reach for something, the impulse begins there.

As you travel through space, notice your own energy and way of walking. Where do you usually focus when you walk? How fast or slow is your walk? What do you look at or avoid? How much energy do you feel? What emotions do you usually walk with? Exaggerate each of these things, taking it to a clownish level of extremes. Gradually begin to veil until you appear to be walking "normally" for your everyday self.

Let's walk again; this time, let's pretend you are feeling on top of the world. You exist there. Walk around a bit now, exaggerating the *on-top-of-the-world-ness*. Perhaps it is hipster, cool, suave. Inwardly reflect on these questions: Where do I focus when I walk on *top of the world*? How fast or slow is this walk? What do I look at or avoid? How much energy do I feel? What emotions do I experience on this *top-of-the-world walk*? Now veil this to be your "secret."

Now, switch back to your everyday self as you walk for a minute.
Now, go back to *top of the world*. Vary how much you veil or unveil.
Back to self. Back to *top*...

Now go back to the *top-of-the-world walk*; exaggerate each of these things.

Switch back and forth several times. Notice what happens to yourself, other actors, and to the space around you.

Pause and release.

 *Journal/Discuss/Flyback*

*Make notes in your journal about your own tendencies, and share your observations and responses to these questions. You may decide to ask a trusted friend or mentor to confirm your self-observation.*

Most people's everyday walks focus downward and tend to be *business-y* or lagging. There seems to be little connection to anyone or anything around them. In the top-of-the-world walk, the whole room often gets brighter, and the atmosphere becomes jovial and light. People look at each other, feel happier, bouncier. There is more rotation in their bodies and more ease all around. They feel less tension in the pelvis and shoulders. There is often a bounce or smiling swagger. The shoulders and pelvis rotate more freely in counterbalance, and there may even be a slight overlap of the steps, or the steps fall closer to a center line. The head tends to float, with less forward neck extension. The breath often flows more easily. Some people even hum.

These adjustments come for many people instantly upon imagining this carefree state. When I am *on top of the world*, my stride is shorter and more centered, my hips rotate, and my shoulders rotate in opposition. I have a very smooth gait. My head floats atop the spine. Students say I look younger, more intelligent, more available, and more powerful. I connect more directly and easily with people.

If we, as a culture, were walking more naturally, we would need fewer hip and knee replacements and have a lot less spine pain. When we do this walk, we engage our best selves and instinctively release many of the ingredients in our piece of the pie. We are shifting effortlessly from our everyday self into our artistic self, who is centered in the higher ego or "I."

Let's intentionally combine our Ideal Artistic Center (IAC) with the *top-of-the-world* walk. Tap your IAC if you like, imagining that powerful sun shining in your chest and radiating to your fingertips, head, and feet. It's as if there are no shoulder bones or hips, just a five-pointed star of light body that rotates lightly and easily and counterbalances right from the center point. Now, imagine you can walk on top of the world, and all the energy to do so is coming directly out of the center point in your body.

> ⚛ **Axiom 12.1: One image unites many details.**

I will briefly talk of "health science" to make the above point: no matter what I say here, in the end, simply go back to the image of being on top of the world, having a great day, and these following technicalities will all happen naturally.

Walking has Triplicity, Polarity, and Transformation (TPT).

Walking has three parts: lift, carry, and place. The proper way of walking ergonomically requires moving the shoulders and hips in polarity to each other for upright counterbalancing. When the right foot goes forward, the right shoulder goes back, the left foot behind rolls through the arch to the ball of the foot and propels your whole body onto your right heel as the shoulders rotate, the hips counter-rotate, stepping onto that left heel as the right shoulder is forward. Completing the sequence transforms you from one place to another.

Well, trying to do this process intentionally can be quite mind-boggling and turn into very geeky moments of lumbering along doing the opposite of what is perfectly natural, so trust me—if you really walk as the hipster I-am-so-cool-on-top-of-the-world—you will naturally activate the TPT counterbalanced walk.

How do you feel when you do it? How do others look when they do it? Most will look lively, intelligent, confident, healthy, powerful, and sexy. Is this a good thing?

Yes and no ... we start to see why little girls and little boys, teens, young people, and others might not want to look that powerful, sexy, or confident. But this is what we humans, with our bodies, are naturally designed to be and feel. It is natural for our whole quantum pie to have access and live this way. It would be so much healthier for our entire body. Our breathing, digestion, spines, heart health, etc.

If you look at primitive peoples who live barefoot on uneven terrain carrying jugs of water on their heads up and down hills and valleys without spilling the water, you will see that they move this way. They have amazingly strong spines and feet, and they have excellent balance.

They don't have a whole lot of chiropractors or pain meds. That rotation is the most efficient use of energy for walking. Try crawling, and you will see how vital polarity and rotation are. Many people skip the crawling stage of their infancy, where the rotation is first developed, and rotation and alternation are essential to balancing the hemispheres of your brain. Many toddlers are placed in "walkers" with a wide strap between their legs, teaching them to waddle like me! This sets up a future of impending joint replacements, slower brain connectivity, and all that comes with poor walking habits.

We might call this *top-of-the-world walk* our *ideal universal walk*. It is available to you—how many hours of the day? Yep, 24 is the magic number yet again. You can access this IAC and walk as if you are on top of the world at any time, which brings you that relief and connection with vibrant and vital sun power. You can make it more subtle, but I would work a long time in the exaggerated form before going subtle in order to rewire your "piece of the pie." In other words, fall in love with your top-of-the-world walk and make it a regular practice until it becomes your everyday walk. The transformation you undergo will change how the world sees you as well as how you experience your personal sense of intelligence, emotional availability, and level of authority.

If you embrace this ideal universal walk, your thinking will be clearer. You will experience improvements in other physical areas as well. You will likely gain more confidence in social relationships and cultivate a stronger professional network. Do you want this?

## Journal/Discuss/Flyback

*Make some notes about how you feel walking like a hipster on top of the world.*

### Homeplay

Let's use this ideal universal walk as much as possible in life, but especially when exploring exercises in artist mode. Imagine the impulse for all your exercises emanating from the IAC and traveling through your body as the natural rhythm and forms of your impulses express themselves. I use a little mantra for myself in daily life: Remember to rotate. I allow easy rotation to enter my whole being when I think that.

## Clearing the canvas

Before we take on a character, it is helpful to "clear the canvas," if you will. Our body and Personal Atmosphere (PA) comprise the canvas upon which our lower everyday self is painted. If we want the audience to experience this specific character revealed through our higher ego self, clearing the canvas helps. In some circles, this activity is thought of as neutrality. When acting the Michael Chekhov way, our word choice is ideal **universality**. The concept is that each genetic form contains the potential for an ideal, a diamond of its own design, filled with the complete prism of colors, as unique from another as DNA.

As we have seen in the Quantum Peek chart (Figure 1.2) only one portion of your ideal has been evolving into your personality, which has been imprinting its psychology on your body and vice versa, thus covering your "canvas" with a clearly defined picture. The canvas reveals your colors of posture, habits, mannerisms, personal atmosphere, etc. It has done this by repeatedly eliminating certain shades and patterns and activating others. When we play diligently with the PPEs, we restore our full potential universality, clearing our canvas for our new creations.

I have a hard time with how clearing the canvas has traditionally been attempted using neutrality as an aim. As a clown, mime, or mask artist, most neutrality work that I have done, taught, or experienced leads to a sense of automation, of robotic inhumanity. The process seeks to reduce our habits rather than free our whole being. In the Michael Chekhov way, we are looking to augment our humanity, restoring all the colors to the clear spectrum of the diamond.

We can then find new patterns specific to the character we wish to reveal in the prism of possibilities. Instead of a neutral slate, we are seeking to allow our ideal artistic image to crystalize from our unlimited sphere of archetypes.

## Universal stance

 Let's play universal you

Find a partner who can help you find your ideal universal stance; otherwise, work with a mirror. Generally, I don't encourage having a mirror while playing; however, it can be very useful in this case. (Take a moment to breathe…)

 The Goblet process

Reconnect with the image of the powerful sun streaming from your chest (IAC) out into the cosmos. You are on top of the world. Imagine that your own bright star way out there sends rays of light into you. Allow that light to travel into the fontanelle on top of your head. Let it travel down your spine and into your shoulders, arms, and hands, down into your pelvis, hips, and down each leg. Place your feet parallel to each other, with your ankles directly below your hip bones. Allow your hands to fall by your side with your middle fingers aligning with your ankles. A long stick at your side may help you experience whether you are aligned and centered. Place the stick next to your ankle and see if it lines up with your pant seam and middle fingers if the palm is flat against thigh. Perhaps you are leaning forward in the pelvis or back. Is the lean from the hip, waist, shoulders or ankles? If your palms are facing back, the thumb will ideally line up with the side seam of a pant leg, and that same seam will fall outside the center of the ankle.

If your hands are falling forward, your shoulders may be rolling in, or you may be leaning forward. This is the most common adjustment people need. Many of us lean forward at the hips and have to counterbalance in the shoulder by relinquishing the arch in the thoracic section of our spine between our shoulder blades. This causes the bottom of the rib cage to extend forward. Try using the Pilates idea of knitting the ribs together at the diaphragm and bringing them closer to the spine. Remember to imagine your energy/light/life body making these changes first. This will make it easier for your physical body to adjust and retain your ideal form.

## ✒ Journal/Discuss/Flyback

*Note the adjustments you need to make to find this on top-of-the-world universal stance. Do you need to lean back a little? Drop your left shoulder? Turn your toes in or out a bit? Roll your shoulders back to keep your hands from hanging forward? Do you need to lower or lift your chin and draw your head back from thrusting forward? Unlock your knees? Take turns with someone, helping them get a sense of their ideal form and the necessary adjustments.*

When we are working in class or rehearsal, this ideal stance is the form to find when you enter the state of readiness to begin. This state of readiness is one of three levels of attention (see Introduction) that we want to engage in our play together.

Try walking as your ideal universal self now with the Actor's March.

Michael Chekhov had his students do a daily activity: *the Actor's March*. Seemingly simple, it is a highly charged activity that can carry us to much greater creativity, physical universality, and joy, building charisma and star quality. It can be used before or after a class, rehearsal, upon rising, before sleeping, or whenever you need a pick-me-up! Lots of us like to gesture while doing this, described below. In Chekhov's day it was done moving in a large circle; however, you can feel free to fill the space as you wish.

##  Let's play the Actor's March

Begin by becoming aware of the golden forces of light within your Ideal Artistic Center.

Imagine being led by your IAC as you walk powerfully and gracefully through the space, often this is done in a circle. As you speak, keep your imagination highly active in visualizing the power within the words. Daily commitment to the *Actor's March* is a path to building charisma and star quality.

## The Actor's March

### I AM a creative artist

This statement zaps any clouds of doubt about our talent. When spoken from the IAC, it truly empowers those who say it with commitment and vision.

### I have the ability to radiate

This statement declares the truth of your ability to give and receive this talented creative artistry. Affirming this is important because we are not actors unless we have an audience to whom we can give and from whom we can receive.

### Lifting my arms above me, I soar above the earth.

In this statement, we commit to our highest goals with passion. We declare our freedom from earthly limitations, expanding physically into space. We can lift our arms as we speak this phrase.

### Lowering my arms, I continue to soar.

Here, we affirm our ability to veil our power and talent without diminishing it. We can lower our physical arms while keeping the arms of our energy body lifted.

*In the air moving around my head and shoulders, I experience the power of thoughts.*

We now affirm that the elements are supporting us, and we remind ourselves that we have strong forces of thought as a resource, and we know where they are located in us physically. We can move our physical arms around our heads in linear forms if we wish.

*In the air moving around my chest, I experience the power of feelings.*

We now affirm that the elements are supporting us, and we remind ourselves that we have strong forces of feelings as a resource, and we know where they are located in us physically. Here we can move our arms in swirling curves around our chest.

*In the air moving around my legs and feet, I experience the power of will.*

We now affirm that the elements are supporting us, and we remind ourselves that we have strong forces of will as a resource, and we know where they are located in us physically. This triplet aligns the trinity of our psychology, helping to bring it into balance. We will discuss this toward the end of this chapter. Here we can strengthen our step and move our arms below our waist with strength.

### I AM that I AM

This final statement affirms your creative individuality. This fuels your star quality, your love, and passion. The sharing of your creativity awakens it in audiences and brings forth healing within you and within them. Here, we can pause with our arms expanding outward.

---

#### Artist to artist chat

Wow! It always amazes me that Chekhov taught this poetic mantra to his students a century ago! It's just the thing to help when self-doubt creeps in. I don't know about you, but I have often felt bullied and challenged by people when I say I am an actor. "Oh, what have you done? What's your day job? What makes you think you're so special? Better get some other skills to help you make a living." All sorts of stuff like that. It hurts and is a bit scary too, because what if they are right? "Why don't you do something important?" Grrrr.

Michael Chekhov went through such severe doubt about whether acting was important that he walked off the Moscow Art Theatre stage in the fall of 1917, at a time when he was a superstar with curtain calls hours long. He left mid-show, nervously laughing, and didn't return for a year. His traumatic breakdown was caused by a series of wars, epidemics, suicides, loss of family members, and political upheaval that was destroying the culture. It made being a famous actor seem ridiculous. His profound studies into the spiritual and cultural role of artists allowed him to reenter society and return to stage and film a year later.

---

Recovery became a turning point in how to train so that, as artists, we can fulfill this higher mission. When we train, we are actors in training. We are not trying to be actors. We are actors first. Actors are creative artists. With every look, breath, and movement, *we write the invisible text*,[1] the unspoken word, that resounds within the hearts of the spectators. This is what the playwright, director, and designers cannot do, and why Chekhov urges us to believe that the "actor is the theatre." So, when we say, "I am a creative artist," we truly are and encourage every cell of our body, mind, and spirit to live and love accordingly.

And here's some bonus news we can take joy in knowing and sharing: *Acting the Michael Chekhov Way* is training you for a strong future anywhere in the world in any profession. The World Economic Forum 2023 forecast the ten most essential skills sought by employers by 2027. Here, we are cultivating at least eight.

> Analytical thinking is considered a core skill…. Creative thinking, another cognitive skill, ranks second, ahead of three self-efficacy skills—resilience, flexibility, and agility; motivation and self-awareness; and curiosity and lifelong learning…. Dependability and attention to detail rank seventh, behind technological literacy. The core skills top 10 is completed by two attitudes relating to working with others—empathy and active listening and leadership and social influence—as well as quality control.[2]

## What does "character" mean for casting?

For professional purposes, let's look at some sticky situations we may face. To a significant degree, the audience unconsciously goes through a similar set of questions that a director or casting director goes through consciously.

The first question casting/directors have is, "Are they the basic type for the character?" Next, "Can they do what the story requires of the character, physically and emotionally on cue?"

After that, it usually falls into the matter of charisma. "Do they have "IT?" "Do I like them?"

Here's a hypothetical unspoken dialogue between "them" and "us."

> Them: Just be yourself in the situation. That way, even if you get nervous and don't act well, you will still always at least be the type.
>
> Us: Well, I can be anyone you want me to be, and I am very different depending on who I am with, where I am, and what we are doing. (I am a very different person when I am out on my motorcycle at a rally than when I am teaching a master class in Milan.)
>
> And besides that, I am an ACTOR—I want to transform into what I am not.
>
> Them: Well, you look like a housewife.
>
> Us: Oh, I am supposed to play the self that I look like I am. Ok. Playing the same "self" based on what I look like, laughing and crying the same way on cue, becomes seriously dull in a very short time. What they are really looking for is the archetype of a housewife.
>
> Them: We don't want you to play a character. People won't believe it.
>
> Us: Aha! They have confused characterization with caricature. No problem. *Acting the Michael Chekhov Way* trains us to create beings who are both wholly unique and archetypally recognizable without being stereotypes. We learn how to express these characters truthfully for the style of the production. If needed, we transform so subtly that anyone who asks us to "just be you" may not even consciously realize that we have transformed. When we transform from our everyday self to a multidimensional character, we cross the threshold from ordinary into extraordinary. This is the world of radiant peak performance. That's when we have "IT."
>
> Them: Wow! You got it.

Now that we know how to create a crystal clear canvas by awakening our ideal universal self, let's dive into the art of transformational characterization.

## Primary Tools for Characterization (#12)

### Discover Moveable Centers

 Let's play discover Moveable, imaginary, or character Centers

Standing in your ideal artistic stance, imagine an impulse in the center of your chest to transform, to play "elsewhere." Pretend that ideal, radiant, sun-like center becomes a yellow Pac-Man, gobbling gleefully through your arteries into your left hip. Feel free to exaggerate this and maybe add sound effects to make it very obvious. It settles in the left hip, leading you this way and that. It wants to talk right from there. Allow your voice to say some numbers or letters right from that yellow gobbling Pac-Man hip.

Imagine that Pac-Man morphs into a jagged dagger thrusting into everyone. Follow that impulse. Allow the voice of that center to emanate right from the dagger hip. Your arms move from there; your eyes look from there.

That dagger morphs into a swirling cloud that floats above your head, hovering about six inches above you. What happens now?

As you play, allow the image of the Moveable Center (MC) to remain the inner focus of your mind. Free yourself from intellectually deciding what it will do or how it will move you. Allow yourself to be surprised by refreshing the image inside you whenever it starts to fade. Pretend it has its own thoughts, feelings, and desires emanating from its location, and all you do is follow it.

Play with as many of these moving centers as time permits. Release and restore your image to the sphere.

 Journal/Discuss/Flyback

*What did you discover with Moveable Centers? Were you able to allow the MCs to influence your voice and movements? Was your whole body engaged?*

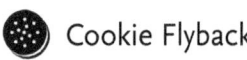 Cookie Flyback

*What did you like overall? What would you do differently? What was your favorite moment?*

## Let's discuss Moveable Centers

The term "center" means the point from which our impulses radiate. Gaze into your imagination or into the world around you, focusing on a person or object. Can you sense that there is a particular locus or power point of energy of that person or even "thing," such as a tree or a truck, that seems to lead them?

Each center has three elements: location, quality, and mobility. Each element influences how the image awakens your creativity. Did you notice that the yellow Pac-Man in the left hip inspired a very different character than the dagger in the same location? Choose juicy images (yellow Pac-Man gobbling, jagged dagger thrusting, swirling cloud hovering) that activate qualities, sensations, and gestures.

>  Axiom 12.2: What to do when imagination fails? Lead it with questions.

When we are seeking to awaken our creativity, our best beginning starts with asking good questions. To explore the possibilities of a Moveable Center, we can lead our imagination with three questions whose answers are as unlimited as our imagination:

1. Location: Where is it (e.g., inside, around, or another person)?
2. Quality: What is it (e.g., sensations, textures, animals, or images)?
3. Mobility: Does it move (e.g., stationary, spinning, shooting, pulsing, or traveling)?

>  Axiom 12.3: Each Moveable Center has three elements:
> - Location
> - Quality
> - Mobility

When we give our Moveable Center a name with its location, quality, and mobility, we are "baptizing" the MC. Once we have baptized the MC with its name, it seems like the image gains more clarity and power in our imaginations. This concept of baptizing names is used in Atmospheres and will be used much more as we go forward toward SynthAnalysis™, Chapter 19.

 Let's improv Moveable Centers

Randomly choose an MC—its location, its quality, and its mobility. State your choices out loud or jot them down, even when playing solo. This helps us be very clear and specific. Choose your improv structure:

1. Choose an étude with no words, solo or with partners
2. Choose a setting with only the Atmosphere as a given. Allow the MCs to inspire the who and what.
3. Choose a relationship and allow the MCs to inspire the Atmosphere (ATMO) and the *what*.

 The Goblet process

**Center** before beginning; ground yourself; align and open yourself. Inhale, imagining the MC forming in the location, and with the quality and mobility you chose. As you exhale, allow its impulses to radiate through your body until the center begins to lead you across the room. Perhaps it brings forth a little laugh or giggle. Then, let it speak a phrase or two to find its voice. When ready, begin the improv. Remember, ideally, all improv uses imaginary character names, careful listening, and follows the "Yes, and…" guidelines. In this case, you might listen and speak from your MC.

Release and restore when done.

 Journal/Discuss/Flyback

*Begin your Flyback by restating the description of your center. Were you able to allow the center to lead you through the improv? Did you focus on one aspect, or were you able to retain all three elements? Were you allowing the image to inspire every body part and your voice?*

 *Overall, what worked? What would you do differently? What was your fave moment?*

 Try several improvs with MCs to build your skills. Repeat the same scenarios as above with different MCs.

- See **Kilroy Improv** Chapter 8 for relentless fun!

### How do we choose a Moveable Center?

When applying MCs to a specific character, we will want to take much more into consideration than randomly choosing a center. Certainly, the style, era, and type of character need to be considered. How then, do we know what to choose?

Here is a "choice-making" pattern we will use for many tools based on the process of awakening the imagination by Leading it with Questions (LQs).

 **Axiom 12.4: Answer Leading Questions with the 3Is:**
- Inspiration
- Imagination
- Intellect

**Inspiration:** When we ask an LQ and suddenly a very clear answer appears, and we know it is a perfect fit, we call it Inspiration. We love it when this happens. Then, we apply this inspiration to our work and flyback to see if it inspires us. And if it doesn't, we turn to our next path.

**Imagination:** With this approach, we engage the Goblet process. We center, ground, and open to the unlimited sphere of our imagination, holding the question in our IAC. This unlimited I-sphere is also known as the higher "I" or "eye" or "ego." Then, we wait in a process known as an *active artistic gaze*. Opening all of our senses, we inwardly repeat the question in our IAC and scan with our "eye" for any impulses, images, ideas, smells, sounds, or anything at all that appears before our gaze. We can accept the first images or discard them and ask for more. We can add additional information to our question, like "Can you zoom into the hands for me?" or "What if the color is red instead of blue?" When something makes you happy, apply it to see if it inspires you. If not, return to the Goblet process and ask your higher ego for more options, changing the questions as needed. Pretending to get answers works! Never fear if your imagination doesn't deliver you happiness, for logic is here.

**Intellect:** By asking a series of logical questions, we can intellectually craft and try options.

The questions we would ask of our logical self will become more apparent as we learn more characterization tools such as Imaginary Body (IB), Trinity of Psychology, Archetypal Character (AC), and Radiating/Receiving. Depending on the relationship a character may or may not have to these tools, their center may be quite logical; then, you can try the rational approach by using location, quality, and mobility as well as their opposites by using the logic of TPT. This intellectual approach will help you make intelligent choices that may satisfy you. Or they may bore you because they fail to surprise you. When this happens, Flyback to see if you are truly imagining the center and let it rule as the tool. Or are you controlling the center to create a specific effect?

 **Let's apply the Moveable Center**

The general plan is to select a character from a monologue or scripted scene. Baptize your MC. Put it on and play with it until you can sense you are allowing it to lead you. Then begin your text. Release and restore. Flyback. Try a new MC for each step below and repeat.

Follow the 3Is to choose your center.

1. Start by pretending that you are inspired by exactly what it is, or use a baptized center you have improvised with.
2. Imagine the Goblet and active gaze process, having the character show you its center. Then, you baptize and imitate it until you feel you are doing what you saw/felt/imagined.
3. Now, logically think about who the character is, what they do, what their personality is like, and where their center would logically be. Check the script for what people say about your character. What body parts are observed as intense and identifiable (Cyrano's nose). Baptize the MC and apply it.

## Journal/Discuss/Flyback

Having tried all 3Is, Flyback, in addition to the core questions of whether you sustained the tool's rule and full-bodied inspiration, also compare how the three different centers impacted the scene and affected how the character was.

> ### Homeplay: POA
>
> Spend some time exploring where your center is. Can you baptize it? Ultimately, we want to compare it to our character's center. If we don't know our center is already in our forehead, and decide the character's is there too, we might overact it. If our center is already very similar to the character's, we might not need to focus on this tool because the tool is designed to help us transform. However, if our center is very different from the character's, we might choose to put extra time into rehearsing with the Moveable Center to make sure we keep our personal habitual center from slipping into our performance.
>
> Bring your active gaze into the world. Baptize the centers of friends, characters in videos, and passersby. The more you play with identifying and baptizing centers you see in the world around you, the faster you baptize the centers that appear in your imagination. You will see the extraordinary range that is truthfully in the world and thus trust extremes when they appear in your "I." The more you have imitated what you have observed, the more fully you will imitate your "Is" offerings. In short, play with your POA process, and you will become adept at connecting very quickly with your higher ego.

### What happens to my IAC when I have an MC?

The relationship between the IAC and the Moveable Center is interesting because we aim for the artist's IAC to be active while allowing the character's MC to inhabit the physical body. So, while the actor seeks to perform through their own balanced, conflict-free Ideal Artistic Center, in terms of dramatic impact, the character's center is the most exciting when off-center.

### Centers in a larger context

In a play, in someone's home, or at any given business, there will be a center from which the activity emanates. We can see it in architecture, design, games, and everywhere in nature. Understanding this will become useful when we explore SynthAnalysis™ in Chapter 19 and in the following book, *Directing the Michael Chekhov Way*.

### Discover Imaginary Bodies

 Let's play Imaginary Bodies

Define your own kinesthetic circle in the space. Imagine an adjoining bubble in front of you.

 The Goblet process

Use the Goblet process, as we did with ATMOs, from your ideal universal stance, connecting deeply with your IAC and the powerful light within. Radiate that light deep into the earth to anchor you. Allow your radiance to travel upward through the ceiling, through the ozone layer into that amazing, unlimited sphere of imagination, your higher "I." Allow this revitalizing force access to you during this discovery; use your eyes as suits you best for imagining—open, in soft focus, or closed.

If you aren't getting any images from your I-sphere, just pretend you are, and make up the answers to these questions that will lead your imagination. Using your active *artistic gaze*, imagine somewhere up there is a character who wants to meet you. As you meet, you see and sense the body of this character. Then, like in *Star Trek*, you beam it down into the kinesphere in front of you. First, the feet appear. What do they look like? Maybe they are bare, worn, aged, and tan. Then, the legs appear. What do they look like? Are they straight or bow-legged, thin or fleshy? What do the muscles look like? Now, the torso appears. What gender is it? What are the genitals like? The buttocks? The navel? The belly? How healthy are the organs inside? How is the spine? What is the waist like? Are they clothed? How so? What kind of chest do they have? How is their heart? Their shoulders, neck, jawline, mouth, lips, ears, nose, eyes, eyebrows, forehead, hair? Clothes, jewelry, arms, elbows, wrists, hands, fingers. Are there scars? What else?

Pretend you can rotate the character in your imagination or actually walk around them in the sphere. What do they look like from all angles?

Now, slip out of your own energy body and into theirs, putting it on one part at a time, stepping into the feet, legs, and torso like a giant Halloween costume. Allow this body to move you as you begin to travel through space. It is as if this Imaginary Body is your puppeteer, and you follow its impulses and guidance for movement and speech. Allow your expression of the IB to be significantly unveiled, and when you feel you are fully responding to its impulses, try veiling by degrees to make it more and more subtle.

As you move through space in your IB, ask it to laugh or giggle through you. Then, repeat the beginning of the silent question aloud by saying, "My name is …" Repeat this, "My name is…" in the IB's voice until an answer flows out. Make it up if one doesn't appear. Follow that with several more identity statements: "What I really like is…" "What scares me most is …" "My biggest dream is …" "I hate it when…" "My favorite food is …."

##  Let's improv IB

If working in an ensemble, improvise with your colleagues. If playing solo, try an étude or improvise a monologue out of the answers to the statements.

After you explore this character, when you're ready, peel it off of you, restore it to the I-sphere, and repeat the sequence with a new character. If you have a leader, the leader might describe a character that you then imagine and adopt.

## Journal/Discuss/Flyback

*Were you able to work with the image from the higher sphere? In what ways do you imagine? Visually? Kinesthetically? Auditorily? Any way is good, even making it up. Were you able to allow the IB to play you? To sense its impulses and allow your body to respond? Were you able to stay concentrated on the IB, or did you lose it or part of it?*

### Let's discuss IB

Have you had to audition with someone who couldn't act? Ever done a monologue where there is an invisible partner or two that you need to imagine? Ever get to play a character who was shorter or taller or had a different shape? An animal, alien, or cartoon? Someone with an impediment, an illness? Someone older or younger?

This tool of the Imaginary Body is perfect for working in all those conditions. We can wear an Imaginary Body or body part or react to an invisible one we imagine in space. If we need to look at a broomstick with a sign that says "HULK" taped onto it on a green screen set, we will be prepared. As we discussed in the section on Style, there are many roles and stories that deal with non-humans and otherly-abled humans, and we need to play them truthfully. We cannot just put on a putty nose and play Cyrano without filling the nose with living energy. Even voice-over artists for animé can put on the Imaginary Body and deliver better performances.

Every character has a unique physical form, just as each human does. When we imagine what this is, we are searching for the Imaginary Body. Using the IB technique provides the artist a singular point of concentration that unites all characterization elements.

Have you ever met someone who seemed much taller or shorter than they actually were? Very often, this is because we each have an image of our own body, which can impact how people perceive themselves. Actual studies have been done measuring the effect of IB on self-perception and on others' perceptions, showing a distinct impact when using IB. It is a powerful and fun tool.

We can picture that this IB already exists objectively in the sphere of imagination, the world of images that envelops the earth just beyond its ozone layer. The images are ready and willing to be expressed through our artistic being. When they come through your body, they blend with your highest self and express themselves through you as your creative individuality. Our goal is to allow them to "play" us as fully as possible. All of the PPEs and the emotional tools have prepared you for this breadth of potential expression. This inspiration can come from objects, animals, architecture, portraits, music, and other art and life forms.

There are many, many ways to play with this wonderful toy.

##  The Goblet process

Here is the basic sequence:

1. Invite the image to appear and study it with your Artistic Gaze.
2. Ask *leading questions* to help "see" or "sense" the body: What are the feet like? Etc.
3. You can start with whatever body part reveals itself first. If nothing pops right out, we recommend starting from the ground up or going from the top down. This gives a logical system to follow in your imagination.
4. You can imagine the whole body objectively and then put it on or put each body part on directly as you discover them. Sometimes, we can only imagine one small part, and it is enough.
5. Put on the IB or a part of it and play.
6. Remember to disconnect and restore your universal self; send the image to the world of imagination, where it will always be available if needed.
7. As you repeatedly access the same IB over a rehearsal period, it can quickly appear with an inhale.

 **Axiom 12.5: The image is subject to your will.**

There is no direction that your character will not do, because it must respond to your will. This means if you are given a direction that seems wrong or undoable, it is most likely that the direction has scared you in some way. Find the Beauty, make friends with the direction, and invite the character to show you **how** it would take the direction rather than **if**. Struggling with direction is usually a lower ego challenge. If you still disagree with a direction after following the above suggestions, consider reviewing the SynthAnalysis™ of the story to see how the direction makes sense to the larger whole. If not, in private, consider making your well-prepared case to the stage manager, who can pass it on to the director. In any case, embrace the final direction fully as if it is perfect so you can fully commit. Directors want the show to work, so they will usually respect an insightful contribution if presented in a respectful way. Build relationships.

## Additional tips for IB

a. Focusing on IB will often instantly produce a Moveable Center and vice versa. Therefore, one doesn't need to do both.
b. The image is responsive to direction, so if you wish to change something that the image presents, ask it to show you what it would be like to be taller, younger, etc. This is important because you must adapt to the needs of the director, text, blocking, etc. The image is always subject to your *will* and must respond.
c. For historical characters, use your creative gaze first to garner as much from your higher eye and then study your research materials and adapt each element or the entire expression. Put on the IB using portraits or photos.
d. Sketches are often available for you to play for cartoon and sci-fi characters.
e. Drawing your own body as you imagine it is a great process to do as a baseline.

## Journal/Discuss/Flyback

*Take some time to review the Chart of Inspired Action and the tools you have already learned. Can you see how having done the PPEs; Three Sister Sensations (3Ss); Qualities and Sensations (Q&S); Beauty, Ease, Entirety, and Form (BEEF); ATMOs; IAC; and MC all prepare you for IB? Flyback on your IBs and describe how Expanding or Contracting they are. Or are they Molding, Flowing, Flying, or Radiating? What Archetypal Gestures (AGs) tend to live in them?*

 Let's play character self-portrait

Gather your drawing supplies and some paper. It's great to have several different kinds of supplies like thin colored markers, colored chalk, pens, crayons, and pencils. If you are working on a scene or play and doing this in a group, position yourself across the room from your primary scene partner.

Choose the character you wish to draw… Wait, are you thinking, "Help, I can't draw! My drawing is worse than a kindergartener's! All I can do is bad stick figures!" Well, guess what! It's your lucky day, because it isn't you who will draw. It's the character creating their own self-portrait. Yes, so that's why you have multiple art supplies; it isn't up to you to decide which ones to use.

 The Goblet process

**Center,** ground, and open to your higher I while sitting with utensils and paper in front of you. Invite the IB of the character to come down upon you and sense it is settling in. Perhaps your eyes are closed or soft focus. When the IB is solidly on in your imagination, allow it to open your eyes and reach a utensil with your hand. Allow it to draw itself. Let go of your own idea of what the character looks like. What it draws may be symbolic, like a tornado or a plant. Keep allowing it to draw itself. Pause and reconnect through your IAC as needed to reactivate the IB. When done, have the character sign its own name, then release and restore the image, and you add your name to the paper.

Tape the drawing up near your rehearsal area (see Figure 12.1).

# Transformational Characterization 181

*Figure 12.1* Imaginary Bodies of characters drawn by scene partners.

 Let's apply IB

Now is the perfect time to rehearse the text for the IB you have drawn. Follow the ground, center, and opening Goblet process while gazing at your drawing. Rehearse the text first very unveiled, overexaggerating the IB, and then gradually veil to the style of the text. Release and restore.

Swap your drawing with another drawing, possibly a cartoon or another IB.

Play with your scene, taking an IB from earlier. Play with an animal, object, or force of nature.

##  Journal/Discuss/Flyback

*Were you able to allow the IB to change the scene or monologue? Did the tempo/rhythm/places of pause and points of emphasis change? What did you discover?*

> *Overall, what did you like about IBs and how you played with them? What would you do differently next time? What was your favorite moment?*

---

### Homeplay: IB

Observe some elements of nature, such as flowers, trees, or architecture, draw them and put on their IBs and play.

## IB for life

How we perceive ourselves changes how others see us. At certain times, if we feel uncomfortable in our bodies, we could be radiating mixed messages to everyone around us. Is this what we want?

> ### Smilin' Jan
>
> Jan, a very tall and large female friend, worked in an office with many other women. Jan was not perceived by many to be beautiful. Her size made her look intimidating, and she was lonely. Jan didn't understand why the other women would avoid her and not be friendly to her. One day, she was in a stall in the ladies' room, unbeknownst to two of the women, when Jan heard them talking about her. They said they were scared of her and thought she didn't like any of them. At that moment, Jan realized she had a very different perception of her own body from what the world saw. She was yearning for connection and learned that because of her height and bone structure, she appeared to them to be frowning. Jan realized she needed to overcome her shyness, so she smiled and said hello first. She had to put on the IB of the friendly initiator of conversation. Jan smiled her way to many rewarding friendships and a lively social life.

Our self-image can affect our mental, emotional, and physical health and happiness. I have never met a person who had absolutely no insecurities about their looks. As a society, we hope to overcome body shaming and all that comes with it. We have also made some progress in expanding our social awareness. However, our inner judge and critic must be transformed into accepting our bodies as beautiful and perfect. We can use Imaginary Bodies to help us rebuild our sense of self and clear the old thoughts out of our piece of the pie. Observe someone you have judgments about. Stop. Breathe. Now, put on their IB. See what it is like to walk a mile in their body. Can we feel more compassion and empathy for them now?

- See **Kilroy Improv** Chapters 9 and 10 for creating from portraits, costumes, and objects, as well as more about IB for life.

## Let's discuss Archetypal Characters

How do you feel about type casting, my dear colleague? If the idea makes your inner two-year-old throw a tantrum, perhaps we can fall in love with the problem. Do you feel type-casting limits your opportunities to play different kinds of characters? If so, fantastic, because what you are feeling is your artistic desire for transformation. The reality is that storytelling requires a certain amount of coherence to tell the characters apart. Each character will fall into some sort of identifiable type. It is through these identities and their clashes that the audience can establish a relationship with the story and invest themselves in the story's players. There are forces of evil and good that battle each other, those who get hurt along the way, those who witness, and those who save the day. By nature, they have certain qualities or tendencies toward behaviors. We know them as archetypes. Their presence allows a story to have universal appeal to the spectator.

>  Axiom 12.6: The presence of Archetypal Characters creates universality.

In this context, the word *archetype* is used as something from the universal ideal realm that represents the classic qualities the ideal version of this type might have. The word *archetype* could apply to gesture (AG), atmosphere (ATMO), or person/character (AC) so in *Acting the Michael Chekhov Way*, here we are referring to the archetypal personality, profession, relationship, or essence a person might have. For example, the teacher, parent, thief, military leader, and healer archetypes can be found throughout all cultures and within all age groups, and each has a set of similar virtues regardless of race, creed, gender, identity preference, era, location, etc. Each one of us has access to all ACs in our higher self. Our lower everyday self, our piece of the pie, may use just a few of them, which may or may not match what we look like. Suppose we want to audition for a military or royal leader AC but most likely won't be cast because it is so different from what we are usually asked to play. We can use this technique to activate that AC in our repertoire of expression and convey it powerfully enough to overcome the limits of our looks.

Michael Chekhov encourages us to explore fairy tales and Shakespeare to deepen our understanding of archetypes.

If you are always cast as "the _____ type," you will do well to fall in love with your type and grow very curious about how to express it uniquely with each opportunity. You are by no means limited to the type your body suggests. However, bursting through the type-casting process will require dedication and stamina. By understanding the energy patterns present in the archetypes you look like you can have, you can embody them truthfully. Then, using MC, IB, and Thinking, Feeling, Willing (TFW, covered next in this chapter), you will be able to express the same AC in a gazillion different ways. When you get great at playing that type with your creative individuality radiating with confidence, people will want to give you more opportunities for various types. This is how you use type-casting as a springboard into a full, transformational career rather than a prison of self-repetition.

Jack Colvin[3] suggested four major Archetypal Characters in most films and television shows. Whether or not this is true for all storytelling, the concept is worth considering. The four major ACs are the hero, the villain, the victim, and the bystander/witness.

Indeed, most bodies can be typed into one or more of these categories. both "leading" actors and the "character" actors are easily placed into these categories. While I believe the best artists are all character actors, defining ourselves as a lead or supporting character is old-fashioned; nonetheless, knowing what the body suggests as its primary archetypes will give us insight into how others will generally want to cast us. Again, embrace your type with beauty and spin it into opportunity.

> ### A hair too long
>
> During the 1980s and '90s, I was such a chameleon that I had to teach the casting people how to type me. To some, I was a dangerous bombshell with wild red hair, and that worked to get me occasional villain parts in movies like *The Last Dragon* or roles like an assassin on *As the World Turns*. On the other hand, I had a very "commercial" look like a mom if my hair was cut a certain length. I was never a mom in real life, yet I could count on making a living playing that archetype. Once my hair got to my shoulders, I no longer looked like the bystander/witness/mom. My bookings dropped accordingly. That short hair also worked for smart, powerful women like doctors and bankers. I needed to choose whether I wanted to fall in love with my "nice and ordinary" castability and pay my rent or enjoy my cascading and apparently villainous red hair and go back to waiting on tables. My hair stayed short all the way to the bank. Through trial and error and a clear headshot marketing approach based on the archetypes, I made a living for 30 years in New York and Hollywood.
>
> I will share more about using archetypes for Headshotology in *Applying the Michael Chekhov Way*.

Let's take the ACs further. There are many personality profiles such as the zodiac, tarot, Meyers-Briggs, Enneagram, mythological and religious deities, Human Design, and by profession or role/relationship in life. Any of these can be used to identify the qualities or essence of an archetype.

We sometimes describe this essence as a "ness."

When we play different types, the "ness" of the type can live in the personal atmosphere. For example, every doctor character must have "doctor-ness," each law enforcer must have "enforcer-ness," and each victim must have "victim-ness" for us to relate to the character in its designated role in the storytelling process. While keeping the archetypal essence in the Personal Atmosphere (PA), the actor can individuate the character through other characterization tools to avoid clichés.

Speaking of clichés or stereotypes, remember Triplicity, Polarity, and Transformation? These laws of composition help us realize that each archetype has a single, perfect expression of its highest aspects and two expressions of its opposite or polarity. This means there can be a range in our choice of three versions of any archetype: the good version and two evil versions, where there is too much or not enough of the *good* version. The perfect parent, the abandoning parent (not enough), the controlling parent (too much). As we play with the archetypes, TPT helps us explore the shadows as they assure us that we don't fall into one-dimensional characters. An example of contemporary use of archetypes can be found in animation and superhero mythologies. There are many TV shows with lots of superheroes who have plenty of flaws. While they may save the day, they are constantly struggling to find the balance of their good powers to make up for their failings.

### Journal/Discuss/Flyback

*Generate a list of a dozen archetypes and create the three aspects of each: the ideal balanced version (loving parent), the shadow with too much of the essence (controlling), and the shadow with too little (abandoning) for each.*

---

### Homeplay: POA

Find examples of at least three archetypes and their shadows in plays, films, or TV shows.

---

### Let's improv AC

Choose an archetype. Identify its two shadows and their contrasting light. Establish a basic location and era.

Use the Goblet process to center, ground, and open yourself to the sphere. Bring the IB of the archetype into a Personal Atmosphere bubble before you. Step into it and fill the air with the archetype. When ready, begin an improv solo or with one or two artists, first as the ideal balanced expression of the archetype. After one or two minutes, switch into one of the shadows for a minute or two and then to the other shadow. Conclude with the balanced version. Release and restore when complete.

### Journal/Discuss/Flyback

*How was it? Were you able to find the extremes of the archetype while retaining the essence of the type? What would you do differently? Does this remind you of anything from a story or life?*

### Let's apply AC

Explore your text and select three possible archetypes that might fit. Explore each archetype by discovering it in the era of the play. For example, Hamlet as the prince, son, and lover, and Ophelia as the daughter, lover, and virgin. After becoming familiar with the IB and PA of the archetype, rehearse the text, focusing on one type at a time. Allow your blocking to change if the archetype inspires you to do so. If you like one in particular, bring in the polarities. Perhaps play the narcissistic royal, abandoned child, reluctant lover, or the seducer. Release and restore. Flyback.

- See **OR 12.0** for Archetype ORIGINS—a deeper discussion on the overall concept of Archetypal Characters and their application
- See **OR 12.1** For in-depth explorations of archetypal characters on your feet

## Discover archetypal objects as Imaginary Bodies

 Let's play Stick Ball Veil (SBV)

For this game, it's really fun if you have access to three items, enough for each artist to share:

1. Straight sticks: three-foot long, ¾–1 inch wide wooden dowels are ideal as they are the same you might use for the advanced tossing exercises
2. Bouncy balls, similar to tennis balls
3. Flowy veils or scarves

Let's start with the sticks. And please remember: safety first! Find space in the room to explore a stick in any way possible. Wonder in curiosity: What is archetypal about it? What makes it a stick and not a hammer or a brush? What is present in every stick? What is the essence of a stick?

When you think you understand the stick, set it aside and adopt its IB. Begin to walk and perhaps even mingle and greet others as a stick with a stick voice and stick movements. Perhaps you test it out on a line of text? When you are satisfied with your stick, release and restore the image. Clear the physical sticks from the playing space and bring out the bouncy balls.

As with the sticks, explore the bouncy balls. What is archetypal about a ball? What makes it a ball and not an egg or a pinecone? What is present in every ball? What is ball-ness? When you have ball-ness, adopt it in an Imaginary Body, mingle, and greet others like a ball. Use ball moves and ball voice. Try the same line of text. When you have gotten a well-rounded experience with that, release and restore. Clear the physical balls from the space and bring out the scarves and veils.

Explore the flowing veils and how they move through the air. What is archetypal about a veil? What makes it a veil and not a towel or a tablecloth? What is present in every veil? What is veil-ness? When you have veil-ness, adopt it in an Imaginary Body and mingle and greet others as a veil with veil-y moves and voice. How does that line of text come veiling out of you? When you have gotten a well-rounded experience with that, release and restore. Clear the physical veils from the space.

## *Journal/Discuss/Flyback*

*What are your observations about this stick, ball, veil exercise? Can you feel there are three very different ways of operating in the world? Can you relate to one of them more than the others? Does one of them feel more foreign to you?*

## Let's improv SBV

Improvise a monologue/dialogue about the weather. If partners are available, teams of three are ideal. Player A starts as a stick, player B as a ball, and player C as a veil. Switch to the next object after 30 to 45 seconds or when a leader calls "Switch." Eventually, players can switch when they wish, with the guideline that no two players are using the same object for their IB. Release and restore when complete.

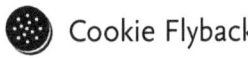 Cookie Flyback

Follow with your cookie Flyback.

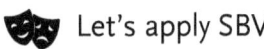 Let's apply SBV

Explore your text once through with stick, then again with ball and then again with veil. Now score your text into three sections, assigning stick to one section; then transition to ball and finally to veil. Repeat the text two more times, assigning each object to a different section. Practice different transitions, such as an instant switch or a slow morphing from one to the other. Partners can choose to play with the same or contrasting IBs. Release and restore. Flyback.

This Imaginary Body/archetype stick, ball, veil exercise has been handed down from at least the middle 1930s. It is an essential initiation into one of Chekhov's most powerful paths of transformation: Thinking, Feeling, Willing.

## Discover Trinity of Psychology

 Let's play discover Thinking forces

Up on your feet with no pen or pencil handy, try to multiply 468 × 273. Don't cheat! That's not the point. Make a concentrated effort to do it mentally while up on your feet.

After a minute or two, freeze and begin your observation.

### Journal/Discuss/Flyback

*What is your body doing? What finger is most active? Where is the energy most dominant? What pattern of movement were you in? Were you pacing in straight lines? Were you rocking forward on your toes or tapping them? Were a lot of your knuckles showing? Were any joints touching other joints, like an elbow on a wrist, knuckles on a jaw, ankles crossed, or if sitting, ankle on knee, rocking back and forth? Were your gestures up near your head and shoulders? What element/QoM was dominant? Perhaps the air is associated with thoughts? Maybe I am an airhead with little thought!*

### Let's discuss T-forces

What we are discovering are the body-language tendencies of a person when they are dominated by their thoughts. While we all have thinking capabilities of some kind, some of us have personalities dominated by our mental capacities. We act based on our thoughts rather than our feelings or will impulses. For our purposes, we will call them *T-characters*. Let's explore what modifications we can consciously make to transform ourselves into a *T-character*.

The instinctive modifications humans tend to make are linear movements, monotone speech, all centered at the tops of each major body part, such as the forehead, shoulders, joints, fingertips, and toes. Picture

Rodin's statue of *The Thinker*. The chin gets tucked away and covered by the knuckles, elbow on knees. Tips of the toes and fingers often tap based on thoughts.

The intellect is thought of as dry and unemotional, very factual. The pattern of movement tends to be direct. We make a point. The sound wave could be imagined as a flat, straight line connecting directly to the point with no melody or feelings. Use the index finger boldly in this exploration. (For the sake of art, forgive each other and yourself for feeling rude. The pointing finger is the true archetype, despite being considered impolite.) Coaches even have public speakers use their thumbs instead of the index finger to make a point. But we know the index finger is the true pointer because so many clichés use it exactly as we are saying. And when we are completely spontaneously engaged in a safe environment, we do point. And in case I haven't made my point yet, do some POAs, observe, and look for these tendencies in the real world. That will help you truly get my point and truly make yours.

There are fricatives and plosives, air-based sounds like K, T, and P made on the inside top of the mouth with the tip of the tongue, lips, and roof of the mouth.

A typical statement by a T-character will over-enunciate the T, K, and P. They will crisp up a D to sound like a T. B can become P, G become K. J may become CH. Z becomes S. Other sounds, such as F, H, and WH, might have more air. Sounds like NS in *answer* might become *antswer*. See how the following sentence changes.

Try to speak your words correctly and then with the exaggerated *T-modifications*.

Dropping arms helplessly complaining: *Gosh, Baby Garlen is just doing nothing but crying.*
Pointing with Finger absolutely monotone: *Kosh, Papy Karlen in chust to-ink nothink put cryink.*

Sound, carried by air, is the dominant physical sense. Word choices often use air and sound-based metaphors. Repeat these phrases with the T-modifications: monotone, factually with the crisp consonants. Imagine each sound flying in a line straight to a point.

Unmodified: *The thought that she is flighty just flew into my head. Yep, that sounds right.*
T-modified: *The thoughT that she is ffflighTy chust flew inTo my HeT. Yep, thaT sounTs HrighT.*

When we first try these T-modifications, it *sounts pritty weirt! Put if we practice ant see them happenink in the real worlt, we will soon pe aple to tdo it peliefaply.*

What body language do we present when we are deeply thinking about a problem? We often wrap our arms around ourselves and bring our shoulders in. And on our face, we "knit our eyebrows." Then, if we don't know the answer and say so with no words, we tend to "shrug our shoulders," lifting them and dropping them. And what else do we lift and drop? Our eyebrows. And when we get the answer, our eyebrows and shoulders fly up with a pointed finger saying, "Eureka!" It's kinda like the eyebrows are the shoulders of the face!

What we are seeing is that the *T-forces* don't just live in the head. They are everywhere in the body, and each body part is a microcosm of the whole body. Figure 12.2 shows one side of a body with the *T-parts* labeled from the shoulders up; the other side has the T-parts in the arms, hands, torso, legs, and feet. When we understand this broader view of T as being throughout the body, we notice it is at the top of each section. **T is tops.** When we look at only the head, T is from the eyebrows up. Looking at the torso, T is in the shoulders. Looking at the foot, T is in the toes. Were you wiggling your toes when trying to multiply those numbers in your head?

T-forces are linear. This means that we can also apply elements of design to the mix. Blue is often associated with thought/air. Scenic elements can reflect the T-force in props, costumes, furniture, makeup, and hair. Sound, light, media, and marketing designs can all reflect the T-forces. More will be discussed in Chapter 19, SynthAnalysis and *Directing the Michael Chekhov Way*.

## 🤸 Let's improv T-forces

Begin traveling through the space as your everyday self for about a minute, then shift into your on-top-of-the-world universal self for another minute and pause. Now, inhale a very T-dominated character that you will exaggerate, very unveiled, as we say. Intense energy in the forehead may lead with a pointed right index finger. Pace in a straight line back and forth, or square off your turns in the space. Repeat the sounds P, K, and T in monotone.

When you feel you have fully adopted all the T-modifications, begin to interact with a real or imaginary water bottle or glass. Create a short étude where you take a sip of the water and walk away. Try to move in a straight line toward it, lift it with the tips of the fingers with emphasis on the index finger, move the arm straight to the water, and lift it straight to your mouth and away.

Find an imaginary or real pet or other artists and improvise a conversation about the weather. Hands may be on hips, joints on joints, and make lots of points as you factually and unemotionally chat about the weather with linear gestures that tend to be from the shoulder up.

Find a partner, real or imaginary, and together, take three minutes to plan an outdoor event, allowing all the elements of *T-Forces* in design to be included in food choices, decorations, activities, etc. After three minutes, take turns presenting your ideas to the group, or, if solo, present to an imaginary "event organizer."

## ✒ Journal/Discuss/Flyback

*Were you able to actively use the T-Forces very strictly in linear movement, tops of body sections, gestures, sound, word choice (sound, air), logical ideas, etc.? What body parts were most challenging to keep engaged if you slipped out? What did they want to do instead?*

## 🎭 Let's apply T-forces

Select a monologue, generic scene, or specific scene to apply the T-forces to. When beginning, play with it unveiled so you can free up the old tendencies and welcome these new forms to play through you. Keep in mind, when we are applying the tools to a text, our aims are to develop our skills with the tools and our appreciation for the transformation that can be facilitated by using the tools. We are not concerned about making sense out of the text. We are not looking for artistic truth based on our logic or understanding of the story. The truth we are looking for is one that surprises us when we fully commit to the tool. Square up your blocking, flatten the expressivity, and make your points. Watch out for over-strengthening the will to force your point. As they said in the old *Dragnet* TV show, "Chust the facts, Chack!"

In the following pages, you will find graphs and charts to help you identify all of the elements visible and audible to the audience that are potentially impacted by our thinking process. These ideas are "tendencies" that archetypally exist independent of culture or gender. They are intended to be a springboard of creativity, not hard and fast rules. As with all of these tools, if you look with concentration through the lens of these ideas, you will see them expressing themselves in life. Do this consistently, and your world will never look the same.

### Homeplay

In addition to your practice-observe-apply activity, build a list of everyday phrases, colloquialisms, sayings, idioms, similes, and metaphors that use thinking-dominated images. Add to the list whenever you think about, read, or hear it.

"This idea popped into my head." "Would you serve as my sounding board?" "I hear you." Make a list of thinking-dominated characters or people you have experienced in shows or in life outside of entertainment.

##  Let's play discover feeling forces

Up on your feet, find a real or imaginary partner with whom to share something unique and wonderful. You can both speak at once; it's okay. If you like, you can listen engaged in your partner's enthusiasm. Talk about something really cool that you did, would love to do, or that you have dreamed about doing. After a minute or two, freeze.

*What patterns were your hands moving in? Are your palms showing? Are your cheeks energized? Is any particular finger most active? Where is the energy most dominant in your body? Were you swaying over the arches of your feet? Were your hands moving in circles near your chest? Were your eyes, cheeks, and upper lips very active? Were any emotions coming up?*

## Discussion of F-forces

Now we are discovering the archetypal body language patterns for when we are dominated by Feeling Forces. Movements tend to curve with the middle of the body, highly sensitive with a watery flow and a sea of emotions. Melody and exaggerated vowels appear. In the macrocosm of the body, the *F-forces* are active in the torso.

In the microcosm of the face, F-forces are active from underneath the eyebrows to the upper lip. Try to smile without using your upper lip. You are now "keeping a stiff upper lip," which we do when we want to block our emotions from overwhelming us. A genuine smile lifts the cheeks and crinkles the skin around the eyes.

For T-forces, our predominant finger was the pointer/index. For F-forces, it is the middle finger.

Draw one middle finger from the tip of your other middle finger through the palm of your hand and up to the inside of your elbow. Is it sensitive? Now, draw one index finger from the tip of the other index finger along the knuckles to the outside of the elbow. What is the difference in the sensitivity level there? Take your middle finger and wipe under your eyes with a curving motion. Take your index finger and rub your temple back and forth. Can you feel the difference between how and where *thinking* energy moves and how and where *feeling* energy moves?

*F-forces* are often imagined to be green or pink colors. The thighs, arches of the feet, and inner arms, from the gut up through the watery organs and heart to just beneath the collarbone, are areas of the body where the *F-forces* are dominant.

Curves are expressed in sound as vowels. A "feeling" character, or *F-character*, will often diphthong their vowels, elongating them musically. "Hlüli! How aaaare you uuu?" In contrast to the thinker who might say: "Yep, thaT sounTs HrighT," the feeler might say: "eYeeaaah I feeeel youuu."

When we first try these F-modifications, it *saaahounds pritteeey weeiirrrd! Buuut, if weee praaactice aaand observe them haappening in the reeeal worurld, wehee will sooune be aaable to dooo it beelievably.*

The designs (within the F-character structure) will focus more on the middles, with more curves, possibly florals, and more fluid or "watery." Blocking will be more indirect. The senses of touch and smell are associated with feeling.

##  Let's improv F-forces

Begin by traveling through the space as your everyday self for about a minute, then shift into your *on-top-of-the world* universal self for another minute, and pause. Now inhale a very *F-dominated character* that you will exaggerate, unveiled. Intense energy in the cheeks and eyes may lead with an open left palm and the chest. Imagine, with each step, your feet curve to their next placement. Repeat vowel sounds in melodic tones.

When you feel you have fully adopted all the F-modifications, you begin to interact with a real or imaginary water bottle or glass. Create a short étude where you take a sip of the water and walk away. Try to move in a curve toward it, lift the water with your palm in the middle of the container, and keeping your emphasis on the middle finger, curve your arm to the water, bending it to your mouth and back away again.

Find an imaginary or real pet or get with other artists and improvise a conversation about the weather. Palms may be on the belly, or you may remain with open arms, and gestures curve and flow like water from the chest area; emotions rise and fall as you chat about the weather. Legs may make curves on the floor as you stand and talk. Melodious vowels carry the flow of conversation. If petting an animal, focus on curved strokes in the body's center.

Find a partner, real or imaginary, and together, take three minutes to plan an outdoor event for a group, allowing all the curvy elements of the *F-forces* to be prevalent in your design. Include food choices, decorations, and activities, etc. After three minutes, take turns presenting your ideas to the group, or present to an imaginary event organizer.

##  Let's apply F-forces

Work with the same text used above for the *T-forces*. When beginning, play unveiled so you can free up the old tendencies and go fully into the curvy, melodic, and emotional *F-forces* with a strong focus on expressive vowels. Allow the blocking to change to suit the *F-force*. Release and restore. Flyback. *Notice how different the same text is when you play the F-force version rather than the T-force version.*

> ### Homeplay
>
> In addition to your practice-observe-apply activity, add to your phrases a new list that uses *feeling-dominated images*. "A sea of emotions." "Flooded with joy." "I feel you." Make a list of *feeling-dominated characters or people* you have experienced in shows or in life outside of entertainment.

##  Let's play discover will forces

Pretend you are two years old and throwing a tantrum. Use your whole body just as a two-year-old would. Freeze.

*What is your body doing? What form is your hand in—maybe a fist? Where is the energy most dominant? What pattern of movement were you in? What kind of energy was in your feet? Were you stomping chaotically and asymmetrically? Was your jaw clenching? Did you drop to the ground?*

## Let's discuss W-forces

Now, we are discovering the archetypal body language patterns of when human beings are dominated by their will force. Movements tend to be angular or spiral, erratic, and asymmetrical, earthy, guttural, and centered in the bottom of things like the heel, jaw, groin, and thumbs. The "terrible twos" happen when a toddler wants something other than for comfort, and often for no apparent reason at all. They just want it, and they won't be happy until they get it.

We see their jaws thrust forward in defiance, and fists clench. They are often quite mobile with their walking and crawling. They can go where they want using their lower body.

Have you heard the allegory of the tortoise and the hare, also known as the turtle and the rabbit, who are in a race? What happens? Who wins? Why? What is the moral of the story? Slow and steady wins the race. This allegory is told in many cultures, sometimes with different animals but in the same situation. It is the story of two different *W-forces*; the hare has erratic, unfocused, and lazy will, and the tortoise has slow and steadily focused will. Learning this is a lesson for how to build concentration, focus, and patience, all founded upon the will force (and all essential qualities for mastering *Acting the Michael Chekhov Way*).

If you were in Rome, how would you express your opinion about whether the gladiator lives or dies? How do you hitchhike? Yes, the thumb is the digit of the will.

Do you recall in Chapter 2 when we did the AGs of Push and Pull, Lift and Smash, Gather and Throw? We noticed that when we engaged the heel of the hand, the power in the legs and groin area changed. When we had weak or disengaged wrists, our lower body had less energy, less *will-force*, and we could feel our jaw tighten or loosen accordingly. Here, we are seeing the correlations yet again between the microcosmic body parts and the larger whole body. The *W-force* is the bottoms. It's the heel of the hand, the heel of the foot, the heel of the face – the chin, and the heel of the torso—the groin.

The colors tend to be more red and earthy, as that is the element for the *W-forces*. The patterns of angles and irregularity might manifest in plaids or chunky spirals in a costume. The design textures might be more rugged or extreme.

Sounds also come from the bottom of the mouth and off the jaw and are guttural—in effect, an inversion of the *T-force* sounds. A typical statement by a *W-character* will over-enunciate the D, G, R, M, N, J, and Z for example. They will dull down a T or TH to sound like Ds. The ultimate cliché is the *"dese, dems, and dose kinda guys."* P can become B, K becomes G. CH may become J. S becomes Z. Other zoundz might have more voice, such as F, which becomes V. Sounds such as the NS in *"answer"* might become *"anzer."* They may take two consonants as in the word, <u>cr</u>y, and diphthong it to *"kuh-ry."*

See how the following sentence changes. Try to speak it correctly and then with the exaggerated *W-modifications*. "Gosh, Baby Garlen is just doing nothing but crying."

(Throwing fists down, stomping.) *"GGozh, Baby GGarlen in juzt doingh nnothingh bud kay-ryingh."*

Sight and speech are the dominant physical senses here. Word choice often involves the use of Earth-based and sight-based action metaphors. *Dude, Loogk here. Word, man. Whada ya zay?*

When we first try these *W-modifications, id zoundz priddy weirdd! Bud, if we bractiz and zee dem habbeningh in da real worldh, we will zoon be able da do id believably.*

 ## Let's improv W-forces

Begin traveling through the space as your everyday self for about a minute, then shift into your *on-top-of-the world* universal self for another minute and pause. Next, inhale a very *W-dominated character* that you will exaggerate, unveiled. Maintain powerful energy in the jaw, and you may lead with the pelvis or heel of the hands. Imagine that your feet move in asymmetrical angles with each step to their next placement or you form spirals, "turning in on someone" or "spiraling out of control." Repeat the guttural sounds.

When you feel you have fully adopted all the *W-modifications*, begin to interact with a real or imaginary water bottle or glass. Create a short étude where you take a sip of the water and walk away. Try to move in angles toward it, lift it from the bottom of the container with your dominant thumb and the heel of your hand, and then bend your arm toward the water, angling it to your mouth and back away again.

Find an imaginary or real pet or other artists and improvise a conversation about the weather. Hands may be in fists; your gestures may be asynchronous, low, beneath the waistline, and your thumb is dominant as you chat about the weather. Your legs and feet may make spirals and angles on the floor, strong heels as you stand and talk. Guttural consonants guide the conversation. If petting an animal, focus on angled/spiraled strokes in the lower end of their body.

Find a partner, real or imaginary, and together, take three minutes to plan an outdoor event, allowing all the angular/spiral, low, asymmetrical earthy elements of *W-forces* in design to be included in food choices, decorations, activities, etc. After three minutes, present your ideas to the group, taking turns, or present to an imaginary event organizer. Release and restore.

 ## Cookie Flyback

*What did you like overall? What would you do differently to double stuff? What was your favorite moment?*

 ## Let's apply W-forces

Work with the same text used above for the *T-* and *F-forces*. When beginning, play unveiled so you can free up the old tendencies and go fully into the angular/spiral, guttural, and asymmetrical earthy *W-forces*, with a strong focus on expressive sounds from the bottom of the jaw. Allow the blocking to change to suit the *W-Force*.

Having applied each of the three forces of psychology to the text, begin now to craft a score using all three in a random pattern, disregarding what might or might not fit. Repeat this several times using each tool in a different location based on random choices. *Flyback* to identify what you discovered in this sequence.

 ## The Goblet process

**Center,** ground, and open yourself to your higher ego. Review the text. Lead your imagination with the question: "How would I like to score this text?" Wait, listen with your *artistic gaze* for a response. If none comes, use your intellect to decide based on the content of the text. Release and restore. Flyback. Repeat as you like until you are happy with your skills and artistic score.

---

### Homeplay

In addition to your *practice-observe-apply* activity, take out your journal containing your phrases and add a new list that uses *willing-dominated images*. Examples could be "Stubborn as a rock," "Iron jaw," "I see you." Make a list of *willing-dominated characters/people* you have experienced in shows or life outside of entertainment.

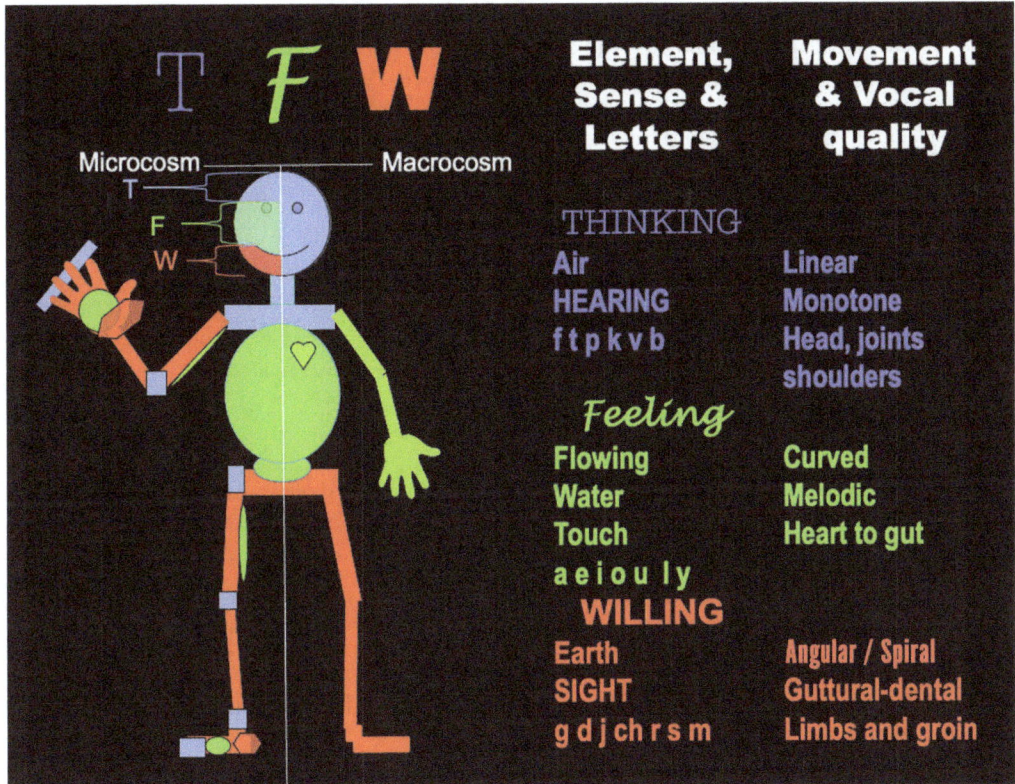

*Figure 12.2* Trinity of Psychology body chart. For the more conceptual-visually oriented person, this may help you grasp and remember the tools available to express the specific psychological composition of the character.

- See **OR 12.2** Trinity of Psychology grid

For the more verbal-auditory-digitally oriented person, this is a table that may help you grasp and remember these tools available to express the specific psychological composition of the character.

## Deeper discussion: The Trinity of Psychology

When I grew to understand the vast ramifications of Thinking, Feeling, and Willing as aspects of characterization, I understood my life in a whole new way. I had not known that there were three distinct forces in us that operate as differently as do our digestive, circulatory, and nervous systems. They all work together as independent systems supporting the whole.

Everywhere we see the prefix "psych" in Chekhov's world, we are using its Greek definition of "soul." Understanding this invited me to explore his technique in a much deeper way. It doesn't mean Jung or Freud's definition. Who knew? TFW are the threefold soul forces humans have that no other creations do as far as we know. We can <u>think</u> in an enlightened way, <u>feel</u> compassionately, and have free <u>will</u> to take action. We can choose good or evil, reflect on our actions, and feel the consequences.

And while these three ToP forces work side by side in us, they don't always agree. For example, "That party tonight feels like fun, but I think I should study my script for rehearsal tomorrow. And my mom says stay home." Which do you choose? What you do is your will, which is either dominated by your thinking force to study, by your feeling force to have fun, or by your will to defy your mom and do anything but stay home.

In perfectly healthy living, there are times when our F-force is the highest choice, others when our T- or W-force is best. The ideal universal being will allow these three forces to shift to the optimal condition to meet the situation. As artists, we strive for this kind of balance. Perfect TFW balance generates an ideal center and is present in our artistic self during peak performance states of inspiration. Conversely, focusing on the ideal center can help unite and balance our TFW forces. However, our characters will be more fascinating when off-center and out of TFW balance to maintain dramatic or comedic tension.

 Let's play who am I?

Let's stand up very, very straight and linear. Have you seen *The Wizard of Oz*? If you were a character in there, who would you be? Yep, the Tin Man. And what would you want? A heart.

Now, remove everything straight and move your body in curves. Who in the Wiz are you now? Yeah, the Scarecrow. And what do you want? A Brain.

Now, hide your thumbs and pull them away from your thighs. Hide your groin, turn your legs inward, lift the weight off your heels, and let your jaw wobble. Who are you now? Great! You're the Cowardly Lion. What do you want? C-C-C-COURAGE!

And what do they all learn from the Wizard? That they had it all along. What shape is every piece of tin on the Tin Man? Round predominates the shape of *F-forces*. And it is fluid oil that loosens him up. He is yearning to know he has feelings, and he does.

What shape are the parts of the Scarecrow? Straight straw, very airy. Perfect for the thinking force, which he uses to help them succeed.

What shape is the Lion? Large paws, a strong jaw, powerful thighs, and a tail. These are all Grrr-ate for the *will-force*, where his courage is alive and thriving.

Let's reflect for a moment on stick, ball, veil. Can you see how they relate to the ToP? Who among the Oz characters starts as a stick, a ball and a veil? Understanding the correlation between the stick and Thinking, the veil and Feeling, and the ball and Willing allows us to easily access the essential modifications that happen instinctively when we play with these tools. Per Axiom 12.1. One image unites many details. Ultimately our dear Oz team finds their balance.

And what about Dorothy? In the beginning, she feels sorry for herself, has no will to help around the farm, and thinks she wants to be anyplace but home (Earth). She has to travel through her various earth, air, water, and fire trials, make friends with her TFW forces, click her heels (her *Will-Force*) three times (don't you just love all these Triplicities?), and state her Will: There's no place like home.

We could say one of the reasons this 1939 film endures all around the world is because it is an archetypal search for Balancing our ToP. Frank L. Baum, the author of the original Oz books, was well-versed in TFW. This Trinity of Psychology is strongly inspired by Dr. Rudolf Steiner and also appears on Stanislavsky's Bases of the System. Its parallel can be found throughout Hindu, Judeo-Christian, Islam, Buddhist, Native American, and Pagan practices. It is present in legal structures such as the US Government: executive, judicial, and legislative branches. It is used in corporate coaching models for problem-solving and marketing: think, feel, do. It can be seen as "head, hand, and heart" in many societies. Again, Chekhov created his system based on observation of universal patterns. Learning how to consciously express in a character what is normally unconscious in our spectators can awaken deep communion with them and open them to transformation.

When coaching Mala Powers on her film roles, Chekhov had two questions first on his list. 1) Is your character predominantly Thinking, Feeling, or Willing? 2) Is your character predominantly Radiating or Receiving? We can see that he placed this tool in high regard. When actors understand their own way of Thinking, Feeling, and Willing, they can then compare themselves with the character and choose to explore and rehearse the **differences**. One can trust that what is the **same** between the character and the actor will reveal itself naturally and needs no additional attention. Let's address the differences by answering the following.

To do as Chekhov suggests, we need a baseline of self-knowledge. Listen to your word choices. Observe your movement and speech patterns. Ask someone who knows you well what they notice.

---

### Homeplay

*Take some time to examine your decision-making processes. Review three different choices you made in the past about how to spend your time and resources.*

 Jot down what the options were, what your T-force thought, what your F-force felt, what your W-force wanted, and which force in you decided to do what you did. This may help you understand yourself more honestly.

 When you fly back over a performance, ask the three cookie questions of each force. Overall, what did I think? Feel? Do?

- Look at two people who have influenced you strongly. Can you get a sense for what their predominance is? How is it different from your own? Often, we either model those closest to us or go to the polarity/contrast.
- Look at two people you sometimes struggle with—maybe you disagree with or argue with. Do you disagree with their thoughts, feelings, and/or will?

---

### Pizza

Well, my husband, Ken, had a very stubborn will and a Mensa (supposedly a very high IQ) T-force. He was constantly battling his weight despite having been a professional-level athlete. To some who sought his approval, his wit and will were devastating and seemingly heartless—a grizzly bear. To me, he was a teddy bear and all heart. One of the things we would argue about was where or what to eat. Living the actor's itinerant life meant often eating out.

HE SAYS: I'm starving.
SHE SAYS: Honey, where do you want to go tonight?
HE SAYS: Oh, I don't know, Sweetie, what do you feel like?
S: Oh, I don't care, Babe. What are you in the mood for?
H: Babe, Really, what'ya feel like? You decide.
S: But I want to go where you want to go.
H: ….

Pretty soon, this lovely conversation is going to get ugly because in three more lines, we will go from hungry to "hangry!"

OK, I am a Libra—hard to make decisions cause there's good and bad on both sides. And he's a Gemini—could go either way. I also know he doesn't always like my ideas and usually has a preference that he won't tell me in case I don't like it. When I understand (T-force) that underneath all those brains and brawn is a feeling-dominated only child who just wants to please me and isn't able to actually identify what he feels like … and that I just want to please him, I <u>think</u> of a new way to <u>do</u> this

> discussion. Even though I don't actually care where we eat, I give him a definite answer, using feeling words which he either agrees with or, without <u>thinking</u>, says what he really feels:
>
> HE SAYS: I'm starving.
> SHE SAYS: I feel like Greek food.
> HE: But I feel like Pizza
> SHE: Let's go!

Our personality will change "tactics" to get its needs met. We will often argue from our predominance first. If that fails, we will go to our secondary and then to the other. In other words, if feeling doesn't work, we will try logic, and then we "will force" our opinion on the other.

If our partner is starting in a different predominance, we will be miscommunicating from the start.

In life, we can use our understanding of TFW to create harmony, better communication, and relationships.

In acting, we can use TFW to create chaos and TPT to enhance storytelling dynamics.

 Let's improv ToP switch

If you are in a class, the group can break into twos or threes, and all practice your skills simultaneously. Alternatively, you can watch one group at a time.

Assign three artists to a group with a different force. Establish that the switch order is T, F, W. So person 1 is T; 2 is F; and 3 is W. Have one outside person who calls "Switch!" randomly, every 30–60 seconds or so. When "Switch" is called, 1 changes to F, 2 changes to W, and 3 changes to T, and so on. Play as best you can, making completely unveiled switches with word choices, enunciation, gesture locations, and movement patterns. When you are happy with that, try with veiling.

Choose any scenario. Oh wait—you want me to choose. Fine! Here's one option: three lost hikers at a fork in the trail with a setting sun and empty knapsacks.

If hiking solo, talk your way out loud through this decision, switching every 30 seconds or so.

An advance on this structure is to have the actors change when they wish. When one switches, the other two have to switch as well, so no one is using the same force at the same time.

Oh, and if you don't *think* my scenario is interesting and you *feel* like you want to do something different—

- See **Kilroy Improv** Chapter 11 for TFW rowdiness!

 Journal/Discuss/Flyback

*Were you able to retain your TFW with your partners in polarity to you? Did you use your feet in a way inspired by the force you were in? Were you able to speak and gesture in the archetypal body language of the force?*

## ToP Leading Questions

- Which soul force predominates me, and which predominates my character?
- How is **my** *thinking force* different from my **character's** *thinking force*?

- How is **my** *feeling force* different from my **character's** *feeling force*?
- How is **my** *will force* different from my **character's** *will force*?

To help answer these questions, let's talk a bit more about the quality or kind of TFW.

## T-forces

We have both conscious and unconscious thoughts that play a role in our personality. For now, we will focus on what we think of as our "daily" style of thinking. Each of us has a quality of Thinking that is our "norm," and we relate to it as logical, regardless of how others perceive it.

If this dominates, your thoughts will be consistently of this kind. It is the T-force in your "piece of the pie."

How each of us thinks may be very diverse. Perhaps you have systematic Thinking, and your friend has associative Thinking. Maybe you know of people who have acute mathematical Thinking with very little "common sense." Here are a few other kinds of Thinking:

| | | |
|---|---|---|
| Analytic | Symbolic | Detailed |
| Abstract | Musical | Illogical |
| Divergent | Distracted | Erratic |
| Idealistic | Witty, clever | Anxious |
| Artistic | Dumb/Stupid | Phobic |
| Reflective | Slow or Fast | Depressed |
| Conceptual | Chaotic or Rhythmic | Spacey |
| Convergent | Big Picture | |

### ✒ Journal/Discuss/Flyback

*Add to this list of kinds of Thinking that you identify with new people you meet in the world and with those you know well. Find a Chekhov buddy to give you some hints about your own quality of Thinking.*

## F-forces

Our Feeling force can also vary greatly, especially the amount of revealed or concealed feeling. Just because someone doesn't look emotional doesn't mean they aren't feeling a great deal. Some people are quickly triggered, and then the feeling is gone as fast as it came, while others do a slow burn and simmer for hours.

For the "feeling life," leading questions can inspire a way to identify and work with different kinds of emotional life.

- Is there a personal atmosphere that has an emotion in it? Optimism vs. pessimism.
- How much do they really feel? Hypersensitive vs. numb.
- How much do they show of what they feel? Overly expressive vs stoic, repressed
- How fast do they respond to triggers? At the mere thought vs. slowly building—have to get hit over the head to feel it.
- How fast do they release the emotions? As soon as they express them vs. linger and stew

## ✎ Journal/Discuss/Flyback

Examine your own Feeling life and that of people around you. Add to the above list any other observations you make about how different people manage their feelings.

## W-forces

The Will force may be the most challenging of the soul forces because, in many ways, it is asleep. So much of our Will is unconscious. When we decide to get a glass of water, we engage our legs and arms—our limbs—to do our Will, but we have no idea how to get each cell of our body to achieve that. How to stop pouring the water so it doesn't spill, how much food to eat to have enough energy to get that water, and how to distinguish between what is valuable in the digestive tract to make the muscle needed to pick up the glass. Of all this action, we are clueless. What we can do is become conscious in our Thinking forces—those impulses that we have—and decide whether to follow them or not. When we are W-dominated, we sometimes don't actually know the "reason" we want to do things. Other times, our wills are clearly in agreement with our rationale, and we believe that thought is right. With a strong Will, we commit to the thought and have a resolute Will.

Here are some LQs for Will with the range of possible answers:

- What is the intensity? High vs low
- What is the consistency? Steady vs. erratic
- What is the direction? Up-forward-side-down-backward
- What is the rhythm? Chaotic, staccato, lyrical, legato, still
- Does it respond more to Feeling or Thinking or to itself?
- What is its relation to morality/ethics? High vs low
- What is its tempo/speed? Slow vs fast
- What is the speed of its responsiveness? Anticipatory, quick vs delayed, unresponsive
- How controlling is it? Totally vs. not at all
- How generous is it? generous vs. stingy
- How focused is it? Myopic vs. dispersed

We can also look at certain states of being as expressed in each of the trinity:

Perhaps Love in the T-force is interest, enthusiasm, and curiosity; in the F-force, affection; in the W-force, courage. Fear in the T-force might be anxiety and worry; and in the W-force, panic and paralysis. This could be useful for a character in a particular state for an extended period. You can play with shifting that state into the TFW forces and keep the creative juices transforming over the arc of the story.

## ToP for productions

We will explore more in Chapter 19 about the application of the TFW for design, blocking, and SynthAnalysis™. Here's a little taste. Every artist can ask the same questions an advertising executive might when creating a campaign for their brand and product:

- **Think:** What do you want your audience to think about your brand (show) and its expertise/authority?
- **Feel:** What emotional response do you expect from your audience, and how do you want them to feel about your brand(show)?
- **Do:** What action do you want your audience to take, and how do you hope to influence their behavior?[4]

## Summary of the ToP

Each person is always a combination of TFW, having a predominance of one that can shift as the character develops or for specific moments. This predominance will affect speech and movement very dynamically and specifically and lead to a host of other behaviors. When we take our course of action based on our logical Thinking forces, we are thinking-dominated. When we take action based on our emotions, we are feeling-dominated. When we take action on our desires and impulses, we are will-dominated.

When an actor knows the basic tendencies in expression associated with Thinking, Feeling, and Willing characters, every movement and sound the actor makes can be crafted to crystallize the characterization. No random patterns of the actor's habitual movement or speech will muddy the image. You will arrive at rapid decisions on how to create unique moments in improvisation, rehearsal, and during performance.

To understand the depth of Psychological Gesture and Characterization, we encourage you to pursue a deep understanding of the Trinity of Psychology, and the physical means these energies use to express themselves.

- See both *Figure 12.2 ToP Body Chart* and *OR 12. 2 ToP Grid* for precise details on how to physicalize these concepts by knowing where centers might be and how Imaginary Bodies might move. Remember to observe life to see these happening all around you. This will inspire you with its truthfulness.

These elements can reflect which trait of the psychology is dominant:

- The direction of the movement: straight, curved, angled, direct, indirect
- The vocal quality: monotone, melodious, percussive, staccato, legato
- The archetypal location of the character center (top, middle, bottom of the whole body) macrocosm, or any given part (microcosm) of the body such as the head, hand, torso, or foot
- The verbal emphasis on plosive or fricative consonants, vowels, or jaw-based consonants
- How characters react to succeeding/winning or failing/losing their objective (the dream or the nightmare)
- The dominant basic sense: hearing, touching, taste, smell, or seeing
- A quality specific to the character—the kind of T, F, W
- Preference of a sense can alter the center, the word choices, and the overall perspective of the character.
    - "Listen!" vs. "Look!"
    - "To touch base" vs. "to get a hold"
    - "What is happening?" vs. "How are you feeling?"

I hope by now that you have a taste of how transformative the ToP concept is in our art and in life. It is possible to simply use the concept of TFW as centers in the head, heart and pelvis. Efficient as it may be, I do caution against making such a reduction for various reasons. This simplification tends to reduce these two tools of unlimited inspirational potential to one tool where you can choose only one of three locations. When MCs are merged with TFW, we fail to ask the leading questions about quality, mobility, and predominance for MCs or for TFW. We tend to forget there are Moveable Centers bearing no relationship to TFW at all. We also lose access to how ToP can apply to blocking and design and an overall life-changing perception.

To help keep the terminology clear, *Acting the Michael Chekhov Way* refers to TFW as the Trinity of Psychology (ToP), using the word *forces* rather than *centers*. After all, it is absolutely possible to have a Will force character with a Center anywhere they will with any quality they say!

Now that you have discovered the ToP, revisit the opening universal artist section of this chapter and explore the Actor's March. You will see that this powerful poem aligns our Thinking, Feeling and Willing, awakening a balanced power that can take us to the top! Daily practice brings vital and radiant life into all we do.

## ꙮ Keep improvising!

**Remember,** the purpose of improv with a tool is to strengthen your skill and expand your understanding of how inspiring it can be. When you know how to use it and what problems it can fix for you, you will seek ever greater mastery of it. That's when life becomes your own piece of art.

- See **OR 12.3-4-5 for Personal, Nature, Observational Character Study Playsheets**

The art of Characterization—with Moveable Centers, Imaginary Bodies, Archetypal Characters and the Trinity of Psychology: Thinking, Feeling, Willing—is the golden pathway to transforming ourselves into the body, mind, and spirit of another being which we co-create through our communions with the author, director, mise en scene, fellow artists and our higher selves. Now that you have trained yourself to safely receive and choose images for transformation, the possibilities are unlimited. Yet, if we apply them without Radiance, our charismatic star quality will remain unseen, unfelt, and unheard. So stick with AMCW to build up your Radiating and Receiving!

## Notes

1. Scottini, Leticia, https://www.leticiascottini.com/ Chekhov Teaching Artist, Member of the Michael Chekhov Studios Cooperative. August 1, 2024.
2. https://www.weforum.org/publications/the-future-of-jobs-report-2023/digest/
3. Colvin, Jack, Direct Student and Personal Assistant to Michael Chekhov 1950–1955. Mentor to Lisa Loving Dalton, 1993–2002. Best known as Reporter Jack McGee in *The Incredible Hulk* TV Show.
4. https://longitude.ft.com/think-feel-do-how-to-use-rational-and-emotional-content-to-get-an-audience-response/

# 13
# Radiating and Receiving Radiance

What is the "IT" factor?

Want to know the key to charisma and star quality?

 Let's play Radiating and Receiving (#13)

When playing solo, perhaps you have a stuffed animal, doll, or portrait of someone with whom you can make eye contact as if they are your imaginary living partner. The advantage of working solo here is, as always, you are building your imagination to be able to interact with invisible partners. This is a standard skill set for working with an invisible imaginary body partner required for monologues and on-camera performances. It helps us develop the self-discipline to work when we have no partner, to prepare for our auditions, rehearsals and performances. Let's fall in love with solo play or partner play either way!

Everyone gets up on their feet. Form a hallway of two lines facing each other, just about arm's length apart from a partner. Let's designate the left line as "A" and the right line as "B."

If solo, try to position your "imaginary body" (IB) partner at eye level. We will consider the IB to be on the left. Designate yourself as on the right.

For everyone, the players on the left (A) will begin as receivers while those on the right (B) start as radiators. We are going to make visible the giving and receiving of energy.

Stand with one leg more forward than the other so that you can lean forward or backward safely.

As you and your partner look into each other's eyes, awaken and energize your whole *life body*, allowing it to fill you with energy and lead you in this exercise. Line B on the right, allow the amazing powerful radiant sunlight within your chest to pour through every pore of your being, giving it lightly and easily to your partner. Lean forward slowly as you radiate light to your partner through every cell of your body. Palms may stay open to your partner and aligned with your body.

Line A on the left, open your palms and allow your inner sunlight to gently receive the golden light energy being sent from your partner, leaning backward as you receive, drawing in this gift.

Remember your connection to Beauty, Ease, Entirety, and Form (BEEF) and breath. We don't need effort to generate this light; nor need we push or pull this light. This process is one of easily allowing your light to flow in one of two directions. Your inner light is constantly replenished in your Ideal Artistic Center (IAC) with your breath and the love you bear for your art. Your personal star, your higher self, streams light from the invisible world.

When receiver in Line A has leaned back as far as they can, we can imagine our energy body can travel about three counts beyond where our physical body has reached its maximum forward or backward motion. That's where we meet our transition point. Then they switch to radiating and slowly start moving forward. When the Line B radiators sense their partners have started radiating, they switch to receiving the light from A and gradually move backward until A reaches their transition point about three counts after they have gone back as far as they safely and easily can, and switch back to radiating. Blink as needed and reconnect.

Take your time going back and forth slowly. After two rotations, keep the energy body moving all the way back to the transition point, while beginning to veil the physical body so that it only goes back and forth maybe three-fourths of the way while the *life body* continues beyond. Veil the body more each round until the energy bodies are still moving fully and visibly; only the IAC in the center of the chest is moving subtly. Keep track of the image of the energy body and blink as you need to. It is not a staring contest. And remember to breathe!

When you arrive at the subtle, veiled radiating and receiving, allow your selves to sustain and then release instantly. Pack up that intensity and send it back up to the unlimited sphere of imagination. Flyback with your partner and then with the group.

## Journal/Discuss/Flyback

*Were you able to maintain your concentration with constant radiating an outward flow of light or receiving the light into you? Were you able to sense when to switch? When veiling, could you keep track of who was radiating and who was receiving? How did you feel? What thoughts came to you? What did it make you want to do (think, feel, will [TFW])? Did you allow, push, or pull? How was your feeling of ease? Your breath?*

## Let's play javelin

Building on this Radiating, stand in a direction with a beautiful view or imagine one in the distance. As you stand in your IAC and universal stance, begin to sense the space behind you. Listen into that backspace as if you can hear only what comes from behind, receiving from the unseen, or from what you have left behind. Imagine the backspace contains amazing power and resources. Listen and receive with every fiber of your being. Receive from the back space for a minute or two. Now step back into the powerful space and grasp an imaginary javelin full of the energy, take three steps, and hurl the javelin way far away over the horizon. Sustain with your throwing hand extended, following the imaginary javelin as it travels across the sky and as the energy streams through you, as if a ribbon of light were attached to the javelin arcing through the air. See it land and release. Step back to your start point.

Step yet again into the backspace, maybe using your non-dominant hand this time, gradually gathering even more power, listening and receiving even more deeply. Radiate the javelin throw a little further, perhaps even naming a distant place, sustaining your extended arm and hand and focus your eyes on the horizon until you sense it land. And release. Step back to your start point.

A third time, listen and step into the backspace and reach even more deeply into the power. Throw the radiant javelin even further, possibly around the whole world. As it is going, begin stepping back to your start point, feeling the stream of light coming in from behind you, through you, to your destination. Imagine you can focus all that is streaming through you to a single point of your choice. Sustain the radiation in the whole physical and *life body*. What if it lands behind you, filled with the power it has collected as it traveled around the world? Release everything when you imagine the javelin landing on its target.

Do you want to practice this tool a bit more to build your understanding and muscles?

## Let's play see spot go

Allow yourself to find your artistic place in the space, using awareness of the whole room and any other ensemble artists. Bring your concentration to your IAC and its radiant power of light vibrating in the center of your chest. Feel free to tap there to energize it if you like. Imagine a high-powered beam of light emanating from your IAC toward a spot in the room. Perhaps your eyes see the spot and then your beam of light connects with it, or maybe your beam leads your eyes to the spot. Radiate your beam of light to the spot for ten seconds and release it. Find another spot and turn on your radiation, sending your beam to the new spot. Radiate for 15 seconds, allowing yourself to breathe as you radiate with ease. Release the spot and find a new spot. Radiate toward that spot in the room for five seconds and then go to the spot. Maintain contact with your IAC and the spot as you travel, adjusting your path to accommodate other people or objects. Remember to rotate in place if you might collide with someone or thing, and adjust your path. If you chose an inaccessible spot, move as near to it as possible. Sustain your radiating for three seconds after arriving near your spot. Release.

Imagine now you can receive a beam of light from an unseen spot behind you. Turn and connect to the spot as if it is drawing you to it, like a magnet. Travel to the spot and if within reach, touch the spot, receiving it into your senses. Receive the sensations and release after about five seconds. Imagine another spot is radiating to you somewhere else. Turn, connect with your IAC and travel to it, receiving its light into you. Sense, sustain, and release. Next time, sense a spot in another direction. Surprise yourself. Will you radiate to it? Will you receive it? Now, see your spot and go! Play as you like. Add a quality to the spot so it is no longer pure light. What are you receiving? What are you radiating? Qualities can be called out. Release and Flyback. Do you feel more skilled at radiating and receiving?

## Let's discuss Radiating and Receiving

Radiating and Receiving is a multipurpose tool, often overlooked in its significance yet essential to the entire Chekhov system.

I was once asked what defines a Chekhov actor? What do Chekhov actors have in common? I believe Rad/Rec is the key answer here. Their creative individuality lives in their whole being and fills the audience with sizzle, excitement and vitality. Audiences walk away filled with energy. There are Chekhov actors who seem to transform very little; maybe we like them but dismiss them as gifted artists, yet they shine at the box office, proving my statements in Chapter 12 about transformation to be foolhardy. Others are so transformational it takes a few moments to believe it's the same actor. And they sparkle in our memories, revitalizing us when we think of their performance.

So what is this Radiating and Receiving? It is an invisible, intangible light that is sensed by everyone in its presence. It exists as an act of our higher ego will force. To have it means we have the will to allow the inner light to come out from under a bushel and be shared with the world. If you have ever had a peak performance moment—which I know you have had because you are reading this book—then you have the ability to radiate and receive. This Radiance is the magical "IT" factor that makes stars.

Whether this light, this Radiance we might call it, is visible or recognizable may be a matter of needing to clear a few clouds around your inner sun or strengthen and clarify your ability to manage it safely. You may need to free yourself from a few ingredients in your "piece of the pie" that are clogging the pores of your personal atmosphere bubble. If you are willing, you can brighten this Radiance and refine its quality and abundance with practice, through your will force and your love. Where focus goes, energy grows.

Stars have a Radiance that appeals to everyone around them. Mr. Chekhov suggests that this Radiance is awakened by our will force when we are doing activity out of our free will. This free-will enthusiasm is our *inner activity*. Anything we do because we *have* to is *outer activity*. Ask yourself at any given moment, "Am I doing this because I have to? Because society or the director or my body requires me to do it? Or am I doing this because I love it, want it, it's who I really am? Am I doing this because it's truly *me* or would the real *me* choose not to do this if I didn't have to.

The trick to cultivating this Radiance, this presence, is to focus your Thinking forces on finding the Beauty in the Forms (circumstances) you encounter so that you are living moment to moment free of judgments which crush enthusiasm. Focusing on the "Yes, and …" approach we use in improvisation and applying it to life can teach our T-forces to be interested in the other, in what is different, rather than judging it, which leads our feeling force into unpleasantness and our W-force into dread, dampening our Radiance.

Radiating and Receiving is like breathing radiant light instead of air. Receiving Radiance brings light into you and Radiating Radiance sends light out to the world. It is similar to how inhaling/receiving air takes the oxygen from plants into you. Exhaling air radiates the transformed carbon dioxide to the receiving plant kingdom. Just as we must always be breathing air, so must our Radiance always be on the in or out flow, if we are to be "alive on the stage." Without the dynamic of continuous Radiating/Receiving, we die on stage. We wind up with "an audience that's dead tonight." No audience enters the room wanting to metaphorically be that. We must accept our responsibility to give all the Radiance we can, free of judging them. We give them life. For some of us, we may not feel worthy, or we might be worried about looking egotistical. A bushel of doubts and feelings weakens our Radiance.

When I was in my early studies with Chekhov, we did the following exercise to help us awaken an unapologetic willingness to be seen, felt, heard, and appreciated for who we are. I clowned it up until I realized I had many insecurities beneath my shiny surface. I was deflecting the emotional impact of being appreciated just for being *me*. Even if you don't have that challenge, please take this seriously and have ridiculous fun doing so.

##  Let's play they love me!

This is a solo or ensemble activity. Activating your ideal artistic center, move to the periphery of the room. Ground and center yourself, allowing light to flow into you from your highest self, the I-sphere. Inhale this light and exhale it across a threshold before you, imagining a great stage, maybe it's a theater for thousands, Epidaurus in Greece, or your local stadium. Cross the threshold and imagine that everywhere you look, the crowds are cheering for you wildly. You don't need to do anything, and they think it's amazing. I wonder what will happen if you walk and fall on your face? They would cheer resoundingly. What if you fart? Again, even more cheers! Be brilliant or stupid, serious and quiet, or holler like a banshee. Allow yourself to receive this ever-flowing appreciation and enthusiasm coming to you. Try to stay for about five minutes. When ready, make a grand exit across the threshold. Release, gather up that celebratory Atmosphere (ATMO) and send it back up to the I-sphere.

For an ensemble deeper dive into "they love me", prepare to set a five-minute timer. One artist steps onto the playing area and stands in the center, arms by their side, open to the audience. The audience applauds and cheers for the entire five minutes, while the artist receives, in silence, with open eyes and open heart. When the timer rings, the artist exits, and another artist enters.

With a larger ensemble, you might spread this out over several gatherings, or you can create groups of five to eight in separate areas of the space, to play simultaneously.

## Journal/Discuss/Flyback

*How was it for you as an artist receiving unconditional appreciation, being seen, heard and felt?*

*Did any specific sensations, feelings or images arise for you? Were you able to sustain your receiving? Were you able to allow your "me" to radiate unguarded? Did you notice anything arise in you as an audience member cheering others on? What else do you notice?*

Cultivating Radiance is the first of five practical skills bequeathed to us via Radiating and Receiving.

>  Axiom 13.1: With Rad/Rec, we can
> 
> 1. Cultivate our star quality
> 2. Define our character
> 3. Define the arc of the character
> 4. Create continuous inner activity with qualities, gesture, and atmosphere for any given moment
> 5. Build listening and contact skills

Let's expand on these applications.

1. Rad/Rec is an overall continuous radiance-creating activity. Our energy is always in motion. What motion? Expanding or Contracting (X/C) or going out and coming in. When we look at that motion on a refined and subtle level, we can say that in peak performance, a performer's energy is either flowing out from their center or being drawn into them. We call the overall concept of energy flow, Radiation: the art of creating Radiance, sparkle, sizzle, charisma, star quality. The act of Rad/Rec is the key and is always present in powerful moments. Some of our exercises, such as they like me!, IAC, Ball Toss, Actor's March, Javelin, Staccato/Legato, see spot go, Focal Points, Beauty, and Golden Hoop awaken this skill. Your Will is the soul force that allows this energy to ebb and flow freely, and Rad/Rec WORKS best using your strong concentration skills.
2. When we get more specific and define the direction of this flow, we subdivide that into Receiving (drawing or allowing in) and Radiating (giving or allowing out). Ideally, each character we play is either Radiating or Receiving at all times. Thus we can add Rad/Rec to our list of Characterization tools. In fact, in private coaching, "Is your character predominantly a radiator or a receiver?" might have been Chekhov's first or second question along with your TFW choices, followed naturally by "And how does that differ from you?"

   It is important to note that the direction of the flow is neutral—not attached to any positive or negative, strength or weakness. If we return to *The Wizard of Oz* for a moment, what would you say about the predominance of Rad/Rec when comparing the Good Witch with the Evil Witch? Or the Wizard as a machine vs. the man-behind-the-curtain? Perhaps Superman radiates and Clark Kent receives. Maybe Batman receives and Bruce Wayne radiates. Some superheroes have powers that radiate, like Spiderman sending out a web. Others can draw things to them like the X-Men's Magneto.

   Marylin Monroe had Radiance, a star quality that seemed to be so magnetic, she drew the world into her in her films and drew people to her in real life (IRL for you millennials and gen Z out there). This is a technique she learned from Chekhov, who coached her until he died in 1955. Susan Strasberg tells a story of Monroe's ability to turn into "Her" with a simple internal adjustment that made her suddenly recognizable on the street.[1] Strasberg is very clear that Monroe knew how to do this before she began studying with Lee Strasberg in 1956. This magnetism is the same Radiance tool but used by drawing the audience, in the opposite direction from Radiating (sending), which Clint Eastwood developed over time during his early Italian films. He truly mastered it in *Dirty Harry*, where his Radiating is so powerful his lines became globally iconic. With Rad/Rec you can "Make my day!"

   In *Unforgiven* and *Bridges of Madison County*, Eastwood breaks from his string of Radiators and is a Receiver. In *Bridges of Madison County*, Meryl Streep is also a Receiver, making it impossible for these two lost souls to unite. In *Death Becomes Her* and *Devil Wears Prada*, Streep is a super Radiator while in her early films, *Sophie's Choice* and *Cry in the Dark*, she is a Receiver.

3. We can use Rad/Rec as an element of composition, revealing the arc of the character.

   In *Kramer vs. Kramer*, perhaps we might observe Streep begin as a Receiver and become a Radiator in the end. Here we see that transitioning from one to the other can create a strong impact, showing transformation in the character. Judy Dench as the queen in *Shakespeare in Love* is receiving her court, taking everything in. But when the queen is faced with a puddle, outside the Globe Theater, she flips into Radiating, insulted by the lack of someone to help her avoid stepping in it!

4. Rad/Rec is the essential tool that allows continuous inner activity to fulfill the actor's primary task: access, select and convey (ASC). In this understanding, Rad/Rec is how the selected image is conveyed/revealed to the performing ensemble and the audience. The image is expressed by Radiating or Receiving it. The image might be a gesture, an Atmosphere, a Moveable Center (MC) or an IB, a Quality/Kind of Movement (QoM), or the Three Sister Sensations (3S). Every tool is an image and can be radiated or received. We have been practicing this kind of Radiating and Receiving with every centering and goblet exercise, with every moment we veil a large abstract expression.

5. Listening with focused intent to receive is an essential act which can inspire us quickly and creatively. We can use Receiving when we practice any listening exercise from any technique we know. Receiving helps us also "listen" or make contact with and respond to the ATMO, the inspiration inside us, the words of the text, a prop or costume and to receive the subtext Radiating from our partners. How we react to our ensemble, our communion with the mise en scene, author, higher self, audience and director is in response to what we receive. The Ball Toss is our first Rad/Rec exercise. Next time you play ball, focus on your Radiating/Receiving.

Receiving, as in listening, is most inspiring when we can quiet our own thoughts about who/what/how something is radiated to us. If we can receive with no preconceived ideas about how we want to respond, or how a line should be said to us, etc., we, as the character, will then be able to spontaneously radiate a response in the moment. We can listen, make contact, and receive through our 12 senses discussed below.

 Let's improv Rad/Rec as characterization

When playing solo, improvise a monologue about a trip you would love to take together and tell an imaginary partner all about it. Decide whether you will begin predominantly Radiating to them or be a Receiving character sharing your story.

When improvising with a partner, decide whether you will begin as a Radiator or a Receiver. Improvise a discussion about a trip you will take together. Your choice can be the same as or polar opposite to your partner.

After a minute or two, switch your Rad/Rec and continue for another minute or two. If time permits play a third time and switch part way through the dialogue. When complete, release and restore.

✎ Journal/Discuss/Flyback

*Overall, were you able to maintain your choice of Rad/Rec? Did you sense the difference between them? How did you perceive your partner when in one or the other? Did the power structure change? If so, did Receiving become weak with Radiating being strong? If so, that might be a tendency in your "piece of the pie." Repeat the improv and try Receiving with power and Radiating vulnerably to expand your habitual tendencies and free up the future applications of this versatile tool.*

- See **Kilroy Improv** Chapter 5 to build your sizzle skills.

Let's apply Rad/Rec for Characterization, Composition, and tools

Select your text for a monologue or scene and use Radiating fully through as an element of Characterization. Repeat now with receiving. *Flyback to observe how it changed your character and what you discovered.*

Now, focusing on Rad/Rec as an element of Composition, try it again switching at two key moments. Reverse that score, so you are Radiating where you were receiving. *Flyback asking how the switches affected the dynamics of the text.*

Focus now upon one to three tools such as ATMO, Archetypal Gesture (AG), MC. Try the text playing with Radiating the tools and again Receiving the tools. You can make this simple or more layered as you wish, by starting with one tool at a time, Rad/Rec. Then using one tool for part A, another for part B etc.

Release and restore the tools, returning to your ideal universal self.

 Journal/Discuss/Flyback

*Were you able to sustain your Rad/Rec? What differences did you notice? Is one easier than the other for you? Take a moment to examine and note when you personally tend to radiate (allowing yourself to go out into the world) and when you tend to receive (allowing the world to come to you). Are you predominantly taking in the world or going out into the world?*

> ### Homeplay: POA
>
> Watch some movies, perhaps some superhero stories and observe their Rad/Rec. Who is Radiating and Receiving, and do they change their Rad/Rec when they are not in super-mode. Practice one or the other while doing household chores such as cleaning or cooking.

 Let's apply Rad/Rec for listening

Using your selected text, situate yourself back to back with your real or imagined partner, or lie on the floor, head to head. Eyes can be closed or open. Speak one line at a time, carefully Receiving what is being said. Whether you are the speaker or the listener, receive the author's words. Pause to allow them to permeate you deeply before moving to the next response. Receive the sounds of individual letters as well as the literal meaning of the words and the subtext. Now, come face to face and radiate the text to your partner simply, and play with Receiving their expression, the sounds they make, and life energy they have. Release, restore. Flyback.

## Let's dive deeper into Radiating and Receiving

Earlier, in Chapter 3, we used the term "Radiating" as one of the Qualities of Movement associated with the element of light/fire/laser. Here we are using the basic word as a higher, more magical concept representing the flow of creative light or Radiance. We can say that Radiating has two uses in the Chekhov world. It refers to the direction of flow of creative Radiance (Rad/Rec) or to the Quality of Movement.

It is important to appreciate that the tool of Radiating/Receiving is a separate tool from the Quality of Movement of Radiating (element of fire/light) as grouped with Molding/earth, Flowing/water, and Flying/air (MFFR).

We can decide what we are Radiating or Receiving at any given moment. We radiate and receive Gestures, Atmospheres, and Qualities. We can even radiate our QoM of Radiating fire! And you can receive so

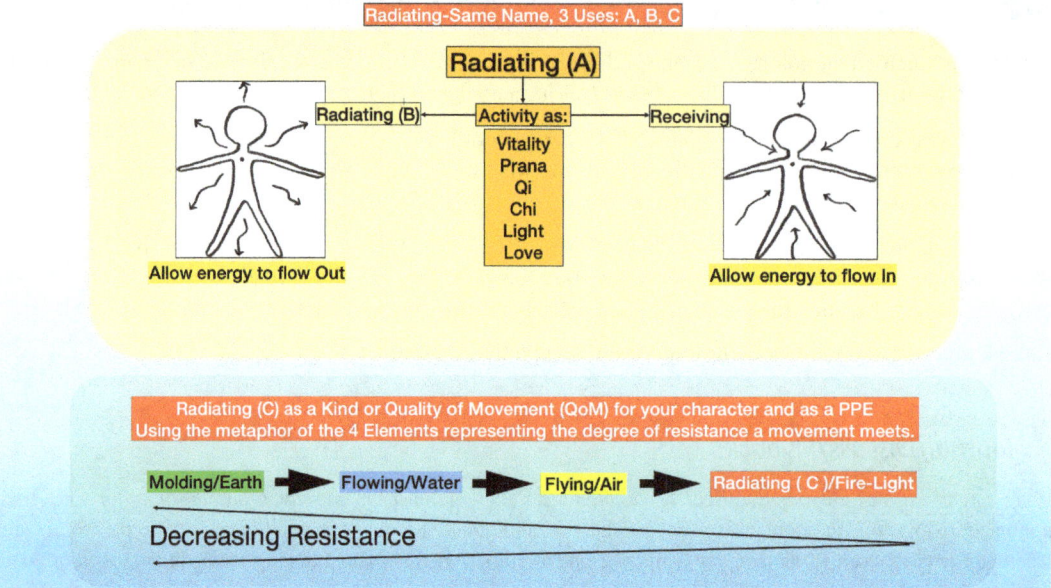

*Figure 13.1* Radiating: Same name, three uses—A, B, C clarifying the multiple uses of the term "radiating." Radiating A is the overall vitality. Radiating B is how a character uses A—as a sender vs receiver. Radiating C is a QoM.

powerfully that you're filled with Radiance like Marilyn Monroe. In her performances, she is Receiving so powerfully that she is "Radiating Receiving." Clint is Radiating fire so powerfully he can be said to be "Radiating Radiating." (See Figure 13.1.)

>  Axiom 13.2: Rad/Rec is different from the QoM of Radiating the element of light/fire.

- See **OR 13.1** Diving even deeper for those who are really curious, we can also explore how to radiate and receive with what Rudolf Steiner, a primary inspiration for Michael Chekhov, introduced as our "twelve senses." See the recommended book *Our Twelve Senses* by Albert Soesman.[2]
- See **OR 13.1** Golden Hoop Deeper Dive: The Golden Hoop, which we did in Chapter 9, Ensemble, is also a Radiating and Receiving exercise. OR 13.1deepens our understanding and increases the artistic training aspect of it, for example, in building our feeling of form.

## The ultimate exercise

As we wrap up this chapter, we have one final exercise, which is considered by many Chekhov artists to be the ultimate exercise, as it can be done in a way that unites and awakens all previous tools. So, if you could only do one exercise, this might be it! Here we present a modified version from the most commonly done staccato-legato sequence (which is well-represented in **Kilroy Improv**, page 60.) This version bridges our next chapter, Tempo and Rhythm with Radiating and Receiving. Chekhov, as you know, suggested we adapt these exercises to meet our needs, so I added in Lyrical, Stillness, and Chaos to the rhythms of Staccato and Legato. And rather than just slow and fast for tempo, I use a 0–7 scale where zero is stillness and seven is as fast as you can safely move. Wil and I feel it is helpful for artists to see an example of variations developed by fellow actors to help with their own specific needs. We encourage developing your own pathway and, as with all artists in *Acting the Michael Chekhov Way*, we are giving you the concepts of play—teaching you how to fish, so to speak.

###  Let's play Staccato-Legato Six directions Radiance exercise

Standing centered and activating your IAC, move in very slow motion with a quality of Legato flow, Radiating your arms out to your right with a slow flowing lunge. Imagine radiant light flowing from every pore of your body at one out of a possible seven speeds with this Legato energy that evenly extends from your IAC right out through the room, the building, and on into space. Sense the light flowing through your eyes, chest, belly, thighs, shins, fingers, and toes. And just as evenly, draw yourself back to center. Pass briefly through center and flow to the left, extending your arms and Radiating through that left wall at a speed of one with a quality of Legato and return to center at the same Legato-one speed. Now, broaden your stance and send your light up to the sky through your arms with that same Legato-one movement. Slowly flow back to center. Then, step a little forward on one leg, plié down toward the earth, radiating your light down and back to center; then, take one step backward as your palms radiate behind you. Flow back to center and radiate your arms forward. Flow them back to center by your side all at Legato-one.

Repeat the sequence again at a speed of two, Flowing. Perhaps Radiating when you extend out from, and Receiving the energy as you return to center. Move right, left, up, down, back, and forward, passing through center in between and continuously moving at Legato-two.

Repeat at speed of three Lyrically, varying whether you are Radiating or Receiving, then at a speed of four, Lyrically, then at five in a sharp Staccato, again at six, Staccato, and at seven, in Chaos. Attempt to find the still point of zero each time you return to center. And remember, you can radiate and receive with every part of your body.

The most common version of this exercise is often done with three moderate legato rounds followed by three fast staccato rounds. The order of the directions can be changed. Also, the images as to whether you are Radiating energy out or Receiving it in can be adjusted to suit your needs. Varying the form or position of the palms may increase or decrease your sensation of Radiation. Pay attention to sustaining the Radiance even when you pick up speed and get sharp and Staccato. We abbreviate this exercise as Stag-Leg 6.

Check in on your feeling of Ease as well. The arms may move swiftly and sharply but there should be absolute lightness and Ease to the touch. If the fingers are curving up, hyperextended, you may be using too much tension. Check to see if your shoulders are hiking up. The shoulders remain light and soft with your IAC pouring energy through the chest into the shoulders, down the arms and through the fingertips, and out into space. Tension will stop the radiation at your fingertips. However, if your fingertips are curving softly downward, for example, you are losing your Radiation. The fingertips are ideally Radiating straight out in the direction of your thrust, with your light raying out like a superhero from every part of your body. Like a martial artist who is about to chop a wooden block, the hand is soft and the energy flows through and beyond. If the martial artist has tension in the hand, the hand will break rather than the block. Ouch!

Stac-Leg 6 is the definitive psycho-physical exercise that encompasses all of the Psycho-Physical Exercises (PPEs) in that it expands, contracts, pushes, pulls, lifts, smashes, gathers, throws, molds, floats, flies, and radiates. It goes through all the rhythms and tempos. It can be veiled and done boldly. It can revitalize you when tired. It can help clear excess nervous energy. It can be reversed and calm you down. It can help you anchor yourself before challenging situations and build your feeling of ease. It can be repeated for a lifetime and never quite be fully mastered.

## Rad/Rec for life

We can fill the imaginary "javelin" with anything we wish and send it energetically into the audience, a casting office, or a friend. With Stac-Leg 6, we can take what is bothering us and send it out of our body with Staccato and refill our body with Ease in Legato. If you are feeling exhausted and need to get energized, start slow Legato and speed up to medium Staccato. If you are overexcited or nervous, start in Chaos and slow it down to Legato. For depression, start very floppy and slow and build up to a speed of three or four with Lyrical crispness. Cultivate your superpowers for enriched contact with people, especially servers, clerks, and passersby. To make contact, receive a person with your eyes. Radiating warmth to a stranger can shift their spirit and yours.

## Conclusion

There are many exercises that have been and can be developed to cultivate Radiating/Receiving.

The Javelin, Staccato-Legato (Stac/Leg 6), and the Golden Hoop are among the favorites and are done in many variations around the world. The most essential concept you can benefit from here is that Rad/Rec is your natural state, and strengthening it creates a magnetic force field that reveals your creative spirit in an irresistible way. Our world is all about relationships. When your light shines effortlessly, people want to experience it. It helps them awaken to their own light.

In Michael Chekhov's *Lessons to His Teachers*, he states very clearly that he wishes us to feel free to revise his exercises and devise our own based on having a clear aim or objective. He loved to say, "What for" are you doing this exercise? His "English as a fifth language" wording is a clue to an interesting approach that might generate a different answer than the question, "Why?" As with all the ideas Chekhov offers us, along with all of the exercises, his advice is well heeded if we wish our creative impulses to blossom. If you are unsure of how you want to do it, try following closely what is given to discover what it offers as is, and then adjust it as you become clearer on your "What for?" The "How?" will flow from your creative individuality as you lead it with these kinds of questions.

## Notes

1. Susan Strasberg tells M. Monroe's ability to turn on an inner light. https://youtu.be/-MLvaskvp1w?si=1eLDDW_nRsWFKmFS
2. Soesman, Albert, Our Twelve Senses, Hawthorn Press; Revised edition, 1998.

# 14
# Tempo and Rhythm

Would it help to know how to get exciting dynamics into your story?
Why do we care about Tempo and Rhythm?

## Rhythm

There's a great answer from De Niro in *AARP Magazine*, February 2024, where the author, Andrew Corsello, observes that De Niro is reluctant to chat about his strong preparation, with the exception of his focus on Rhythm. He is referring to both the character's Rhythm and the interplay of Rhythms between characters. De Niro comments about how finding the Rhythm helps the backstory, psychological complexity, and motivation fall into place.[1]

 Let's play Rhythms—Stillness/silence

If just starting today's artistic play, take a few moments to make friends with the space, cross the threshold, and awaken and energize your creative imagination and body. Maybe you play with some Psycho-Physical Exercises (PPEs), do yoga, or perhaps put on a little music for some freestyle dancing. When you are energized, find your artistic place in the space and center in your Ideal Artistic Center (IAC).

By the way, do you remember the letter étude we did while Expanding/Contracting in Chapter 1? Well, today we will revisit that, and you may prepare by placing an actual folded piece of blank paper somewhere nearby or work with an imaginary one.

Breathe gently in Stillness. Sustain that Stillness as you take inventory of how you experience it. Imagine silence as Stillness of voice.

*What is it to not move? To have your body still and your voice silent? What Thoughts, Feelings and Will impulses arise?*

Now imagine you can move with inner silence permeating all you do and say. Pretend you can speak in Stillness/silence that can be heard by an audience. Travel through the space in Stillness, and with Stillness in your voice, greet someone or something, say a line or two of text. Can you allow the sounds to emanate from you with Stillness? Practice a simple étude of walking to a chair, sitting, picking up a letter, closing it, and returning to your start point, all with a Rhythm of Stillness. Take your time and find within the blocking those moments where you pause completely. When motionless, are you aware of any moving body parts? Bring them to Stillness. Can you hold your eyes still without glazing over into soft focus? Sustain and then release Stillness.

DOI: 10.4324/9781003512745-20

✒ *Journal/Discuss/Flyback Stillness*

What does absolute Stillness awaken in you? What does it awaken when you see another person in absolute Stillness? When is this Rhythm useful? What does moving in veiled Stillness awaken? When is this Rhythm useful? Is this Stillness something you do often, or rarely, or never? When do you do it? What happens to the power of Stillness if a random body part remains in motion? Do you listen to music with much silence in it? What was your imaginary letter about?

Seek the answers to these leading questions to engage your will to master this Rhythm of Stillness.

 Let's play Legato

Starting with your hands, simply begin to move them in a steady, continuous flow. This is the Rhythm called Legato. Legato is sustained, non-stopping, and smooth. Bring it into your entire body with abstract movement. Move your feet across the floor with a Legato Rhythm. Feel the flow in the word Legato itself. Be sure you are filling your entire body with Legato flow. Flow in Legato through the space. Improvise greeting someone real or imagined. Speak a line of text with a Legato quality, connecting all the words together, regardless of their punctuation. Play your letter étude now with Legato. Keep the same blocking and this time, make no full stops, no pauses. Stay in constant steady movement. Sustain your Legato and then release it.

✒ *Journal/Discuss/Flyback Legato*

What does moving with a Legato Rhythm awaken in you? What does this sense of continuity of flow feel like for you? When would it be appropriate for a character? What does it awaken when you see another person in continuous Legato motion? When is this Rhythm useful? Is Legato movement something you do often, or rarely, or never? When do you do it? What happens to the power of Legato if a random body part is motionless or Staccato? Was your letter the same as in Stillness or did it change?

Seek the answers to these leading questions to engage your will to master this Rhythm of Legato.

 Let's play Lyrical

Now, with Legato flowing hands, add a lilt to the pattern, giving it lyricalness. The Lyrical movement has a sense of lightness and Ease. Perhaps your hands move in little gestures that flick or punctuate your moves like breaking waves splashing at a shore. Now engage the feet with lyricism, perhaps like a waltz, moving in a repeated pattern. Lyrical has Legato moments with the surprising little sparks of Staccato. The word derives from the harp-like instrument called the lyre. Perhaps an internal hum of a waltz may help you find the lyricality we hope to experience. Check every part of your body, especially your hand life, eye life, and foot life. Are they moving lyrically? Switch back to Legato with no interrupted motion—steady and continuous. Then pause in Stillness. Resume Legato movements and then fully unveil Lyrical, lilting motion. Sometimes distinguishing Legato and Lyrical is tricky, so switching back and forth can help us understand in our body these two different Rhythms. Play with greeting someone, some lines of dialogue, and your letter étude moving lyrically. Sustain and release.

✒ *Journal/Discuss/Flyback Lyrical*

What does moving with lyricalness awaken in you? How does it differ from the steady, continuous flow of Legato? What does it awaken when you see others or hear others in Lyrical? What moods or thoughts seem to fit Lyrical?

*How often and when do you move lyrically? What are you feeling in those moments? Did the imaginary content of the letter change? Did you become a different character with the letter, or was your character in a different mood when they went to the letter?*

 Let's play Staccato

Now start moving in choppy, Staccato movements. They are sharp, short, cut movements. Check every part of your body, especially your hand life, eye life, and foot life. Feel the sharpness in the word Staccato itself. Add sound in Staccato fashion. Try to keep it very choppy in all body parts and in your speech. It doesn't have to speed up. It is about the choppy disconnectedness. Play with greeting someone, some lines of dialogue, and your letter étude moving with Staccato. Sustain and release.

 Journal/Discuss/Flyback Staccato

*What does moving with a Staccato Rhythm awaken in you? What does it awaken when you see others or hear others in Staccato? What moods or thoughts seem to fit Staccato? How often and when do you do Staccato moves? What are you feeling in those moments? Was there a change in the imaginary letter content? Did you become a different character with the letter or was your character in a different mood when they went to the letter?*

 Let's play Chaos/pandemonium

Now move with Chaos, pandemonium every which way, anywhere, you don't even know where next. One moment it is Legato, then erratically Staccato, and then Still and who knows what next. Add sound in Chaotic fashion. Try to keep it very choppy in all body parts and in your speech. It doesn't have to speed up. It is about the energy of pandemonium. Play with greeting someone, some lines of dialogue, and your letter étude moving with Chaotic pandemonium. Sustain and release.

 Journal/Discuss/Flyback Chaos/pandemonium

*What does moving with Chaos awaken? What does it awaken when you see others or hear others in Chaos? What moods or thoughts seem to fit pandemonium? How often and when do you do chaotic moves? What are you feeling in those moments? What kind of person did you encounter when you were greeted with Chaos? Did your text change its meaning? Was there a change in the imaginary letter content? Did you become a different character with the letter or was your character in a different mood when they went to the letter? When you reflect on all five Rhythms, are there one or two you favor and some you don't like or understand? This may be a clue about what the Rhythm ingredients are of your "piece of the pie."*

## Let's discuss Rhythm

Don't know if you have noticed, much of Chekhov's work is inspired by music. Music is often considered among the highest arts as it bypasses intellect and language, creating an actual sonic wave that permeates the listener. Remember in our introduction we discussed that Chekhov, in effect, looked at what principles and energies are present in peak performances. It seems quite natural that he would embrace Rhythm as an essential concept for us to master as performing artists. Because the Staccato-Legato Radiating exercise we did in Chapter 12 was a favorite handed down, many people think only of these two archetypal

Rhythms when it comes to training our everyday self to become storytelling gymnasts of human thoughts, feelings and desires. In *Acting the Michael Chekhov Way*, we expand the kinds of Rhythms to include lyrical, chaos, and stillness/silence. When we use our Chart of Inspired Action as a prompt reminding us of what leading questions (LQ) we can ask to energize our imagination, having five options for Rhythms gives us a greater variety to explore. The more, the merrier! All sound and motion can be described with these five.

## Tempo

Rhythm and Tempo are often taught and referred to as one tool: Tempo/Rhythm (TR). I encourage us to define them individually to understand the value of each. Tempo is time. It is the speed of movement. Rhythm is the pattern of the movement.

 **Axiom 14.1: The music of movement (#14)**

**Tempo = Time/Speed**

**Rhythm = Pattern**

Mastery of Tempo/Rhythm is key to being able to deliver the rising and falling action of the climactic moments of the composition. Chekhov suggests that the director's most significant job is to modulate the T/R of the show. If you reflect on shows you have seen or worked on, you may recall notes about "picking up the pace." Or perhaps you have heard, "Slow down your speech." These are specifically notes about Tempo.

It can be helpful to use scale to clarify things, using a phrase that you may have heard of before, "On a scale of zero to ten…" So, for example, a director might say "On a scale of zero to ten, your movements are at about a four. Would you agree? Let's try it again at a six. I use zero to seven for Staccato-Legato six directions because I personally can't do the sequence ten times.

Using a scale makes for easy note taking and clear communication when it happens between two Chekhov-trained artists. From this point forward, we'll define our scale by referring to it as a "10 scale" or a "7 scale."

And, if you are such an artist who has done Staccato-Legato six directions (Stac-Leg 6) with increasing speeds, you will take that direction with ease in the following "drills." With Beauty, Ease, Entirety, and Form (BEEF)!

 **Let's play Tempo**

Begin to move through the space with soft focus at a moderate, natural walking speed. Remember to rotate/spin in place until an opening appears if your path is leading you too close to another artist. In other words, please don't crash! Stay safe. Fill the empty spaces as you mill around, moving from center to periphery, in all areas of the room.

Let's establish this moderate speed as five on a 10 scale, with zero being absolutely still, not even a hand wobbling after you stop and ten being as fast as you can safely move. If you have difficulty running, stay in place and move your hands at the Tempo indicated. If you wish, you can do this entire exercise seated and using hands. Whether playing solo or with an ensemble, have one person call out numbers between zero and ten. Begin by moving gradually up and down the scale and then change up the Tempo, sometimes jumping from zero to ten or ten to one. You may keep soft focus in your eyes. Be as precise as you can be with absolute speed or Stillness.

After a few minutes of familiarizing yourself with the full range of speeds, begin again, and now make as much eye contact as possible and improv a greeting. Add your text, allowing it to radiate from you with the same Tempo as the movement. Pause.

Now try your letter étude, choosing one set Tempo throughout. Try this three times and then try switching to different Tempos at three different parts. Use the law of Triplicity and Polarity to score your étude. Release and restore.

## ✎ Journal/Discuss/Flyback

*Did emotions change with the speed? Were there Tempos that were easier than others? Do you simply not do a certain range of Tempos comfortably? Was slow motion or Stillness more or less difficult than fast? What changed when you shifted from soft focus to making direct contact? Were you able to hold contact at different Tempos? Was there a different inner sensation when greeting at different Tempos? How did the letter étude change? What did you discover?*

## Let's discuss Tempo

Tempo, as speed, often seems to awaken changes of energy in ourselves and in our audiences. When music gets faster, our inner Rhythms such as our heart and breath seem to go faster too. This energizes certain sensations that may then awaken feelings such as calmness when slower or excitement and anxiety when faster. When extremely slow it might awaken sleepiness or boredom or impatience. When extremely fast it might awaken panic or rage. What it awakens in you is partially archetypal and partially specific to your piece of the pie. It is important that we as artists are able to move through the complete scales in Tempo and Rhythms if we want to be versatile performers. We will want expand our piece of the pie by developing a feeling of safely doing the things we don't normally do. What if we don't?

Regarding a 10 scale for Tempo, zero to three are often most challenging for younger people while eight to ten are hardest for senior and mobility-challenged artists. The majority of people today are operating at a faster default speed than ever before.

Imagine you are driving down the highway in 1970 at the speed limit of 55 mph. This feels fast. Cable TV is growing, and the launches of MTV and the computer age are ten years away. Then the speed of life changes in 1985, with *The Golden Girls*, where the number of edits in a 22-minute sitcom goes from 175 to 400 because the actors are too funny to not be seen. Then comes the digital age! Today, the highways are 80 mph, and our brains are wired for hyper-fast interactions in sound bites on social media.

Imagine if your 80-mph car (think "brain") could not slow down below 50. How would you park without crashing? It may seem a silly example but not for an actor whose art is expression. Without being able to go slowly and be still, we lose 50% of our expression range. If we can't slow our speech, we can't be understood. If we can't slow down our sitting down or standing up, the camera can't follow us. If we can't pause, we will never get a laugh. If we can't hold for a laugh, we won't get a second laugh. If we can't sustain a slow fall, the audience's tears will rarely follow.

Trust me when I suggest that you will be well compensated for the effort it may take to "fall in love with the problem of slowing down." Michael Chekhov suggests that the most powerful moment in a performance is in the absence of all outer movement, in the presence of a complete pause. And we will talk about that in a few moments.

- **Five universal Rhythm patterns**
    1. Legato—flowing continuously
    2. Lyrical—patterned Legato/Staccato/Stillness (waltz)

3. Staccato—chopped
4. Chaos—unpatterned Legato, Staccato, Stillness (pandemonium)
5. Stillness/silence—pause, no motion of sound or body

- Tempo 0–10 Scale

   0 = Motionless
   1 = Slow as you can go
   5 = Normal walk
   10 = Fast as you can safely go

## Carnivàle

I was thrilled to be cast in HBO's series, *Carnivàle*, episode three, as Mrs. Crabb. It was a small role with one major scene with Nick Stahl at the beginning of the episode and a few minor visual moments elsewhere and would shoot for two days. My back story is that I have been walking with my little granddaughter, who was lame all her life, through the dust bowl of the depression, trying to find and thank the man who healed her. My ardent adoration causes a frenzy when the whole town discovers Nick's character has magical healing powers. The scene triggers the entire episode.

In preparing my scene, I thought the script was redundant and twice as long as it should be. Of course, we want as much screen time as we can get, but it was hard to memorize because my character grows to be so excited that she praises Nick and the Lord before, in between, and after the important lines. So, I fell in love with the redundant problem. I isolated all the story-driving facts that needed to be heard. I set about learning it as a monologue that was interrupted in a few places by Nick trying to quiet me down. I then focused on learning precisely where I said Glory to God vs. Praise to God, Glory to Jesus, Praise the Lord, Glory to the Father, etc. creating specific images for God, Lord, Jesus, Father and detailed gestures for praise, glory, thank you, etc. connecting it to the facts I was revealing. Since it was circus-y, mystery period drama, I didn't know how heightened they might want me to be. I practiced section by section, starting with the last beat, working to the first beat, changing the Tempo, Rhythm, volume and emotional excitement level—rehearsing how much to veil or unveil.

On the day of the shoot, they hoped that my scene would be done before lunch, but that didn't happen. The morning was all focused on Nick, and I was directed to start very, very, slowly, (exhausted, dusty, at a Tempo of two out of seven.) The young artist playing my granddaughter was a look alike to the actual artist who played the character in episode one. They clued me in that they chose her for her looks, and I would need to "help" her and them to get a credible performance from her. At times like this I am so grateful for Chekhov's strong encouragement to be well prepared. I had to be guiding her with hand signals and whispers at the opening of the scene while trying to act my own character and hit my marks and getting her to hit her marks, and while building the atmosphere of desperate stillness, then discovery, building to a frenzy. The director had me do all the lines very slowly, hardly speeding up. So I used my breath, volume, and Rhythms to create the arc. Finally, we broke for lunch and the director took me aside. He asked if I thought the scene was long. I immediately shared my thoughts, with due respect for the writing. He asked if I would trim the scene and bring him my cut over lunch.

Back in my trailer, I quickly cut the redundant praises and kept all the essential information. When I brought it to him, he was pleased and sent me to the script supervisor to give her the new text. At this point, they expected that since it took three hours to shoot my point of view on him, that it would take three hours to shoot the reverse. Especially since I had a new version of the script to memorize. After we did a camera rehearsal for the new setup at the same Tempo as in the morning, the director came to me and asked if we could try it a little faster. Absolutely! How about I start slowly and pick up the pace gradually into manic excitement? He loved it.

After an hour of various set ups, he said "Ok, you're done for the day!" The first assistant director came running over, "Wait! Isn't there some coverage you need to get?" "No, we got it." "How about some inserts?" "No, we got them." "Isn't there anything else you want to try?" "Why do you keep asking me? We got everything we need." "Well, because now we're two hours ahead." Later that evening my agent called. "They want to extend your contract to a full week, are you up for it?"

My week with them was a gift they gave me, paying me my full performance rate and featuring me on camera while I did little more than appear as atmosphere at the subsequent tent meetings. Of approximately 24 hours of programming from which to edit the 3:32 minute, IMDB trailer, my scene and dialogue made the cut, about 2:08 minutes in.[2] Strong preparation made the action effortless. Glory be to Michael Chekhov's technique!

 Let's play Tempo/Rhythm

Since Rhythm is a pattern, it can be done at any Tempo. Therefore, we can have Legato one to ten, Staccato one to ten, Lyrical one to ten. We can have slow Chaos. Let's try some. Begin with the hands again, moving Legato, (connected flow) at a Tempo of five on a 10 scale. Now, slow it down and then speed it up to a 10, keeping your movements all connected and Legato. Add the whole body as you are able or decide to stay with the arms and hands. Try the same with slow Staccato and gradually increase the Tempo to superfast. Now try Lyrical, then Chaos from slow to fast. Release and restore.

    Now, find a seat, center and imagine you discover in your creative I-sphere, an actor going to the Oscars. Inhale the image and put it on. Your chair is now a limo seat. You are now this Academy Award nominee, getting out of a limousine, walking down the red carpet. You are approaching the step and repeat banner and a gazillion cameras and reporters. What is your body's outer Tempo/Rhythm? Now you realize you urgently have to pee. What is your inner T/R? Work your way to the other side of the room, cross the threshold out and find relief! Pack up that image and restore it to the I-sphere.

    **Center** once more and imagine you discover, in the I-sphere, a store clerk mechanically rapidly scanning groceries. Inhale the image and step into it. Cross the threshold into the grocery story, and begin rapidly scanning. What is your outer Rhythm? Maybe it is a Staccato 7? Now, pretend you are inwardly at the beach. What is your inner Rhythm? Perhaps its Lyrical 3. Release and restore the image to the I-sphere.

## Let's discuss Tempo/Rhythm

Hopefully, you now can see how these two combine to form a multitude of possibilities. Yes, the Rhythms tend to have a default Tempo, however that is not a law, and we can mix and match when we are well trained. And the T/R inside of us may be very different from our outer T/R.

 Axiom 14.2: Every character has an inner and outer T/R that can match or contrast.

## The Pause/Stillness/Silence

It's time to discuss the **pause**! Yes, this is a golden gift to master. In a pause, we have an inner T/R that is often in contrast with the outer Stillness. When well done, the inner power radiates so that the Atmosphere becomes electric. This happens in an arc, where the tension expands, rising to a peak and then begins to turn in a new direction. Our task is to find that pause, radiate through it, sustain it (also known as "milking" it), drive the turn and launch into the next action, releasing the pause. In a scene, the pause can be within one character's performance or between two characters, or among a whole ensemble. In some plays, the biggest climax is when the entire cast is in a pause on the inhale. What will happen next? It is sometimes also, the perfect act break!

>  **Axiom 14.3:** A pause before an event calls our attention to it. A pause after an event deepens its impact.

Understanding this axiom allows us to see how a pause works to manage the audience's engagement. In comedy, Rhythm is key. It is mathematical law. It is the one place where every actor is encouraged to take a line reading because if you miss the Rhythm, the laugh dies.

Set up, set up, pause, punch. It is the law of threes with a pause before the third.

Ok, let me pause for a moment.

Can you please exhale and then laugh? Ha ha ha.

And can you now please inhale and then laugh? HA! HA! HA!

Thank you. Hopefully you can hear much more laughter following the inhale.

That's why we need a pause before the punchline. In the pause, the audience has time to inhale. They are prepared for what follows the pause. And, when you set up the laugh, you will then need to pause afterward just long enough for the laugh to rise and begin to turn, or fall. That's when you launch out of the pause into action. Look for more on comedy techniques in the *Applying the Michael Chekhov Way*.

For drama and tragedy, the pause after becomes essential to allow the depth of an event to sink into the Feeling forces of the audience. Keys in suspense/horror—a slow Tempo with intermittent speed—and farce—a fast Tempo with Staccato freezes/pauses—serve us well.

It is also possible to have an incomplete pause, which may appear as a lag in voice. For example, dragging out a word until you have figured out what the rest of the line is:

Weeeeellllll, I don't think so!

An incomplete pause may also be one where some specific body part remains in motion, hopefully intentionally. Take time to study some performances only for the pause to grasp more fully its powerful potential as an element of composition. Imagine two people about to kiss for the first time … or not. What do their hands do?

##  Let's improv T/R

Keeping in mind that our aim in improv is to deepen our skill sets with the tools, we suggest you do improvs in four sets: 1) Tempo, 2) Rhythm, 3) outer T/R, where your focus in on the physical and vocal T/R, and 4) inner/outer T/R, such as legato 2 inside and staccato 8 outside.

Select a scenario that you have used before or create a new one. Consider having a pile of random props for this so you can work with handling props with T/R. You may also have a caller for each player, designating their T/R and switching. Remember to use zero or pause in your improvs and to make them as complete as possible or to designate them as incomplete. Here are three suggestions: strangers moving in as roommates, siblings sorting parents' estate, shoppers at a big sale.

 Cookie Flyback

*Overall, what did you like? Were you able to do the tool and sustain it? Did you adopt your partner's and lose yours? How would you double-stuff to make this better? Top cookie: What was your favorite moment?*

Our favorite kind of music has its own T/R. We can add a whole other dimension to this section on T/R with musical genres. Listen to snippets of various music styles: country, hip hop, opera, rock, grunge, heavy metal, show tunes. Allow yourself to fully embrace the energy of the music. After moving through the various genres, turn off the actual sound and imagine the genre as someone calls each of them out. Follow the same processes of greeting each other, applying to text, and improvising in a scenario. Release and restore.

- See **Kilroy Improv** Chapter 13 for a musical extravaganza.

 Let's apply T/R

Using the same four sets above, rehearse your text and make sure you find at least one pause in each run-through, changing its location each time. You also can do your text with a caller, randomly giving you the T/R. Remember to Flyback with each run-through.

- See **OR 14.1** to dive deeper into T/R for Rhythmic Repetitions in the story, your acting, Rhythms of life and more.

> ### Homeplay
> 
> Explore how Rhythm plays a role in your daily life. What do you do repeatedly? Do you eat at a certain time, or does it change a lot? Do you rest, exercise, clean, study, rehearse at certain times, or is it random. Would your life become more or less manageable with more or less awareness of T/R? Do you have rituals that are Rhythmic: Every weekend I …, Every winter, I … What do these Rhythms do for you?

## Conclusion

Rhythms are an essential tool that unites many of Chekhov's gifts and brings us to marvel at the beauty of his circular, holographic Chart of Inspired Action, where the whole is found in each part. Rhythm, as a pattern, can be done at any Tempo (speed), and these can be inner or outer movements, which means the potential combination offers a bigger mathematical potential than my little brain can handle! The art of pause is essential to be mastered. Rehearsing your text and blocking with contrasting T/R is one of the fastest shortcuts you can make to prepare for performance, especially in quick-turnaround film situations. By cultivating Ease and appreciation for all the possibilities, you are prepared to take any direction. Sometimes, lighter, louder, faster really is all that's needed to awaken a peak performance; and when we master T/R, we will take that direction right to the bank.

## Notes

1  Visit AARP for the story, https://www.aarp.org/publications/magazines/aarp-the-magazine-february-march-2024/
2  *Carnivàle* 2003-05 IMDB HBO https://www.imdb.com/title/tt0319969/?ref_=ttep_ov_i

# 15
# Focal Points of Concentration

Hey, do you ever wonder where you should be looking at any given moment during your performance?

How does it feel when your partner looks at you constantly?

What does it mean when someone is looking out a window or at their watch instead of making direct eye contact?

## Let's discover Focal Points for characters

 Let's play Focal Points (#15)

Gather as a group very tightly in the middle. Imagine this is the inner circle of five concentric circles.

Above you is a pin spotlight shining down, only lighting you up and forming one small circle of just your body (FP1). You are literally able to look only at your body. You see nothing else. This is your focus. As you look at yourself, point to your body with your index finger and repeat several times, "*I am one. I see me.*"

Speak some lines of a scene or a monologue, looking at yourself without focusing on anything else but your body, clothing, etc. You are not contemplating or being "into yourself." We are literally talking about what your eyes can see regardless of anything else. Maybe you are picking lint off your sweater, cleaning your fingernails, or tying your shoe while casually conversing with someone beside you.

Step out to the second circle (FP2). Imagine the stage light overhead has expanded so you can see and hear your partner and nothing else. Look at your partner. Perhaps you point at them with two fingers. Say several times, "*You are two. I see you.*" Speak some lines of a scene or a monologue, looking at your partner without focusing on anything else but your partner. Do not look away. Stay looking at them only.

Step back into 1, say, "*I am one,*" while looking at/pointing one finger to yourself. Step out to FP2, say, "*You are two,*" looking/pointing with two fingers at a partner. Step out one more circle to FP3. Imagine all the lights of the stage are on now so you can see the walls, the sets; you can hear the sound cues. Look at anything you can see. Point with three fingers at the walls and say, "*This here is three. Three is all I see.*" Focal Point three is anything sensorial that you can experience. It could be sound coming from the other side of the wall, but it is here in your sensorial range. Say some of the same monologue or dialogue while looking in three. If you were using the idea of a fourth wall, what is on that wall is FP3.

## Focal Points of Concentration

Step back into FP2 to review and imprint the pattern, then 1, 2, 3. Repeat the words while pointing one, two or three fingers at the area of focus, changing your Focal Points as you cross into the next circle and back again. Now step out to Focal Point four (FP4) and say, *"There is Focal Point four. It's not here. Four is out the door."* Use four fingers to gesture back toward your temple. FP4 is something specific out there that you have in mind, an internal image that is not present in 1, 2, or 3. Move forward to FP3.

Step forward into FP2, then 1, 2, 3, 4. Repeat the word and point the fingers, change your focal points as you cross into the next circle and back again. Now step out to Focal Point five (FP5) and say, *"Five is I don't know where."* Throw your five digits to the sky. FP5 is everywhere and nowhere. It is Duh! or Help! Blankness, the unified energy field, vast emptiness or anything that is not here and not specific. FP5 is a place we go to only for short periods of time.

### Let's discuss Focal Points

See Figure 15.1 Focal Points for character.

In real life, we look in many different places in any given conversation. We don't usually stay in direct eye contact (FP2) for very long before we look elsewhere. Sometimes it is for practicality and safety (FP3), like when we are walking beside someone in a conversation. Sometimes we will look at our watch (FP1) while talking. Other times we are trying to avoid the direct contact, trying to remember something (FP4), to intentionally enjoy the scenery or get a mosquito off our arm. And sometimes we go to an unknown place (FP5) that seems to be everywhere and nowhere at the same time. One of the tendencies that actors have

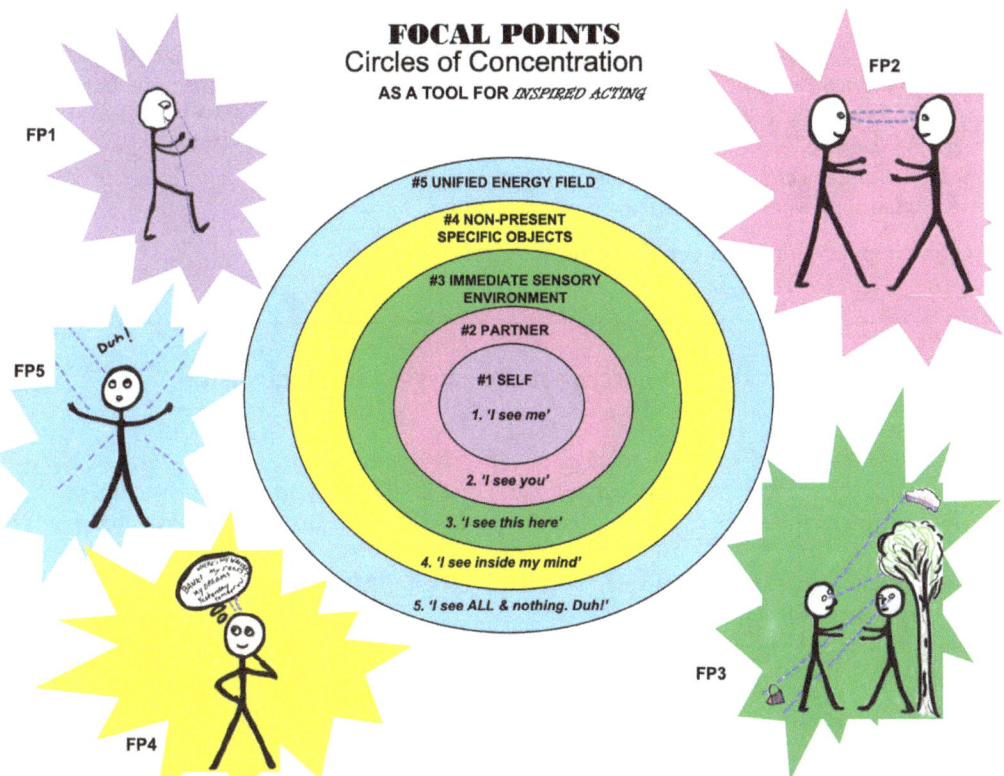

*Figure 15.1* Focal points for character: Where should I be looking right now?

which makes their performances seem untruthful is an overuse of direct eye contact, FP2. If you have this training or tendency, take some time to practice, observe and apply FPs.

> ## Homeplay
> Study the people around you to see how much time they spend looking directly at the person they are talking to. This is great to do in a restaurant where, from a distance, you can watch people sitting across from each other where it is easiest to look straight at each other. *Does the listener more often look at the speaker? Does the speaker look more at the listener? What is the effect when one looks more directly than the other? What seems to be happening between them when eye to eye, and does that change when the FP changes?*

To further clarify between FP1 and FP4, FP1 is literally looking at your body, your shoe, etc. In the present moment, you see a material body part. It is not an internal state. That is FP4, which can be a memory, a problem you are solving, a name you are trying to recall, a person you want to call, where you left your wallet yesterday, etc. FP4 is looking at something specific that is not present. It could be future or past or just somewhere else right now, and you are trying to locate it in your imagination. FP4 is "there" not "here" which is Focal Point one on your body, and FP3 is the present place you are in.

The thing that distinguishes FP4 from FP5 is that FP4 is a specific thing you have in mind. Say some of the same monologue or dialogue while looking in FP4. If you are looking out at the audience or to something specific over their heads and speaking to them/it as if they/it were your partner—that would be FP2. If you were looking out into blankness while recalling and picturing the story you are telling, that is FP4. If you are doing neither of those while looking out, you are in an artificial construct of the stage outside of human behavior and perhaps justified by the style. For example, in musical theater, we might turn out to the audience, in effect being in Circle 2 with them while we are looking over their heads perhaps at our dreams or yearnings in a distant FP4. Try to justify such blocking by finding something in FP3 or FP4 to bring it into humane behavior. For certain styles, like alienation, this artificial disconnection may be useful. Awareness and intentionality are what make magic.

As a tool for inspired acting, focus on the points in Axiom 15.1.

>  Axiom 15.1: Focal points are what the physical eye focuses on.
> 1. Our body—I am one. I see me. *Point one finger to chest.*
> 2. Our partner—You are two. I see you. *Point two fingers to partner.*
> 3. Our present environment—This here is three. Three is all I see. *Point three fingers to walls.*
> 4. Some non-present, specific object—That there is four. It's there, in my mind. *Point four fingers to temple.*
> 5. I don't know where five is: the void, God, the big whatever—Somewhere is five. *Five digits open and are flung to sky or earth.*

Repeat these mnemonic phrases while moving from circle to circle to help remember the five Focal Points.

Review the entire sequence with big physical movements until you have it memorized. Play with a partner exchanging simple lines in the five circles. Notice how the meaning of the lines change depending on where you are focusing.

Suppose I am in FP1, picking my nails and saying, "Gee, I really like you." How does that make you feel? How seriously will you take me? How sincere do I seem? How sincere do I feel saying it that way? Maybe I mean it and am terribly shy. Or maybe I don't care about you at all and don't have the time of day for you.

 Let's improv: FP

Practice improvisations using Focal Points. When playing solo, improvise a monologue about the weather, choosing an imaginary partner with whom you are planning a weather-dependent activity. Switch your FP about every 30 seconds, without talking about the fact that you are changing where you are looking. The topic continues, though how it goes may shift.

For two actors, use the same scenario, each with a partner off-stage who calls out the number of the Focal Point for their player. Be sure to have the off-stage voices be distinct from one another, so the players on stage can recognize when the caller is addressing them. When the callers give the players their starting FP, the actors begin. Stay strictly with the FP no matter how difficult or against the grain it may seem. Allow yourself to keep the storyline continuing even when the FPs change. Guide the callers to keep their actors in the fifth circle only briefly.

 Journal/Discuss/Flyback

*How does changing the Focal Point impact the story the audience sees? How does it change you as a character? What did you discover about your ability to stay in one FP for an extended period of time?*

- See **Kilroy Improv Chapter 14** for FP ball toss chaos, callers, and more!

🎭 Let's apply: FP

1. Let's start a memorized monologue, changing Focal Points as you go, boldly unveiled, using an arbitrary score (sequence) starting in Circle 1 to 2, 3, 4, 5, 4, 3, 2, and back to 1. Gradually veil the movements to make them more subtle while staying precise with your eye; focus and play with the monologue multiple times, using different scores of Focal Points. Be very strict with yourself. Circle 2 in a monologue is the imaginary person you are speaking to. In Shakespeare, that could be to another part of yourself, the audience, or another character.
2. Apply Focal Points in a generic scene with six to ten lines total, and play the same "calling" game. Try it again, declaring what your score will be in advance. Then, simply play the scene intuitively, shifting FPs where it seems appropriate to the story.

Here's a sample generic scene that can be done by anyone:

A: Hi, How are you?
B: Hi, How are you?
A: I am fine.
B: I am fine, too.
A: I didn't expect to see you here.
B: I didn't expect to see you here either.
A: I missed you.
B: I missed you, too.

## ✏ Journal/Discuss/Flyback

*Did the "story" change with each variation of the Focal Points? Did a relationship or situation begin to appear? Did an Atmosphere arise? What are you noticing about the power of each of the five FPs?*

3. Apply FPs to a specific scene with arbitrary scores at first, and then craft two contrasting scores that produce a completely different subtext for the scene. Allow the blocking to reflect the inspiration from the FP score.

## Let's dive deeper into FPs

Focal Points are part of our artistic process of crafting the character's eye and hand life, which explore the unique ways each character uses their hands and eyes; the way they touch their clothes or props, habitual mannerisms, etc. As with other aspects of Chekhov's approach, he developed these Focal Points as a variation of Stanislavsky's three circles of concentration. This set of tools appears on his hand-drawn Chart of Inspired Acting that he gave our teaching partner, Mala Powers. However, like the Three Sister Sensations, they are not generally found in Chekhov's own writing. This work was handed down to me orally from George Shdanoff and Jack Colvin, who stated that Chekhov added two more circles. Having more circles gives us more variety of expression.

Some artists are doing lovely work with a "second-circle" focus, which is serving a very different purpose than the above FPs. Their second circle is a bit more metaphoric and brings the artist into contact with the other, inspiring the actor to focus on their partner, giving to them, receiving from them; and, as such it is perhaps more akin to Chekhov's Radiating and Receiving, with a touch of the Four Brothers of Art, Beauty, Ease, Entirety, and Form. This second-circle work will complement Chekhov's five FPs, Rad/Rec, BEEF, and vice versa.

**How do you know what is appropriate to the story? How do you choose the best FP?**

Focal Points are a specific means of creating power in how we relate to other characters, as well as a means of organizing our lives in general. Anytime we don't know where to focus, we can check in with our objective and ask, "Which Focal Point will move me closer to achieving my objective?" Exploring objective is our next chapter. Meanwhile, let's play with what we already know about objectives.

##  Let's play or homeplay

Through the Goblet process of centering, envisioning the unlimited sphere of your imagination (I-sphere), ask your character to reveal to you its FP score by inviting the character to appear before you and play the scene. You observe the scene objectively noting on your script where the character is focused. Now, play the scene imitating precisely where the character was focused even if you don't understand why.

*What did you discover?*

Play the scene again, choosing the opposite of what you just did to experience the difference.

*What was new, and which did you prefer?*

Try this with another pair of actors watching to see how different the scene is to them in its subtext.

Witness their scene after yours. This same process can be done with a partner for your monologues.

> ### UFO self-discovery
>
> I watched an actor in an emotionally confrontational scene while they were in FP2, eye to eye. I saw the actor's eyes darting off to what looked like their partner's ear or aura, an *unidentified focus on* (UFO), if you will. The actor was completely unaware that this was happening and thought they were in FP2 the whole time as intended. Unfortunately for their partner, it was difficult to stay connected with them.

Fortunately, this tendency is in most cases a habit, sometimes neuroatypical, that can be improved or even fully transformed with a little bit of awareness. It is usually unconscious. To an audience, it can appear evasive and lacking in focus. It is often physically revealed while acting with eye patterns that avert, dart off to the right or left, or drop to the floor. If an artist has this unconscious pattern, becoming aware of it is an easy first step to dissolving it. If you are an artist with this process of eyes moving away from your intended partner, it is important for you to discover it as soon as possible. It might take a bit of courage and your strong will to "fall in love with the problem." Perhaps you are not aware of it; and perhaps people don't know how to talk to you about it. If you are willing, ask your scene partners and your coach to help you recognize whether you have any eye life that has moments of UFO. We really do want the best for each other and will help if you ask.

 Journal/Discuss/Flyback

*If you do have these moments, are they only when acting or also in other areas of your life? Do they happen at certain times, when certain topics are being dealt with? Certain emotions, like rage, eroticism, shame, fear, tenderness? Or is it completely random? Try some concentration exercises where you look at an object for two minutes without taking your eyes away. You could even self-tape looking at a person next to the camera.*

*You will want to take personal time, outside of class to look deeply into this physical "dis-click" in your biological imprint. Reach out to a life coach or counselor to help you clear this habit from your body. Building your confidence, sense of purpose, and feeling of safety in those situations is critical to you being cast in the future. It will also play an important role in all personal and public relationships.*

*Remember that these biological imprints likely began early in your life, and you can free yourself from them if you know about them. If you feel confident in your partners, friends, or mentors, you could ask them to give you a private hand signal or cue if they notice when you are doing it. Then, you are free to use your will to keep your eye on the target.*

> ⚛ Axiom 15.2: Where focus goes, energy grows.

## Focal Points for life

We can approach *Acting the Michael Chekhov Way* as a problem-solving technique.

This section is the result of leading my imagination with the question, "How can the five FPs be used as an inspiration in everyday life, and help me solve some problems?"

> ### The universe will have its way!
>
> I was working very hard during my career in New York and Hollywood, going on sometimes 125 auditions a year, spending a lot of time driving in traffic, and terrified of leaving town for a day in case I might miss something. I needed a better sense of balance and BEEF. I wasn't prioritizing other aspects of survival very well. When I did pause my efforts to get more acting work, I felt guilty. Inevitably, a stunt job crippled me. That got me to slow down big time. I finally applied *Where Focus goes …* to my life. I hope you can find more Beauty and Ease with this tool, learning it the easy way and avoid crashing into a cliff like I did.[1]

Looking at Figure 15.2, we see Circle 1 is the *character*. When we are playing a character, our focus is where the character is looking. We are wholly invested in what's happening as the character.

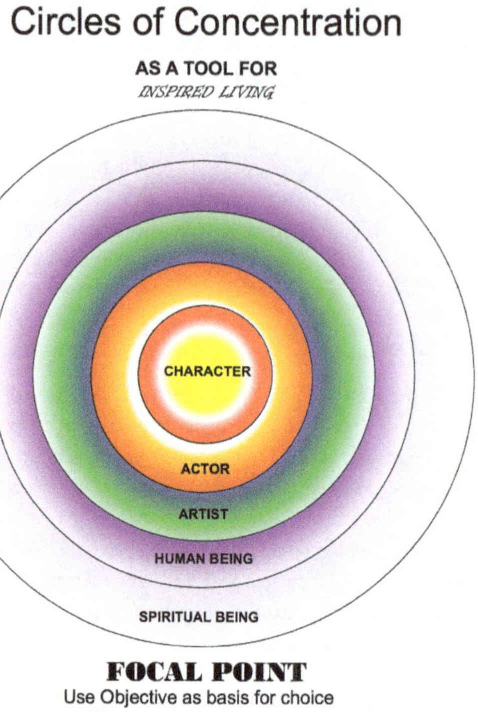

## Circles of Concentration

**AS A TOOL FOR**
*INSPIRED LIVING*

(Concentric circles from innermost to outermost:)
- CHARACTER
- ACTOR
- ARTIST
- HUMAN BEING
- SPIRITUAL BEING

**FOCAL POINT**
Use Objective as basis for choice

*Figure 15.2* Focal points for life as a piece of art: Where should I be focusing right now?

In Circle 2, we are the *actor*. Our focus is meeting the aims of the art of performing such as doing the blocking, trying new techniques, remembering lines, selecting tools to use. While we are the character, the actor is simultaneously working to meet its aims.

In Circle 3, we are the *artist*. Our focus is on building opportunities to live as an artist, getting headshots, getting an agent, going to auditions, networking, doing a showcase to be seen. This is happening simultaneously with the character and the actor.

In Circle 4, we are the *human being* who encompasses the artist/actor/character. The human being needs to eat, rest, make love, shop, pee, play, see family, make personal connections, and pay the rent. Ideally all of that happening in this circle can support 1, 2, and 3, and vice versa.

In Circle 5, we are a *higher self/spirit being* encompassing a human experience who is an artist who loves to act their characters who are struggling with life threatening problems in their own imaginary five circles. All 5 *beings* are present inside the I-sphere of our higher self.

At any given moment, each of these five beings has needs and objectives. Ultimately, they must all find balance. When a family member is on their deathbed (4), it might not be the time to excuse yourself for a commercial audition (3). When you have been doing scenes in class for ten years (2) but still haven't made a headshot and resume (3), it might be best to put your time and resources elsewhere to get that agent and put your actor on the line. While you are performing the character (1), it's not the time to play tricks on the other actors (4). If you can't pay your rent (4), it might be time to stop taking class and get a job (2/3). Robbing a store to get money (4) isn't going to meet your higher self's objectives.

Each circle has its needs, and if we can align them so that Circle 5 permeates and supports 4, and 4 supports 3, and 3 supports 2, and 2 supports and aligns with 1, then we are "happy" not just on the stage. We have a sense of life, of balance, of community, of purpose. We no longer fear turning down a career opportunity because we understand that we are in the perfect place in time and space. Chekhov would ask, "Of what shall we think when we are on our deathbeds?" Will it be of our stuff? Or shall we rest with Beauty and Ease for who we have been within the Ensemble of our lives?

At any time when life feels out of balance, or things are tugging at you in different directions, you can pause and review your life with this chart. Identify your objectives, and prioritize your needs with freedom from angst and shame. The universe will align to support your dream when you are internally aligned. Synchronicity—magical random moments—happens more frequently. There are days when buying that ice cream cone is just more important than the calories and cash! It's moment's like that when you might get discovered by a director who likes the same flavor.

To help you understand, here's how these two versions of the Focal Points chart compare:

 **Axiom 15.3: Focal Point circles of concentration chart**

**As a tool for inspired acting**

1. On our selves
2. On our partner
3. On our present environment
4. On some non-present, specific object
5. On the void, God, the big whatever

**As a tool for inspired living**

1. On our character
2. As an actor
3. As an artist
4. As a human
5. As a spiritual being

## Summary

Choosing the right Focal Point at the right time in character or in life can help you accomplish your objective. When you begin working with these FPs for acting, dare to be bold and disciplined so that you can identify which ones are most challenging and practice them a little bit more. It will help you learn about your own *eye life* and enable you to create characters with a very different *eye life*. Imagine the way Othello uses his eyes vs. Richard the III does, or Juliet vs. Lady MacBeth. Perhaps observe or recall someone you know well, like your Auntie Su and Uncle Mark around the house versus your best friend, Scott, and you out on an adventure.

Take some time to review your life in all five circles to see if you are well balanced. And when you get stuck on where to focus, check in on your objective. Where focus goes, energy grows.

## Note

1   Dalton, Lisa Loving, *Falling for the Stars: A Stunt Gal's Tattle Tales*, Sojourn Publishing, 2017.

# 16
# Objectives "What for?"

What's my Objective?

How do I get my Objective out of my head and into my body, into the scene?

Objective: ~~I want to understand!~~ Oops! That's not an actable verb.

The moment we get an idea to do *something*, an image is living inside us of that *something* coming out perfectly. This ideal outcome or goal fulfills us in some way. This image of our future glory engages our will to move forward, perhaps despite the many steps that we must take to reach that ideal. The image gives us hope, and when we have hope, the audience does too. For example, your hope to be an inspired artist brought you to this moment in this work, and your image of the ideal success of that will carry you up onto your feet toward mastery. This impulse to do *something* is generally identified as an *Objective*. We also can call it an *aim*, *goal*, *task*, and other words which we will look at shortly. For now, we will default to the word *Objective* (#16) as Chekhov wrote it on the Chart of Inspired Acting.

In an ideal world, my favorite way to learn is experiential. It's a bit tricky trying to have a discussion about Objective experientially. However, **Crumpled Paper Tag** is a great way to experience hope and images of Objective fulfilled. To take a deeper slower dive into reflecting on how we personally relate to Objectives, our Will Force and how that might be different from others, gather some folks to play too.

- See **OR 16.0** Crumpled Paper Tag.

In our everyday lives, we are rarely conscious of what our more profound Objectives are that are driving us forward. However, Chekhov encourages us to be as clear as possible about our character's Objectives, even if De Niro says, "Sometimes it's easier when characters don't know themselves." We, as the artist, do want to know the character so we can raise the level of impact our storytelling has on audiences.

>  Axiom 16.1: We live with an image of our Objective fulfilled.

## What's the problem?

In contemporary psychology, having a dream to inspire us is called "towards motivation." The hope, yearning, and excitement for succeeding, winning, or achieving victory keeps us moving toward the goal. When we are clear on the character's Objective or aim, we are able to identify the rise and fall of the character's journey toward fulfilling their dream.

Rather than think logically to find our Objective, Chekhov encourages us to use the Goblet process to ask the character to show you it's Objective. Then incorporate that image to sense what the image was telling you. For answering all of the questions posed in this chapter and forward, ask your images first!

As previously mentioned, Chekhov often asked "What for" is the character doing this? Some attribute this word choice to his English as a fifth language. However, it does potentially offer us a richer understanding of an Objective. As a leading question (LQ), "What for?" might lead me to begin my answer with "For pursuing my dream," or "For fixing my problems."

In fact, Sharon Marie Carnicke, who in my opinion is the foremost English–Russian speaking scholar on the subject of Stanislavsky (KS), gives strong justification for understanding Stanislavsky's Russian word *zadacha* as *problem*, despite it being historically translated as *Objective* or *task*.[1] Carnicke quotes an analogy KS gives as "[T]he circumstances in a scene present the character with a *zadacha*, just as a mathematics teacher presents a student a *zadacha* to solve[2] (SSII: 1989)."

When an actor understands what the character's *problem* is, and that there is at least one in every scene, the world of "dynamic response" expands easily. Now we are energized to meet the challenge, to solve the *problem*, including the various smaller steps that need to be taken to solve their biggest problem. Linking this with the idea that the character immediately imagines themselves successfully solving the problem (*toward motivation*), one can then explore how each moment of the text is either moving the character closer to their safety/victory/good (+) where they overcome the problem or closer to danger/defeat/evil (–) where the problem crushes their dreams.

We can increase the tension in this battle between good and evil if we also have "away motivation." A classic example of *away motivation* is a lion chasing you. The lion is the problem you are running from. Think of this lion as a nightmare. When a character (or any human) is only running away from their nightmare or lion, as soon as the lion gets too tired to chase them, they can stop all forward motion. Meaning once the *away motivation*/nightmare is resolved, all forward momentum is lost. There is no reason to go forward.

As a path of self-development, focusing on *toward motivation* creates a healthy concentration on a dream that lies ahead. Your love for the dream keeps you moving forward with health and hope.

However, in storytelling, we want to have conflict (problems) times three: conflict within, between, and from without. So, having both *toward* and *away motivation* gives us the dream and the nightmare, and then the story is about dealing with the problems we meet in fulfilling the dream and avoiding the nightmare.

A classic use of Objective applies a hierarchy to the overall story: there's the Super Objective (SO), and then smaller Objectives for acts, units, scenes, and beats. Each of the smaller Objectives is a stepping stone to meet the higher ones, all the way up to the SO. This creates the "spine" that unites the elements of the character or the story. Generally, the language used to state the Objective is required to be an action statement followed by an active, infinitive verb: *I want (to + an active verb)*. The intent in stating the Objective is to help the artist understand the character's motivation. For most of us, the statement remains in our heads and doesn't make it into the *life body*, the Imaginary Body (IB) of the character. This is our *actor's problem*. What we need is a way to awaken in us the character's urge to action, to create high stakes/extreme consequences for success or failure of the action that live in us from moment to moment.

*Acting the Michael Chekhov Way* offers us tools to fix this problem. That's the "what for" Objective of this chapter!

## Objective statement

Here is a template for a classic American Stanislavsky-inspired Objective statement:

**"I want *(to + an active infinitive verb)* despite *(obstacle)* so that *(intended result)*.**

Let's use a character from William Inge's *Picnic*. Rosemary is a spinster yearning to be married. The actor might say Rosemary's Objective statement is

"I want *to get* him *to propose* to me despite his resistance *to marrying* me,

so that I *won't die* an old maid."

 Let's play an Objective (#16) experiment

There are two major parts to this experiment.

For Part I, your aim is to compose a Stanislavsky Objective statement and then get it into your body so it will be living there as you play the scene. If you are currently working on a character, you might use that for this experiment. You may use any character you feel you know well enough to form the statement. For a short cut, use Rosemary's statement above and pretend you know her story.

1. Take a few moments to figure out and write down the statement, using the template above. Keep your statement a secret until the end.
2. Perhaps you self-record or choose a colleague to be your audience. Once you know the statement, speak it out loud privately so your audience doesn't hear it, and then start your text, monologue, improv, or scene, allowing it to guide you. ❋ When you finish, do a short Flyback and then get ready to keep experimenting. *Did the statement help you? Did it make the rehearsal more exciting for the audience? What did your audience think it was?*
3. Find movements that convey this statement with no words to the camera or your audience. Perhaps it's a bit like you are playing charades. If you like, start a timer to track how long it takes you and your audience to get connected with the character's Objective. ❋ *Note in your Flyback to what degree you sense the character's dreams, wants, and nightmares in you. Perhaps you ask now or wait a little bit longer to hear what the audience thinks is your statement?*
4. Try the text once more to see whether having physicalized the statement helps you. ❋ *Flyback with your own self-evaluation and then listen for any helpful offers from your audience, or go to your video tape. What did the audience understand about your character, and did it awaken anything in them?*
5. Release and restore yourself.

I don't know if you found satisfaction in the above sequence. Perhaps it was helpful, but you feel there is more. When I view Rosemary's statement above from Chekhovian wisdom, I am reminded that I experienced a few problems with getting this from the page to the stage:

- The phrase: "get him to propose" is vague and uninspiring.
- The obstacle: "his resistance to marrying me" is passive and unactable.
- The intended result: "So I won't die an old maid" is *away motivation* with no forward motion and offers very little with which to act. What drives her forward is hope.

So for me, my Rosemary statement was not so inspiring, regardless of whether or not it was accurate.

I am ready for Part II of this experiment!

For Part II, let's *Chekhovize* this statement, using gestures as expressions of will. In creating gesturable verbs, we are preparing to embody Chekhov's belief, which the next chapter will examine, namely that

Words are symbols of Objective, and the Psychological Gesture, as the crystalized Will, is the Objective.[3]

Using gesturable verbs in our Objective statement is a practical way of getting intellectual ideas to live urgently in our bodies. We can describe what gesture we are doing; what gesture is being done to us by the problem, and what gestures are happening in the outcome. This way, you can literally practice the scene doing those gestures unveiled and then veil them while energizing your body, and the character's IB as well as your partner's.

In a moment, we will shift a few of the words in the template, rewrite our Chekhovized Objective statements and try our scenes again.

First, however, I want to share a very frustrating thing that my intellect decided was a big problem in the fundamental need for the Objective to be formed as an infinitive verb, whether gesturized or not.

Do you remember that idea of a hierarchy of Objectives with the highest one being the super Objective? This is either the single most important "infinitive verb" the character wants to accomplish either in the story or beyond the story, in the scope of their existence. Knowing the SO should answer all questions of "why" the character does what they do.

Hang on. Seems to my mind that every actable infinitive I find for a character can still provoke the question, *Why?* And, if there is another *Why?*, then my current SO must not be at the top of the hierarchy. Why does King Richard need to kill all those people? Because he … Why does Lady Macbeth need to be queen and kill all those people? Because she… Why does Rosemary need to marry a man? Because she … Why does the Empire need to kill all those people? Because they …

AMCW Objective statement:

**"I want to *(gesturable verb)*, despite *(gesturable problem)* so that *(gesturized expression of Dream over Nightmare)*.**

*Here is one example of using gesturable verbs for Rosemary:*

"I want to *pull a proposal* out of him despite him *pushing* me *away* so that I *won't shrivel* into an old maid."

Using this phrase, as the scene unfolds, Rosemary tries to pull him to her. She may use her vulnerability, her sexuality, her authority to pull him to her. She can watch everything he does—his body language or his blocking—looking for signs that he is coming closer, physically, emotionally, etc. She can react to his pushing away, whether she sees him physically distance himself or it is evident in his body language, text, or emotional distancing. And with his every push away, she shrivels just a little bit more. Her partner will have his own gestures, and as artists, they can stay completely in the moment, Radiating and Receiving the gestures, sensing whether they are closer to their dream or nightmare.

I started exploring the relationship between Thinking, Feeling, and Willing forces and emerged with the idea that there is a *state of being* that we are seeking to experience. It changes from person to person, though there seem to be a few states that are truly archetypal: we wish to be in a state of happiness. All our actions are to overcome the problems that keep us from being happy.

What makes us happy? Many things, and here's one approach. To be in that *happy state*, we want to stay biologically alive, feel safe, have a sense of belonging, a connection to others, sense our and other's value, experience aesthetics, and meet our full potential (You be the best you).

These are essentially psychologist Abraham Maslow's Hierarchy of Needs,[4] which justifiably may be found in most global cultures though not necessarily in the order listed. My point here is not to endorse Maslow but to acknowledge that this question of motivation has lingered in the minds of humanity. Notable people have observed that our Objectives move us toward a state of being.

So why are we not asking, "What state of being is my character moving toward?" And "What state of being are they experiencing now because they aren't in their most desired state?" When we identify the state of being, it is not in an actable infinitive verb. So, I called this a "life wish."

I queried some highly trained Russian teachers about this question: Was there something above and higher than the character's super Objective that is not an actable verb, but is a state of being? "Oh yes, that's the super-super Objective." Aha! The SSO is the character's life wish.

When we know the character's life wish—their deepest dream—we can lead our imagination with questions that will inspire in us everything we want to know. Ask, "If my character succeeds in this action, how would that get them closer to their life wish?" "What action must they take to get their life wish to come true?"

Using the law of Polarity, "What is the nightmare they fear if their dream doesn't come true?" Another way of asking is, "If they aren't living their dream now, what nightmare are they experiencing?"

We can ask questions using Thinking, Feeling, Willing (TFW)—how does their life wish affect their *thinking*? How are they *feeling* about getting or not getting their life wish and how do they show or hide those feelings? How do they use their *will* to get what they wish?

The answers you generate can become powerful images that activate the character's urge to do what they do to get what they need. Understanding the life wish can also lead you to discovering the "seed of the need," an experience the character might have had where the nightmare was or almost happened that may be driving them to revenge or over achieving. We will talk more of this in the next chapter.

With all of that said, here is my proposed Chekhovized "What for" statement where we include the action, counter-action, and states of win/loss (*toward and away motivation*).

>  Axiom 16.2: Chekhovized "What for" statement
>
> "I *wish* to (gesture phrase) despite (counter gesture/problem) so that I (life wish/dream + nightmare/ fears)."

Here is a sample for Rosemary:

"I wish to *pull a proposal* out of him despite him *pushing* me *away*, so that I will *float* happily in his arms, and I *won't shrivel* into an old maid."

With this statement, I can make a gesture for each section. Using Polarity, I start from the last image, which is my fear: shriveling. Then I reach out to pull him (action); then I react to his pushing me away (counter action) by pulling harder. Maybe he gives me a sign of hope, and I start to float (reaction, using a quality of movement to convey my state).

### 🎭 Let's apply part II of our Objective experiment

1. Revisit your previous Objective statement and Chekhovize it into a "what for" statement.
2. Create big, unveiled gestures and movements for each part of your statement. Without text, try them in various orders, using Triplicity, Polarity, Transformation (TPT). If working with a partner, you can interact. Perhaps a new gesture comes from your improvised playing. If solo, freely react to imagined counter gestures.
3. Try the text with the fully expressed gestures.
4. Gradually veil the gestures until you are as physically expressive as the Style suggests.
5. Release and restore.

### ✒ Journal/Discuss/Flyback

*Did you feel inspired by the gestures? If you watched other artists, were you as an audience more actively engaged? Rooting for or against a character more than before? How was the Atmosphere? If watching the video replay, is there a difference between the scene with the Stanislavsky Objective statement and the Chekhov "What for" statement? Were you able to sense when your dream was disappearing or getting closer? Did it to change the Tempo or Rhythm of the gesture? Did new or different gestures want to come with tactical changes?*

## Conclusion

Chekhov encourages Stanislavsky's system of analysis that uses the concept of Objective as a basis for composition. Well-defined Objectives/problems with extreme consequences for the whole production, the story, the character, the smaller units and beats, will propel the dynamic composition. Keep this in mind when making choices.

>  **Axiom 16.3: A well-chosen Objective will have the possibility of succeeding brilliantly or failing miserably.**

In our AMCW, if the "What for" of the character is deeply compelling, driving the character toward the dream with the possibility of failure endangering the character's existence according to their psychology, then we have very exciting performances. When these images radiate in the imaginations of the actors, it can trigger all emotions to rise and fall depending on the success or failure of the dream.

Objectives/aims/What fors/problems as we now know them are not just for the character. We use them throughout the production process. In sum, we begin with

- What problem will writing/doing this show solve?
- "What for" do we choose this script, here and now?
- "What for" did the author write it?

We will go deeper into these in Chapter 19 on SynthAnalysis™.

## Notes

1. Carnicke, Sharon Marie, *Dynamic Acting through Active Analysis*, page 112, Methuen Drama, GB, 2023.
2. Stanislavski, K. S., *Sobranie sochinenii II [Collected Works]*, 9 vols., page 212, Moscow; Iskusstvo, 1989. As cited in Carnicke, 2023; xiv.
3. Chekhov, Michael, *On the Technique of Acting*, Harper, 1991.
4. Maslow, Abrahm, American psychologist, https://en.wikipedia.org/wiki/Abraham_Maslow

# 17
# Psychological Gesture

How cool would it be to snap into the character in one breath?

How do I get my character's objective to live inside my body?

How does my objective affect my walk, talk, and body language?

 Let's play go green

Gather into a circle standing a little more than shoulder width apart. Imagine everyone is standing on a spot in a circle of spots. Be able to step to the right, taking the place of the person beside you. When playing solo, imagine 20 Imaginary Bodies standing on the spots around the circle with you. Select a person to clap a "Go" signal. Playing solo, set a timer to go off every 15 seconds or use your inner sense of tempo to determine the time to "Go" to the next spot.

 Using the Goblet process, ground yourself deep into the Earth below, feeling the solidity of your talent supporting you. Allow the sun center in your chest to energize your ideal artistic center (IAC). Imagine you can radiate up through the ceiling, the clouds, the Earth's ozone layer and beyond, into your unlimited higher ego, your sphere of imagination (I-sphere) above you. Today it is overflowing with characters of a special color, all of whom want to show themselves to you. They all want to fill your goblet!

When you hear the "Go" cue, immediately create the gesture of a character in green as if it instantly comes to you. Give it a full-bodied, clear beginning, middle, and end. It may or may not have sound. Sustain it for three seconds and release.

On the next "Go," everyone steps onto the spot on their right, into a new path of inspiration. Go again instantly. Another character in green. A new gesture pops in, and you sustain it. And release. Go again. And yet again. And again. Go 21 times if you can, without repeating anything. When done, release and restore all of those incredible characters in green back to the I-sphere where they will eagerly await the next artists who invite them.

*Journal/Discuss/Flyback green characters*

*What did you discover? Was it fun? Did you use your whole body? Was there a qualitative difference in how you expressed your first few characters and your last few? Did you notice anything you wish to share? If there was anyone watching, any observations? Did you get bored? Did you worry about what you would do next? Were you able to be surprised? Did you hit a wall and go blank?*

DOI: 10.4324/9781003512745-23

Many of us will hit a wall and think we are empty of characters in green. Then suddenly, light breaks through and even more creativity floods. By the time we are at 21, we know we could go to 121. Our endless creativity will provide for us if we trust it and if we know a few more tips.

##  Let's play Psychological Gesture (#17)

Standing in a circle, shoulder to shoulder, follow a leader for the next five minutes or so, silently imitating what they are doing or as much as you can see of what they are doing. When playing solo, lead yourself in a sequence something like this: Begin in ideal universal stance with your arms at your sides, your feet hip width apart.

Raise one hand and point forward. Pause three counts to sense how this affects your thoughts, feelings, and will. Adjust the left foot pointing out. Pause three counts to sense into this new position. Shift your weight onto your left hip. Pause. Place your left hand on that hip. Pause. Shift your center with hand on hip. Pause. Raise your shoulders. Pause. Drop your shoulders and bring your right hand up to wave, with your wrist forward and the palm of your hand cupped, facing out. Pause. Release your left hand on hip to the side. Pause. Raise it and place your index finger on your bottom lip, then on your top lip. Pause. Switch your thumb for your index. Pause. Drop your left hand down. Pause. Straighten your right hand that has been waving a little bit in front of you, without changing the arm, just the hand, so that your palm is down, and your fingers and thumb are aligned straight up and out to the horizon. Pause. Restore the hand wave, Pause. Return to the straight hand, Pause. Now, rotate the palm upward and cup it. Pause. Release.

## Journal/Discuss/Flyback Follow the Leader

*What did you notice? How did the different moves affect you? Did images arise? What were they? Were you surprised by how powerful a minor body change affected your psychology?*

When we can sense how much change can happen psychologically by a simple cupped or straight hand, turned-in feet versus parallel feet, or a weight shift. We begin to see how many sensations whose form we interpreting are traveling through our body. The exploration of the impact of body language on how we think, feel, and desire helps us to appreciate that, as we work to find the ideal forms here, we could be very close and just have a finger out of place. Keep this in mind as we move forward.

## Let's discuss the Psychological Gesture (#17)

What can I say about the PG but that it is certainly the cherry on the top of the Chekhov cake. Everything we have done has been leading up to this masterful all-encompassing tool that is both the most famous and most misunderstood aspect of Chekhov's work. The Psychological Gesture (PG) encapsulates everything you need to snap into performance level in one breath. Gesture, as we mentioned in Chapter 4, is a movement + an intention (Will). A PG adds the Thinking and Feeling Force to incorporate the entire trinity of psychology (ToP) into the movement.

In many ways, a PG is like a moving or "living logo" for a character. A logo is the most concise expression of everything the company who owns it represents. One brief look at the swoosh logo immediately awakens the energy of Nike, Greek goddess of victory, and inspires us to want to buy Nike products.[1] Do you get hungry when you see golden arches? Yes, visual logos are powerful. Doing a pose for two minutes can also empower you, as 25 million people have seen in Amy Cuddy's 2012 TED talk.[2] Chekhov takes this idea further by offering us a movement. Because the PG begins in one position and moves through to another position, it can create a longer lasting power than a pose. One challenge in the past that students of Michael Chekhov have struggled with is that it is very hard to convey a moving sequence in a book.

Readers saw poses, were confused, not understanding that some of the more known PG illustrations were in fact a sequence of three images showing the beginning, middle and end of a gesture. These were often interpreted as separate gestures/poses for different characters. The result of this is that many are in effect doing a psychological pose rather than a movement. The power of the PG is awakened by the effort to move from the start point, through to the end point. The transformational power is in the transition itself, rather than the final pose.

Taking Chekhov's idea that all images exist independently in the higher I-sphere, we can pretend the PG is up there, and we just need to find it. Remember, our job is to train our body, mind, and spirit to play fully, revealing our creative individuality. To accomplish this, we ASC the image: access, select, and convey it to our audiences. And now that we have trained our bodies—physically and energetically—we are masters of conveying transformation; therefore, once we access the image, we will be able to convey it. When we complete our study of SynthAnalysis™, we will have all the tools to make the greatest selection to convey. If this technique were music, we could say you have learned your scales and now you are ready to play a melody.

>  **Axiom 17.1:** The purpose of a Psychological Gesture is to transform you instantly into your character's Thoughts, Feelings, Desires, and Imaginary Body.

PG is a full-bodied gesture, like the Archetypal Gestures in Chapter 4, and has the same guidelines, BBEEP, reviewed below. The PG to which we just referred is visible (physically accomplished) and eventually will become less visible or entirely invisible (veiled while being done in the imagination with the etheric life body).

>  **Axiom 17.2:** All well-done PGs engage BBEEP:
> - Breath—One inhale and exhale. If you have excess breath at the end, increase the resistance.
> - Body—Make full use of the form, especially the pelvis, legs, and heel of the hands.
> - Extreme polarity—The movement begins in the polar opposite direction of its ending.
> - Effort—Make 100% commitment of the will (key to star quality) with real tension easily done.
> - PASS—Be prepared, acted, sustained, and stopped with clear beginning, middle, end.

## Differences between AG and PG

Now that you have a greater understanding of the Trinity of Psychology (ToP) from Chapter 12, it may help to have an AG vs. PG review from Chapter 4 and note a few new thoughts.

- The AG awakens an urge, a *will* to act that has no reason or consequence for its success or failure (AG = Will). It is executed objectively with no emotional *how* and with no thought of *why*. The will is in the present and in motion.
- The PG adds to the AG, an *image, a thought* (T) of *why* we are doing this gesture and a *quality/feeling* (F) that expresses *how* we are doing it. We add reasons and consequences.
- The PG is not universal or objective. It is heavily filled with the subjectivity of characterization and a "what for" that makes it so specific that it is used for this one character and no other.
- Remember that the Archetypal Gesture is a training technique and is never used in performance. When an actor applies the AG of push, for example, the character and context of the story will add their own T-force + F-force. Instantly the AG is transformed into a PG, colored by this character's Trinity of Psychology—Thinking, Feeling, Willing (TFW)—in this moment.

- All gesture, when eventually veiled (made invisible when we apply it), then enjoys freedom from time and space limitations. You can reach for years in your imagination and suddenly smash 50 times in one second.
- Emphatic and habitual gestures are the body language of the character visible to the audience and may or may not be influenced by or consciously expressing the PG. It is most powerful when the body language is psychologically connected with the character via a veiled PG.
- Try a few minor adjustments if you feel the form of the PG is close to inspiring you, yet not quite there.
- If it isn't working, ask yourself if you have BBEEP'd your gesture, making it extremely physical before veiling it.
- To experience full transformation, commit fully to doing your PG.

 Axiom 17.3: A half-done gesture does half the job!

## How AG becomes PG

An AG (pure W-force) transforms into a PG when you add T-forces + F-forces to the W-force.

When a *what* (will), *how* (feeling), and *why* (Thinking) are added, the formula can be abbreviated as such: **AG+T+F=PG.** Add terror (F) to throwing (AG/W) in order to protect (T-reason) and we have a PG for a character trying to throw off a detective who suspects them of murder.

## How the ToP works in PG

Here is how each aspect of the trinity of the psychology is impacted by how you do the PG:

- The stronger and clearer the image of the meaning, the reason for—*what for/why* the gesture is—the more fully your Thinking Forces will be awakened and aligned with the character's thoughts. This is the T in Thinking, Feeling, Willing (TFW)—the Trinity of Psychology.
- The stronger the quality you do the gesture with—*how* the gesture is done—the stronger your Feeling Force will be awakened and aligned with the character's emotional state. This is the F in TFW.
- The stronger the physical force you use in fullness and dynamically—the *what*—the more deeply you will want what the character wants, imprinting the will-force of the character on your Will. This is the W in TFW.

## The application process

There can be as many PGs for a character as there are objectives. This means there can be a super-super PG that expresses the life wish or the ultimate state the character desires. Then, there can be a super PG, or an overall PG that encompasses the action and nature of the character in this story. There can be PGs for acts, units, and beats. There can be reaction PGs that are responses to the gestures coming toward you from your partners, from the atmosphere, from the internal conflict.

There can be PGs for the play, for the theme, for the cast to the audience, for the atmospheres. We will discuss these in Chapter 19 on SynthAnalysis™.

Once we find the PG, we perform the PG ideally three times to awaken and anchor it into our beings and can then proceed in different ways.

One application is to use the PG as a springboard. Having done it three times, we spring into the performance with the energy created by the physical doing of the PG and ride the waves of that through the scene, segment, act, etc. invisibly.

Another way is to use it while in the scene as a stepping stone, by imagining all or part of the gesture, so that it continuously fuels our performance by energizing our life body. At any given moment when we feel less connected to our character, we imagine doing it in our energy body right then. We ride that until we need more "juice" and imagine the gesture anew. In truth, every moment of the story might change the Tempo/Rhythm or urgency of the gesture. This keeps it always in the now.

While we may be using the super PG throughout the story, we can use a reactionary PG or unit, act, or beat PG as needed for sections. As an example, if we return to our kids-on-the-bus improvisation (opening of Chapter 4) as a parent, our super PG may be a very protective embrace. However, for that scene, we may use a punishing, firm push, and then a sugary pull accompanying a promise of candy to achieve the objective of getting our child onto the bus safely and quickly.

To get a little more familiar with the basic idea, let's create some random PGs and see if they can inspire us in an improvisation.

 ## Let's improv building a PG from an AG

Let's make up a PG for a scene. Find your own creative spot in the playing space. Center and ground yourself. If you wish, radiate a pathway up through the ceiling, beyond the clouds and into your unlimited sphere of imagination.

- Ask your IAC to select a generic character such as a teacher, doctor, thief, or orphan. This process of looking into your I-sphere is called the Artistic Gaze. Wait patiently if answers don't pop up immediately and then just pretend something came and make it up. When the answer arrives, whisper or speak the selection out loud. That signals your body that your selection is clear.
- Our next leading question (LQ) is "Which basic AG would be fun to play with now: push, pull, lift, smash, etc." Speak that answer aloud also.

For purposes of clarifying the steps, let's pretend your answers were *thief* and *push*.

- Now lead your imagination by asking "*What for* are you pushing?" Pause until your I-sphere sends you an idea, or just make it up. "Aha! My thief is trying to push their friend Jordan into helping them steal something!" Whisper that aloud.
- Now try "imitating" that image with a large physical push as if you are trying to push Jordan into stealing. What quality are you using to push? Try gently, flirtatiously, threateningly, pleadingly. Try different Tempos and Rhythms. Allow the Form of the gesture to reflect your character and morph its form so it is no longer like an AG, symmetrically balanced with an impulse from the IAC, but rather starts from some other place in the character and has a freer, unique form. Clarify in your mind (T-force) why you are "pushing" and "how" (F-force) you are pushing, and use strength to push (W-force). Give it a clear beginning, middle, and end.
- When you are satisfied with one or more of your versions of the PG, improv a scene. With a live partner, you can keep your character and PG a secret. Do the PG three times, with your backs to each other, then veil your PG, turn, and enter the game. The improv will reveal the circumstances each of you has. Play for two to three minutes. Release and restore. If playing solo, improvise a monologue or dialogue with an invisible partner, Jordan.

Flyback to see if the PG is inspiring you in your improv

If necessary, start again and unveil the PG so it is more physically expressed in your body. If there is a big difference in your voice and energy when unveiled, keep practicing the larger expressions and veil gradually until you can stay connected to the images and allow them to be conveyed by your voice and body. Remember to release, restore, and Flyback with each round of activity.

## Deeper dive into finding your perfect PG

When we are applying the PG to a specific character, the most common question is "How do I, the artist, find the right one and how will I know it's right?"

 Cookie Flyback

Chekhov suggests that when you find the right PG, you will know it immediately and for the rest of your life. Building your skills to quickly recognize that Aha! moment "when it feels right" is the value of the Cookie Flyback technique. That asks us to identify our favorite moments. When "it" is working, "it" will immediately excite you, and maybe surprise you. Remember that you being surprised is an ingredient in all peak performance. The perfect PG will continue to inspire you every time you do it or even think about it. We just need to find its form, and here we have … guess how many ways? Yes, three per the Law of Triplicity.

> Axiom 17.4: Answer leading questions with 3Is: Inspiration, Imagination, Intellect.

These are the same three ways that answer all your leading questions, and here is how we specifically use them to answer the LQ: "What is my character's PG?"

## The 3Is

1. **Inspiration**—Sometimes even before we can form the LQ, we are instantly inspired. The character image and traits appear effortlessly and rapidly. I love when this happens. The answers just happen and are perfect choices. When we did our go green circle, we could say that we were instantly inspired. When it comes to PGs, it happens when we see a story board, or hear the idea or read the script. We suddenly have a knowing. Then we imitate or incorporate them—we put them on and try them out. Do some lines or a scene with your inspiration and Flyback. If it doesn't surprise us, excite us, inspire us, no worries. We can turn to our second "I."
2. **Imagination**—Chekhov has a strong preference for using our imagination rather than our intellect to find the character's objective which is a central ingredient of the PG. So, try this before moving to the third "I." That's why we have used this imagination process many times, where we awaken our Ideal Artistic Center, ground and radiate up to our unlimited sphere of imagination, our higher I/ego. We ask the LQ, and using the *ARTISTIC GAZE*, we wait patiently for the images to appear. We might develop it further here.

    Invite the character to reveal the PG and wait, patiently gazing. If it won't deliver the goods, ask it to show you some behavior, perhaps some activity that appears in the script. Then we inhale the images and exhale their expression. We imitate them. Incorporate the behavior trying to see if you can inwardly feel the PG. After you see, feel, sense, or hear your PG, imagine you can show it back to your image while it watches. Listen to any adjustments it makes to you as you do it. Try it several times and apply the same line used earlier. If we need to adjust something, we can converse with the image and ask it to make changes. We can zoom into a body part to get a close-up of what it's doing or rotate it in space. We can have it reverse its motion and go backward, or speed up, etc. Say some lines or run through a scene with your imagined PG and Flyback. Sometimes our imagination requires seeds to be planted that grow and blossom a day or a week or two later. When you are developing your character, consider connecting with your IAC before going to sleep at night and asking some LQs to appear in your dreams. And be sure to ask to be able to remember them when you awake. Keep your journal or recorder handy. As we are artists 24/7, our *higher I* never sleeps. If nothing shows up or it doesn't surprise us, excite us, inspire us, no worries. We can turn to our third "I."

3. **Intellect**—This third approach may not be the most desirable. However, it is pretty surefire, and that makes it worth doing. Sometimes I work with it even when I am confident in my first or second "I" just to see if it affirms those gestures and perhaps reveals even more clarity to me of why they work.

In this Intellect-based approach, we are asking a series of three leading questions. We will create a PG for each answer. Then, we will have what we call a "Compositionary Gesture" (CG). This is a sequence of gestures that combine to express multiple aspects or situations a character might use. We can then condense the three-part CG into one super PG. This process is built upon the "what for" objective statement we learned and composed earlier. You might want to use that same character to practice on in this process.

To develop a Compositionary Gesture we ask the LQ:

1. *What do I want? What is my aim, my purpose? "What for" do I want this? How do I try to get this?* One way to find this answer is to stand up and talk about your character to someone who can witness you or self-record as you do. They can ask you the questions, and you answer them, actively using your hands and body language as you talk to help make what you are saying clear to them. Stand up if possible. This will support you best.

   Meanwhile, the witness watches you describe the character and what they want, making note of the small gestures you are making, perhaps unconsciously. When you are done, Flyback and ask whether you noticed any specific gestures starting to happen. Then your witness flies back to you, affirming or helping you become aware of what gestures you repeatedly did. These micro-gestures are veiled PGs already living in your vast creative self. They are the seeds of your full PG.

   Now, try taking the most frequently repeated of these small gestures and begin to unveil it. Perhaps your witness coaches you with these LQs. *What are you doing? Can you expand it? What happens if you give it more polarity? Could you use more of your whole body? Is there a sound? Can you use more force? What if you change the Tempo or the Rhythm? Do you want to try one of the other gestures you were doing?*

   Remember Rosemary from *Picnic*? Let's say I am talking about her/as her (*my body language is in italics*). By the way, we can do this where we put on the imaginary body and speak in the first person: "I, Rosemary," or we can imagine looking at her in our imagination and speak in the third person: "she, they." For this section, we shall use "I, Rosemary."

   > I've been this school teacher for thirty years (*I seem to be pointing my finger*) and dating this guy for a long time who just won't make a commitment, (*now my hands fall to my side in hopelessness*), and then I see the young lovers (*my hands clench*) and I'm so jealous (*I start reaching out*) and I just want to get this guy to marry me (*now I am urgently trying to grab him*), to take me away from this lonely life. How I get him is I let go of my moral standards and have sex with him to trap him into feeling guilty. (*ooh, now there's something interesting—I do a trapping gesture—yeah that's the sweet spot, the moment when my creativity gets excited! My primary* How *is to trap.*)

Now I play with various ways "to trap" until I come up with a well-formed version that feels like the way Rosemary would trap. This trapping gesture is now what we will call the *how* or *core* gesture. It is the underlying action living in Rosemary throughout the play. It is *how* Rosemary tries to solve her *problem*.

 Let's apply

Before we launch into this training sequence, remember, working with the material in this book, that we are artists who are seeking to build healthy skills and learn a practical preparatory sequence for disciplined, professional work and for healthier, happier lives. We are not trying to do this one scene as a perfect fit for the whole play. We aren't trying to *get it right*. We will save that for the actual production, using SynthAnalysis™, Chapter 19.

Create a sequence/étude of physical actions your character does or might do and apply this gesture to it three times, non-verbally. *Flyback each time to note what you liked, what seemed to remain uninfluenced by the gesture that you might double stuff (your suggestions for how to enhance your play), and what your favorite moment was. With each rehearsal, try to keep your previous overall likes and favorite moments in the scene, while integrating your suggestions.*

Next step is to add the dialogue. Try this three times, first using a very expressive, unveiled Gesture, then half-veiled, and finally, revealing just the tiniest bits of the gesture in the body language, maybe keeping it more expressive vocally. *Flyback as above. Release and restore.*

2. Having found the *how* or *way* our character works, we want to identify the *win*, the character's dream, their *toward motivation*, and the transformed state of being. In a sense it might be a gesture for the fulfilled super-super objective. We can call it various names such as the dream, the win, the transformation, the SSO or the victory gesture.

    Once again, solo or with a witness up on our feet, we ask LQs to the character and we and they respond. *What will it be like when you succeed with your core gesture? How will you respond when you get what you want? What would be your dream come true? How will you feel when you have your life-wish fulfilled? What is your victory gesture?*

    Here's me as Rosemary, in first person answers: I will be so happy, I can finally relax. (*My arms open peacefully.*) When he marries me, I will be the best wife he could ever want. I will make him happy with delicious meals. (*I rub my hands together with yumminess and then give an imaginary plate a food to him.*) And I will kiss him hello and goodbye every time I see him. (*I open my heart and palms and then lean into him.*)

    Hmmm, I am noticing that I am opening and lifting my heart and palms to him. It's very gentle, tender, and playful. I begin to explore the gesture, making it bigger and bigger. Maybe there is a phrase, statement or sound that is there? When I have found the essence of this glorious gesture, I feel so happy I could cry tears of beauty. I give it a clear beginning, middle, and end that is prepared, acted, sustained, and stopped.

Try the same silent étude as previously, three times fully unveiled and working to the degree of veiling that the show might use. *Cookie Flyback, and remember to retain the sparkling moments, those favorite ones of yours, and then juice up the parts that aren't quite inspired, sustaining the best aspects of the last "take."*

Add the dialogue, rehearse three times again with our sequence of unveiled full expression, half-veiled to veiled to the style. Flyback and refine. *Double check in your Flyback whether you are allowing this sense of victory to play throughout with no possibility of defeat. This may force you to work completely against the dialogue and/or the situation. Committing to doing it polar to the customary sense—what we usually call "wrong"—may surprise you in the best way. Release and restore.*

3. For our third part of the compositionary gesture, we now want to awaken and align in ourselves the polarity of the victory gesture by discovering the loss of the character. This is the deepest fear or nightmare the character has—the problem with its worst outcome. It is the trigger or seed of the character's need. It is the original wound that the character wants to get rid of, avoid, escape, or heal. On some level, it is the threat of a horrendously painful physical or psychological death. This generates the *away* motivation. It is the lion at its hungriest.

Once again, solo or with a witness up on our feet, we ask LQs, and we respond. *What will it be like if you fail with your core gesture and never succeed? How do you respond when you don't get what you want? What would be your nightmare come true? What scares you the most? What is your defeat gesture?* Another approach which may generate different answers and therefore different gestures is: *What happened in the past that you never want to re-experience? What pain is your problem causing?*

If you find your nightmare/loss gesture based on the failure of not getting your dream, try this several times. Try a second one that focuses on the seed of the need, a triggering event that happened in your character's past that you swore would never happen again. Take this also through the skill-building sequence and then compare both loss gestures. Using the cookie Flyback, one of them will likely "click" more than the other. That being said, maybe one works for one section of the script, and the other for another part of the story. As you do this, remember to keep your personal identity separate from the character's.

> Here's me describing Rosemary, this time in third-person answers, as if I am a camera experiencing her in my imagination: She will be so lonely, she can hear people whispering, "She's an old spinster nobody wanted." (*My arms shove something down like garbage.*) He'll abandon her (*more throwing down*). She will sit in her rented room until she withers in loneliness. (*I shrink my chest and wrap my arms trying to hug myself.*) She feels unlovable. She thinks she's a slut. He used her and threw her away. No one will even notice when she's dead. Her life has been pointless (*more discarding trash gestures.*)

Well, it seems pretty clear that my image of Rosemary's nightmare is total abandonment. When I try to do the gesture I am contracting, my torso is falling, collapsing while I am throwing my arms and upper body downward as my knees crumble inward. I refine this and try the étude.

When you refine your character's loss gesture, try the étude and then the scene using the same unveiled-to-veiled sequence and then add dialogue, using your Flyback skills to empower each rehearsal.

 Let's improv rehearse!

Having found now the three gestures, rehearse your scene with callers who randomly call "win," "loss," or "core" as you play. If you have short names for your three gestures, those can be used in place of the generic term. For Rosemary it might be: giggly give (win), trap (core/how), wither (loss).

## Uniting the Compositionary Gestures

With these three gestures, you now have the dreams and nightmares of the character imprinted in you, and the main method your character uses to achieve their dreams and avoid their nightmares which is the spine of the character's arc.

We can put these together in sequence in any order depending on the story. We can keep them as three separate gestures that compose the life of the character.

- Try starting with the nightmare, then the core gesture, and then the dream fulfilled. Suppose the plot is that your character is failing at everything, then they find their *how* gesture, overcoming their problems

# 18
# Improvisation/Jewelry

Would you like unique moments in your performance to sparkle in the audience's mind long after you are done?

Would you like to feel spontaneous in all that you do, regardless of how many times you have done it?

## Jewelry (Improv) (#18)

Don't we artists just love to create that special quirk or idiosyncratic behavior for our character? Yet how often do we fall into the clichés of hair twirling, toothpicks, and cigarettes? Sometimes we pick random things out of desperation to be creative and they make about as much sense is wearing a gold-studded bowtie with a tank top. If we are doing broad comedy, we might get away with it. Most of the time, that choice desperately screams "Look at how creative I am … please?" I think I mentioned much earlier that I made a lot of silly choices trying to prove, perhaps to myself most of all, that I was talented.

Let's have more faith in our creativity! If we learn to Improvise our scenes with tools, allowing *the tool to rule*, we can discover the psychologically perfect mannerisms and behaviors. These moments are what Chekhov calls "Jewelry," and we want to be able to *wear our Jewelry* regularly when we express the character. When we discover the jewel through Improvisation, its source is from our higher creative ego. When we recognize and choose a jewel, it can become iconic in society, like "fava beans and a nice chianti," Anthony Hopkins' line in *Silence of the Lambs*. And we want that. These moments are your jewels, and you want to wear them as they sparkle.

We are just now focusing on Jewelry because it is, in a sense, a finishing touch on the character. With Moveable Centers, Imaginary Bodies, Archetypal Characters, TFW, Radiating/Receiving, and Psychological Gesture (PG) we have a deep box of tools to explore and craft our characterization. This is like getting the basic outfit on for going to the grand party. Sometimes though, you discover a jewel very early and design the outfit/character to fit it perfectly. Have you done that? Where you have a cool piece of Jewelry and need to find the outfit to match? There are times when we discover very early, something like a hand movement or way of walking or a way to say a certain line that always works. Through rehearsals then, we assemble the rest of the outfit (the characterization) to match the truth of the jewel. Yes, what allows a jewel to sparkle is its feeling of truth.

The Jewelry puts the finishing touches on and makes the whole outfit shine, whether it's a necklace, watch, earrings, tie tac, or tie itself, it is uniquely your taste. And in a sea of formal black evening attire, it is your Jewelry that sets you apart.

Jewelry is one of the two most memorable elements about any performance. The other most memorable aspect is the Overall Atmosphere (OA) of the experience. Think about a great show or film you saw a while back. Do you remember an especially cool moment? Do you remember the general vibe of the show, the Overall ATMO? How much else do you recall? Often, we have to spend more time "racking our brains" to access more specific details. It's the jewels that sparkle in our memory (T-force) as the Atmosphere (ATMO) radiates through our soul (F-force). And that makes our day!

How do we discover our Jewelry? Through Improvisation, Chekhov puts us at ease by helping us find unique behaviors and body language that are absolutely psychologically founded in the character. Rehearsing with the PG fully expressed, then veiling it, can lead to finding Jewelry—small, special touches on your character that are mannerisms, how you use your props, costumes, hands and feet that evolve organically from the psychology of the character.

Using Rosemary as an example, suppose as I rehearse the scene with my loss gesture of shrinking and withering, I notice that I tend to use my left hand to nervously gather the collar of my blouse on either side of the front buttons, making it more "uptight;" my eyes avoid him. Then, I notice that when I am trying to trap him through sex, I tend to release my hands, gathering my blouse and slide it down, molding my hand lower as if to open a button. And I look straight at him. When I Flyback, I observe that I really liked the left-handed fidgeting closing the collar and could use that as a habitual mannerism. The hand sliding down to open a button, I will save for that one moment when I desperately need to snap the trap shut or lose him, and maybe it will be both hands when I do. The evolution from nervousness to daring seduction will be a lovely arc to act. I have learned something about my eye and hand life as well.

I hope you can see this is where that Flyback skill is so important. Remember asking, "What was my favorite moment?" You have been building the skill to recognize when you Flyback the moments that sparkled. By now, I bet you're a pro at it.

 ## Let's apply Improv with our super PG

Using a previously created Psychological Gesture, developed through Inspiration, Imagination, or Intellect with the Compositionary Gesture, rehearse your text again with some specific stage direction or activity. Use a prop if you can, along with a costume element. Focus on how you can use your eyes, hands, props, and costumes to reveal the PG. In what way does the PG affect how/where/when you look, how you handle the props or the way you touch, adjust, ignore your costume? Flyback and repeat several times if possible to develop your favorite moments.

 ## Journal/Discuss/Flyback

*Were you able to imagine your PG altering your eye patterns? Your use of props? Hands? Costume? Was there a particular moment or way of moving that interested you more than other moments? Did a jewel sparkle for you? Overall what did you like? What would you do/what did you do differently in each "take"? What was your absolute favorite moment?*

 ## Improvisation

If what defines Improvisation is a sense of happening for the first time in an unplanned way, then from a Chekhov point of view every rehearsal and performance, no matter how tightly directed and crafted should in fact be executed with a feeling of Improvisation. Indeed when you let the tool rule, you may experience surprise at how you sound and move, in the same way one does in a peak performance. Keeping this in mind, will keep the jewels fresh and sparkly. This boosts your unique creativity and makes your characters deeply memorable.

There are multitudinous ways to trigger inspired action through Improvisation. I encourage you to view Improv in an expanded way. When acting the Michael Chekhov way, every time we explore or rehearse our text with a tool, we are Improvising.

 **Axiom 18.1: All inspired action is Improvised.**

Regardless of whether it is scripted, blocked or made up on the spot, good acting is *happening* in this one moment. Acting is a time art—it lives in the now as do all performances: dance, music, opera, and sports. Even if it is captured on camera, it still has happened only once. Improvisation earns its place on the chart as the key to "moment-to-moment" acting from the character's truth. This is distinct from other acting techniques that seek "moment-to-moment" truth through the artist's lower ego/personality/memory.

## Improvisation in scripted/directed applications

We must be able to play the same scene or monologue again and again on stage or on camera, with the same dialogue and with the same activity and do so each time as a new time. When we focus on a particular tool each time, our aim is to use the tool in our imagination, our life body, and our physical body, right then. If we are remembering how that tool impacted us last time and acting out that result, we may deliver intelligent yet uninspired performances.

We strive to be in this moment, Expanding or Falling, for example, or allowing the Imaginary Body (IB) to guide us. And, since this expansion or fall can only be right now, and since the independently existing image is ever changing, no two expressions of this text and blocking will ever be "repeated." The use of the same tool each time will deliver both consistency and spontaneity. Use of different tools for the same spot can also produce inspiration. When Yul Brynner performed the *King and I* for some 5000 performances, he used a different Chekhov tool from night to night. Chekhov played Hamlet with at least five different PGs depending on how his higher ego guided him in relation to the audiences' needs. When we use the exact same text to practice different tools, we are training ourselves to be able to literally *play* the same text in a new way each time.

In Chekhov's *To The Actor*, there is the famous "Exercise 12" that is an extraordinary process for developing this sense of "moment to moment." We could even consider it Chekhov's psychophysical equivalent to Meisner's repetition exercise. This could be the singular focus of a very patient, advanced class for several months with an astute teacher. Or you could do this as your own private Chekhov muscle-building process. It could evolve into a show. I wrote in detail about this exercise in *Michael Chekhov and Sanford Meisner: Collisions and Convergence in Actor Training*, edited by NMCA-certified teacher, Anjalee Deshpande Hutchinson, Routledge 2020. (Chapter 19, "A Psychophysical Path to Moment to Moment—The Gift of a Lifetime. Chekhov's Repetition Exercise 12-13," By *Lisa Loving Dalton*.)

## Improvisation to learn the tools

*Acting the Michael Chekhov Way* regularly uses games and Improvisations for learning the tools and expanding our perspective on them. Chekhov's classes in Hollywood included an Improvisation night every week. Remember, **knowing our objective defines the application of the tool.**

- We sometimes use Improvisations to introduce a tool. This allows you, the artist, to experience the tool and become aware of it during the Flyback and discussion following. The kids-on-the-bus Improv before teaching the AGs is an example of this.

- Whenever possible, we encourage Improvising on some level soon after the tool has been discussed. Here it is important to prioritize yielding control of the moment to the tool. We want our clever minds to rest and release ourselves from the need to be funny, entertaining, dramatic, or interesting. There is no need to prove you are a good, unique, or creative artist. No need to follow Thinking, Feeling, Willing (TPT) or any Laws of Composition. The sole goal is to concentrate on the tool and allow it to "rule" by moving you and speaking through you. This can be as brief as speaking a line with an imaginary Center or on a Push. It can be games or structured Improvisation.

Here are useful tips:

- Set the grounding guidelines using safety first and "Yes, and …" (No denial.)
- Determine which, if any, dialogue is to be used (silent, three-word max, gibberish, verbal)
- Given circumstances can be, but do not need to be, defined. We can start with no objective, no characterization. As players we can simply focus on the tool and the inspiration coming at the moment from the images and from our partner. It might be as simple as this:

    *"Player A, please use Thinking forces. Player B, please use Willing forces. GO!"*
- Flyback when the Improv is completed and ask, *Did I yield control to the tool? Did I maintain contact with the image and my partner? Did I listen and respond through the image? Overall, what did I like? How would I "double stuff" for next time, making it juicier? What was my favorite moment?*
- For three- and four-person Improvs, it's easy to use tool sets that contain three or four elements such as the Qualities/Kinds of Movement (QoMs), Three Sisters, and the TFW Trinity of the Psychology.
- For ensemble Improvs, try playing with the unlimited number of centers, IBs, or ATMOs both overall and personal, Archetypal Characters and PGs.

Wil Kilroy's *Improvisation the Michael Chekhov Way* developed in partnership with this pedagogy and is a brilliant resource for deepening understanding and skill with fun Improvs, using the tools of our Chart of Inspired Acting.

## Improv as an entertainment form

There is a whole world out there of short- and long-form Improvisational entertainment that is specifically a performance style. All the tools and principles that you are learning here will expand your repertoire and skillset for this style of performance. There is much more to say about how terrific you can be, switching up characters, listening carefully, and rapidly accessing your imagination. However, we will delve more deeply into Improv as entertainment in *Applying the Michael Chekhov Way*.

Improvisation/Jewelry, box 18 on the Chart of Inspired Action, is the last tool in the box before putting it all together into Composition/SynthAnalysis™. Many artists learn the tools of Chekhov system, but few are given a clear sequence of how to integrate the tools when building a specific production of a story. Congratulations on making it this far. With what we are about to explore, you will be prepared to deliver inspired action in the audition, rehearsal, and performance.

# Part VI

# Putting it all together

*Putting It All Together* means fulfilling the goals of our training with *Acting the Michael Chekhov Way*. Our aims have been to solve the problems we face as artists with a healthy sequential approach that builds our skill sets for our art and for living our lives as works of art. Two final chapters are about the composition of our performances and our lives, respectively.

The task now is to synthesize all we have learned and to put on a show! This way we harvest the healthy balancing benefits of our sequence for growth (T-force), our wish to radiate to and with audiences (W-force), and be "happy" on the stage and in life (F-force).

Chapter 19, SynthAnalysis™ for the Part-Composition, offers us the pathway to falling in love with the problems of production. The SA process is the result of three decades of weaving the Stanislavsky system of analysis into a sequential approach for storytelling via stage and film, in a teachable way, that lifts table work onto its feet, from page to the stage. Table work is the century-old challenge of analyzing the script around a table, sometimes for a year, often leading to "paralysis by analysis." (We are so in our heads that when it's time to get up on our feet, we can barely act.) Also, traditionally, the actors do what the director says, and there is very little interaction between the design team and the performers, many times leading to stressful interactions because actors don't understand the director's and designers' overall vision. It seems to culminate in a crisis a week or so before opening the show, when technical teams and actors converge, and the curtain call hasn't been staged.

SynthAnalysis™ brings all creatives into communion with each other with clarity of shared vision via multidimensional practices, unconventional rehearsal techniques, and practical engagement of higher ego principles.

SA helps us prioritize our tasks in the rehearsal process, drawing attention to the most significant aspects of production and of the story itself. *How* one "draws attention to" what is significant is found on the Chart of Inspired Action in the Composition section. However, what is implied in the original chart[1] where it states "Composition" is often incomplete. To address this, our *how* is based on the *why/what* found in the Stanislavsky system of analysis and then synthesized with Chekhov's indications in Chapter 8 of *To The Actor, To the Director and Playwright* and *On the Technique of Acting*.

As a side note, most of Chekhov's students knew analysis already, and since Chekhov liked the basic Stanislavsky system, his teachings focused upon what Chekhov could improve upon—synthesis. Having studied with a dozen of Chekhov's students, and interviewed many more, I observed that Chekhov's students primarily focused on teaching the exercises and principles as he taught them, without including the system of analysis. Very little actual scene study was done and even less directing of his trained actors by a Chekhov-trained director. This left a fundamental gap between practice and application to a full text. This gap widened as the generations passed, and it manifests as a systemic weakness that SynthAnalysis™ and dynamic directing address. *SynthAnalysis™ the Michael Chekhov Way* is forthcoming to address this fully. Here we will focus on the actor's point of view for a specific role.

The structure that follows is modeled upon the analysis plan as taught to me by directors Dmitry Boudrine and Andrei Malaev Babel, to whom I owe deep gratitude. They are both alumni of the Vakhtangov School in Soviet era Moscow. Historically, Stanislavsky is said to have felt Vakhtangov was the best teacher of his system and Michael Chekhov the actor who most exemplified it. Chekhov was also head of the Vakhtangov school after Vakhtangov passed away.

Our final chapter, Love, Laughter, and the MC Way Hereafter, aims to solve the problem of what do next and how we do it, as artists living in the "real" world.

Both chapters help us recognize in our thinking, feeling, and will forces what needs our attention, which is our single greatest choice as human beings. **Where attention goes, energy grows.**

## Note

1   Chekhov, Michael, *On the Technique of Acting*, Harper, 1991, Preface by Mala Powers.

# 19
# SynthAnalysis™ for the part-Composition

"I loved that show!!!" Isn't this music to our hearts, we who create shows? We love to hear both audiences and the production ensemble sing the praises of our shows, and we hope that this love will live in all of us for our lifetimes. It happens with the best of shows, whether on stage or camera.

## Composition/SynthAnalysis™ (#19)

How do we create such powerful storytelling experiences? With SynthAnalysis™ (SA), we can take a mighty leap in this direction. The aim of SA is to raise the standards of artistic achievement in production so that audiences experience deeper transformation, so that being a spectator of our shows becomes a significant event in their lives. In meeting this goal, we, as creators of the event, also experience creating and giving the performances as a significant event in our own lives. And we do so with Beauty, Ease, Entirety and Form, each step of the way.

## Images arise

When we get the part, we intuitively begin to synthesize all of the images arising into our performance. From the very first images we weave our way to rich, more nuanced discoveries until a deep satisfaction begins to sparkle within ourselves and among our ensemble. Ultimately SynthAnalysis™ is seeking to inspire us as artists, clarify our vision, and unify our creativity toward the single focal point for the benefit of the audience in a harmonious flow of production. This process awakens a deep sense of collaborative ownership, led by a respectful and clear director. It is also a practical model for devising/collaborative creating with or without a director, and script writing, as will be addressed in *SynthAnalysis™ the Michael Chekhov Way*. SynthAnalysis™ has applications specifically for every member of the production team, for actors, directors, scenographers, designers, dramaturgs and writers. This version is angled to the actor, with some references to what the director and designers might do with a cast and crew for context. Modifications for scenes and monologues follow. The process is useful for on-camera and live-performance story telling.

Imagine acting the climactic highlights of an entire story in three minutes as a warm up before a performance? How would it be if you could rehearse your full character arc in those three minutes, aligning yourself with the Thinking, Feeling, Willing forces of your character, with their dreams and nightmares, their Imaginary Body with all of its sensations and gestures pulsing through your creative body? This is the purpose of this chapter. We call this pre-show, or pre-rehearsal warm up a SynthAnalysis run-through (SART). The SART unites all the elements of the Chart of Inspired Action, expressing the composition of the specific story being told and each character's journey in it. While developing the SART may seem to be time consuming, it becomes the most rapid rehearsal process available.

On stage, dedicating four to six hours of first rehearsals to crafting the elements of the SynthAnalysis run-through could save you 10 to 15 hours later. On camera, where you often have only a few moments of rehearsal before filming, you will bring great confidence to the set, ready to make a clear offering to the director regardless of where in the script you are shooting, needing fewer takes, saving the production precious time and resources.

As we proceed, imagine that actors, directors, and designers might follow this process privately before they begin their collaboration and then repeat it together as an ensemble where synergy will multiply the creativity.

## Feeling of Entirety

> "For a good actor must acquire the director's broad, all-embracing view of the performance as a whole if (s)he is to compose his(her) own part in full harmony with it."
>
> Michael Chekhov, *To The Actor*, 2002, page 93.

All amazing actors will understand they are playing a part of a larger whole. Knowing the whole picture will help the artist play the part perfectly to enhance the story. That is everyone's common goal. When artists have the feeling of the entire story, then they can contribute in a way that will make the whole even grander.

For learning purposes, we will use *The Wizard of Oz* as our model since it is one of the most well-known stories around the globe. If you have a play script you are preparing to perform or are studying a scene or monologue, you might apply this process to that.

To prepare, you will want to have drawing supplies handy, colorful if possible, and a mix of media such as chalk, ink, markers, crayons, and pencils. Also, this process is exciting to capture on camera, so you might encourage pix and video, especially if you have a social media sharing point for your art and/or your ensemble. Consider the composition of any photos as their own works of art, with foreground (connecting stone), focal point and background, angle, light, etc.

Since the transformative element of SynthAnalysis™ is getting us up on our feet, it's a great idea to prepare our bodies and imaginations to move and play before beginning. If working with an ensemble, now is the perfect time to review the Rock Garden principles of form in Chapter 8 both for composing a harmonious grouping, and for expressing the theme.

Stanislavsky, Vakhtangov, and Chekhov all recommend making a list or column of first impressions after your first reading of the text. In SynthAnalysis we multi-dimensionalize this process in non-linear fashion with drawing, crafting, sound, and gesture. Later you can reflect upon these to see if there is anything you want to add, that you lost sight of, or that was not ready for inclusion earlier.

As an artist, your greatest preparation for beginning rehearsals could be doing this process solo, before your very first rehearsal. Study the following sequence, read your script and begin step one. You might even begin step one after reading just the first scene or first act and return to your image collage after each section until the end.

Note that if working with a cast, this process ideally happens prior to the first cast read-through.

For demonstrating SynthAnalysis™, I focus on *The Wizard of Oz* because it is a well-known story. However, images and examples include other scripts (see Figure 19.1).

## SynthAnalysis™ sequence

### Step 1. Read and respond with first images collage

Read your script from the perspective of an audience member, for the story, with no character in mind the first few times. During and after each read, jot, draw, sketch, and create a **first images collage** randomly on a

# SynthAnalysis™ for the Part-Composition

*Figure 19.1* First images collage of a character from a play *Sing Me to the Other Side* by Gwen Flager, courtesy of Merri Brewer. The character is covering a terrifying shame instigated by her abusive, racist husband by focusing on her crystalware and hosting the perfect Mother's Day brunch, which literally goes down in flames.

sheet of paper, in a journal or on a sketchpad. Disregard lines and organization as you do this. Write/draw as fast as you can, free of worry about how it looks. Just go! Accept every image (Yes, and …), even if it seems disconnected or irrelevant to the story, draw it anyway. Fast. Keep adding images to this paper. Keep adding until you are out of images. You may also use fabric, feathers, glitter, and other decorative elements to make a three-dimensional collage. Now, stand up and *gesturize (imitate)* these images, using full body and sound. If working with a cast, take turns drawing and gesturizing with sound or silently (see Figure 19.1 for a solo character collage and Figure 19.2 for cast collage).

Pause, center yourself with the goblet process. Perhaps you close your eyes, maybe tap on your ideal artistic center (IAC), connecting with your unlimited sphere of imagination (I-sphere). Ask the story to show you anything you might have forgotten. Listen through your higher ego—IAC. This is your time to artistically gaze with patience. Add any new images and gesturize them. When you run out of ideas a second time, pause again, connect with your highest self and ask, "What else?" Allow the images to pour into your creative goblet and into the drawing.

Guided by our law of triplicity, when we enter our goblet process a third time, waiting patiently in our Artistic Gaze, we penetrate into our superconscious ever more deeply, to see if something comes.

Draw your new inspirations until you run into another empty spell. Keep interspersing your gesturizing with sound. Have fun and feel free to get silly even if the story is a tragedy. Working as a group, it's really fun to have everyone jostling around the drawing board and gesturizing each other's images too. No worries if the same image appears multiple times. Take some selfies and Us-ies too.

*Figure 19.2* Castmates cocreate their first images collage for *Becky's New Car* by Steven Deitz.

### ✎ Flyback over your first images collage

*When your first images collage is complete and you have gesturized the images, step back and study the whole collage for a few moments. Ask these question: Is this a show I want to play? Is this a story I'd like to tell? Does this story seem like it will be exciting for the audience? Did creating the images excite me to want to act in this? Did gesturizing the images help me feel the possibilities in my body? What did I like overall about this process? What would I do differently? What was my favorite moment in this activity?*

As we move on in the sequence, we can add any images that arise. Save these drawings for review later and for inspiration at any time. Keep in mind, as actors, we are still exploring getting our feeling of entirety for the story and are not yet focusing on our part.

### Step 2. Find the theme

For our purposes, here's how we will define Theme:

 Axiom 19.1: Theme = what the story is about.

What are the **themes** of this story? What is the story really about? On a fresh canvas, jot down any themes in words, pictures, sayings. When all of your thoughts are transferred to the paper, ask for more through the goblet process. How many times do we ask leading questions (LQs)? Yes, as you know by now, when in doubt as to how many times to do anything, try three.

For this sequence of three rounds, for curiosity's sake, we can write them on the canvas using one color for each round, such as blue for the first, red for the second, and green for the third. It is possible that 30 to

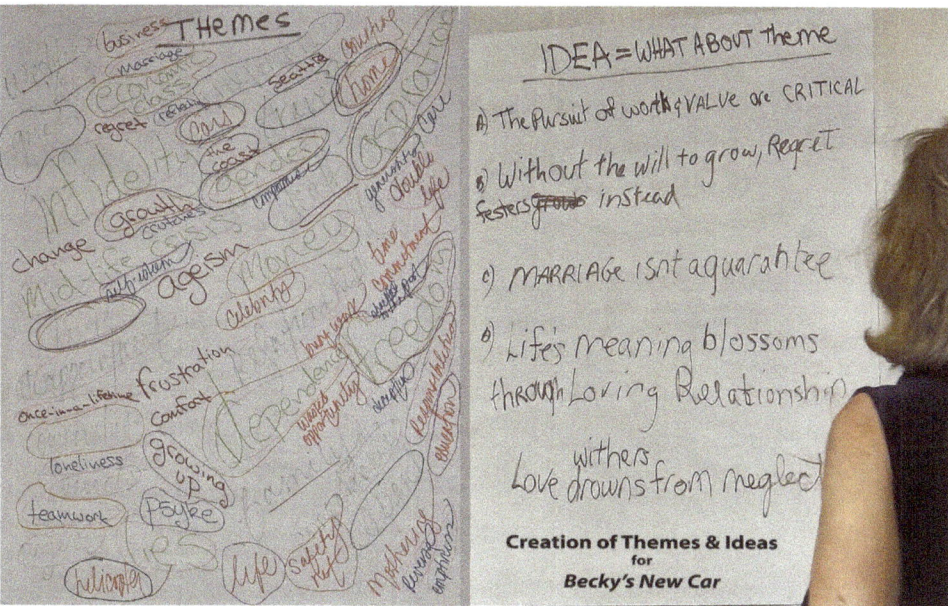

*Figure 19.3 Becky's New Car themes on the left, ideas on the right.*

40 themes may emerge. To satisfy that curiosity, you might discuss whether each round brought forth a meaningful difference (see the left panel of Figure 19.3).

## Flyback on themes

*Is there anything to note about the nature of the themes that rapidly appeared from the surface of our minds in round one? Is there any difference, and if so what, between that and rounds two and three, where we went deeply into our artistic gaze from our IAC rather than "off the top of our heads"? Which, if any, of these themes interest you most?*

With careful examination, we might notice that many of the themes have a commonality among them, that they all might be sub-themes of perhaps three to five overall categories or *super themes*. Baptize (give a name to) one overall super theme at a time. This might be "feeling of belonging," "money," "life purpose," "egotism."

## Step 3. Find the super theme and create harmonious groupings

Identify any theme on the canvas that might fit into one of the super themes by using another color, such as black, to encircle them. We can choose to make the color symbolic or random. For example, perhaps all words or phrases about *money* will be circled in black. All about *belonging* will be circled in pink. *Life purpose* will be in purple. If I were to choose that color scheme, I might already be judging money as a dark force compared to the other two themes, or not. Some words may relate to more than one category and are circled as many times as appropriate. Some may not fit any category and may warrant their own baptized super theme.

 Let's play super theme Harmonious Grouping

As with the first images, gesturize the three to five super themes. Perhaps you add to your collage a specific image for each of these.

Going further, if you have an ensemble, create a Harmonious Grouping (HG), keeping in mind the Japanese Rock Garden (RG; Figure 8.5) principles we learned in our feeling of form in Chapter 8. When creating your HG, welcome into your imagination the many smaller themes it contains. For example, the category of *belonging* might encompass words such as *abandonment, judgement, marriage, status, sex* and *family*. A harmonious grouping for *belonging* might express a combination of these. *Egotism* might encompass *pride, greed, selfishness,* and *condescension*. Keep in mind there are no Chekhov police so if you feel or sense there is a connection, trust yourself and circle it.

HGs will be created for each super theme. As a solo artist, aim for creating a gesture for each super theme. You can also use a prop for your gestures.

When playing with an ensemble greater than eight, you might split into groups of three or more in each team. Teams might each create one or two HGs as needed.

Define where the audience is so you know where downstage and upstage are. After this is established, consider working in silence. Creating harmonious groupings can be surprisingly effective using silence as a working tool, boosting spontaneity, trust, efficiency, and fun, while circumventing thinking/planning/directing. Perhaps the most essential compositional principles to employ are about levels, especially for a cast.

- Stay low to the ground when closest to the audience.
- Stay high when upstage.
- Be on a different height and distance from the audience than anyone else unless you are a unit.
- Express specific eye, hand, and foot life to direct focus.
- And no worries if we don't get all five stones (focal, connecting, conflict, support, and background) of the Rock Garden represented when we do this. It's more important that we commit and sustain whatever we do with confidence, knowing its perfect.

When playing solo, choose a different location in the playing space for each super theme gesture, using the same audience orientation. You might choose intentionally where you want to create any given theme. For example, for *belonging*, downstage left. For *egotism*, upstage center. You also might decide to randomly select a theme and improvise where in the space you want to create it.

For groups, each team finds their spot in the space so the HG can be seen both by an audience and the other groups. If there are three teams, A might be downstage left, B might be upstage center, and C might be downstage right, all oriented toward the same location for an audience. In a classroom structure, perhaps each group is oriented from a corner toward the center of the room. Center is now downstage, and the corner is upstage.

The next step can be done by all groups at once or taking turns, each watching the other from their space. Clarify this sequence so everyone knows the plan. When all are in place, assign one of the baptized super themes to each group just before they are to begin. If working in silence, one representative can point to the super theme on the chart/board.

To prepare for discovering the gesture of your theme, awaken your ideal artistic center and listen from there, in a state of readiness. In the three-count pause following discovering it, allow the images to stream from your I-sphere into your IAC and the instant you hear or see "Go," move.

As soon as a theme is given, pause silently for a few counts and on "Go," move in three or four counts to the final form and sustain. A member of the team or someone outside the group can call the theme and time out loud or use hand signals and a clap or chime for the stop and go. "Belonging, 6-5, and Go 3-2-1- stop and sustain." Trust and pretend your form is perfect, resisting any urge to make adjustments after the "Stop" is called. Snap some pix! If all groups go at once, have them sustain for a few counts, snap pix and then one at a time, take a peek at each other's HG. Release and restore. Post pix later to your sharing point (see Figure 19.4).

*Figure 19.4* Harmonious grouping from *The Wizard of OZ*. "Wizard is a Fake!" (Photo by Author, from European Theatre and Film Institute, Brussels.)

When playing solo, guide yourself to also make quick spontaneous gestures. Maybe write your themes on pieces of paper, pick one randomly and go.

###  Journal/Discuss/Flyback super theme HGs

*Did we move with Beauty and Ease into our form or were we hesitant, worried? Were we able to commit to our impulse and immediately stop as an ensemble, trusting our form? Or did we make some adjustments, correcting ourselves, trying to get it right? Was an inner Feeling of Ease present? Were we secretly trying to direct others to do what we wanted done? How successfully did we apply the Rock Garden principles? Overall, what did we like about the HG we created? What might we do differently next time? What was our favorite moment in the process? Did the HGs capture the super themes? Which theme is most exciting? Which theme do we most want to feature in our story? Are you more excited about playing this story for an audience? If you Flyback with pictures taken, what do you observe? Are there any uneasy tendencies you notice that you might strengthen?*

### Step 4. Find your Idea and create an active HG

For our purposes, we will define the Idea in relation to the super themes.

> Axiom 19.2: Idea = what we are saying about the super themes. What *idea* are we putting forth?

To develop the Idea, now ask what is being said about these themes? What **ideas** are being put forth? What is the message of the story? If *selfishness* is a theme, what is being said about it? What if the theme is *belonging*?

Follow the same process of connecting with your IAC and ask it to reveal the *ideas—what message are we giving to the audience about selfishness or belonging*? Jot down the various ways you might phrase the ideas. Make up one Idea for each super theme. Perhaps somehow they combine (see the right panel of 19.3).

For *The Wizard of Oz*, perhaps one Idea might be: "Selfishness destroys our sense of belonging."

When you arrive at ideas for each of the themes, create solo gestures or Harmonious Groupings using the same sequence as before with this addition: Find a starting HG and allow it to morph or transition into an ending HG, showing a transformation. We call this an Active HG. Create the HG, sustain for a moment, then take three counts to morph it into the ending HG. For example, from our universal stance, we move into a *belonging* HG; pause for a moment, and then with *selfishness*, we begin destroying *belonging* over a period of about three counts. Our final form is *supreme selfishness*.

Perhaps we'd like a positive message, so our Idea might be "Helping others heals the wounds of *abandonment* and creates a sense of *belonging*." Now we can begin with an Active HG beginning with *abandonment* and transforming through helping others into *belonging*. Is this a message you would like to share with an audience?

### Flyback/Discuss Idea and Active HGs

Upon completion of the Idea's Active HGs, choose the Idea that best represents the story you feel today's audience needs most to experience. Ultimately this will be the director's final choice, and hopefully when you do this with a director, the whole cast will sense ownership and the unity of a common vision. All of the dynamics embodied in the telling of the story ideally support the Idea.

## Step 5. Reading for your character images, drawing, and gesturizing

Having now explored the feeling of the entire play and chosen an Idea, it is time we looked specifically at our parts through the lens of the message. Prepare your own personal canvas upon which to create just for your character, perhaps even draw as your character.

- Read the play several times just from your character's point of view. Jot/sketch/write images that arise about your character and the other characters through your character's lens. Keep asking your IAC: "What else?" Gesturize these character images (see Figure 19.5).
- Character theme: Add to this or a new canvas the responses that stream in when you ask in your IAC, "What are the themes and qualities that you focus on, dear character. For example, in *The Wizard of Oz*, the Good Witch: *protection, kindness, guidance, lightness, beauty, calmness*. Gesturize these as you go. Your character may change their focus over the arc of the story. For example, Dorothy begins with *poutiness, irritability, spoiled, self-centered, disrespectful, spitefulness, boredom* and later becomes *caring, helpful, giving*.
- Ask your character what their function is in the plot of the story and the Idea. For example, the Good Witch might reveal, "*I help Dorothy overcome selfishness by giving her challenges that require her to help others.*"

## Step 6. Identify the basic plot structure of good vs. evil

All stories are essentially a battle between good and evil. Everything that happens to lead the forces of good to victory are on the **throughline of good**. Everything that seeks to defeat good, and bring evil to victory is on the **counter-throughline**.

*Figure 19.5* The first images by Kelsey Harrison playing Romy in *Grotesque Lovesongs* by Don Nigro. (Courtesy of Kelsey Harrison and NMCA.)

Looking now at the whole story, who or what are the forces of good? Who or what are the forces of evil? Traditionally, the lead character is called the protagonist, and the one who causes the trouble is the antagonist. For our purposes, allow yourself to think outside the box of "protagonist versus antagonist" as referring to specific characters. Perhaps *virtues* are the true heroes, and *vices* are the true evil, and the lead character has some of both. Maybe things are not so simple today regarding the whole plot. We have lots of flawed heroes and lovable bad guys.

Keep in mind, the brilliant actors will always make choices to help the story be brilliant. Other actors make choices to make themselves great. Be a brilliant actor and understand where your character falls on the throughline of good and the counter-throughline of evil. Create a PG for the force of good. Create a PG for the force of evil.

## Step 7. Find the nine major events

A major event is a moment, **a specific point in the script,** where the direction of the plot changes. It affects all major characters and without this particular moment, the story cannot continue on the course that it does. These events are climaxes, the direct points of *conflict* between good and evil, as determined by the Idea and its throughline. An event is not a scene. **It is a moment in a scene.** When we identify the major events, we "baptize" them by giving them a short name that quickly reminds us of what the plot point is. For example, when Toto reveals the man behind the curtain in Oz, we might baptize that moment as "betrayal" or "how dare you!?"

Using the Law of Triplicity, the story has three parts. In Act 1, it begins as the seeds of a battle are planted. In Act 2, the bud of battle grows in intensity, forming or blooming into a transition. In Act 3, the fruits of transformation ripen. Each act has one main event or climactic moment. Within each act, three smaller parts with smaller climaxes are also present. All in all, each story will have nine major events (three events × three acts).

Find the nine major events that serve as the switching points on the track of the plot. The plot needs these nine events to unfold as it does. The more specific you can be about exactly where each major event is, the more useful this process will be. If it were a video, you could freeze-frame it at the precise point where the pinnacle of tension shifts. There will be many minor events in every story. What qualifies as a major event may vary depending on the Idea of the play and ultimately is a director's decision. We are discussing this very briefly here, so that you can understand how to create your own set of "character events" that will ultimately support the dynamics of the whole story.

## Step 8. Find the pre-event and post-event

There are two more events we would like to identify: The pre-event and the post-event. These are not usually in the story that the audience will see.

 **Axiom 19.3:** The pre-event forces the story to open on <u>this</u> day of <u>all</u> days.

The **pre-event** is something that happens before the story begins which forces the story to open on *this* day of *all* days. What is it that has happened that forces the story to start when it does? Why does the story take place now and not 100 years ago? Why didn't the story start yesterday or why wouldn't it start next week? For *The Wizard of Oz*, is it Dorothy's parents dying? Is it the weather forecast? Or is it that her dog Toto has bitten Mrs. Gulch? What drives the forces of evil to challenge the forces of good *on this day of all days*?

The **post-event** is a fantasy event that happens after the story ends. What happens to your character after the story is over? What happens in the imaginary world of the story? Perhaps in our version of *The Wizard of Oz*, Dorothy is happily helping on the farm. Here is an example of the nine plus pre- and post-events of the story, identified using the Idea and good and evil.

## Step 9. Baptize the main Overall Atmospheres (OA)

A major atmosphere will envelop each major event. These are usually "baptized" by the director with the cast. List the events and atmospheres. Below is an example list with the OAs connecting the events.

### SynthAnalysis™ of *The Wizard of Oz* events and Overall Atmospheres (OAs)

OA: selfish boredom
    0. Pre-event: Toto bites Gulch
OA: frightened loneliness
    1. Dorothy decides to run away with Toto.
OA: terrifying tornado
    2. House KILLS wicked witch of east.

> OA: bright blooming wonder
>   3. Glinda protects Doro with shoes from Wicked Witch of the West.
> OA: clawing anticipation
>   4. Doro and three friends promise to go to Oz, together—We're off to see the Wiz
> OA: mysterious forest
>   5. Wizard demands the broom—get the broom.
> OA: menacing danger
>   6. Monkeys capture Doro and Toto—I've got you my pretty.
> OA: desperate heroics
>   7. Doro saves Scarecrow and kills Witch—I'm melting
> OA: victorious hope
>   8. Wizard is a fake (see Figure 19.4).
> OA: shocked disillusionment
>   9. Doro wills herself home—three clicks.
> OA: determined concentration.
>   10. Post event: Doro is happily helping on the farm.
> OA: familial warmth

## Step 10. Develop your Actor's SynthAnalysis™ Run-Through (A-SART) chart of character's events

While the director will identify what the good and evil is for the whole play,[1] the actors can create their characters' points of view. Identify your character as the heroic good in their own life, independent of the plot. Who or what are the forces of good and evil from your character's perspective? This may be the same as or opposite from the play as a whole.

Create a chart with *good* labeled at the top and *evil* at the bottom. Draw two lines vertically, creating three sections on the chart, Act 1, Act 2, Act 3.

Draw one line horizontally across the middle. This mid-line divides the good above it from the evil below it.

Upon this graph, we will place each event either above or below the mid-line. The better an event is for the character, the closer to the top (good) we place it. The worse it is, the closer to the bottom (evil) we place it. No two events are the exact same distance from the top or the bottom. This way, we can easily see the most significant moments of the character's life.

In *The Wizard of Oz*, the Wicked Witch doesn't perceive herself as evil. For her, Dorothy is an evil murderer of her sister. For the Wicked Witch, good is anything that creates pain for Dorothy. Evil is anything that brings joy to Dorothy. Though we don't see the Witch in every major event, each major event moves the Witch closer to her goal of destroying Dorothy (good) or further away from it (evil).

*What are the events that affect your character? What are your character's most important turning points that define their life in the story?* Depending on the size of our role, there maybe three to nine. No worries, we can be completely creative here, imaging things that happen to our characters "off stage" that the audience never knows about. Imagine your character has a reaction to everything that is happening, whether in the story or not. If you are playing Auntie Em, in your imagination, you have a whole life that is going on that Dorothy and the audience don't know anything about. Perhaps Auntie Em is watching Dorothy, unconscious in her bed in Kansas, and Dorothy is tossing and turning with each danger she dreams of, or perhaps Dorothy relaxes, even smiles a bit when wonderful parts of her dream are happening. Auntie Em's good rises with Dorothy's relaxing and falls when Dorothy is restless.

## Step 11. Research and create character backstory

In basic Stanislavsky analysis, we take the time to research the life of the author, the historical era in which the story was written, and the customs and politics of the era. **Chekhovize this approach by researching all of these questions in your imagination before going to external sources.** Then ask yourself, "How can this research inspire my creative expression of my character?" If it offers no inspiration, the research is irrelevant. The value of research is in how it transforms your performance. This way you will be creating first from your higher self and then you can adjust your ideas if you discover they are too different from the recorded *truth*.

Another common preparation is to write a backstory of the life of the character which can help us justify why the character does what they do and how. I love doing this and tend to write twice as much as a director might ask me to. However, like the value of research, unless the elements of the backstory are visible or audible, they are irrelevant. This means that any incident I say happened to my character has meaning only if it changes how I walk, talk, use my hands, feet, eyes, relate to my clothes, etc. All biographical facts are important only if they change how I act in a way the audience can experience. For an alternative to writing a logical backstory, we suggest using Palaces, which were introduced in Chapter 8. Sometimes variations on Palaces are called corridors, matrices, or castles. The central idea is that you create a safe space which you can enter that can be anywhere or anytime, with no time or space limitations, with as many interior or exterior, real or fantasy worlds or rooms as your imagination discovers in the moment, based on the theme you baptize your palace with. Choose themes that will help you connect with your character and the story being told.

 Let's play Palaces

We can create a Palace with any theme. Perhaps you create a palace where one area is the character's fears, another area is their dreams; or, one where an area is their past, another is their future. In these versions, imagine putting on the imaginary body (IB) of your character and then stepping into the palace as them.

 Use your centering Goblet process to bring down the IB from the I-sphere. Inhale the Palace of images across the threshold. Step into the palace as the character. Explore all the images that arise; and if your imagination is blank, just pretend something is appearing for you and make it up. Have patience, actively wait, and trust your creative gaze.

Take about 20 minutes in your palace and allow 10 to 20 minutes for your Flyback. Having done the earlier SynthAnalysis™ steps, much may flow to you and be useful for the next steps in identifying your character's problems and needs, strengths and weaknesses, etc. Palaces can be used at any point in your rehearsal process to deepen your artistic contact with the character.

## Journal/Discuss/Flyback

*What did you discover? How does it influence your character's body, movement, voice, habits, and mannerisms? Did any images appear that you want to add to your collage? Do you feel more connection with your character?*

## Step 12. Identify and graph the character's major events

Find a pre-event in your character's life. What has happened that makes them have to get what they need when they first walk into the story? We will identify that as event #0. Find the post-event. What is the character left with at the end? We will identify that as #10. Place them on the Character's Graph, defining what is good at the top and what is evil on the bottom.

SynthAnalysis™ for the Part-Composition    263

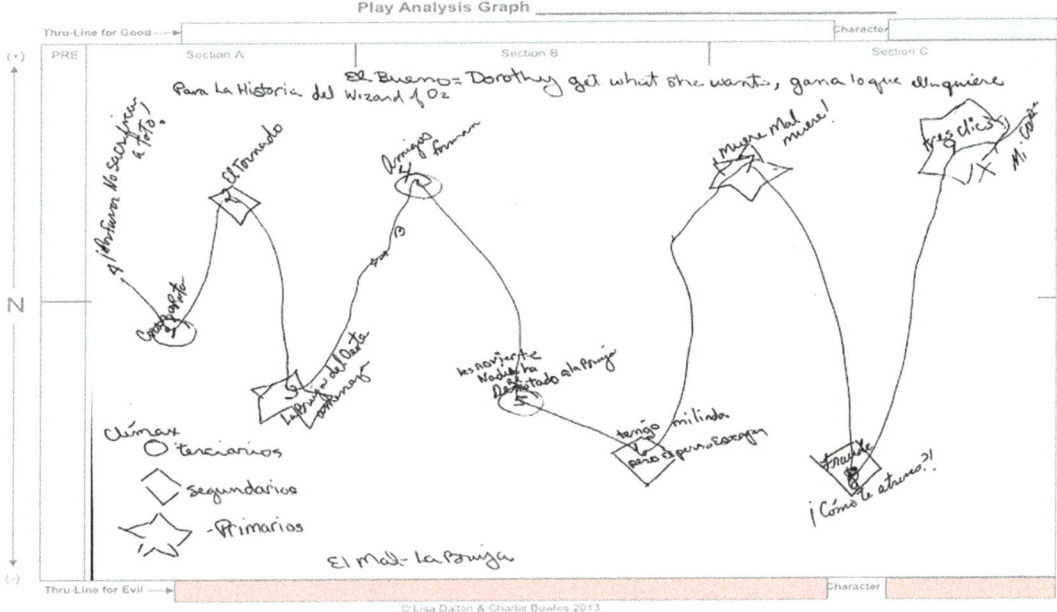

*Figure 19.6* Director's SART Chart of *The Wizard of Oz*.

Figure 19.6 shows a Director's SART Chart for *The Wizard of Oz* based on *what Dorothy wants* as good and anything that blocks Dorothy as evil. Thorough steps for finding the events and creating the director's graph will be detailed in *SynthAnalysis the Michael Chekhov Way*. The next chart, Figure 19.7 is the role of Dorothy. We could say the higher the point is on the line, the closer she is to having her dream fulfilled. The nearer the events are to the bottom, the more nightmarish they are for her. In this case, the artist has

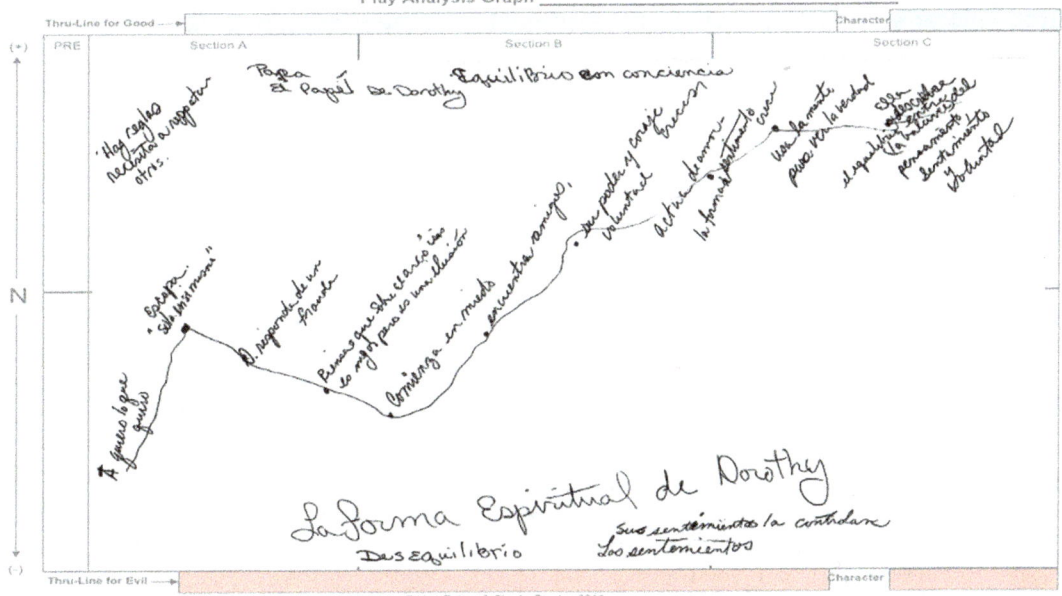

*Figure 19.7* Dorothy's A-SART chart graphing her spiritual journey in *The Wizard of Oz*.

chosen to graph the "spiritual" life of Dorothy, which Dorothy's everyday personality doesn't know about. What is good is "balanced Thinking, Feeling, and Willing" and what is evil is "anything that affirms Dorothy's imbalance". Dorothy begins selfishly, behaving disrespectfully, predominated by her self-pity. Over the story arc, she is challenged to help others, be respectful, balance her will, feelings, and thoughts with compassion. In this graph, we can see the polarity within her journey.

## Step 13. Baptize the Qualities and Sensations and create your A-SART

The director will baptize the Overall Atmospheres around the events for the entire cast. For your Actor SART, identify the predominant emotional state around each of your character's events and create your graph (see Figure 19.7).

## Step 14. Walk the line

Imagine taking string or chalk and laying it out on the floor in an imaginary replica of this graph you have drawn. Counting the steps, walk the mid-line from beginning to end. Let's say it is ten steps straight across the graph. Now, walk the story arc you have drawn and count the number of your steps. The greater the difference between these two measurements, the more dynamic the story arc is. If walking the graph is now 30 steps, it will be more interesting than if it is only 18. Try to make the story arc reach in to all areas at some point on its journey, switching above and below the midline to varying degrees. After all, don't you love roller coasters that sometimes start mild and then go to sudden change, give you a little break, and then get really wild?

When you have arrived at a dynamic arc that excites you and invites you to want to play it, try moving on the imaginary graph in different Tempo/Rhythms. If your director has created the graph for the whole show, notice whether/when your character contrasts or harmonizes with the story's good vs evil graph. Notice the difference between Dorothy's personal graph and the director's graph.

## Step 15. Transpose the graph to the floor, gesturize the events, baptize sensations

Write the baptized name and number of each of the events on separate pieces of paper. Place these cue sheets on the floor in the approximate place they would be if the graph were superimposed on a stage. Arrange it so the evil is downstage nearest the audience and the good is upstage. The beginning of the story is stage right, and the ending is stage left. Your #0 pre-event cue sheet would be on the stage right edge and #10, the post-event cue sheet, on the stage left edge.

Now, we are going to develop a Psychological Gesture (PG) for each event, starting with #10, the last event, first. If you have created a Compositionary-PG sequence with a nightmare, a dream, and the way you get from one to the other, you can use this as your basic PG. Each event emphasizes one moment in that sequence, based on whether your character is closer to or further away from victory (upstage, top of chart) or defeat (downstage, bottom of chart). You can use very symbolic forms or even mime forms of activity. The important element is that the gesture you choose is one that energizes you with the character's thoughts, feelings, and desires for that moment. Here is how this process can be done.

When you have placed your 11 events on the floor, go to the last event, your post-event #10. You can stand on the cue sheet or above it. Create your PG for this event. Dorothy's post-event is "happy farm life," and the PG begins with Dorothy holding her heart and throwing it open. In her imagination, the PG is joyfully tossing food to farm animals. It represents her being a helpful and happy part of the farm family life. Note especially the overall sensation that fills her, baptize the sensation, and jot that down on your SART chart on the section of the line connecting event #9 with the post-event #10. Perhaps the sensation is *delightful enthusiasm*. You can also make a separate sensation cue sheet and place it on the stage, connecting #9 and #10. If I have written my events on white paper vertically, I might write my sensation cues on green sheets, horizontally. This way I can quickly tell which paper represents an event with a PG and which is a sensation that I will move with between the PGs. When you travel from one event to the next with a sensation, consider unveiling the sensation and even becoming an abstract molecule that might make a sound. Have fun with it and overact it.

Now move as that molecule of *delightful enthusiasm* from event #10 to event #9. When you reach event #9, create the PG for it. For Dorothy, we have baptized the #9 Event as "three clicks." It is when she clicks her ruby slippers with Triplicity, aligning her Thinking, Feeling, and Willing, by clicking her *heels* where the W-force is active. Her sensation is *hopeful anticipation*. Her PG begins with arms expanded and one foot outstretched, and then her hands grasp the hope from the air and contract to her heart as the heel of her extended foot contracts and clicks the other heel. It is a polarity to the beginning. Instead of running away from home, now she wants to be there.

Now, from event #9, as a molecule of *hopeful anticipation*, move to event #8, adding a cue sheet with *hopeful anticipation* on the line connecting #9 to #8. Create your PG and identify your sensation for #8, continuing with this same sequence of creating a PG for each event, jotting down the sensation and adding a cue sheet connecting the two events. Traveling between events as unveiled molecules until you arrive at the pre-event #0. For Dorothy, the pre-event is *Toto Bites Mrs. Gulch*. Dorothy's gesture is one of terrible loss as she imagines Toto being killed by Gulch. Her sensation is *desperation*.

Now, we have created eleven PGs for the life of our character in the story, starting from the end and working our way to the beginning. Now start from the beginning, the pre-event (#0), do PG0 and sustain it for a beat; then move as a molecule to event #1, do the PG1, sustain, and move as a molecule to event #2, do PG2, etc. until you arrive at post-event #10, PG10.

For your first time creating your Actor's SynthAnalysis Run-Through (A-SART), try it again. Now, from the end (post-event) to the beginning, and back again. As you move from post-event #10 backward to the pre-event, when you get to event #1 PG, you move with the sensation from event #1 to the pre-event PG, and then move offstage right, as a molecule of the pre-event sensation. Then, come right back on as the same molecule and move into the pre-event #0 PG; then, move as molecules of the sensation for event #1 to event #1 PG, etc. to the end.

If time permits, run it backward and forward for a third time to help you remember your choices.

## Tips for SARTs

You can allow your A-SART to morph over the rehearsal period and eventually relocate the PGs to where those moments actually happen on the set.

Before a performance, you might do your A-SART starting from the end, moving toward the beginning, and then step on to the stage, letting the performance be the forward flow.

In an ideal world, you as an artist would have a director who would create a DA-SART (Director's Active SynthAnalysis Run-Through) for the whole story, using the whole cast in Harmonious Groupings with Atmospheres connecting the 11 events. And the director might then help you with your A-SART.

However, we want to be able to play with these ideas even if we are the only artists who know acting the Michael Chekhov way. You could create your A-SART before your first rehearsal, though that might not be realistic; however, you could give it a try and tweak it as you go. Again, no worries about getting it right, it will be perfect, and you can change it if you discover something better.

- See **OR 19.1** for Kelsey Harrison's complete actor's SART for Romy in *Grotesque Lovesongs*.

## Benefits of the A-SART

- In creating your A-SART, you now are very clear on the major journey your character goes on in the show.
- You know where your character is coming from when the story opens and where your character is going to when the story ends.
- You know when the character is winning and when they are losing and the major sensations they experience because of this.
- By starting at the end, and working backward, you come to know the story "backward and forward."
- Most actors find memorizing to be easier.
- Before every rehearsal you can use your A-SART as an energizing warm-up.
- When you rehearse out of sequence, or one small section, your body and soul will know exactly where this small section fits into the whole story.
- You have a very practical connection to the emotional throughline of your character.
- By practicing unveiled molecules and full gestures, your psychophysical body will be a well-trained gymnast of your character's thoughts, feelings, and desires.
- This process will allow the nine most significant moments to radiate powerfully.

## Reversal of rehearsal

One of the more radical Chekhov ideas for preparing a part is what we call **reversal of rehearsal.** Here is Chekhov's observation:

> It is an erroneous impression that rehearsals of a play should start with the very first scene and continue in undeviating succession; it is prompted by habit and not inspired by creative necessity. There is no need or reason to start from the beginning if the whole play is vivid in the imagination. It would be better to start with scenes that express the gist of the play, then proceed to scenes of secondary importance.[2]

It is this very idea that inspires us to start at the end for our SART. We can essentially do the same for blocking and memorizing. Consider how often the opening of a play gets over-rehearsed and the biggest climax in the last act gets lost in time as technical needs gain priority before opening. It is actually very logical to work on the most complicated part of the show first. It's done that way in film frequently. Even when building a highway, the complicated interchanges and bridges get built first, not the entrance ramps. Let's play smarter by letting go of the linear habit.

The SynthAnalysis™ process is the tool to identify and awaken in our bodies the vivid images of the story and its most important parts. Using Chekhov's suggestion of rehearsing these parts first might look like this for a director:

Following creating the SART, read through with the cast and then block and memorize the major climax of Act 3, the ending plus the curtain call, then major climax of Act 2, major climax of Act 1, and the opening. These five sections are the most essential. As time gets tight, finish the smaller connecting scenes, which are less significant and generally easier to develop. We will in effect direct ourselves.

For us as actors, even if the director is blocking from the beginning, we can begin memorizing our last scene first and working our way to the beginning, so the hardest and most significant parts get the most attention. We are then driving into our strength rather than toward the least rehearsed and known part of the show. We also sense very clearly the conditions of our character at the end and can make strong choices to contrast that for our beginning scenes, creating the greatest character transformation. We can craft more Polarities, Triplicities, and Rhythmic Repetitions in the earlier part of the script when we are very clear on the ending.

## The crisis

In most stories, the most challenging parts to perform are the climactic moments, the ending, and the beginning. It is fairly common to see actors develop anxiety about being able to "hit" those moments. By rehearsing them right off the bat, it circumvents the buildup of such tension, and can help prevent the seemingly unavoidable *week three crisis*.

What I am referring to here is the ever-so-common situation where, in a four-week rehearsal period, around the third week, a crisis of health, personality conflict, financial restriction, personnel changes, and/or set or costume disasters seems to threaten the very stability of the show. It seems like the climax and finale will never get rehearsed.

While in most cases the show magically assembles itself in the nick of time, wouldn't it be easier to undertake a creative approach that prepares for such a possibility? When director and cast already have the climax and finale firmly implanted in their artistic souls, the crisis that slows everything down appears much less threatening. Thus, folks are less likely to exacerbate the situation and more likely to respond with a Feeling of Ease and creativity that can be applied for resolving traumas. Yet another example is that strong preparation makes the action effortless. I go so far as to block my curtain call first, before any of the scenes!

Remember that the crisis phase will come. If you start feeling your inner tension building, talk to your director, stage manager, or teacher. Let them know what, and even who, you are worried about. If they are aware, they may already be working on fixing the challenge. If they are unaware that it is happening, they will now be able to help. Either way, communicating directly with your leader is a win–win. Gossiping with your buddies may contribute to this atmosphere of crisis. Take responsibility to create an atmosphere of Ease in all you do and say.

**Lack of preparation is the casting directors' and directors' biggest complaint about actors.** We can be well prepared by using a mini **SynthAnalysis™**.

## SynthAnalysis™ for monologues/scenes

To apply SA to a monologue, identify your character's good throughline (their dream) and evil (their nightmare) counter-throughline, and the three climactic points (#1, #2, #3) in the text where the story turns toward one and away from the other. Choose a pre-event (#0) to establish why this must be spoken now and a post-event (#4) of the outcome of having spoken. Baptize each event with the dominant emotional quality or ATMO.

Place these on a SART Chart. Transpose the SART Chart to the floor. Using reversal of rehearsal, start at the post-event, create your PG or CG for (#4) and move backward to #3 with the quality/ATMO into the PG, then to #2 PG to #1 PG to #0 PG and then forward. Repeat the reverse SART sequence and when you arrive at #0, begin moving forward with your text, ending somewhere between #3 and #4. Adjust your gestures, qualities, and T/R. Flyback each time until you are "happy."

Apply the same concept for scenes, modifying the number of climaxes pending the length. For example, a seven-minute scene may have three primary events and two to four secondary events.

- See **OR 19.2** SA for scenes, short one-acts, and monologues.
- See **OR 19.3** for blank SynthAnalysis™ run-through chart template.

## Enriching composition with homeplay and rehearsal activities

**Strong preparation makes the action effortless.** Do you remember this axiom? When we are cast in a role, it is essential that we prepare for each rehearsal. Great actors bring exciting ideas to the director, and they are ready to show them options and just as easily take any new and different directions given. Here are some ways you can prepare.

**List activities/stage business.** Write out a list of each piece of business your character does. *Walk to a table, enter stage. kiss their hand. Etc.* When you see in the script exactly what the character does, it can help you understand who they are. You can begin improvising those activities using any of the tools that seem interesting. You can ask your imagination to show you how the character does the activity. Try the activities with different tools. When you have lots of choices, try them as if you believe each is the best, then do a Flyback to see which one tickles your heart most! Choose that one while being ready to give it up for the director's idea, and be ready to show your other ideas.

Ask your Ideal Artistic Center to reveal the answers through the meditative process you have learned. Play with your list of business, allowing your answers to these leading questions to flavor *how* you do the activity. Flyback over your personal rehearsals and make notes on your script.

## Plus (+) and minus (–) as a means to character relationships

When we are clear on our character's aims, life-wish/seed of the need/super-super-objective and the actions it takes to accomplish these aims, we can craft multidimensional and vital relationships among the characters in the story. For this process, it helps to have our compositionary gesture with the character's win/loss and main PG.

Imagine that each character ends as a + (*plus*, good for you, is "fer ya") or – (*minus*, evil to you, is "agin' ya") to your character. A "+" is anyone who helps you, intentionally or not, toward your aim. A "–" is anyone who blocks you, intentionally or not, and is an obstacle to your aim. It is possible for someone to be neutral, but why not make a more interesting choice?

Invite your character to reveal which other characters end as a plusses and which end as minuses. Ask whether these characters change over the course of the story. If possible, you will want the degree of plus or minus to vary. It is also possible that your character doesn't know whether someone is a + or a –. That in itself is an exciting situation for characters who are clear on their aim.

You can create the greatest transformation by using Polarity and viewing your minuses as plusses in the beginning of the story and the reverse. This will allow you to have the greatest change in relationship to other characters. If a soon-to-be enemy can begin as your best friend, the dramatic tension will be higher than if they are neutral or even a nasty minus at the start.

Invoking the Law of Triplicity, ask your IAC to reveal three moments that trigger the changes (for example, the transitions from + to –) in relationship to each main character.

Once you identify the moments of transition, ask the character: "*How do you mask or reveal this moment?*" "*Where in your imaginary body does this change anchor itself?*" "*How does this character affect your equilibrium?*"

If you can, try one whole rehearsal just dedicated to exploring the + and – of relationships and their transformations. You can try one scene completely unveiling the affect the other characters have on you as they help you win your objective or help you lose it. For example, using the Three Sister Sensations (3S), for this run-through, you or some part of your body will fall every time your character has a minus. You will teeter when you don't know, find yourself hanging in the balance, on edge, and weightlessly float on top of the world when you get a plus. You might also do your main PG in the scene until you know this person is a +, when you begin to do your win gesture or a –, doing your loss gesture.

Score your script with + or –. You can even note truly strong points if you wish, +++ or – – –. Develop this shorthand and position it (always in erasable pencil) on a script very quickly, experimenting with whether it helps to mark it before the section, so you know what is coming or inserting it right at a particular spot or some other way you like best.

## Crafting a score of tools

For this process, we recommend printing your script in the center of the page on the front of a full sheet of paper. Place the script in a binder with firm covers so you can write on the paper while holding the binder. Allow space around the text to make director's notes for blocking on the left and acting notes on the right. On the blank sheet facing that text, print or draw five (or more) columns and label them by category. Having built familiarity with abbreviations comes in very handy now, enabling you to make quick notes. With each application of a tool, using an erasable pencil, write notes in the column opposite the part of the script where you are using it. Jot down what it is and how helpful it was. Draw an arrow down the column beneath the note to show the segment to which this tool applies. This is to track the effectiveness of any given tool. If the tool can work for a long time, that's great. Sometimes, however, we might need a tool for one quick moment. It's all perfect!

Baptize the columns as you want. For example, I might baptize Column 1 as Atmosphere (ATMO). Column 2 will be gestures (X/C, AGs, PGs), Column 3 is characterization (IB, MC, TFW, R/R), Column 4 is emotional life (Q/S, 3S, PA, MFFR), Column 5 is Composition (T/R, FPs, +/-) (see Figure 19.8).

There is no set order for applying tools to your script. If you have a favorite, you might start there. For example, Chekhov's first questions to Mala Powers when he coached her were about the trinity of psychology and radiating/receiving.

- "Are they primarily a Radiating or Receiving character?"
- "Are they primarily a Thinking, Feeling, or Will-dominated character?"
- "How do your own real-life Radiating/Receiving and your TFW differ from your character's?"

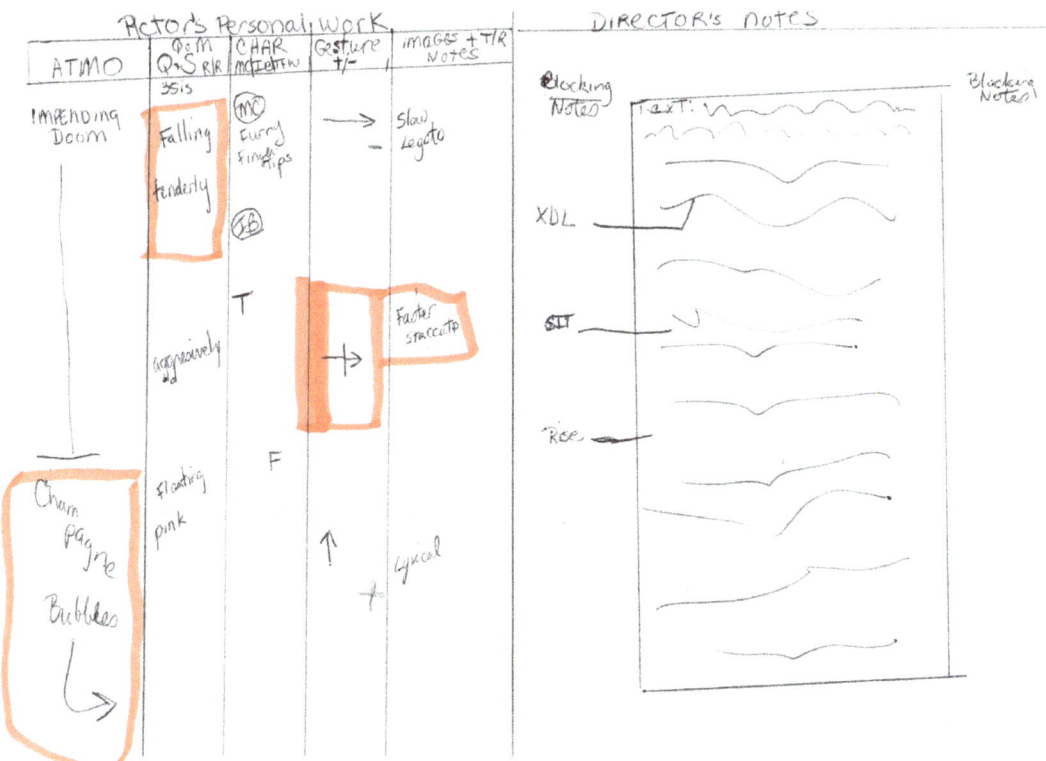

*Figure 19.8* Score of Chekhov tools on left page opposite text with blocking and director's notes on right.

- Work on different tools for each run or rehearsal, one at a time. Jot them down in one of your baptized columns on the script. Flyback afterward to make notes of what you liked. They will layer themselves naturally.
- Remember our Feeling of BEEF (Beauty, Ease, Entirety and Form)? We won't need every tool for every role.
- Create a score of Atmospheres Using Triplicity, Polarity, and Transformation (TPT). Each scene starts with a specific OA that transforms one or more times by the end of the scene. Starting from the final OA working back to the opening OA, run the whole score as a molecule of the OA. Take a section you have questions about and play with mismatched OAs that are a different style or tone and then come back refreshed to what might support the feeling of entirety, the director's vision, and the feeling of Truth for the story. Add the score to the ATMO column with the baptized name of the OA and then draw an arrow through the section where it works. Remember to use pencil so you can make changes. If you like, you might use different colors of pencil for different sections.
- See **OR 19.0** for a sample score of OAs.
- Ask your character, "How do you change in this scene? What is different in the beginning from the end?"
- Early on, begin making friends with your business, costume parts, especially shoes and props. Chekhov suggests wearing the shoes of the character as soon as possible in rehearsals because of how the shoe affects the walk and the will force.
- Practice Tempo and Rhythm shifts to build to climaxes. Is there an important moment that needs a pause before or after? Do you have a behavior or text that repeats itself? If so, does it crescendo, diminuendo, or sustain the same expression?
- What is my character's main problem in this scene? Can you generate all three sources of conflict at once (inner, outer, between)? These might become gestures to explore and add to the score. Add + and – relationship notes.
- Where would the perfect place be to shift dominant characteristics such as Radiating to Receiving, Willing to Feeling, etc.?
- Every tool on the chart is a prompt for a question: What is my Center, Quality of Movement, Imaginary Body, Gesture?
- Check back on your collage of first images from time to time and especially one week before you open. See what has been lost and what has transformed and allow it to re-inspire you.
- Trust that your creative ideal artist will synthesize all of the images into each other. If we have played with many tools, when we focus on one strongly, all of the others appear effortlessly.
- If other actors think you are weird when you do gestures or movement as preparation or are jealous, bring them into your process. Find the Beauty in their vulnerability. Trust that you can get your work fully explored and maintain the social graces. Play at home with the tools and include your favorites in rehearsal. If you are able to create an Atmosphere, for example, your scene partner will sense it, and you will both be more powerful.
- If you don't like your partners, find something to appreciate about them. Cultivate non-judgment and compassion, BEEF. If you don't like the space, the set, costume, props—if you are nervous, scared or uncomfortable, *make friends* to free your talent. Remember the plus or minus of relationships is true in life too. Everyone can help you or sabotage you. Who does what will be based on what you do to whom.
- As we get closer to performance, our role and the whole takes clearer shape. We want to build consistency in ensemble with the director and cast. At any stage, if you have found the best tool for a section, make a note on your score and keep using that tool through your rehearsals. You might discover that certain sections just happen for you without any specific tools. That's perfect. We use tools to fix actor problems. If it ain't broke, don't fix it. Our goal is to play freely and turn to a tool only when a problem appears, or inspiration strikes you to do so.

## Highlight your final score

By the time you begin full run-throughs of the whole show, it's great to pick your favorite tool for each section. If that one tool can work for a whole scene or several pages, good. As we said, sometimes we need a quick one here and there. Take a highlighter (or other colored pencil) and highlight your favorite tool for the section along with the arrow drawn beneath it through the column until you switch to another tool that works best for the next section. Now, highlight that new tool and the arrow in that column until you reach another point in the script where you like another tool best. Proceed with highlighting just one tool in any given place through your whole script. When finished, you can now look at all of the left-sided pages and quickly see the sequence of tools you can use for every scene of the script (see Figure 19.8). If you wish, you can add one new piece of paper and list the tools, either from first tool to last or last to first. You can separate them by scene if you wish.

## Pre-show score whip-through

Using reversal of the rehearsal, before the show, you can do a **score whip-through.** This is where you start by doing unveiled, psychophysical expressions of the very last tool for a few seconds, then the next-to-last, working your way to the beginning tool with which you started the story and back again to the end. This imprints into your body-mind-spirit, the abstract, energetic flow of transformation you will perform. The score whip-thru might take five minutes or less. You can do this before, after, or in place of your A-SART, which will refresh the whole story of the character, their dreams and nightmares. The combination is powerful, and you can change the order you want as you apply this process to your dress rehearsals. You might also only do the score whip-thru or A-SART from *end to start*, so that your performance is the forward version.

By the time the show opens, you might have chosen your best preparation ritual. Some artists keep changing it up over the run of a show to keep it fresh and to integrate their discoveries from each performance.

## Significance

"Significance" as a stand-alone concept for the artist is rich with inspiration. "Insignificance" is essential as its polarity. A drum roll well-placed in the midst of a rock song is significant in its crescendo, building us to the heights of frenzy. However, if the whole song is just the drum roll, with no insignificant moments before or after, the contrast of crescendo-diminuendo disappears, and the emotional arc audiences love goes with it. We want our stories to take our viewers on the rollercoaster ride that inches slowly, tumbles quickly, turns sharply, dips dramatically, and soars over peaks just enough times for us to be satiated by the thrill. As builders of this roller-coaster, we also want the construction to flow in polarity to the story. We pray for ease, harmony, and joy, minus the surprising or anticipated scares often found in the course of production.

When you think about actors who win awards, they are not usually actors who only go through extreme emotions. Rather they are artists who render multidimensional performances with nuance and specific ways of expressing those extreme emotions and the subtle ones. It is the artist who creates a character that the audiences loves to root passionately for or against.

To create superior dynamics in the climaxes, there are a number of tools and combinations of tools that can be used. Dynamic tempo and rhythm changes include the following:

- Reversing Radiating, and Receiving
- Switching Thinking, Feeling, Willing
- Emphasizing the loss aspect of the PG
- Pausing to engage the audience.
    1. A pause *before* prepares the audience for what is to come; they inhale.
    2. A pause *after* deepens the impact of what proceeded it; they exhale.

## Focal Point as a tool for significance

In the same way that a character can have a Moveable Center, so too does a story. This is the Focal Point (FP) of the story. Where earlier we used the Five Focal Points as a tool to define where the character is looking, and alternatively, as FPs for tools for living, here we are using it for the FP of the mise en scene. Where do we want the audience to focus at any given moment of the story? In film, the position and frame of the camera determine what the storyteller wants the audience to focus on. On stage, the audience's attention can go anywhere, including to other audience members. The storyteller can draw the audience's attention to the most significant moments through awareness of where the story's FP is at any given moment. In this case, *the storyteller* includes the entire cast, crew, designers, and director. Here is an example of a mid-phase rehearsal process to help everyone be clear on where the FP is at any given point in the story.

## The Ball Toss run-through—keep your eye on the ball

**The Ball Toss run-through** integrates all of the earlier SA elements of the creative process. When done at least a week prior to tech for the show, having the designers and technicians participate allows them to make adjustments to support the discoveries.

Using one ball only, rehearse with the actors tossing the ball to whomever or wherever the audience should pay most attention, to the most significant element of the story being told at that moment. The ball would be where the deepest impact is being made on the audience. In a play, the ball would follow the throughline of the story as the battle between good and evil play out. Perhaps, do this with one scene first to get "the hang of it." Prepare for very little "good" acting to occur since our priority is on this FP task. A good teammate (stage manager, assistant director, self-tape) to take precise notes of this can be very helpful.

For the solo artist, you can secretly imagine where the ball is at any point in the scenes you are in. Knowing when the ball is "in your hands" will help you to give and take focus in the perfect way.

Confused where the ball should be? Perfect! The ball toss run-through is doing its job when we discover we don't know where the ball should be at any given moment. Take a pause to examine the scene in relation to the whole story. Refer to your SART Chart with nine events and your Atmosphere score. *Where is the climax of the scene? What moments build up to it? What does the audience need to experience in this scene to "fall more deeply in love" with how this story is being told? Do we need to awaken sympathy or antipathy for the villain? Do we need to strengthen our forces of evil to get the audience to cheer the hero onward? Do we need to give the audience a resting moment with a seemingly calm and tender breath? Do we need a laugh or a tear here? An inhale or exhale? When does the atmosphere transform and what moment causes it to change?*

We are now able to make adjustments in the scene to clarify what is most significant.

Here are some means to modify significance of a scene or moment: Tempo and Rhythm, Crescendo, Diminuendo, Staging with the Rock Garden Principles, all as used in movement or Stillness, within the mise en scene of live performers/set/props/costumes/technology.

When the actors know exactly where the Focal Point is at every moment, they can consciously, creatively, and intuitively support the storyline. When the director's clarity of vision is shared with the designers, technicians, and actors, their talents are tantalized by the opportunity to participate in all means possible. All raise the limits of their past artistry and take it to new heights, collaboratively. We love this. Spectators love this. This is what Chekhov, in his audio lectures from 1955, means when he speaks of attention as a kind of love that we want to foster. *Where attention goes, love grows.*

## Conclusion

Our entire SynthAnalysis™ process is health building. Each participant yearns to be seen, heard, and felt in community and opens up to the other when they feel safe. SA engages and respects the creative voice of each person, ultimately nurturing the soul of the creative individuality in body, mind, and spirit from author to audience. We know the audience has come to us, opening to us to receive this radiance from us, to love us, and to love this show. When we deliver on this level, storytelling becomes a significant life event for all involved.

## Notes

1. See Chapter 8 in *To The Actor* for creating the director's graph of the nine events of the entire story. Much more detail will be forth coming in *SynthAnalysis™ the Michael Chekhov Way*. Here we wish to focus on a character SynthAnalysis™, which ideally would weave itself into the Director's SynthAnalysis™.
2. Chekhov, Michael. *To the Actor: On the Technique of Acting*, page 105, Routledge, 2002.

# 20
# Love, laughter, and the MC way hereafter

How do you feel about your art, about acting, being an actor?

What do you feel when you are in the flow, in the happy moments?

What do you hope for your audience?

There really are only four letters to answer these questions, l-o-v-e.

## Love

Is that L-word awkward? For many of us it is something embarrassing or shameful. Let's see if we can shift our view and step into the light this incredible force can give us. Here is a spin on Chekhov's 1955 "Love in Our Profession" Lecture.

As we look at this one English word, "love," there are three words in Greek that can help us understand a few of the different kinds of love.

1. *Eros*—erotic, intimate love between lovers
    a) This kind of love has a higher ego expression as *romantic love*
    b) Its lower ego expression is *raw sex*, a phantom we mistake for love. This is not the topic for today.
2. *Philia*–virtuous human love
    a) This also has a lower ego expression where we "love" <u>my</u> family, <u>my</u> partner, <u>my</u> pet, because they are <u>mine.</u> We love <u>ourselves</u> in the other.
    b) There is a middle level of this one, where we are still self-oriented. It is a tribal love for <u>my</u> state, <u>my</u> country, <u>my</u> culture, again, because it is <u>mine</u>. These two are self-referential.
    c) The highest of the human love is the love we have for any human regardless of our even knowing them, independent of where or who they are. We love because they are human, without reference to ourselves.
3. *Agape*—divine-love

This streams from the highest forces of all creation. This love is beyond our greatest comprehension, and someday I hope we will all know it, though it is not our focus today.

*Philia*, the highest of human love (2c) is our topic. This virtuous love exists just because it does. Here, we are speaking of our love of acting.

Chekhov isn't asking us to love. He is asking us to admit that we already do love. We love acting. We love the process of creating the show. We love our characters as if they are our babies. We love the struggles and the victories, the flops and smash hits. We love the people who show up to our shows. We love staff and crew, those who help us be seen, heard, costumed, propped. We love those who write the words, promote the show, take the tickets, send out the emails. We hope the audience leaves our show having loved it. We love it all.

This love is a practical tool. It is the very love you experience for the art, for your characters, for your ensemble, and for human beings that leads you through endless hours of technical rehearsals. It is your love that drives you to create for no money, to even pay to perform despite the unfairness of that. The more we acknowledge and share this love, the more powerful it grows and infuses everyone around us with that same passion for action.

*When did you first notice this feeling? This interest? This curiosity?*

For most actors, something happened at a very young age that made you want to be seen. It might have been just a fleeting moment when you saw a performer and inside you lit up in recognition that you wanted that, that you would love to do that. Exactly when the "want" came is hard to say because it didn't just begin at that moment you recognized it. It must have begun much earlier.

## Where did it come from?

Who knows? So many of us feel we were just born with it, with this love of performing, regardless of how long it may have taken to act on it. That it is part and parcel of the highest part of us that unites spirit and soul in our bodies. It must have come from the divine forces. It really is part of our spiritual DNA. Could you possibly be you if it weren't there? Could someone come and surgically remove it from you?

Love really is a key starting point in finding the answers here. Chekhov speaks at length about this in his audio lecture series, which I highly recommend. Here are highlights along with my take on love and how practical it is for you as an artist to use as an active, actionable tool.

This love is a force of action, not just a romantic feeling. When it fills our thinking force, it inspires curiosity. Filling our feeling force with love transforms it into compassion. Penetrating our will force generates courage. Love, when absent from our will, leaves us with fearful cowardice. Love's absence from our thoughts, leaves us in fearful doubt. Fearful isolation arises when love is absent from our feelings.

## Thoughts about being an actor

Are you enthusiastic about being an actor? Enthusiasm is intense interest and enjoyment, coming from the Greek words for being inspired by a god. When we have enthusiasm for being an actor, we are much more likely to succeed in our training and career. When we love our job and are proud of what we do, feeling it has great purpose, enthusiasm comes easily. That's not always the situation though, is it?

One of the actor's greatest fears is of loving a useless and vain profession. I believe all human beings seek to be of value to others. The artist inevitably lives with an inner critic who screams into our psyche, "Why don't you do something important?!!!" Thinking that what you love is irrelevant, maybe even a life sentence on social "death row" is often projected onto us by our family and friends.

**It's time to speak, slowly and commandingly, right back: "Whoa! Doing this is necessary to my life."**

We come into this world with the love and compassion to do this. We are highly capable people who could work many jobs, and often do. We sacrifice ourselves, and gift our body, mind, and spirit to our audiences—and to each other and to our directors, writers and producers. What we have after all of that giving is nothing but the joy of having given. And what a joy it is. We love it. Who could stop this love?

People say, "Go into medicine, law, or education—something important with a stable income." Yet, every five minutes that someone spends in a state of appreciation of our art boosts their immune system for over six hours.[1] And, through our stories, we will teach more people than any teacher, defend more causes than any lawyer, and heal more people than any doctor.

Chekhov had a deep spiritual crisis where he questioned his super stardom in relation to the horrific turmoil of a world war, revolution, and pandemic. His path out of this was to commit to developing the integration of one's higher self into the role of the artist. He began taking social responsibility for helping the culture by choosing specific stories produced with a higher set of standards which he has passed to us. We create understanding and communication; and, we heal culture clashes. We help build peace.

And we are big business, to boot! In 2021, the performing arts and film industries contributed $82.3 billion to the US economy.[2] The second-largest export of the United States, a couple of years ago, was entertainment. It was second only to the theater of war.

Yet, 95 percent of performers do not make a living wage at this. We do this because we love; and with every performance, our noble intent is that the spectators be happier, healthier people.

We make others laugh. We make them cry. They come to us to feel connected to something. They come to disconnect from their world and give their world a break. They step into our story, and something changes in them. They come to us to be different when they go.

Our profession will never die, though the means for us to reach our audiences may change. The professions around us may fade, but ours will not. We are noble and should be treated as such. We are safe being humble. We are safe being proud to say *I am a creative artist. I am an **actor***. There is no such thing as an aspiring actor though we actors may aspire to being properly paid for our work. And if we are not to be bullied, insulted, mocked, or torn to shreds any more, we must stop any dysfunctional behavior. Then we will command the level of respect needed to rise in society.

## Training for stardom

Only a very few make it to the very top, and what happens when we get there is often terribly distorted and confusing. Who prepares the spirit for stardom? Precious few—and that must change. The more you *allow* your sunlight to shine through, the more brightly you will shine. Your charisma will soon lead the world to recognize you as a star. You are that star now, and you must learn to live that truth whether the world sees it or not. Still, you will always put your underwear on one foot at a time … at least until someone else has to do it for you. Cultivating your higher ego is essential.

There are very practical achievements that our love will bring when we are aware of its existence.

## Seven gifts we receive from awareness of love

1. All of our creativity is generated from the innate love we bear. To neglect our love will poison the field of creativity. To recognize our love is rich, organic fertilizer for the field.
2. The essence of all acting is giving. The essence of love is expanding. Are they not the same, to give, to love, to expand?
3. We are born to give, and not to hog our art. Giving brings a path of tranquility and poise, and no creative effort is possible without it. From love the fire of inspiration is ignited.
4. The artist who doesn't give is at unrest, tearing their nerves. Withholding suffocates us. Restlessness is tiring us today.
5. When we love every character, especially the evil ones, we then love to hate on the stage and the audience loves to hate the characters too. This is fun and healing. If we bring actual hate on the

stage, real hate energy creeps into the audience and also lingers in us. We bring the street onto the stage, and vice versa, confusing our everyday self with our artistic life. We begin acting in life, creating lies upon lies and awakening fears. Audiences feel dirty and less than, contracted, the same as we become.
6. We carry within us the seeds of love *and* of evil. When we cultivate love, it grows. Failure to be aware of love kills its flower. Failure to be aware of evil allows its weeds to strangle love.
7. Love will be a constant help to us, directing us in every detail, filling us with enthusiasm and the will to create.

Chekhov is not the only leader who sought to bring this highest aspect of humanity onto the stage. Nor was he the only one whose spiritually infused work was intentionally blocked from being shared with you who need it most.

In *The Routledge Companion to Stanislavsky*,[3] edited by R. Andrew White, Dr. Sharon Marie Carnicke, noted Slavic theater scholar, reveals how even the most recent translation of Stanislavsky,[4] the most influential teacher in the art since 1900, includes a specific choice to reduce key words conveying spiritual concepts to simple logic. Carnicke writes:

> It is interesting to note that "soul" (*dusha*) and "spiritual" (*dushevnyi*) remain in Stanislavsky's censored books and also appear in Elizabeth Reynolds Hapgood's seriously abridged translations; but Jean Benedetti rejects both words in his more complete 2008 translation by consistently translating *dusha* as "mind" (um) and *dushevnyi* as "mental" (*umnyi*).

To change "soul" to "mind" and "spiritual" to "mental," in my opinion, is an egregious wound that undermines the artist yet again.

We need this higher ego/spirit to help unite our love with our body.

The real, practical ways to strengthen the higher being within you start with believing it has value. Only then will you want to consciously grow its power.

As Candace Pert Says in *Molecules of Emotion*,[5]

> Some of my best insights have come to me through what I can only call a mystical process. It's like having God whisper in your ear.... There's a higher intelligence, one that comes to us from our very molecules, and results from our very participation in a system far greater than the small circumscribed one we call "ego," the world we receive from our five senses alone.

The higher ego gives us context and allows us to make sense of our love and our role. It inspires us to hold fast in the flood of fame and the drought of invisibility. It bridges audience, author, and artist with the story. It sustains our will to create and to live. It is what grants us the flow, puts us in the gap, fills us with "IT" and happens through us in those happy moments.

## ✏ Journal/Discuss/Flyback

*Compare your start point. As you read this now, reflect on where you were when you began this journey. Flip back to your first pages in your journal where you assessed your artistic life. Take some time to sit back and fly over your own level of participation with the offerings contained in this book and course. Answer those questions from the Introduction again today. And here are a few more.*

 *What did you like overall about how you participated in your discoveries of this approach? What was your favorite part of what you brought to the mix? Did you play all out? To what degree does the amount of commitment you made reflect the results you experienced? What would you do differently? What do you want more of? What do you not understand or "like?" What was your favorite moment?*

Reach out to those around you when you are clear on what you need help with or need more of. Surely others will want more of that too, and if they can help you fill in your gaps, I bet they will be willing to help you as their ensemble colleague, as I am sure you will, if someone comes to you.

## Personal PG and apps for life

*Having an amazing artistic experience while life is falling apart?*

*What would it be like to live life artfully? To make your life into its own peak performance art?*

No matter how fantastic your ability to act or do any other creative activity, if you have a painful, unfulfilling life, your artistic glory will be short-lived. We have no artistic need to be in pain. Yes, we can have a peak moment through pain just like a rat cornered can suddenly find inspiration to escape, and live to brag about it. Joy, love, and freedom are infinitely more inspirational and sustainable and, well, more fun!

Living with peace, expanded clarity, healing, and health can create more frequent, peak happy moments in art and life together. It all depends on whether you want that enough to choose the awareness and action possible. Here, we have offerings for you through the Chekhov-inspired approach that you can engage to bring your whole life into an active, living playful art.

As the course itself wraps up, your life continues, and we now accept the truth that your artistry does as well. In a practical sense, there is no possible way to just be an actor and do nothing else. After all, we have to eat, drink, stay healthy, pay bills, and have purely unrelated social times. We have to get a life to reveal a life in our art. And ultimately, the number of actors who love this art and pay the rent with it are few, and those who pay a mortgage with it are even fewer. Those who will move into other ways of generating income are the majority. Nonetheless, you will be an artist still, even if you don't perform on a stage or in front of a camera ever again. This love of which we have spoken will not fade. It is like the fiery sun that can only be obscured. To keep your love from burning up all that blocks it, you have the opportunity to live an artistic life by applying the tools we have learned.

If you are amongst the few who do sail through life in the eye of the public in any field, you will endure a scrutiny unlike any other way of existing. You will live at the fingertips and on the tongues and in the eyes of the world, and your every vulnerable moment may be plastered across the internet beyond your control, falsely or accurately. For you, it is even more critical to embrace this happy approach to peak performance as a way of living. Your clarity of love as an action and an experience of centered, unceasing stability and inspiration will carry you through your private pains that you may want to shield from the public eye.

Your understanding of the role you have chosen, the role that sacrifices a private world to be on the public stage, this awareness of your destiny will be that which fortifies you when no one else stands near. When you are surrounded by those who need you, want you, adore you, and demand of you so much that you have no reality check to bring you to your senses. When you don't know whose love to trust, you will always have your own.

You must train for fame and success to be able to stand on the pedestal when you are placed upon it, and be able to step off without breaking your neck so you can pull down your pants and take a dump when you need to. As fast as fame will deify you, it will vilify you and then crucify you. This is what so many famous people cannot survive, why they struggle and die in needless pain.

Love of who you are, love of why you are who you are, and a practical know-how to be who you are in all circles of your life will bring you enthusiasm, courage, and joy. What follows are ways to achieve this using some specific tools now as a path of continuous artistry for peak performance living.

## How do I know where I can best spend my time and energy?

Since our greatest creative power is our ability to choose our thoughts, where to place our attention, managing this becomes our greatest protector of our life. Mismanagement of our thought and attention becomes the greatest enemy we face. Yes, the enemy is within—and the hero is as well.

Review the last section of Chapter 15 on focal points: *Where thoughts go, energy grows*. As a human, choosing the most appropriate FP leads to peak performance living. While there are five basic Circles of Concentration of where we can physically "look" with our eyes, we can focus on the metaphoric circles of our lives: #1: character, #2: actor, #3: artist, #4: human, #5: spirit.

How one decides where to focus, whether this decision is for the character or for the self, is to identify the objective, the "what for?" When one is clear on the aim and purpose one is pursuing, the choice of where to focus becomes clearer.

Because we have an objective in each life circle, we could say that we also have super objectives, and a super-super objective. This means we have a want, a will-force intention for each circle. One distinction we can make in identifying the "what for" of our lives is to source our love. Ask, *In what way will this expand love? How does my intention strengthen love in this circle? How can the powers of love support me in this area?*

## Ultimately love is an act of will—are you willing to love?

If all the circle's intentions line up, things are going great. This happens when the largest circle's will, the spirit #5, permeates the human #4 will, which inspires the will of the artist #3, whose will infuses the actor #2, whose will creates the character #1. This happens in the opposite direction when the smallest circle's will, #1, the character, goes to meet the will of circle, #2, the actor, which goes to meet the will of #3, the artist, #4, the human, and #5, the spirit. When we get all of the aims of each part of our life together, things work. Those different parts of us that battle, for example, over where to spend that extra moment or dollar, can come to harmony. This will keep you from getting crazy over how life is going when you get scared that it isn't "right." It will help you find the Beauty, Ease, Entirety, and Form (BEEF) continuously.

>  Axiom 20.1: 100 percent of the will, aligned, will align the misaligned.

## Gotta love those Psychological Gestures!

Developing the flexibility to choose a tool and instantly allow it to inspire your next actions and speech is a skill applicable in nearly every moment of life. *Acting the Michael Chekhov Way* helps you become comfortable expressing powerful energies in a safe controlled environment and to turn them on and off at will. You have learned that you can shift your undesired emotional state to its opposite with movement qualities and breath. You know how to change the atmosphere around you and how to lighten your Personal Atmosphere. You can move with Ease and seek Beauty to uplift yourself. At any step of the following process, you can step out, clear and restore your ideal self.

Metaphorically, as human beings, we can drift into that sixth circle of unconsciously disconnecting, the "I don't know" unfocused life with mood alteration and aimlessness. Again, staying conscious of our goals in each area of life helps us prioritize time, energy, and all resources. Use Chekhov's question "What for" are we doing this?" to lead your imagination to your path to peak performance in acting and in life. Also, as a general concept, taking ourselves too seriously can lead to contraction. All great spiritual teachers recommend laughter. We can lighten our attitude and bring a sense of humor to help us expand our sense of love as an action. Keep this in mind with the following activities. Have fun even when it gets intense. Be ready to laugh at yourself and with others.

## Power Gestures: Deeper dive into gestures for personal growth and healing

I have benefitted greatly by applying Chekhov tools in my life and have developed applications in my life coaching practice as well. This section steps one through some of the possibilities as an option for any interested parties. Please skip to the circle below if it ain't yer cup o' tea!

See Lisa Dalton on Power Gestures at https://youtu.be/_4tBkJF2NAg.

> ### Homeplay daily Power Gesture
>
> Some folks create a new psychological gesture every morning to express how they would like their day to go. We like to call this personal application a power gesture. Then, when things go awry, they repeat their daily PG, veiled or unveiled as circumstances invite. This helps them get on track toward their intentional outcomes.

 ### Let's play Compositionary Gestures for your life circles

Use the 3I's to create your personal compositional sequence of psychological gestures for each circle of concentration for your life. This will help you get clear on what you want in each life circle. Sometimes finding the words to say it is difficult, and somewhere in your body, the answer is there.

- Create your own expression of the obstacle or condition that keeps that from happening. These obstacles or conflicts can be from three sources, just like a character or a story: inside you, between you and others, or with the outer forces you cannot control.
- Create a PG for the thing you do to cope with or overcome that obstacle or condition.
- Create a PG of your biggest dream come true in that area of your life that activates the love in you.

### Journal/Discuss/Flyback

*Allow yourself to Flyback on what you have experienced and journal or chat with a confidant about your thoughts.*

### Conflict resolution

*The following suggestions are for manageable stressed states. If you sense you are beyond that, please seek professional support from a qualified individual, such as a guidance counselor or a mental health care coach within a professional setting of trust with the specific intention to support healing and self-development with a "do no harm" ethic. Please use these exercises carefully, preferably with a witness to hold space for you and with ample time for Flyback.*

See Peak Performance Living with Lisa Dalton on Conflict Resolution https://youtu.be/VY8uagWtxS4

Some of us fear the future and get visions of failure or loss. When invited to focus on a positive outcome, we just don't have the biological imprint inside us. Perhaps our bodies don't know the feeling of "good." To help free ourselves of these inner limitations, we can improvise a situation we may face in the future and play out the potential loss we fear and can easily imagine. Then, we can follow that by reversing the improvisation so that we win big, way BIG. Trying this in this order can be an outstanding preparation to increase the likelihood of a positive outcome. By improvising the scene of the ideal outcome, of complete success, a new neurological pathway is formed. Your whole being now knows it is possible for it to experience success. By improvising the complete failure, our fear can no longer be denied or repressed. In our personal stories of good vs. evil, the expression of the good increases its strength. The expression of the "evil" releases its unseen strength for the good.

 Let's improvise our nightmare and our dream

- Create the PG of your biggest fear/nightmare expressed, using your whole body.
- Create the PG of your biggest love-based success/dream expressed, using your whole body.
- Replay these in a sequence, beginning with your worst nightmare and transforming into your most awesome dream.
- Replay the whole movement sequence, filling the victory with more and more energy until the energy of worst nightmare is no longer activating you, and you spend less and less time in that state.
- Hold the energy of joy and love of the dream fulfilled longer each time until you can no longer feel any negative energy in the nightmare and can feel it all fully in the dream.
- Flyback and remember if at any time your old negative thoughts return, you can do a mini-gesture of the dream to pull you up to joy.

## We'll be one part of *us*

When we played with Thinking, Feeling, Willing, we might have noticed that each part of us can have a different task and, indeed, opinion about how to handle a situation. It can be very helpful acting out the different parts of us, imagining that we have a higher self who witnesses and assists us in weaving all of the revelations together and hatching a plan. We see emotional parts exemplified in the Disney-Pixar animated film series, *Inside Out*. The concept of identifying conflicting parts is also used in Jungian parts therapy and voice dialogue, where one takes on the specific part, allowing it to express in its own voice and imaginary body, saying exactly what it wants to say from its own space in the room. Every part has the super objective of protecting us and therefore has the same dream. Each, however, has its own nightmare of what will happen if you don't listen to it. Create the dream gesture of safety and joy. Then, allow each of the most active parts within you to express their nightmare and then transform it into the dream gesture as we did in the previous improvisation. Allow your higher aware ego to Flyback and unite all the parts with a gesture of gathering and integrating into your heart.

The energy in our anxious parts will calm down when it feels seen and heard, even if you choose to take a different action than it wants. You can negotiate a deal once you know its concerns and honor them as real. Remember, every part loves you.

## We'll be *them*

Switching identities is an improvisational tool to increase empathy and diffuse conflict with others. We can do an improv playing the conflicting person or event or situation as if we were *them*. We may discover an understanding on a deeper level than being told about them. Here is one of many ways one can play with this. Put on their imaginary body or moveable center. Impersonate them seriously or judgmentally, even exaggerate what you find unpleasant. Now, pause and ask yourself to find beauty and love in them, to imagine their pain and their dreams. Now, once again, put on their Imaginary Body (IB) or Moveable Center (MC) with honor, free of judgment. Reveal that beauty you found in them. *Flyback with the lessons you have learned.* Perhaps you even try putting on the imaginary body they might have for you and their judgments they might be projecting onto you. Release and Flyback. *How does it feel? What do you love?*

*Life is an Improvisation, and once we know we cannot control it, we can find the love, go with the flow, and enjoy it. We can choose love-based perceptions and respond joyfully if we decide that is our aim.*[6]

## Coming full C.I.R.C.L.E.

George Shdanoff was a Russian actor/director who became Michael Chekhov's dramaturgical colleague in Dartington and New York. He was eventually Chekhov's co-director of the Chekhov Theater Players. He continued developing his teaching in Los Angeles, coaching into the late 1980s, when I trained with him. I co-produced the documentary, *From Russia to Hollywood: the 100-Year Odyssey of Chekhov and Shdanoff*.

George spoke of the "grounds" of the actor in the same way I use the term "tools." He frequently repeated this axiom:

- *You must always have as your primary grounds three things: Concentration, Imagination and Radiation. If you are missing any one of these three, your inspiration will fail.*

Let's unpack this statement to discover the treasure it contains.

## Concentration

**Concentration** is the grounding point for all inspired action. It is so fundamental that, when Chekhov drew his chart for Mala, it was not even included. One could say it was the very paper upon which the chart was drawn. We begin to play with any tool only when being grounded in concentration. And, as the ever awe-inspiring chart reveals, every exercise we play with is in fact a concentration-building exercise. Chekhov dedicated much of the content of *Lessons for Teachers* to concentration. He adapts most of Rudolf Steiner's six basic exercises for spiritual development into his teaching.

Today, many of us are increasingly challenged with focus and concentration skills, and even Chekhov suggests we will get bored doing simple exercises blatantly stated as "concentration exercises." With our playful approach, we can make concentration skills a highly desired by-product. And we certainly do want the super powers of concentration. When we discover the scientific effect that concentration has, how athletes use it, doctors use it, people of all natures create through it, it gives us reason to believe in its power. Remember, it is a muscle that builds by repeating challenges. Use the gesture and the axiom "A unified field of focus is present in all inspired action." Repeat this frequently. Use silence as a working tool.

 ### Let's play radiate the gesture

Here's a quick, fun game to play with a partner, live or online. (Sorry, shy of working with a cat, I haven't figured out how to play this solo; so let me know your ideas for that if any arise!) Give yourselves enough space to move up, down, back, or forward safely. Both artists can begin by centering first or try it without centering and see how effective it is and then center and play again.

Player A has eyes closed and is at least 10 feet from Player B and far enough away for Player A to not feel the light, air, or movement of Player B. Player B radiates gestures to lift, lower, push or pull Player A in various directions. Keeping eyes closed, Player A receives and responds to Player B's gesture. Player B can begin radiating veiled gestures and unveil as necessary if that doesn't work. Play in silence so you are both working with the invisible forces traveling through space. Play for several minutes, release, Flyback and switch positions and repeat. Then, clear and release.

## Journal/Discuss/Flyback

*Begin your Flyback with a good laugh about the whole thing and whatever you wish to share for about a minute. Here are some prompts to follow that.*

*How was it? How was your concentration level? Did you feel your will force engage? If you tried it without centering and then centered, did being centered first help?*

*Player A, did you sense anything? Were you able to develop trust in your sensory receptivity? How was your feeling of ease? How does "not knowing" if we are getting the signals affect us psychologically? What else came up for you?*

*Player B, how receptive was Player A? How did the how success and failure affect your emotions, your gestures? What else came up for you?*

## Imagination

To make concentration valuable, we must have a target or object upon which to concentrate. For our purposes, we define that object as "the image." As artists, we have several skills to develop in regard to images:

- The ability to access and sustain images of many natures such as fantasy, memory, or projection, in literal or abstract terms, in multiple modalities such as visually, aurally, kinesthetically, and auditory-digitally.
- The ability to psychophysically express the images. All basic Psycho-Physical Exercises (PPE's), sensations, and tempo/rhythm exercise build this skill.
- The ability to lead the imagination with questions. The Chart of Inspired Action is itself the reminder of the many questions that will stimulate an undeveloped or blocked, creative imagination. IBs, centers, and sphere of images are key tools here.
- The ability to identify useful images, discard clichés, and choose the ideal. The laws of composition and SynthAnalysis™ cultivate this skill.
- Images can be of the lower ego's reality of past or present personal circumstances such as affective memory (biography), sense memory (taste, touch, etc.), of current life (substitution of real personal relationships and needs), of observation/imitation of "real life," or of fantasy and pretend.
- Images of fantasy and pretend are the center point of *Acting the Michael Chekhov Way*. We support the image that our sub and super conscious self is like a laboratory that purifies all of the above and unites it with the Jungian idea of collective consciousness and the existence of archetypes. We recommend going from our Ideal Artistic Center (IAC) to the sphere of images and sourcing this first. Fleeting images of past or present personal life may arise and are allowed to pass and are never used to stimulate the artistic impulse. Observing unlimited images first allows your creative individuality to offer the first and freshest objective ideas. External observation and past experience can validate or offer minor adjustments afterward, thus not limiting the initial discoveries.

## Radiation

To reveal the ideal images upon which we are concentrating, we need radiation. This is the skill, developed through the will of the player, which expresses to our audiences the images needed to convey the story. It requires a continuous flow of energy in (Receiving) or out (Radiating). It is the element identified as charisma, star quality, and the "IT" factor. Key tools are all Veiling exercises, the Four Brothers of Art (BEEF), love in our profession, making friends with, IAC activating exercises, ideal artistic stance, staccato/legato six directions radiation sequence, and incorporation from the sphere of images. Truthfully, all the tools work to build it.

**We must *concentrate* on an *image* and *radiate* it.** Concentration on multiple images will radiate a mess. Radiation of an image in conflict with the Style and Truth of the story will be a mess. Inability to concentrate on a specific image will cripple radiation. We need all three to ground the Goblet of our artistic being and to create a vessel to receive Inspiration.

These three grounds form the beginning of the word c̲i̲r̲cle. Now let's flesh out the entire word.

## Centeredness

From the earliest parts of the training, we focus on awakening an awareness of the Ideal Artistic Center. Identifying it instinctually, we cultivate the act of allowing our artistic impulses to emanate from this point. More recent developments have supported the success of imaging through the IAC as opposed to through the mind. We also emphasize that the Ideal Artistic Center is its own locale rather than the heart or heart chakra. It is not a specific organ, though it is most closely located near the thymus gland.

The ideal artistic stance and stroll have developed to help anchor the IAC in everyday living. This frees the biology-limiting imprint of our off-centered lower ego. When we allow our body to rotate in the shoulders and hips as we walk, we return to nature's counterbalancing system used when we walk barefoot on natural surfaces. It is the exact same free flow of rotation that is instinctively done when we feel "on top of the world" and is used by power walkers for maximum efficient use of energy. Centeredness in our physiology improves our ability to concentrate and radiate. Centeredness in our higher ego unites and synthesizes our creative acts as referenced in Chekhov's audio lectures and Five Guiding Principles.

## Love/Lightness/Laughter, and Ease

Lightness and Ease are frequently paired in Chekhov's teaching. They are the qualities present in everyone who is in a state of inspired action. Inspiration seems to be flowing effortlessly, lightly, and easily into the artist. Artists appear to effortlessly radiate even those characters who struggle in chaos.

We have spoken of ease at length, so here we discuss expanded interpretations of lightness. Lightness is part of the light of radiation. It generates sparkle and sizzle in the action and actor. Lightness of attitude gives the artist a sense of humor and fun that is central to play and to *Acting the Michael Chekhov Way*. When we *lighten up*, we can recover from moments of uneasiness. We can be more objective about the flow of our career or life. We allow ourselves more freedom to fail "perfectly" and to recover with ease. In fact, lightness allows us to rename failure and to baptize those seeming moments of disaster as a perfect experience, perhaps different than our own expectation, leading to a growth opportunity or a way of being guided by higher forces.

Lightness and Ease create a magnetism that draws to you a powerful ensemble of like-hearted people. And, as previously mentioned, it heals! Laughter and humor are essential elements in the life of those who seek to live through their higher self. When we can laugh compassionately at our foibles, we can move love into action more regularly. If you find yourself out of sorts, check to see if you are missing any ingredients in the C.I.R.C.L.E. (See Figure 20.1.)

Ultimately we *concentrate* on *images* and *radiate* them with *centeredness*, *love/lightness* and *ease*.

We hope you will bring this full C.I.R.C.L.E. with you in all aspects of your life and share it along your inspired path.

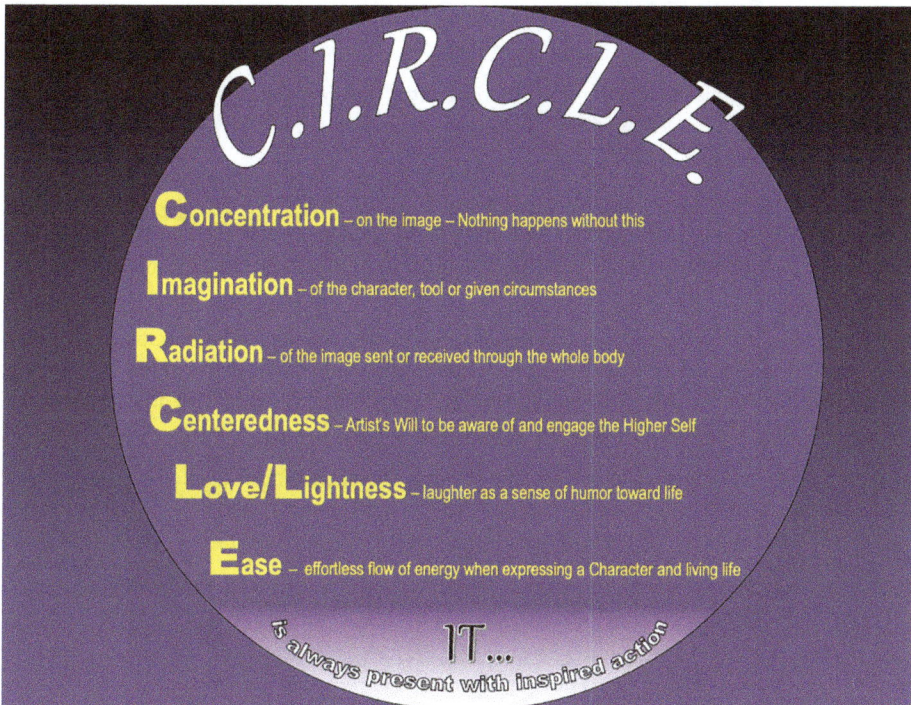

*Figure 20.1* The image of the C.I.R.C.L.E. as a unification of the core elements of *Acting the Michael Chekhov Way*. (Courtesy of NMCA, Dalton & Bowles.)

## Five Guiding Principles

In the Introduction, we discussed Chekhov's Five Guiding Principles. Reviewing these now may help you see what was not so clear when we started. I want to delve a little more deeply into the fifth guiding principle (GP5), "Ask each tool in what way do you free my talent?" Seeking the answers to this question is an act of love. It leads to falling ever more deeply in love with the truths Chekhov identified and transformed into a practical application process.

Can you see that love frees us from our inhibitions? That the Four Brothers of Art calm our nerves and expand our love? That without being able to do Expanding and Contracting, we might not even recognize when we are out of flow? Akim Tamiroff, a dear friend of Chekhov, was a Russian compatriot who hosted Chekhov gatherings in Hollywood during the 1940s and 1950s. Tamiroff was known for his aggressive, often intimidating performances. One actor asked a question about what to do with directors with whom you don't agree. Tamiroff—whom everyone expects will tell a director exactly what to do—instead reinforces Chekhov's guidance to find the beauty by saying that he "dips" the direction in his own creative will. There he finds freedom. Freedom is necessary for all true "peak" performances. Any acting offered by force—meaning because you have to do it—you are driven by habits, fears, and social necessity—will lack true spontaneity and creativity. Forced activity lacks love, which must be freely given to awaken full freedom. My wish is that you fall in love with each tool and find freedom.

## It's a wrap!

We began with "making friends with," a simple activity that builds our love of where we are at the present moment. Way back in our early ball-tossing days, we learned that "strong preparation makes the action effortless" and "repetition is the growing power." "Practice, observe, and apply" daily because you are a creative artist 365 days a year.

You can activate your unlimited sphere of imagination with leading questions and gaze patiently and artistically until images appear. You know how to compose with triplicity, polarity and transformation and use tempo/rhythm to drive the dynamics.

You have *thought* critically to gain understanding of many powerful ideas. You have played fully to *feel* the power of these tools. You have *done* many tasks to explore these tools and have many reasons to want to gain mastery. Your Thinking, Feeling, and Willing forces understand in every cell, the role you play in the theater of humanity.

You have resources for honing your transformational acting skills, revealing your native talent, applying it in innumerable styles and to your life itself. You know how to be a continuous artist, the Goblet itself, seeing love and beauty in the forms around and within you, meeting challenges with ease-filled commitment. You create atmospheres that radiate the soul of the story to the audience.

You know how to make friends with your ensemble of inner characters, family, colleagues, and business associates. You know how to form relationships that will be a plus in your life, and you know how to be that for others. You understand that this giving and receiving aspect will nurture you in all circles of life and spirit.

You know in your heart that it all begins and ends with the love you already have inside.

### Homeplay: Four daily deeds of love

There are four daily deeds that Chekhov encourages us to do that will have many benefits. He specifically gives us these four deeds to do in our everyday life because we are always artists, and he asks, "Why shouldn't we use our daily life to strengthen these happiness-building daily deeds of love?"

When we view love as a verb, we have no need to wait for a feeling or emotion to move us toward loving acts. Thus, these four suggestions on how to cultivate Love in our lives are a call to daily action.

1. The first suggestion is to look for opportunities to show kindness by doing thoughtful things for other people. This might be opening a door for someone, creating an open space for a trucker to change lanes, giving a donation to someone in need, or a simple smile to someone you pass on the street. The action need not seem very significant, but when you do it with the intention to help someone have a better day, it is cultivating in you a stronger sense of human love. We don't need to worry about whether we feel love for this or that person before we act. We do a loving deed and the feeling will follow. If we wait for the feeling before acting, we will miss many opportunities to grow more joyous and creative.
2. The second suggestion is to cultivate the Feeling of Beauty we spoke of in Chapter 8. When inner judgement arises for people, places, situations, and conditions, choose actively to find the positive aspect in the situation. If something is unpleasant and ugly to you, engage your concentration and employ your will force to extract some element of goodness and beauty. Choose that to focus on the bright side of life. More love will flow within you and toward you.
3. The third suggestion is to listen closely to your thoughts and speech to notice how you use the self-referential words like I, me, mine. When we listen to others over the day, are we waiting for them to say things we agree with? Are we thinking of what we are going to say back to them? Can we practice listening objectively to them from our higher self? Can we listen without tracking whether we approve or disapprove? Can we base our relationship with others on their humanity rather than on how much we agree or disagree with their opinions? By inviting our everyday selves to notice our own self-referential responses, we may over time grow more and more loving.

4. The fourth suggestion is develop a continuous awareness that each person we encounter has a higher self within them. When we allow ourselves to recognize the higher being before us, we awaken our human loving self, and we invite theirs to appear. We need not try to envision their higher self through a whole conversation. If we can allow a flash of awareness when we come together, that is all that is necessary. Bearing in mind that this person has a higher self will help us apply the first three suggestions more easily, regardless of the situation we find ourselves in.

These four simple suggestions awaken the Four Brothers of Art, which are present in all peak performances. Applying these four deeds daily will transform your life into a loving piece of art.

 **Axiom 20.2: Four Daily Deeds of Love**

1. **D**o random acts of kindness.
2. **E**xtract beauty from ugliness.
3. **E**xamine your everyday lower ego and self-referential language.
4. **D**evelop awareness of the higher ego of others.

You have the power of concentration, the wisdom to choose where to focus and when, and the love to infuse you with the will-driven courage, thinking-infused enthusiasm, and feeling-inspired compassion.

YOU ARE READY! YOU ARE PREPARED! USE THE FORCE!

**P.S. Actors, will you stay ready? Here are resources that will help.**

- See **OR 20.1** AMCW technique review.
- See **OR 20.2** Think you know it? Test yourself with two quizzes.
- See **OR 20.3** Actor-led syllabi for six *Acting the Michael Chekhov Way Workouts*.
- See **OR 20.4** Video links for lessons online.

**Teachers, for additional online resources, see**

- **OR 22.0** A teacher prepares the MC way
- **OR. 22.1** Study questions for *On The Technique of Acting*
- **OR 22.2** Comparing/weaving Chekhov with other approaches

## Notes

1. Hearthmath.org
2. https://www.arts.gov/news/press-releases/2023/new-data-show-economic-activity-us-arts-cultural-sector-2021# The motion picture industry…contributed nearly $68.9 billion in 2021…. Performing arts presenters (such as performing arts venues and festivals) contributed just over $14.3 billion to the economy….
3. White, R. Andrew, Carnicke, Sharon Marie. *The Routledge Companion to Stanislavsky*, Routledge, 2014.
4. Stanislavsky, Konstantin. *An Actors Work*, Benedetti, Jean (trans.), Routledge, 2008.
5. Pert, Candace. *Molecules of Emotion*, Simon & Schuster, page 315, 1999.
6. Watch *Peak Performance Living with Lisa Dalton on Conflict Resolution* video on YouTube for more information. http://www.youtube.com/watch?v=VY8uagWtxS4

# Appendix 1
# POA Journal-Flyback Playsheet

Name:             Today is             POA #

For _____ minutes, I practiced/played with the tools and techniques of _____
*Remember to use the Rock 'N Roll DVD to help you with the exercises if needed.*

This morning, I observed the tool expressing itself in life as _____

This morning, I applied the above techniques, doing it while I _____

This afternoon, I observed tool expressing itself in life as _____

This afternoon, I applied the above techniques, doing it while I _____

This evening, I observed tool expressing itself in life as _____

This evening, I applied the above techniques, doing it while I _____

Through my practice, observation and application today, I have created a **piece of art** and I am excited to have discovered _____

# Appendix 2
# Wil Kilroy's rehearsal outline

## Courtesy of Wil Kilroy and the NMCA MC technique playbook

Blocking, line memorization, and the Four Brothers—
Ease, Beauty, Form, and Wholeness—should be incorporated throughout the play sessions.

1. **Characterization**

    Transformative tools: *Molding, Flowing, Flying, Radiating, Centers, Imaginary Body/voice, Images, Thinking/Feeling/Willing, Radiating/Receiving*

2. **Objective/gestures**

    First: Try a variety of objectives

    Tools: *Expanding, Contracting, Pushing, Pulling, Gathering, Throwing, Lifting, Smashing, Tearing, Penetrating, Dragging, Reaching, Psychological Gestures*

3. **Atmospheres/qualities**

    Create: *Overall Atmosphere, Personal Atmosphere, Qualities leading to Sensations leading to Feelings*

4. **Dynamics**

    Investigate: *Tempo/Rhythm, Staccato, Legato, Floating/Falling/Balancing, winning/losing, and Radiating/Receiving*

5. **Composition**

    Investigate: *Triplicity, Polarity, Rhythmic Repetition, Spirals/Lines/Curves, Rock Garden, variety of levels, Psychology of the Stage: downstage future, center present, upstage past, Feeling versus Thinking versus Willing*

# Bibliography

Brown, Theodore L., LeMay, H., Eugene Jr., Bursten, Bruce E., Murphy, Catherine J., Woodward, Patrick M., Stoltzfus, Matthew W., Lufaso, Michael W. *Chemistry Central Science*. Pearson Higher Education. 2013.
Carnicke, Sharon Marie. *Dynamic Acting Through Active Analysis*, page 112, Methuen Drama. 2023.
Chekhov, Michael. *To the Director and Playwright*. Compiled by Charles Lenard. Limelight Editions. 1984.
Chekhov, Michael. *On the Technique of Acting*. Ed. Mel Gordon, Preface and Afterword by Mala Powers. HarperCollins Publishers, Inc. 1991.
Chekhov, Michael. *To the Actor: On the Technique of Acting*. Routledge. 2002.
Chekhov, Michael. *On Theatre and the Art of Acting: The Five-Hour CD Master Class Lectures Recorded by Michael Chekhov in 1955*. 4 CDs. Working Arts. 2004.
Dalton, Lisa, Wil Kilroy, and Charles P. Bowles. *Michael Chekhov Technique Playbook*. Peak Performance Publishing. 2017.
Dalton, Lisa Loving. *Falling for the Stars: A Stunt Gal's Tattle Tales*. Sojourn Publishing. 2016.
Dalton, Lisa and Frederick Keeve. *From Russia to Hollywood*. Pathfinder Pictures. 2002.
Dalton, Lisa. *Murder Of Talent: How Pop Culture Is Killing "IT"*. Peak Performance Living Pubs. 2017.
Delgado, Ramon. *Acting with Both Sides of Your Brain*. Harcourt School, 1985.
HeartMath Institute. *Science of the Heart*. An Overview of Research Conducted by the HeartMath Institute 2016. HeartMath.org; https://www.heartmath.org/assets/uploads/2024/09/blog-todays-stress-is-different.jpg
Hutchinson, Anjalee. *Exercises for Non-traditional Staging: Chekhov Reimagined*. Focal Press. 2017.
Hutchinson, Anjalee Deshpande. *Michael Chekhov and Sanford Meisner, Collisions and Convergence in Actor Training*. Routledge. 2021.
Kasponyte, Justina. *Stanislavski's directors: Michael Chekhov and the revolution in Lithuanian theatre of the 1930s*. MPhil(R) thesis, University of Glasgow. 2011. Original images found at the archives of Lithuanian Theatre, Music and Cinema Museum, Vilnius.
Kilroy, Wil. *Improvisation the Michael Chekhov Way*. Routledge. 2024.
Meisner, Sanford and Longwell, Dennis. *Sanford Meisner on Acting*. Random House. 1987.
Earl Nightingale. *The Strangest Secret*, Sound Wisdom. 2019.
Pareto, Vilfredo. *Cours d'Économie Politique* (in two volumes). F. Rouge and F. Pichon. 1896–1897.
Pert, Candace. *Molecules of Emotion*. Simon & Schuster. 1999.
Rein, Glen, Mike Atkinson and Rollin McCraty. "The physiological and psychological effects of compassion and anger." *Journal of Advancement in Medicine*. 1995; 8 (2): 87–105.
Sagan, Carl. *Cosmos*. Mass Market Paperback. Random House. 2002.
Schechner, Richard. *Performance Theory*. Routledge. 2004.
Montelle, Yann-Pierre. *Paleoperformance: The Emergence of Theatricality as Social Practice*. Seagull Books. 2009.
Stanislavsky, Konstantin. *An Actor's Work*. Translation by Benedetti, J. Routledge. 2008.
Stanislavski, K. S. *Sobranie sochinenii II* [*Collected Works*]. 9 vols. page 212. Iskusstvo. 1989.
White, R. Andrew, Carnicke Sharon Marie. *The Routledge Companion to Stanislavsky*. Routledge. 2014.

## Online resources

Abrahm Maslow. American psychologist. https://en.wikipedia.org/wiki/Abraham_Maslow
*Carnivàle* 2003-05 IMDB HBO https://www.imdb.com/title/tt0319969/?ref_=ttep_ov_i
Coggins, Guy, Founder of Auraphoto.com. Aura Imaging Photography.

http://actorsmovementstudio.com
https://actorstoolkit.co.uk/the-ultimate-guide-to-acting-movement-practitioners/
https://en.wikipedia.org/wiki/Swoosh
https://longitude.ft.com/think-feel-do-how-to-use-rational-and-emotional-content-to-get-an audience-response/
https://pmc.ncbi.nlm.nih.gov/articles/PMC7551835/#sec4-behavsci-10-00137
https://www.aarp.org/publications/magazines/aarp-the-magazine-february-march-2024/
https://www.secondmedic.com/blogs/which-part-of-the-body-has-the-most-nerve-endings
https://www.weforum.org/publications/the-future-of-jobs-report-2023/digest/
https://www.youtube.com/watch?v=Ks-_Mh1QhMc
Johns Hopkins. https://www.hopkinsmedicine.org/health/conditions-and-diseases/immunoglobulin-a-deficiency
Scottini, Leticia, https://www.leticiascottini.com/ Chekhov Teaching Artist, Member of the Michael Chekhov Studios Cooperative. August 1, 2024.
The Hand in the Brain By Til Luchau [The Somatic Edge] https://www.abmp.com/textonlymags/article.php?article=2244#:~:text=Your%20hands%20are%20truly%20sense,are%20finely%20attuned%20to%20pressure.
www.EurythmyOnline.com

# Index

*Note*: Page numbers in italics refer to figures.

3Is 30, 176–7; LQ 239, 243; *see also* Inspiration, Imagination, Intellect
3S 28, 85, 87–94,110, 113, 115, 117, 136–7, 143, 180, 206, 224, 268–9; Falling 87–8; Floating 88–9; Balancing 89–90; examples: *Wizard of Oz*, Hamlet, Seinfeld, Friends 93; they walk in improv 92; three applications 93; *see also* Balancing; Falling; Floating; Three Sister Sensations
5 GP 3, 14–15, 133, 136, 284–5; *see also* Five Guiding Principles

AAA: Activity/Action, Archetype of Character, Atmosphere for Auditions *see also* audition
AC *see* Archetype: of character
Access, Select, Convey *see* acting job description; ASC
acronyms, purpose 6, 34
acting job description *see* ASC
Actor's March 162,171–2, 199, 205
actors gym/gymnasium 1, 32
AG 14, 27, 72–84; aim to awaken urge 78, 80; BBEEP guidelines 79; building a PG from 236–8; definition 81; differences between PG 84, 236–7; Drag, Reach 83; *Symbols* 83; Form 78; Imaginary Body 180; invisible 67; learning curve 81; life 80; Lift, Smash, Gather, Throw, Penetrate, Tear 82; neutral 75, 82; PPE 27, 57, 113, 143, 182; pure will 76; Push and Pull 77, 82; Radiating 207; Style 157; subtext/tactic 81; veiled as free of time/space 78; voice 75; as "why" 74; *see also* Archetypal Gestures; BBEEP
alley: silent 16–17, 39; *see also* Form; hallway
AMCW: *Acting the Michael Chekhov Way* 200, 213, 233; To the Teacher 3; technique review 287
American Film institute 1, 22
Andrees, Joerg ix
anticipation 42, 90, 92, 96, 102–3, 114, 261, 265
Antidote to AI 7; *see also* OR
archeological research 7; see also Montelle, Yann-Pierre

Archetypal Gestures (#4) *see* AG
Archetype (-al) 215, 231; of Character 29, 81, 173, 182–5, 200, 245, 248; meaning 81, 182; motion 60; objects: SBV 185–6; Rhythm 213; shadow 184; TFW body language 187–91, 196, 199; *see also* AC; orphan
ASC 25, 27–28, 32, 34, 44, 46, 143, 206, 236, 283; *see also* Access, Select and Convey; acting job description
ATMO 28–29, 85, 99–112,143; Archetypes 115; in Beauty 131, 134; combine OA/PA *104*, 107–9, *112*; in life 105, 110, 137; Radiating/Receiving 207; rehearsal 289; *see also* Atmospheres; OA; PA
Atmospheres (#7) *see* ATMO; OA; PA
audition 35–6, 67–8, 105, 117, 141, 178, 183, 226, 248; missed 22; *see also* AAA
aura 29, 44, 79, 106–8; photography 112n2, 224; *see also* ATMO, PA
away motivation 229–30, 232, 242; *see also* CG; PG; toward motivation; win/loss
Axiom 6, 9, 11–12, 14, 15, 17–19, 21, 23, 25, 27, 32–4, 39, 41, 43, 52, 59–60, 63–4, 74, 76, 78, 81, 84–5, 93, 96, 102–3, 109, 114, 121, 126, 131, 133, 136–7, 143, 149, 156, 168, 174, 176, 179, 182, 194, 205, 208, 214, 217–18, 222, 225, 227–8, 232–3, 236–7, 239, 247, 254, 257, 260, 267, 279, 282, 287

backstory 262; *see also* Palace
Balancing teetering sensation 89–91; metaphors 89; *see* 3S
Ball Toss 19, 26–9, 36–8, 40–3, 54, 75, 79, 141, 145, 205–6, 223; perfect ball drop 37–44, 49; receiving 42; run-through 272
Baptize, -ing 70, 98, 175–7, 262, 264–5, 267, 269–70, 284; ATMO 104–5, 110, 134, 259–60; balls 44; Palace 134, 159, 176–7; Super Theme 255–6
BBEEP 79, 81, 236–7, 244; *see also* AG; Ball Toss; Breath, Body, Extreme, Effort that is P.A.S.S.ed; PG

Beauty: chairs 131–2; chart 219; choice, Axiom 8.5 131–4, 227; C.I.R.C.L.E. 284; Feeling of 14, 16, 31, 64, 131–7, 180, 204–5, 214, 224, 241, 257; homeplay, on set 134, 136; for life 144, 183, 225; Love 279–82, 285–7; Palace of 134–5; POA 33, 134; for Rad/Rec 201; rehearsal 289; Shakespeare 161; Style 155, 158; SynthAnalysis™ 251, 258, 270; taking direction 179; Walking in-Navajo blessing 135; *see also* BEEF

Beauty Ease Entirety Form *see* BEEF

BEEF 29, 113–37, 180, 224; Axiom 8.6 133; Beauty, Ease, Entirety, Form, peak performance 133; chairs 127; C.I.R.C.L.E. 284; Ensemble 143; Communion 144; homeplay, on set 134,136; "IT" factor 284; life 144, 225; Love 279, 284, 287; Palaces 134; purpose 29, 85, 137, 139, 143, 214, 224, 284; QoMs 133; Rad/Rec 201; rehearsal 289; SynthAnalysis™ 270; *see also* Beauty; Ease; Entirety; Form; Four Brothers of Art

belief 7, 149, 155–6, 161, 230; beliefs 49, 159

body language 30, 37, 42–5, 49, 54, 55, 57, 60, 72, 74, 80, 84, 86, 92, 96, 150, 159–60, 162, 167, 171–2, 174, 198–9, 201, 203, 208; modifications for TFW 186–96; PG 231, 234–47, 249, 252–3, 255, 258; Style 155; *see also* emphatic gesture; habit; mannerism; Thinking, Feeling, Willing (TFW)

Bowles, Charlie 2, 9, 48, 285, 290

breath, -e 8, 118, 158, 168, 170, 279; ATMO 35, 100–2, 115; Beauty 132; Ease 122–4, 133–7; Ensemble 141; Gesture 73–81, 234–6, 243; habit 49; IAC 46; life 182; PASS 19; Q&S 28, 95–8; Rad-Rec 201–4; Rhythm 211, 215–16; 3S 87–93; X/C 65; *see also* AG; BBEEP; PG; Q&S; 3S

Breath, Body, Extreme, Effort that is P.A.S.S.ed *see* BBEEP

Bridges, Dorothy 124

Brynner, Yul 247

bubble *see* PA

Carnivàle 216

Center *see* IAC, MC relationship

Centeredness 133, 284

CG 240–2, 246, 268; life 280; *see also* away motivation; CG; PG; toward motivation; win/loss

chair, -s 35, 91, 97, 217; étude 211; game of 125, 127, 129, 131–3, 141; modification 59, 156; *see also* BEEF; étude

chalice 51; *see also* Goblet

Chaos 16, 30, 213–17, 284; Balancing 90; creating 196; Improv 223; Stac/Leg 6 209–10; *see also* Pandemonium; Rhythm; Stac/Leg 6

Character, -ization 16, 28–31, 150, 165, 167–200; active gaze 176, 229; arc 18, 205, 242–3, 270; AC 182–5; casting 173; clearing 170; communion 117; danger of staying in 117; Goblet 52; FP 30, 220–5; Images 251; Imaginary Bodies 177–82; Improvisation 248; Jewelry 245; life wish 231–3; moveable, imaginary or character Centers 173–7; multidimensional 160; names 175; Palace 134; PASS 39, PA, aura 29; PG 236; play the difference 24–5, 106, 195–7; posture 158; Quantum Peek, Pie 48–50; Rad/Rec 205–7; release 67; score 269–71; SBV 185–6; synergy 45; 3S 83; TFW 186–99; *see also* Transformation

Chart of Inspired Action 1–2, 6, 14–15, 31–2, 33–4, 54–5, 60, 66, 70, 74, 141, 165, 180, 228, 248–9, 251, 283; Concentration missing 2, 282; floor plan of actor's gym 32; Focal Point 224; holograph 136–7, 148, 219; map to happiness 25–7; prompt 60, 214

C.I.R.C.L.E. 282–5; *see also* Concentration, Imagination, Radiation, Centeredness, Love/Lightness/Laughter, Ease

Circle of Concentration 224, 227, 279–80; *see also* FP

Coggins, Guy 112n2; *see also* aura, photography

Colvin, Jack 34n6, 81, 144, 151, 224

Communion, Five Communions 25, 29, 30, 117, 141, 144–5, 148, 194, 200, 206, 249; *see also* contact

Composition 18, 26, 30–1, 128, 137, 184, 206–7, 214, 218, 233, 248–9, 283; for the Part 251–74; psychological 193; *see also* CG; SynthAnalysis™; TPT

Compositionary Gesture *see* CG; SART

Concentration 9–11, 15–17, 24, 26, 33, 59, 63, 92, 103, 122, 130, 139, 146, 225; attention 16, 179; C.I.R.C.L.E. 282–7; contact 144; dream 229; FP 30, 220, 275; *gesture* 10, 54; life 280; missing from Chart of Inspired Action 282; Rad/Rec 202–3, 205; Stanislavsky circles of 224; T-force 188; W-force 191; *see also* C.I.R.C.L.E.; FP

Concentration, Imagination, Radiation, Centeredness, Love/Lightness/Laughter, Ease *see* C.I.R.C.L.E.

conflict, -ing: avoid 90; betraying signals 37; free 91, 177; life 280–1; Overall Atmospheres 103, 108–10; personality 267; Radiation 284; resolution 280–2; Rock Garden 256; three kinds 144, 161, 229, 237, 243, 270; SynthAnalysis™ 259; *see also* away motivation; evil; nightmare

contact 12, 71, 130, 205–6, 215; communion 139, 141–5, 248, 262; eye 38–44, 67, 142, 201, 221–4; life 147, 210; Openhearted 26–7, 148; see spot go 203; 12 senses 206; *see also* Communion; Golden Hoop; Rad/Rec

contrast, -ing 77, 108, 184, 186; PA 108; score 62, 65–7, 83, 92, 97, 143, 224; themes 128–9; T/R 219; *see also* Polarity; TPT

Cookie Flyback *see* Flyback

Crescendo 142, 270–2; *see also* Composition
crisis 267, 276
criticize 20; *see also* evaluate; Flyback
crossing threshold 15, 99–102, 107, 131, 134, 156–9, 204, 211, 217, 262; consciousness shift 16, 43, 54; of truth 148, 150, 173; *see also* ATMO; OA
curiosity 13, 151, 254–5, 275; beauty 132; creative thinking/T-force 172, 185, 198; PA 107

Dean, James 11
Dench, Judy 206
Deshpande Hutchinson, Anjalee 151, 247
design, -ers 7, 30–1, 66, 172, 177, 187–8, 190–2, 198–9, 245, 249; esthetics 139; SynthAnalysis™ 251–2, 272
Dickens, Charles: Scrooge 150; X/C graph 61
Diminuendo 142, 270–2; *see also* Composition
Drag *see* AG
dream 241–3, 251, 264, 267, 271, 280; Dorothy 261, 263; life 281–2; Palace 262; universe aligns 227; *see also* CG; PG; toward motivation, win/loss
*dusha see* soul; Stanislavsky, Konstantin
*dushevnyi see* spiritual; Stanislavsky, Konstantin

Ease 16; AG 76; BEEF 29, 33, 144, 162, 180, 201–3, 214, 224–7, 251, 257, 270–1, 279; Bridges, Dorothy 124; C.I.R.C.L.E. 284; Feeling of 36, 91, 121–37, 144–8, 152, 209–12, 219, 267; Love/ Lightness / Laughter 284–5; Style 158, 162; *see also* BEEF; C.I.R.C.L.E.; efficient; peak performance
Eastwood, Clint 11, 24, 30, 205, 208
efficient, -cy 9, 15–17; abbreviations 27; energy management 26, 39, 72, 169, 256, 284; Ball Toss 40, 42–3; *see also* Ease; peak performance
emotional life 28, 85–137, 143, 161; kinds of 197; score 269; *see also* ATMO; BEEF; F-forces; PA; OA; Q&S; Thinking, Feeling, Willing (TFW); 3S
emphatic gesture 74, 79–80, 237
energy body 9, 24, 28, 33, 35, 41–2, 44, 46, 50, 62–4, 75–6, 79, 82–3, 87, 106, 112, 115, 135, 145–6, 168, 171, 178, 201–2, 229, 236, 238, 247; *see also* aura; etheric body; kinesphere; life body; light body; Rad/Rec
enneagram 183
Ensemble (#9) 16–17, 25–7, 29, 65, 132, 139, 141–7, 178, 203–4, 214, 218, 251; audience as 142–3, 206; benefit for artist 144–5, 227, 284, 286; building 35–54; daily life 147; Golden hoop 145–6; for Improv guidelines for 248; Love 2; Radiating/ Receiving exercises 208; vs self 67, 77; Style 154, 157–8; SynthAnalysis™ 252, 256–7, 270; theatre troupe 78; truth 148
enthusiasm 12–13, 189, 198, 204, 265, 275, 277–8, 287

Entirety 16, 29, 31, 127–34, 180, 201, 214; feeling of, ensemble 141, 144; FP 224; higher self 48; lacking in Truth 152; Love 279; Style 162; SynthAnalysis™ 251–2, 254, 270; *see also* BEEF; Feeling of the Whole; Four Brothers of Art; overacting antidote
environment 15, 30, 37, 49, 57, 102–3, 157–8, 187, 222, 227, 279
essence 88–9; acting, love 276; gesture 241; as PA 29, 61, 108, 183–5; star quality 162; truth 81
etheric body *see* energy body, kinesphere, life body, light body.
étude 65–6, 72, 83, 92, 104, 108, 175, 188, 190, 192; Letter 65, 97, 162, 211–13, 215; for Psychological Gesture 241–2; score 215; *see also* sequence
eurythmy 78, 161; *see also* Steiner, Rudolf
evaluate, -ion 20; self 8, 20–1, 26, 32, 34, 46, 130, 143, 153, 230; *see also* criticize; Flyback; self-reflection
everyday personality 28, 41, 47, 50, 60, 264; *see also* lower ego
evil 117, 182, 192, 268, 272; antagonist 259; away motivation 229; conflict 161, 229, 259; graph 262–4; life 281; love 276; SynthAnalysis™ plot structure 258–64; two kinds 184; Witch 205; *see also* away motivation; Compositionary Gesture; conflict; dream; nightmare; Psychological Gesture
Expanding/Contracting (#2) *see* X/C
eye aversion 224–5

F-forces (Feeling Forces) 186, 189–90, 192–200, 204, 249; atmosphere 246; audience 193, 218; -character, -dominated 189–90, 199, 269; how, PG 235–8; love 275; soul 246; touch and smell 189; *see also* Thinking, Feeling, Willing (TFW)
Falling yielding sensation (3S) 87–8, 90; metaphors 88; *see* Three Sister Sensations
fantasy 99, 116, 159, 160, 260; vs reality 151, 283; *see also* Imagination, pretend
Feeling of the Whole *see* BEEF; Entirety
Feelings 5, 174, 189, 275; conceal 42, 197; crisis 267; doubt 6, 10, 18, 47, 50, 66, 83, 171–2, 204; Love 275; Tempo/Rhythm 213–15; Tin Man 194–5; veil 194; *see also* BEEF; emotional life; F-forces; Thinking, Feeling, Willing (TFW)
Five Guiding Principles *see* 5GP
Five Tibetan Rites 45; *see also* warm-up; yoga
Floating weightlessly sensation (3S) 88–9; metaphors 88; *see* Three Sister Sensations
Flowing/Floating (#3 MFFR-QoM of water) 28, 69–72; BEEF 133; IB 180; Legato 215; PG 246; POA 33; PPE 113; rehearsal 289; Stac/Leg 6 209; Style 156–9; 3S, different from 91; *see also* QoM

Flyback: Cookie 20–1, 22, 29, 31, 66, 77, 82, 97, 122, 142, 174, 186, 192, 219, 239, 241; feedback 22; self-reflection 6, 8, 22, 72

Flying (#3 MFFR-QoM of air) 28, 69–72; BEEF 133; energy 9; POA 33; gestures 75; Imaginary Body 180; PPE 113; rehearsal 289; Style 156–9; T-force 187; 3S, different from 91; *see also* QoM

Focal Points of Concentration *see* FP

focus 9–11, 25–6, 122, 270; activating 30; AG 77–8; attention 11, 15–17, 117; Ball Toss 38–41, 44, 272; BEEF 122–34, 136; Ease 10, 36, 38, 122–5; gesture 9, 38, 54; love 274, 279–87; Pareto Principle 136–7; peak performance 103; Penetrate 82; rehearsing 92, 97; split 10, 76; on understanding 57, 65–7, 251; *see also* Concentration; FP

Follow the Leader 13–14, 26; PG 235

follow-through 19, 39, 41

Form 9, 29, 125–9, 208; alley: silent 16–17, 39; BEEF 121–37, 201, 214, 224, 251, 270, 279; character 179–80; clearing 170; Feeling of 125; Ensemble 144; exaggerated 169; hallway 39–40, 43, 73, 201; HG 256–8; Improv 248; PG 237–9; physical 179, 235–9; RG 252, 256–7; Style 139, 155–62; TFW 190, 192; Truth 152; Universal 170; *see also* alley; BEEF; chairs; hallway; HG; RG

Four Brothers of Art (#8) *see* BEEF

FP 10, 17, 30, 128, 137, 148, 159, 165, 205, 220–7; for character 221; for life 225–7, 226, 279; significance 272–3; *see also* Focal Points of Concentration; RG

FP1: Focal Point 1; theme stone 128, 252; *see also* RG

freedom 16, 20, 54, 61, 64, 90–1, 116, 150, 171, 237, 244, 278, 285; from shame 227; to fail 162, 284

friends: make with 29, 35–7, 40, 54, 105, 124, 136, 145, 270, 284–5; TV show 93

*From Russia to Hollywood: the 100-Year Odyssey of Chekhov and Shdanoff* iii, 32, 282

Gather *see* AG

gaze artistic/creative 71, 94, 134, 157, 159, 174, 176–80, 192, 238, 239, 253, 255, 262, 286; *see also* IAC; What else?

genetics 8, 49

genius 11–13

Gesture: definition 74, 81; eurythmy 78, 161; subtext 80; transitional 93–4; *see also* AG; CG; emphatic gesture; focus; habit; HG; mannerism; PG; Power Gesture

Goblet 3, 26, 27, 51, 151; aim of process 54, 224, 229; as artist 286; C.I.R.C.L.E. 284; erecting exercise 27, 50–4, 52–3; Objectives 229; Palaces 262; PG 234; process 99–102, 106–8, 158–9, 170, 175–81, 184, 192, 206, 224, 284, 286; Rad-Rec 206; SynthAnalysis™ 253–4, 262; *see also* I-Sphere

Golden Hoop 29, 145–8, 205, 208, 210; bring down 146–7; *see also* Ensemble; Rad/Rec

gravity, -ational 14; Balls 40–2; 3S 28, 87–91; *see also* 3S

grounds: as tools 282, 284; *see also* Shdanoff, George

habit, -ual 47, 49, 66; desires 80; eye aversion 225; gesture/mannerisms 37, 80, 118, 155, 159, 162, 170, 224, 237, 248, 262; linear rehearsal 266; *see also* body language; emphatic gesture; mannerism

hallway 16–17, 39–40, 43, 73, 201; *see also* alley; Form

hang time 16–17, 79; *see also* three levels of attention

happening: as art 5, 33, 41, 135, 152–3, 222, 225, 231, 246–7; as events 29, 33, 92, 103, 116, 199, 224–6, 261, 267, 280

happy, -iness 5–7, 15, 18, 26, 32, 46, 51–2, 54, 84, 96, 108, 110, 125, 129, 135, 191, 176, 182, 192, 196, 226, 231, 249, 267, 274, 277–8, 286; Dorothy 264; map to 24–5; not happy 133; Rosemary 241; *see also* peak performance; the zone

Harmonious Grouping *see* HG

health, -y 7–8, 17, 20–3, 29–30, 32, 34, 49, 64, 85, 91, 113–18, 139, 168–9, 178, 182, 194, 229, 241, 249, 267, 273, 276, 278–80

HeartMath Institute 45, 46, 113–14, 114

HG 29, 128–9, 132, 252, 255–8, 265; *see also* Harmonious Grouping, SynthAnalysis™

Higher Ego x, 41, 45, 48, 133, 142, 144, 146, 148, 168, 170, 176–7, 192, 203, 234, 247, 249, 253, 274, 276–7, 284, 287

HomePlay 32–6, 57, 60, 92, 98, 104, 110, 133, 136, 149, 169, 177, 181, 184, 188, 190, 192, 195, 207, 219, 222, 224, 267, 280, 286; *see also* POA

Hopkins, Anthony 245

Human Design 183

I-Sphere 27, 54, 87–90, 92, 95, 102, 109, 134, 150, 156–61, 176–81, 202, 204, 217, 224, 226, 234, 236, 238–9, 253, 256, 286; *see also* Goblet; Imagination

IAC 15–16, 29, 33, 54, 62, 76, 79, 90, 154, 176–7, 204, 211, 220, 253; Actor's March 167–73; ask 238, 240, 253, 255, 258, 268; C.I.R.C.L.E. 284; Goblet 51, 99–101, 159, 180, 233; Golden Hoop 145–7; grounding 23, 107, 109, 234; *HeartMath* 46; Imagination 283; life 152; listening 256, 268; location 45–6; MC relationship 177; Radiance 162, 202–3, 284; Stac/Leg 6 209; star/sun 64, 201–2; 3Is 239; Transformation 29; Truth 148; veiling 24; "What else?" 154, 258; "Who me?" 45, 54; *see also* Ideal Artistic Center

IDEAL 15, 283; AG 81; form 121, 171, 182; reach for 228; *see* IAC; universal

Ideal Artistic Center *see* IAC

ideal self/stance 167–73, 270, 284
Imaginary Body 161, 167, 176, 178, 184–6, 201, 229, 247, 251, 262, 268, 270; life 280–2; PG 236, 240, 243
Imagination(#1) 35–55; artistic sensitivity 25; Atmosphere 101–4, 112; benefits of 50, 247, 261, 266; C.I.R.C.L.E. 284; cultivation of 9, 15, 28–31, 35, 48, 60, 117, 201, 222, 240; free from time and space limits 237; kinds of 17–18, 171, 283; LQ, 3Is 176–80, 192, 214, 225, 232, 239, 246, 268, 279; memory as 115; moving energy with 9, 77–9, 236; pretend 116; as research 262; to stimulate 79, 94, 174; Style 158–61, 282–3; unlimited I-sphere 27, 87–90, 95, 109, 116, 134–5, 156–7, 202, 224, 234, 238, 253; unity with body 52, 55, 67, 70; versus Intellect 239; warmup 38, 121, 149, 156, 211, 286
Improv 26, 63, 245–8; AG 73–4, 77, 81; Archetypal characters 184; ATMO 106, 109, 112; BEEF 133; book series iv, 27; chart 31; Ease 124; entertainment 248; F-forces 190; FP 223; games and 65–6, 71; guidelines 65; happening 247; for IB 187, 182; Jewelry 245; Letter étude 162; life 281; Moveable Centers 175; Objective 230; PG 238–9; purpose 31, 200; Q&S 97–8; QoM 71; Rad/Rec 206; RG 128; rehearse 242; role in pedagogy 6, 27, 34, 246–7; Stick, Ball, Veil 185; Style 157–8, 162; T-forces 188; 3S 91–2, 94; ToP 196; T/R 215, 218–19; W-forces 191–2; win/loss 243; X/C 64–6; *see also* Improvisation (#18); Kilroy, Wil
Improvisation (#18) *see* Improv
in action 16; *see also* three levels of attention
Inspiration, Imagination, Intellect *see* 3Is
inspired action iii, 67, 145, 247–8, 282, 284; *see also* Chart of Inspired Action

Japanese Rock Garden *see* RG
Javelin 202, 205, 210; *see also* Rad/Rec
Jewel, -ry, -s 21, 31, 139, 178, 245–8
Jungian parts therapy 281, 283; *see also* Power Gestures

Kane, Sarah ix
Kasponyte, Justina ix, 52–3
Kilroy, Wil 3, 4, 9, 27, 34n8; Improv 66, 71, 81, 94, 98, 106, 112, 133, 175, 182, 196, 206, 208, 219, 223, 243, 248, 290; rehearsal outline 289; warm-up 44
kinds of Imagination 17–18, 43; *see also* kinesthetic
kinds of Movement *see also* Qualities/Kinds of Movement
kinesphere *see* aura; energy body; PA
kinesthetic: imagination 18, 43; circle 177; *see also* kinesphere; kinds of Imagination
Konstantin Stanislavsky 6–7, 30–1, 45, 117, 229–30, 233, 249, 252, 262, 277, 287

L.E.A.D: Lines, Emotions, Activity/Action, Desires, SynthAnalysis™ 251–74
Langhans, Jobst ix
Laughter 31, 230, 250, 275–87; *see also* C.I.R.C.L.E.
Law of Change *see* transformation
Law of Threes *see* Triplicity
Laws of Composition (#19): Triplicity, Polarity, Transformation *see* TPT
Leading Center *see* Improv, Moveable Center
Leading Questions *see* LQ; 3Is
learning curve 25–6, 81, 97
Legato 30, 63, 70, 209; TFW 198–9, 209–18, 284, 289; *see also* Rhythm; Stac/Leg 6
*Lessons for Teachers* 282
life body *see* energy body
life wish 231–2, 237, 241, 268; *see also* toward motivation, win/loss, Compositionary Gesture, Psychological Gesture, SSO
Lift *see* AG
light body *see* energy body
Lithuanian Theatre, Music and Cinema Museum, Vilnius 52
little piece of art 17, 126; life 121, 200, 226, 287; POA 288
Love 31, 274–87; acting 87–8; attention, fear 11, 96, 117; creative power 114; evil 117; fall in 40, 139, 155, 169, 183, 201, 285; Four daily deeds 286–7; genius, perfectionist 13–14; higher self 116; inhibitions 285; lessons 20; problem 144, 182, 215, 225; of our profession 9, 115, 183, 284
lower ego 41, 48–9, 115–7, 133, 179, 247, 254, 274, 283–4, 287; *see also* everyday personality
LQ 79, 94, 121, 174, 210; Focal Point for life 225, 229; Imagination 176, 178–9; I- I-sphere 286; life wish 232, 279; Moveable Centers 199; Psychological Gesture 238; Rhythm 212, 214; 3Is 239, 243; SynthAnalysis™ 268; TFW 197; Theme 254; *see* Leading Questions
Lyrical 30, 198, 209–15, 217; *see also* Rhythm

magnet, -ic, -ism 46, 132–3, 203–5, 210, 284; *see also* HeartMath Institute; Radiance; Receiving
make friends with *see* friends
mannerism 159, 162, 224, 246; of daily POA 57; tactics 80; tendencies 206; tension 122; *see also* body language; emphatic gesture; habit
Marshall, Kevin 146
Maslow's Hierarchy of Needs 231
Mayer, Louis B 32
Meyers-Briggs 183
MFFR 57, 70, 113, 136, 143, 156, 158, 160, 207, 269; *see also* Flowing/Floating; Flying; Molding; Radiating; QoM; Qualities/Kinds of Movement

Molding (#3 MFFR-QoM of Earth) 69–72; BEEF 133, 136; gestures 75, 82; Imaginary Body 180; PG 246; POA 33; PPE 113; rehearsal 289; 3S, different from 91; *see also* Qualities/Kinds of Movement
Monroe, Marilyn 11, 30, 205, 208
Montelle, Yann-Pierre 7, 290; *see also* archeological research
*Murder of Talent: How Pop Culture is Killing "IT"* 118–21; *see also* emotional life, F-forces; teddy bear
mythological 183

"naïve", -té 12–13, 89
National Michael Chekhov Association *see* NMCA
naturalism 152, 155, 156–8, 162; Meisner 29
Neal, Patricia 162; *see also* Oscar(s)
neutral, -ality 42, 147, 170, 268; AG 75, 82, 84; life 147; QoM 70; Rad/Rec 205; universal canvas 170; X/C 60, 66; *see also* universal
neutral stance *see* universal, stance
Nicholson, Jack 14, 117
Nightingale, Earl 12
nightmare 116; vs dream 30, 199, 229, 231–2, 242–3, 264; life 267, 281; *see also* away motivation; Compositional Gesture; Psychological Gesture, win/loss
NMCA 3, 9, 26–7, 33, 34n7, 70, 78, 134, 146, 151; *see also* National Michael Chekhov Association
nonverbal communication 63, 123, 142; *see also* silence

OA 99–106; baptizing 104, 175, 206; crossing threshold 99–102; definition 103; discovery 99–101, *104*, *112*; key concepts 110; molecules 102; score 270, 272; soul of the story 102, 286; Sphere of Emotions 112; stylistic truth 149, 152, 160; SynthAnalysis™ 264–5, 270–2; threshold 99–102, 107; two collide improv 109–10; *Wizard of Oz* 260–1; *see also* ATMO; Overall, objective, general Atmosphere
objective, -ly, -ity 21, 28, 29, 70, 84, 93, 97, 118, 283; Atmosphere 103, 105, 110, *112*; existence of image 179; higher self 286; love 284
Objectives (#16), "What for?" 9, 25, 29, 30, 57, 115, 228–33; AG 73–4, 78, 80, 84, 108, 143, 152, 237, 240; choice of tools 247–8; life 165, 210, 279, 281; dream/nightmare 199; embody 234–41; exercise 210; finding 229; Focal Point 224–7; Problem 231; Statement, Super 229–33, 268; Super-Super (SSO) 231–2; win/loss 268
*On the Technique of Acting* 26, 108, 249; study questions 287
Online Resource Centre *see* OR; Routledge Resource Centre 3
OR 3, 7, 15, 31, 33, 44–5, 61, 66, 78, 84, 94, 104, 112, 116, 143, 159, 161, 185, 193, 199, 200, 208, 219, 228, 265, 267, 270, 287; *see also* Online Resource Centre; Routledge Resource Centre 3
Orlandi, Janice 162, 163n2
orphan 14, 178, 238; *see* AC; Imagination
Oscar(s) 29, 45, 118, 217; least screentime winners 162–3; nominee Michael Chekhov 162; *see also* Neal, Patricia; Straight, Beatrice
over the top 23, 152; *see also* overacting antidote; Truth
overacting antidote 23, 152; *see also* Entirety
Overall, objective, general Atmosphere *see* OA

PA 29, 85, 90; of archetype 185; aura 29, 44, 108; discovery *104*, 106–7, *112*; essence list 108; bubble 44, 106–8, 112, 177, 184, 203; clearing 170; SynthAnalysis™ 265; *see also* ATMO; Personal, subjective, individual Atmosphere
Palace: Beauty 134–5, 158; backstory, research 262; Style 158–9; *see also* crossing threshold
Pandemonium *see* Chaos; Rhythm; Tempo
PASS 19, 26, 34, 39, 54; AG 75, 79, 81; PG 236; *see also* AG; Ball Toss; BBEEP; PG; Prepare, Act, Sustain, Stop
Pause 21, 35, 37–8, 125–6, 132, 218–19; ATMO 100–2; after, before 270–1; Form 125–7, 129, 131–2, 141; life 227; no 212; PG 235; Rhythm 211; SynthAnalysis™ 253, 256–8; *see also* Silence; Stillness
peak performance 5, 7–10, 13–15, 17, 22, 26, 29, 33, 38–9, 41, 44–5, 48, 54, 64, 72, 103, 123, 133, 136, 151, 173, 194, 203, 205, 213, 218–9, 239, 246, 278–80, 285, 287; *see also* happy; the zone
pedagogy iii, ix, 3, 78, 248; *see also* sequence
Penetrate *see* AG
perfect *see* Ball Toss
Personal, subjective, individual Atmosphere *see* PA
PG 15, 30, 234–46, 165; BBEEP 79, 236; CG 240–3, 264; conflict resolution 280–1; concept, purpose 235–6; counter, reactionary 232, 238; crystalized will 230; difference from AG 79, 84, 236–7; emphatic, habitual gesture 237; good and evil 259; half-done 237; Horatio 94; how many 238; Jewelry 245–6; life 278–80; as living logo 235; Power Gesture 280–2; Rosemary 230–2, 240–3; Super PG 238, 243; SSO 237, 241, 279; SynthAnalysis™ events 264–8; TFW 199, 237; 3Is finding PG 239–44, 246; Triplicity 238; *see also* AG; BBEEP; CG; Power Gestures; Psychological Gesture; win/loss
piece of the pie 27, 48–50, 60, 80, 89–91, 155, 206, 213, 215; life 168–9, 182–3, 197, 203; lower ego 115–16; *see also* Quantum Pie

pizza 195; *see also* F-forces; Thinking, Feeling, Willing (TFW)
playdates 33
plus or minus (+/-) 61, 70, 125, 144, 150, 268; life 270, 286; *see also* SynthAnalysis™
POA Journal-Flyback 32–4, 57, 72, 92, 104, 133–4, 165, 177, 184, 187, 207; Sheet 288
Polarity 18, 26, 79, 168–9, 184, 186, 196, 215, 232, 236, 240, 242–3, 264–5, 268, 270–1, 286; *see also* contrast; TPT; yin/yang/opposites
Power Gestures 280–2; *see also* CG; PG
powerful organic artist 33
Powers, Mala 3, 9, 21, 24, 26, 34n7, 134–5, 152, 194, 224, 250n, 269, 290
Prepare, Act, Sustain, Stop *see* PASS
pretend 6, 10, 12, 14, 17, 27, 38, 41, 45–6, 48, 54, 63, 71, 88, 95, 97, 106–7, 109, 116, 122–3, 134–5, 148–9, 151–2, 158, 163, 167, 173–4, 178, 190, 211, 217, 230, 236, 238, 256, 262, 283; *see also* reality
problem 229; acting 7–8, 25, 28, 113, 115, 120, 249, 262; Carnivàle 216–17; Focal Point 222, 225–6; if it ain't broke 270; life 151; objective 30, 228–33, 241–3, 270; PG 241; solvers 54, 144, 156, 159, 173, 182, 200, 215; style 155; thinking 187, 194; *see also* Objectives (#16), "What for?"
prototype 81
Psychological Gesture (#17) *see* PG
Pull *see* AG, Gravity, PG
pulse of creation *see* Expanding/Contracting
Push *see* AG

Q&S 28, 85, 95–8, 102, 113, 115, 180, 203; baptize 264–5; breathing patterns 96; Layer Atmospheres 110; Moveable Centers 174–6; PG 232, 236–8, 267; principles 96–7; *radiate image* 112; Style 157; TFW 197–9; *see also* Qualities and Sensations (#6); star
QoM: artistic medium 70; BEEF 133; degree of resistance 70; IB 180; implied question "how" 70; improvisation 71, 136–7; POA 33; PPE 27, 57, 69–72, 113; Rad/Rec 206–8; Style 157; ToP 186; warm up 156; *see also* MFFR; Qualities/Kinds of Movement
Qualities and Sensations (#6) *see* Q&S
Qualities/Kinds of Movement (#3) *see* MFFR; QoM
Quantum Pie/Quantum Peek 26–7; chart 48–50, 54, 170; *see also* piece of the pie
Quinn, Anthony 11

Rad/Rec 30, 201–10; characterization 165, 176, 194, 200, 208; 245, 269–71; as charisma, sun, vitality 15, 45, 51, 162, 168; gestures 231; Goblet 156; good will 146, 210, 224; rehearsal 289; sending 39, 43, 53, 79, 139, 142, 145, 182–4; Staccato-Legato Six Directions 209, 213; *see also* Radiance; Radiating-QOM; Radiating and Receiving Radiance(#13); Radiation; Receiving
Radiance 62, 64, 162, 178, 200, 203–5, 207–9; Marilyn Monroe 208; *see also* Rad/Rec; star
Radiating and Receiving Radiance (#13) *see* Rad/Rec
Radiating-QOM 28, 69–72; BEEF 133; difference from 3S 91, 208; IB 180; PG 246; PPE 113; POA 33; rehearsal 289; Stac/Leg 6 209; Style 156–9; *see also* QoM
Radiation 283–5; Clint Eastwood 24; javelin 202; losing 209, 284; magnetism 133, 205; as part of C.I.R.C.L.E. 282–4; *see also* Rad/Rec; star
Reach *see* AG
reality 116; check 278; vs pretend 151, 163, 247; *see also* pretend
Receiving 30, 64, 79, 139, 142, 144, 162, 182–3, 201–10, 224, 284; catching ball 42; characterization 162, 165, 176, 194, 200, 206, 208, 245, 269–71; gestures 231; Goblet 54, 156; good will 145–6, 210, 224; javelin 202; listening 206, 256, 268; love 286; Marilyn Monroe 208; as preparation 43; rehearsal 289; Stac/Leg 6 209, 213; *see also* Rad/Rec; Radiance
religious deities 183
repetition: growing power 32, 50, 67, 77–8, 110, 150, 159, 161, 183, 286; Chekhov vs Meisner 247; with reflection 22–3; rhythmic 219, 266, 289
RG 127–8, *128*, 132, 252, 256–7, 272, 289; *see also* Form; FP; Harmonious Grouping; Japanese Rock Garden; Rock Garden
Rhythm, -ic 18, 30, 63, 92, 126, 165, 181, 211–14; AG 82; BEEF 131–2, 136, 141–2; breath 95–7; choices 19; De Niro 211; five rhythms 198, 213, 215–16; heart 46; inner/outer 162, 217–18; of pedagogy 27; repetitions 266; ritual 146; Staccato 63, 199, 212–16; Stac/Leg 6 208–10, 214, 284; style 150, 160; TFW 197–8; transitions 61; universal walk 169; voice 67; *see also* Chaos; Legato; Lyrical; repetition; Staccato; Stillness; Tempo; T/R
Rock Garden *see* RG
Rock Guitar 13
Rosemary: CG 242–3; objective statement 230–2; PG 240–3; *see also* CG; dream; nightmare; PG; win/loss
Routledge Resource Centre 3; *see also* Online Resource Centre; OR

SART 251–73; actor's 261–6; A-SART chart *263*; director's D-SART chart *263*; Director's Activated DA-SART 265; monologues and scenes 267–8; *see also* SynthAnalysis™ Run Through
SBV 10, 185–6; archetype of TFW 194; *see also* Stick, Ball, Veil
Schechner, Richard 34n1

score 61, 266–7, 157, 223–4; Atmospheres 270; crafting 269–71; definition 61; Goblet, IB 192; objectives 78; plus or minus 268; reversed 207; *sample monologue 62*; *sample scene 269*; SBV 186; SynthAnalysis™ whip-through 271; TFW 192; TPT 215
Scottini, Leticia 200n1
Scrooge *see* Dickens, Charles
seed of the need 268; trigger 242; *see also* Compositionary Gesture; Psychological Gesture; win/loss
self-reflection 6, 8, 22, 72; *see also* Flyback; evaluate
self-talk 21
sequence, -tial: AG 77–81; CG 240–3, 280–1; composition 30; Goblet 179; Ensemble 142; étude 65, 66, 83, 92, 97, 104, 108, 162, 175, 178, 188, 192, 211, 212, 213, 215; FP 222; physical actions 66, 72, 83, 123, 125, 129, 132, 141; MFFR 69, 71; out of, reversed 266; PASS 39, 45; pedagogical, training iii, 1–2, 6, 14, 26–7, 34, 92, 97, 241, 248–9; PG 235–44; score 61, 104, 223, 271; Stac/Leg 6 208–9, 284, 214; SynthAnalysis™ 230, 252–67; 3S breath 90; warm-up 45; walking 169; *see also* pedagogy
Shakespeare 62, 126, 134, 150, 153–4, 158–9, 161, 183, 206, 223
Shdanoff, George ix, 32, 124, 224, 282; *see also* grounds
Significance 72, 271–2; your role 7; Radiating/Receiving 203
Silence of the Lambs 245
silence,-tly 121, 134, 141, 156, 158, 178, 204, 241; improv 248; *of the Lambs 245*; Pause 218; Rhythm/stillness 211–12, 214, 216; receiving 42–3; as a tool 16–17, 59, 71, 97, 235, 253, 256, 282–3; *see also* Stillness
Smash *see* AG
SO 229–33, 268, 279; *see also* Objective, Super Objective
soul 6, 246, 266–7, 273, 275; *dusha* 277; forces *see* Trinity of Psychology; "psych" 193; Stanislavsky 277; story *see* Atmosphere
speech *see* voice
speed, -ing 12, 43, 240; AG 82; dating 81, 162; Floating 88; life 162, 215; scale 209; as Tempo 30, 63, 66, 82, 198, 211–19; traffic 73; warm-up 44; *see also* Rhythm; Tempo; T/R
"spine" as arc 229, 242
spirit, -ual 6–8, 18, 26, 30–1; art 152, 172; body, mind, soul unity 38, 41, 44, 236, 271, 273; character 134, 200; creative 15, 51, 210; define 49; DNA 275; Dorothy's journey 263; *dushevnyi* 277; FP5 226–7, 279; free 11; higher ego 277; intangible 90; lifting 120; Love 275, 286; performance 102; Steiner, Rudolf 282; traditions 132

SSO 231–2, 237, 241, 268, 279; *see also* life wish; Objective; Super Super Objective
Stac/Leg 6 162, 208–10, 213–14, 284; *see also* Rad/Rec; Radiance; Rhythm; Staccato/Legato Six Directions Exercise
Staccato/Legato Six Directions Exercise *see* Stac/Leg 6
Stanislavsky, Konstantin 6–7, 30–1, 45, 117, 229–30, 233; analysis 249, 252, 262, 277
star/stardom 50, 115, 149, 276; body 168; Goblet 50–3, 151, 170; quality 30, 45–6, 79, 151, 162, 171–2, 200–1, 205, 236, 284; *Star Trek* 156, 178; *Wars* 158
state of readiness/standby 16
Steiner, Rudolf 78, 161, 194, 208; Six basic exercises 282; *see also* eurythmy
Stick, Ball, Veil *see* SBV
Stillness 30, 212–18, 272; Stac-Leg 6 209–11; ATMO 104; *see also* Rhythm, Silence
Straight, Beatrice 9, 162–3
Style (#11) 154–63; *Actors' responses to 155*; Atmosphere 159–60; attitude 156; Belief 156; as Form 126, 129, 139; Genre 161–2; images 160–1; language 160; Mannerisms 159; musical theater 222; naturalism, realism 7, 152–8; Palace of 156–8; Posture 158; Radiance 162; SynthAnalysis™ 270; and truth 29, 133, 149–54; veiling and 24, 26, 74, 90, 117, 181, 232, 241; *see also* Form
Super Objective *see* objective; SO
Super Super Objective *see* objective; SSO
Super theme 255–8
Sustaining 1, 19, 39, 41, 43, 47, 69, 75, 79, 81, 106, 129, 131–2, 144, 202, 209, 241
SynthAnalysis™ 3, 31, 116, 128, 144, 160, 165, 175, 177, 179, 187, 198, 233, 236–7, 241, 248–9, 251–73, 283; Actor's SART 264; Atmospheres 260–1; backstory, research 262; Baptize Qualities and Sensations 264; benefits 266; character graph 262; *collage of images 254*; Directors' SART chart 263, 283; *Dorothy's A-SART chart 263*; entirety 252; good vs evil 258; Harmonious Groupings 255–6; Idea 257–8; images arise 251–2; monologues 267; 9 events 259–61; Palaces 262; reading 258; reversal of rehearsal 266; SART 261; scenes 267; theme, super theme 254–7; Tips for SARTS 265; Walk the line 264; *Wizard of Oz* 256
SynthAnalysis™ Run Through *see* SART; SynthAnalysis™

T-forces (Thinking forces) 33, 57, 79, 186–91, 193–8, 204–5, 236–8, 248–9, 275; list of kinds 197; memory 246; stick 194; *see also* Thinking, Feeling, Willing (TFW)
T/R *see* Rhythm, Tempo
Tamiroff, Akim 124, 285

tarot 183

Tear *see* AG

teddy bear 118–20, *119–120*, 195; *see also* emotional life; F-forces, *Murder of Talent*

Tempo 30, 70, 181, 198, 208–9, 211–19; AG 82–3; BEEF 136; breath 96–7; dynamic 44; ensemble 142; freedom 61; inner/outer 162; scale 217–19; slow 88, 91–2; 3S 92; Transformation 165; Truth 149–50; voice 67; *see also* Rhythm; Speed; T/R

Thinking, Feeling, Willing (TFW) 7, 30, 33, 93, 165, 167, 183, 186–200, 202, 231–2, 236–7, 243, 245, 248, 250–1, 264–5, 269, 270–1, 281, 286; *body chart 193*; production design 198–9; soul forces 8, 30, 193, 196, 198, 205, 246, 273; *see also* curiosity; F-forces; T-forces; W-forces

Thomakos, Jeff 146

three levels of attention 16–18; *see also* hang time; in action

Three Sister Sensations of Equilibrium (#5) *see* 3S

threshold *see* crossing threshold

Throw *see* AG

*To the Actor* 108

top-of-the-world 14, 268, 284; walk 29, 167–71, 191; *see also* IAC; universal, self

toward motivation 228–9, 241; *see also* CG; PG; seed of the need; win/ loss

TPT 18–20, 25–7, 168–8, 176, 184, 196, 232, 243–4, 248, 270; *see also* Laws of Composition (#19): Triplicity, Polarity, Transformation

transform, -ation, -al 18, 26, 29, 45, 57, 150, 198–200, 203–4, 206, 232, 236–7, 241, 243, 285–6; audiences 167, 194, 251; characterization 165–247; energy 9; love 275; personality 48; PG 281; Style 158; SynthAnalysis™ 252, 258, 260, 262, 266, 268, 270–1; walking 168–9; yearning desire 50, 139, 165, 173, 177, 182–6, 188; *see also* Law of Change, TPT

Transform, Inform, Perform (TIP) xi, 126

Transition, -ing, -s 16–17, 61, 63, 67, 71, 92–4, 103–5, 118, 186, 202, 206, 236, 258, 260, 268

Trapped Image Game 47, 49, 51, 54, 57, 84

Trinity of Psychology (ToP) *see* Thinking, Feeling, Willing (TFW)

Triplicity 18, 25–7, 184, 215, 218, 239, 253, 260, 265, 268, 270, 286; *see* Law of Threes

Triplicity, Polarity, Transformation *see* TPT

Truth (#10) 26, 29, 148–53; of axioms 6; of actor's purpose 7, 276, 278; acceptance of 65; of archetype 81–3; artistic 188, 245, 247, 270; and Atmosphere 149; as C.I.R.C.L.E. 284; and consequences 154; Feeling of 152–3, 245; emotional 93, 113–14, 118, 137; as esthetic139; Golden Hoop of 148; inner 127; loss of 76, 116, 130, 284; and Meisner 29, 247; Nine Diamonds of 149–51,162; relative to Style 156, 159; of surprise 66–7; veiling 158

Unidentified Focus on (UFO): atypical eye patterns 224–5

universal, -ality 41, 70; AG 79, 84; appeal 182; emotions 96; neutral canvas 170, 199; PG 236; Rhythm 215; self 171, 173, 179, 188–91, 194–5, 199, 207; stance 62–4, 75, 79, 170–1, 177, 202, 235, 243, 258; tools 163; truths 152; walk 169; *see also* neutral

veil *see* SBV; veiling

veiling 23–4, 29, 63, 65–7, 71–2, 74, 76–9, 82–3, 87–97, 105, 109, 130, 146, 150, 157–8, 160–1, 167, 171, 178, 185,196, 202, 206, 209, 212, 216; PG 236–8, 241–6, 280, 283–4; un- 24, 63, 90, 105, 108, 167, 178, 181, 188, 190–2, 196, 223, 231–2; unveil PG 238–46, 265, 268, 283

voice 6, 8, 12, 14, 20, 26, 28–30, 44, 51, 62–7, 69–71, 73, 76, 78–9, 88–91, 94, 96, 105, 108, 118, 130, 134, 150, 155, 157–61, 167, 173–5, 178–9, 185–6, 191, 195, 199, 211, 213–15, 218, 239, 262, 273, 279, 281, 286; *see also* speech

W-forces (Willing forces) 13, 30, 33, 76, 93, 183, 190–4, 197–200, 203; Archetypal Gesture pure WILL 76, 83–4; align 279; attention, focus 9, 146, 250; ball 186, 194; *body chart 193*; character 194–5, 197, 199, 270; Golden Hoop 146; improvisation 247; kinds/leading questions 198; legs 10, 191–2; love 275, 279, 283, 286; objective 228, 231–2; PG 236–7, 243; tactics 196; *see also* Thinking, Feeling, Willing (TFW)

warm-up 1, 26, 43–5, 148, 160, 251, 266

"What for" *see* objective

What else? 130–1, 134–5, 154, 157, 178, 253, 258; *see also* gaze; IAC

whip-through: Chart of Inspired Action 13–14, 26; score 271

Who me? 45, 54; *see also* Ideal Artistic Center

win/loss 93, 228, 232, 241–3, 246, 265, 267–8, 271; life 280–1; *see also* Compositional Gesture; dream; nightmare; Psychological Gesture

*Wizard of Oz* 93, 117, 194, 205, 252, 257–64, *257*

Works-in-Progress (WiP) 11, 43, 155

The World Economic Forum 2023 172

X/C 59–68; Actor's March 171–2; basis for all AGs 82; with BEEF 136; black and white 60, 84; energy 62–3; 5GPs 285; Imaginary Body 180; Improvs 64–6; Homeplay 60; letter étude 65; light, love 276;

neutral 60, 66, 70; PPE xi, 27, 57, 113, 143; POA 33; in the now 31, 151, 247; Rad/Rec 205; rehearsal 289; scale 63, 157; scoring 269; Style 156–60; voice unity 67; "what" 70, 74–5; warm up 156; *see also* Expanding/Contracting; pulse of creation

yin/yang/opposites *see* Polarity
yoga 26, 44, 45, 211; *see also* Five Tibetan Rites; warm-up

zadacha 229; *see also* objective; problem
zodiac 183
the zone 5, 22, 41; chart as path 26; as happy 46; safety 151; *see also* happy; peak performance

For Product Safety Concerns and Information please contact our EU representative GPSR@taylorandfrancis.com
Taylor & Francis Verlag GmbH, Kaufingerstraße 24, 80331 München, Germany

www.ingramcontent.com/pod-product-compliance
Lightning Source LLC
Chambersburg PA
CBHW080408300426
44113CB00015B/2439